My Maman sent me this prayer in 1980.
What foresight she had!

Prayer to Our Lady of the Meetings
Our Lady of the Meetings,
You, who were often called to the service of God and of men,
On the highways and the byways full of unexpected twists,
Teach me the art of the meetings,
Be they short or long,
Enriching or unpleasant,
Or perhaps full of consequences
For the direction of our lives.
Make me welcoming, but cautious.
May I always have my heart 'on my hand',
But keep it well 'in hand'.
On my lips, put a smile that overcomes distrust
And the right word to make me brave.
May no one suffer from having met me,
But may they take with them some joy
From having had contact with me.

Written by F. Lelotte S. J.

TRANSLATED BY M. BELLA AND C. TRANCHANT

GW00775736

Graphic Designer: Katie Farmer
Website: http://www.bootstobliss.com
Author: Claude Tranchant
Editor: Clare McEniery

First edition published in Australia in 2012
Second edition published in Australia in 2013
Third edition published in Australia in 2014

Printed and bound in Australia by Clark & Mackay
Rocklea Queensland 4107

ISBN 978-0-646-58587-1

Cataloguing-in-Publication entry is available from the National Library of Australia.

http://catalogue.nla.gov.au/

Some of the names have been changed to protect privacy.

Prologue
'My motivation, desires and preparation'

After completing the Saint James' Way pilgrimage and upon returning to Australia in 2010, I was encouraged to write about my journey. With the thoughts and prayers of my friends in France and Australia, I will share with you my wonderful story.

In 2006, I was approached by my friend Anna from Melbourne to walk 240 kilometres of the Saint James' Way. Oh la la! I thought. 240 kilometres seemed to me a long way. As I did not want to say no straight away, I asked her when she was planning to do this walk. 'In a few years', she replied. I was off the hook for a while, at least. I secretly hoped that Anna would forget all about this adventure of hers. Little did I know, however, the seed was already planted and gradually it germinated in my mind and heart.

The following year, I went to see my father in France, as he was not well. He left this world in 2008, and every day I treasure the precious time I got to share with him. I had missed that sharing with my mother before her passing, as she had had Alzheimer's. They were two beautiful human beings. At the end of their journeys on this earth, they left a lovely message for all of us to hear: love one another.

As I was staying with my sister, Michele, while I was in France during this time, I informed her that I was thinking about walking the Saint James' Way. To my astonishment, Michele laughed and laughed when she heard me say the walk was 240 kilometres. She said that I had no idea of the real length of the walk and she asked me where I had got my information. As I had never bothered to check it out, I could not give her any answer. My ego was bruised.

The next morning, the local paper from Orleans was lying on the kitchen table. Usually I never really bothered to read it, but something stronger than me made me open it. I could not believe it: there in front of my eyes was an article about the Saint James' Way. My heart beat rapidly. What a coincidence! After reading the article I found that the real length of the walk was not 240 kilometres, but in fact it was over 1,900 kilometres, depending on where you started. Oh my goodness! My eyes nearly popped out of my head. I understood now why my sister had laughed so much when I told her of my plan. I took note of this article and promised myself that on my return to Australia I would do more research. How strange. It would seem the newspaper article was not a deterrent, but a stimulus.

One month or so after returning to Australia, I told my French friend, Dominique, what had happened in France and what I was planning to do. When I had finished, she asked me to repeat what I wanted to do. I thought to myself, 'My goodness, here we go again!' Then, to my surprise, she told me that she had a French friend whose parents had walked the Saint James' Way in 2006. She also added that they were currently in Brisbane, but were leaving the next day. I was relieved: Dominique did not think I was mad, after all. That same afternoon, I met Monique and Claude from Reims in France, not knowing that a few years later they would play an important part in my pilgrimage. Was this course of events mere coincidence or something else?

After doing some research on the internet, I discovered

that the Easter of 2010 would fall on my birthday, which was another sign for me. In addition, I discovered that 2010 was also going to be a Holy Year. Saint James' feast day is on 25 July and when that date falls on a Sunday in a particular year, it is a Saint Year or Holy Year. The previous Holy Year was 1999. In some Christian countries in Europe, a feast day is a very important day and it is usually a public holiday for certain saints such as Saint John, Saint James or Saint Anthony. Maybe there is a hierarchy among the saints. Who knows? Since the Middle Ages, these holidays have been special occasions for people to go to church, have a rest and enjoy themselves. In those days, however, there were no paid holidays!

The article in the paper in France and my meeting with Dominique, who introduced me to Monique and Claude - the lovely French couple who were visiting Brisbane - were not accidents: these were messages. I was certain 'someone' was directing me to do the Saint James' Way. Why? I did not know, but I felt I had to do it. From then on, every single day, I thought about the pilgrimage and I did research on it. I kept my secret close to my heart, yet strangely enough, people would come out of the woodwork to inform me that they had done the walk or part of the walk, even though they did not know of my intentions. It was an overpowering feeling: I had to do the pilgrimage.

After months of research, I informed my children of my decision. They were stunned by my resolve. Was I surprised by their reactions? No. After all, their mother wanted to cross France and Spain on foot with a backpack at the age of 64 and all alone, as my friend Anna could no longer join me for personal reasons. It was a shock! My daughter raised her eyes to the ceiling. I could guess what she was thinking. 'Oh dear, my mother is going through a mid-life crisis or she must have fallen on her head!' Her husband, my son-in-law, was so stunned that he did not say anything, keeping his thoughts to himself. Eventually, they adjusted to the fact and when my daughter realised that I really meant it, she said, 'You can do what you want Maman, but be careful. Remember we love you'.

With regard to my son and his wife, after the initial shock, which lasted a few seconds, they said, 'Good on you, Mum. We know you will be fine. Enjoy yourself and please keep in touch every day. We love you'. Despite their brave words, however, I could see fear as well as pride in their eyes. They were all afraid, as I wanted to walk the pilgrimage alone. On top of that, they were well aware of how bad I am with directions. In fact, I have no sense of direction at all! When I would look for a road in a street directory, my children used to say, 'Oh dear, we will end up in Africa. Be prepared!' It was lucky for them that we lived in Australia, a huge continent totally surrounded by water, as sometimes we could very well have ended up in Africa, for sure! To quell their fears, I promised to stay in touch with them as often as possible. After all, modern communications are meant to make such things easy nowadays, are they not?

So why did I want to walk alone? Some books mentioned that walking with friends could be more of a hindrance than an asset, considering the fact that the group would be spending so many weeks together. I read as well that if you want to lose friends, you should walk the Saint James' Way with them. Not everybody walks at the same pace or has the same endurance or the same personality. One person could get sick or get hurt. What would I do if faced with such a situation? Would I quit because my friend could not keep on going, or if I were the one to become injured or ill, could I honestly be a burden to someone else? If failure was going to be my partner, I wanted to experience it alone, without a witness. On top of these thoughts, a little voice inside me said, 'You have to do it alone, like a real pilgrim', and deep down I wanted to face this pilgrimage alone, feeling instinctively that I would be safe.

When I told my friends of my plan, some were surprised, but all encouraged me. They asked me why I wanted to do this walk and such a long walk. I told them that I would be 64 the following April and I wanted to celebrate the official end of my working life with a bang! I needed to know what our ancestors would have experienced crossing country after country on foot and in contact with nature, without the help of a car, a bicycle or a plane. I explained to them that the path is not so dangerous nowadays, compared to the Middle Ages, though there are still some wild beasts such as boars, dogs and bears in some areas of France and northern Spain and in the Pyrenees, where they had been re-introduced a few years ago! I shared with my friends the coincidences I had experienced and told them I felt I could not ignore these signs. I was ready for a new challenge in my life. The worst thing that could happen to me would be that I would fail to complete the walk.

I informed my workmates of my project at the last minute and their reactions were mixed. The women were surprised, though supportive. It was a different matter with the men, as some of them decided to bet on my failure and I could see their grins. Some of their comments were along the lines of, 'Claude? She won't make it, and alone for sure she won't make it'. Hurt by their attitude and comments, my frustration grew. I did not have to prove anything to them, but I was stung and I could hear myself saying, 'I will show you, mates! Yes, I am a mature-aged woman and on the chubby side, but why couldn't I achieve this challenge? I might be stronger than you think'. I knew I did not need anyone's approval, but their comments did hurt.

My children, their partners and my grandson put aside their fears and gave me their blessings and I promised to stay in touch as often as I could via text messages, phone and the internet. I left with my children's love and the good wishes of my friends and all my workmates, even those who did not believe in me. I was ready for the challenge ahead. I was going to realise my beautiful dream, carrying everyone's love within me. I was not scared at all, for somehow I knew, deep down, that I would be safe. Apart from the physical challenge that awaited me, I was oblivious to what was in store for me along the way and how my adventure would turn out.

So, after all of this, who is Saint James? What is it that he did that so many millions of pilgrims 'a travers les temps' ('through the ages') have walked these paths? Legend or truth, I will leave you to decide. His story is in the New Testament. Saint James is also known as James the Elder. He was the son of Zebedee and was one of the twelve apostles and his brother was John the Evangelist. The two brothers and their father were fishermen. One day, as they were repairing their nets in their boat on the shores of the Sea of Galilee, Christ approached them and the two brothers followed Him. According to the Christian tradition, after His resurrection, Christ appeared to his twelve apostles and told them, 'Go throughout the whole world and preach the good news to all mankind'. Saint James went to Iberia, which is now made up of Spain, Portugal, Andorra and Gibraltar. Some scholars argue that Saint James did not convert many to Christianity. Eventually though, Saint James reached the north-west part of Spain, Galicia, and it was likely he had more success in that part of Spain, as Galicia was full of Celtic mysticism and perhaps more open to new thoughts and spirituality. Around 42 or 44 AD, Saint James decided to return to Jerusalem with two of his disciples, leaving the others to keep on doing his work in Iberia. After they arrived in Judea, King Herod Agrippa I had Saint James beheaded and he became the first Christian martyr mentioned in the New Testament. One night his two disciples took his body and sailed back to Iberia. Due to the fierce winds and dangerous sea currents, they landed at Iria Flavia (called Padron nowadays) on the coast of Galicia. The body of Saint James was carried to Santiago de Compostela where it was buried. His tomb was forgotten for a long time and not found until approximately 800 years later. A hermit named Pelagio had a vision and saw some bright lights over an area. Digging in that very spot revealed some human remains. On 25 July 812, the bishop of Iria Flavia declared that the remains found were those of Saint James. This was the beginning of the pilgrimage.

For Christians, the Saint James' Way pilgrimage became as important as those in Jerusalem and Rome. To walk towards the Atlantic, the Romans used to follow the line of the Milky Way and later the same road was used by the pilgrims going to Santiago de Compostela. 'Compostela' itself means 'field of stars'. It is so beautiful and poetic.

In October 1987, the route to Santiago was named the first European cultural route by the Council of Europe and became a UNESCO World Heritage site. I was overwhelmed by the thought of walking this pilgrimage and joining my footsteps to those millions of other pilgrims. I had a challenge ahead, but what a wonderful one!

I flew from Brisbane to Paris via Seoul. On my first morning in Paris I was up at the crack of dawn and I could not stay still. I was in Paris! It was freezing, but I did not care and I went for a walk through the deserted streets, without a map mind you, with my good sense of direction! It was almost as though I was at the beginning of my pilgrimage.

I was re-tracing my footsteps to go back to the hotel when suddenly I was in front of Notre Dame Cathedral. I could not believe it. How had I managed to do that without a map? I surprised myself so much. It was a great feeling to lose myself in the capital of France without any worries. I was in Paris, absorbing it all. I walked along the bank of the Seine and it was spectacular. I had stars in my eyes; I felt so free. In a way, it was like I was in Heaven.

Back at the hotel, I had my French breakfast of juice, coffee and the traditional croissant, then I collected my luggage and took a train to Orleans to visit my sister again - my first visit since 2007. Orleans is a town on the Loire River, about 100 kilometres south-west of Paris. In France every city or town is full of history. Orleans was the town that Joan of Arc liberated from the English on 8 May 1429.

My sister was quite surprised that I still wanted to walk the Saint James' Way, even though I had told her many times over the telephone. She was convinced that I was completely mad and just the idea of me walking alone was a trigger for her. 'You have no idea', she would say. 'You do not realise the danger in France. Things are different nowadays. I thought you were going to do it with a group? Alone and carrying your backpack! Do you know there are companies that carry them for you?' And so on and so on. Meanwhile, I was saying calmly to her, 'I will be alright, do not worry. Nothing will happen to your mad sister! I will be protected, I assure you, and I am strong. I have worked hard in my life. I will be ok'. Nothing I said would calm her. For the sake of peace, after seeing her in distress, I promised to send her a text message before I left each morning with the names of the different places I would go through, and another text message when I arrived at my destination. All these compromises felt like a burden. My children's worries came back to me and I felt a little bit guilty about wanting to do this pilgrimage alone. No matter what, however, I knew I had to do it alone and do it my way as I was totally confident that nothing would happen to me. I felt like a teenager taking on a great adventure for the first time, believing in her lucky stars and telling her parents that everything would be fine. A part of me felt sorry for myself: here I was on the verge of living my dream and I was being treated like a child. I informed my children that they could sleep peacefully as I would have daily contact with my sister. I was so grateful for modern technology, but I was still annoyed and I did not comprehend their worries. I was like a little brat: I wanted to be alone, to walk alone. I was not mad. I knew from the bottom of my heart that I would be looked after, no matter what. Putting my frustration aside, it was nice to feel so much affection. My heart felt the hand of love passing over me. I was so blessed to have such a beautiful family. It made me feel so very special.

After a few lovely days with my sister, I spent time with my brother in Rennes. The winter and early spring were fierce in Europe that year, and every day I was dressed like an Eskimo. To keep up with my training, I walked through the narrow, cobbled streets of Orleans and Rennes, re-discovering the beauty of the area. I was seeing it with new eyes and I did not want to miss or forget anything. I filled my lungs and my mind with big breaths of the French atmosphere, absorbing every detail and marvelling at the beauty of the architecture of the buildings, churches and cathedrals, wrapping it over myself, like a cloak.

I observed the interactions of the French people sipping their coffee on the terrace of a café, even in the cold and windy weather, or those doing window-shopping. I thought to myself that they must be mad! How could they drink coffee outside on the terrace in such cold weather and go strolling in this icebox? After living in Brisbane for so long, the 'Brissie Girl' was freezing and my body felt like ice, but I marvelled at everything, re-discovering my country of birth. How strange that was. I never forgot anything about France after I left at the age of 33 to migrate to Australia. Do you think you can forget your country of origin? No, not at all. But somehow it seemed I

14

had some catching up to do in my mature age. It was a strange feeling.

After a few lovely days with my brother, I left Rennes on a TGV train for my home town, Aix-les-Bains, a town built on the edge of Lake du Bourget in Savoy in the lower range of the French Alps and part of the Rhone-Alpes region. It is also a spa town. The Knights Celtic tribes discovered its sources of hot water on the slopes of Mont Revard and the reputation of the healing properties of its waters are still renowned. Aix-les-Bains was once under the dominion of Rome and there are still Roman ruins and Roman baths to see and visit. People from all over Europe and around the world, including writers, poets, composers and ordinary people have come to drink its water. Queen Victoria used to come to Aix-les-Bains under the name of Countess de Balmoral. She loved the town so much that she wanted to buy the hillock called Tresserve and turn it into a piece of England in the middle of France, but this privilege was rejected. When I think about it, as my parents lived there, I could have ended up being an English girl!

The train line into Aix-les-Bains follows the edge of Lake du Bourget, the biggest natural lake in France It looks as though it is snuggled into the arms of the surrounding mountains. There was still snow on the mountains when I arrived. It was majestic and my heart swelled at seeing such beauty. Tears flowed. I could not stop them and I realised how much I was still connected to this place and how much I had missed it. My thoughts went to my parents; I was coming back home for a little while as I had done years before, but this time my Maman and Papa would not be there waiting for me. The realisation was too great to bear.

I am always asked whether I feel French or Australian. In truth, I have a profound connection with both Australia and France. My life may have started reluctantly enough in Australia-the idea of bringing a young child to a strange country was difficult to accept-however, I love both countries equally and I cannot make a choice. Both countries are dear to my heart and I think as human beings we are universal. Our ancestors and humanity itself have created these divisions between human beings through greed and control.

In Aix-les-Bains, I met and stayed with my school friends, Francine and Alain, and bathed in my past. I walked through the town, re-living my youth and climbing 'my' mountains to keep up my training, as well as absorbing their beauty to the fullest. My sister, her partner and my brother came to Aix-les-Bains and we spent time together. In the church where my siblings and I were christened and had our Holy Communions, families on both sides were reunited and we all attended a special mass for the ones who had passed away and the ones still living. We were together as one, which was very touching.

On a miserable, cold and rainy day, my brother and I went to my parents' grave in the cemetery of Tresserve that overlooks the lake. In front of their tomb I felt their love and support all around me. My heart ached with how much I missed them and I cried.

In Aix-les-Bains, my sister and I met with my sister's friends, Francoise and Jean-Claude, who had walked Saint James' Way to Santiago de Compostela from their house a few years earlier. They did their best to reassure Michele that I would be alright. Amazingly, Francoise was born the same day and month as me, but not the same year. They were really happy for me and they re-lived with us their pilgrimage, which was still deep in their souls. A pilgrim is always a pilgrim.

Soon, it was time to leave Aix-les-Bains and begin my journey. I had had a lovely time with everyone and received a lot of encouragement and good wishes. My cousins could not believe their ears when they heard what I wanted to do, however, they were very proud. For me to migrate with my family to Australia was one thing, but this was adventure! As they said, 'She will always surprise us!'

WEEK ONE

The beginning

I left Aix-les-Bains for Reims. I was crossing France for a second time in a TGV train and I was getting a bit tired. Claude and Monique, who had previously done the walk and who I had met in Brisbane, were waiting for me at the railway station. We had kept in touch since our first meeting in Brisbane and a special bond had been created between us because of our connection with the Saint James' Way.

In France, four different routes will take you to the end of your pilgrimage at Santiago de Compostela: from Paris, from Le Puy-en-Velay, from Arles or from Vezelay. The route from Vezelay is divided into two branches and you can either walk through Bourges (northern branch) or through Nevers (southern branch). I wanted to start from Vezelay in the Yonne region, taking the southern route, as it is the most ancient path through France, though I know some would disagree.

The relics of Saint Mary Magdalene are held in the Abbey of Vezelay. Even from an early age, I saw the injustice she suffered, though I did not understand exactly what she had done. I could not bear the thought that a human being could be stoned to death for whatever sin they may have committed. I felt sorry for her, as the harsh judgment of one human being towards another, with or without justification, never sat right with me. Some of us, including myself, feel such injustices keenly, even from our first years. In Mary Magdalene's case, hysteria had probably overtaken the crowd and it would have been too late and too difficult to stop the stoning. Some were most likely too scared to intervene, but Christ arrived and saved her, saying, 'Whoever has not sinned can throw the first stone'. As a child, I read books about the lives of the saints and I used to read a particular picture book distributed by the chocolate company 'Suchard'. After school, French children would eat a few squares of chocolate with a piece of bread. A real treat. In those days, books were a luxury. I loved these Christian stories and I read many during my younger years.

Whatever the reason, I wanted to start my journey at Vezelay. In 2006, Monique and Claude had also started their pilgrimage from Vezelay, going via Bourges. As I was a new pilgrim, Monique had decided to walk with me for the first four days to get me started, and we would take the route from Vezelay through Nevers, adding about 40 kilometres to the journey. On the fifth day, I would walk alone while Monique and Claude would drive ahead and wait in Nevers. They took me under their wing and I was deeply touched by their kindness.

I was close to Reims train station and was getting a bit nervous; I wondered if I would recognise them, as it had been two years since I had last seen them in Brisbane. The train pulled into the station and I found them without a problem. It was so nice to see them again. Straight away, I noticed their worried looks at seeing my bulging backpack. I had packed more than was advised, taking into account that I would cross France in spring, which was really winter for me, and would finish my pilgrimage in July, summer, which meant two types of clothing.

With pride and love, Monique and Claude showed me their town. Rain and freezing weather did not dampen our spirits and I tried to absorb as much information as possible. The city of Reims had played an important role in the history of France, as it was the traditional place for the Kings of France to be crowned. It also has the most impressive Gothic cathedrals of France. Reims is the capital of the Champagne region and is approximately 130 kilometres from Paris.

Monique, Claude and I went to a massive mountaineering shop to get a pair of trekking poles, which were going to be my precious travelling companions. Later that evening, I emptied my backpack on their dining room table, as Claude wanted to make sure that I had what was necessary for the walk. He was quite satisfied, but was scrutinising all the contents of my backpack because he thought it was too heavy. I had a strange thought: perhaps he felt I was carrying a make-up case or something like that. Hmm! As if I would! He advised me to cut down on the number of pairs of socks I was carrying. I was not keen on this at all, as I was planning on wearing two pairs of socks every day to prevent blisters: one light cotton pair and one thicker woollen pair. I had to wash them every day and have an extra pair in case of rain. Reluctantly, he accepted and then he asked me what the head-net was for. To his astonishment, I told him that in some areas mosquitoes and insects were bad and a head-net was advisable, to which he replied, 'No use. Leave it here'. In a weak voice I explained, 'It only weighs 100 grams!' I put it back in my bag, deciding to ignore him. He pointed to the two bottles of organic spray for bedbugs and advised me to get rid of them because they had never had a problem with bedbugs. Of course, I kept them. I did not want to run the risk of bedbugs spoiling my nightly sleep or causing me to be constantly itchy and scratching. I was expecting a reprimand for all the tablets that my brother had sent to Reims, but no. I thought this was going to be it. Good, he was finished. Then a bomb shell: my mattress! 'A mattress?' he asked. 'What for? You will never need it'. Claude asked me what it weighed. I told him it weighed 700 grams and that I wanted to bring it in case I had to sleep outside or if I could not find any lodging. Plus, it was on the list of things to bring on the pilgrims' association website. Claude put his hands over his head in disbelief and said to leave it with them as I would never need it. In a flash, I saw myself sleeping on rocks in the forest or on the hard bench of a church, feeling all the bumps and the discomfort of not sleeping in a warm bed or a bunk. The thought gave me shivers. No way! I could not dump my mattress. Then he asked, 'Did you ever walk with such a heavy bag during your training?' Quietly, like a child caught doing the wrong thing, I told him that I had only trained with six kilograms on my back. With despair in his voice, he told me that I was going to ruin my back, but he knew I would not change my mind and I saw a cheeky look in his eyes, telling me, 'You will think twice about this mattress, I know. I shall wait and see!'

The evening before our departure, I rang my children and their partners. I have to admit I felt quite emotional, though I still did not realise what was ahead of me. I reminded them of my love and told them I would walk with them in my heart. They sent me words of encouragement and, most of all, their love in return. I was still sure that nothing bad would happen to me.

Before leaving Reims, Claude and Monique gave me a guide-book. It is one of the guides that the pilgrims carry with them as a directory and this one detailed the route from Vezelay to Saint-Jean-Pied-de-Port, a little French town right near the Spanish border. I was so touched by their kind-heartedness and generosity. They dismissed my thanks, for when pilgrims have completed their pilgrimage, they, in turn, give back to other pilgrims what they have received along the way. What a blessing! I started to feel part of the community of pilgrims and I knew I would never be alone, no matter what.

The guide-book had been written and researched by Madame Chassain and her husband over a period of ten years. Each section covers a day's walk with thorough information about the length of each stage in kilometres, when to turn left or right or to go straight ahead, where to find lodgings with addresses and phone numbers included, and details about food shops, cafés and historical places along the path. It also outlines the difficulties of the walk with detailed aerial maps. These leaflets were going to be my bible. It would have been a mammoth job to compile so much information for the pilgrims. In my heart, I thanked the Chassains for their work, not quite comprehending, at that time, the extent of what they had done.

We went to bed and I slept like a baby, full of dreams. On 3 April we left Reims by car for Vezelay with my heavy backpack and my mattress in the back of the car. The day was grey and it was very windy, but my heart was light. I was so full of expectation for what was ahead. Not even the weather could diminish my happiness.

Vezelay is a small town in the Burgundy region, which is famous for its excellent wines, including Pinot Noir, Chardonnay and Melon de Bourgogne, to name a few. One might have trouble finding the village on a map, as it is so small. There is no railway station and it is only accessible by car, bus, bicycle or on foot. Approximately seven kilometres from Vezelay there is a railway station called Sermizelles, and some pilgrims walk from there to Vezelay just as a warm up.

After a few hours of travelling along highways and the French countryside, there it appeared as if by magic at the top of a majestic hill: Vezelay and its magnificent basilica. It was my first glimpse of the village and it looked just beautiful. My heart started to beat so hard that it felt like pain. Very soon, I will be there, I thought. I was overcome by mixed feelings, for after so many years of preparation, the moment had finally arrived. It was hard to believe that soon my dream would become a reality. The weather was still horrible, but I was over the moon.

To reach the basilica we drove along a very steep cobbled road. It was cold when we arrived, but I was still so happy to be in the company of Claude and Monique and looking forward to the task ahead. We had a lovely lunch in a very typical French restaurant called 'Le Pot' situated in the village square. Claude took some photographs, then, as a warm up, Monique and I started our eight-kilometre walk in the fierce wind and rain. The area is very pretty with its wooded hills and its mountains rising to over 300 metres above sea level. The height of the mountains is not noticeable as they are round like the mountains in some parts of England. However, when you have walked them, it is a different matter. We were following the same pilgrims' path from the eighth or ninth century, which produced in me an overwhelming feeling. Our first walk was difficult with its steep hills and the tracks were full of water, mud and slippery stones. At times we had one or two kilograms of mud stuck under our shoes. We had to be careful not to fall, especially with our backpacks-mine weighed more than 14 kilograms without my water bottle, which I had to carry. I was learning to walk with trekking poles for the first time. In front of me, Monique was walking with hers so gracefully, as if they were an extension of her arms. For me they felt hard to handle. I could not walk properly and it annoyed me. By the end of the walk, however, I did not feel so hopeless and the trekking poles became my companions. I realised how useful they were going to be in relieving pressure on my upper body and back. Hanging from my neck was a digital camera in its case, a present from my dear friends Charlie and Paul from Brisbane. This camera would be the visual witness of my pilgrimage, recording where I walked, places I would see and the people I would meet along the way.

We arrived at Pierre-Perthuis in more rain and wind. I felt very cold, but I was happy and excited. As we were crossing a bridge, a car stopped on the other side of the road and a young woman got out carrying a bottle of water. She approached us and offered it to us. I was witnessing first-hand the kindness on the path. She told us that she did the pilgrimage a few years ago and she had decided to do the first stage in one go, that is to say, 36 kilometres in one day. Oh dear, I thought. During the last eight kilometres of that initial day, she told us that she was in so much pain that each step was an agonising experience, so much so that she nearly abandoned the whole thing. Through her experience, she knew what we would be going through and wished us 'bonne chance' ('good luck').

Further down the road, Claude was waiting for us in his car. He asked how we felt and I replied, 'No sweat! Easy, in a way. If every walk is like that, it is going to be a piece of cake'. We went to the basilica to have my credential signed. A credential is a small official folded document. It is also called a passport and identifies you as a pilgrim. It contains details such as your family name, Christian names, date and place of birth, address, nationality, passport details, your photograph, signature, where you started your pilgrimage and whether you are doing it on foot, by bicycle or on a horse. It also has a place for stamps, which you can collect as you pass through each town or village. This document allows you to sleep only one night in each refuge, shelter, convent or monastery along the way and records the details of where you stay overnight. The stamps on your credential show your progress and police can track you in case of an accident. At the end of your journey, when you arrive in Santiago de Compostela, on presentation of a credential that has been correctly stamped along the way, you receive a certificate called the 'Compostela', which is proof that you have walked the Saint James' Way.

While standing in front of the basilica, which is dedicated to Saint Mary Magdalene, my eyes marvelled at such splendour. It is the largest Romanesque church in France and is only just shorter than the Cathedral of Notre Dame in Paris by a mere three metres or so. In 1146, Saint Bernard de Clairvaux preached the Second

Crusade in front of the basilica at Vezelay, and it was also here that King Richard Coeur de Lion of England and King Philippe Auguste of France met and joined their armies for the western invasion of the Holy Land from 1189 to 1192. In 1946, another great event occurred here: the Crusade of Peace for reconciliation after the Second World War. Two extremes: war and peace. There are wooden crosses in the basilica in commemoration of this latter event. In 1979, the basilica and Vezelay became part of the UNESCO World Heritage list.

All the details of each pilgrim who starts their pilgrimage from Vezelay or is passing through are registered in a large book in the basilica. The lady at the counter at the entrance to the basilica, Pierrette, asked me where I was going to finish the pilgrimage. When I told her it would be Fisterra, she advised me to go on to a place called Muxia, which was only a few days further on. At that early stage I was oblivious to the challenge of the number of kilometres I would have to cover and I agreed: Muxia would be the end of my journey.

When I had finished with Pierrette, Claude approached me and suggested that from now I should be called 'Claude the Australian'. This is how I came to be known along the path. It was quite clever, as it was easier to remember 'the Australian' instead of my family name.

I was wandering around inside the basilica when suddenly a woman grabbed my arm and took me aside. I smiled and followed her. She started to talk to me in a language I could not comprehend. I know English, French and could manage Italian, but it was none of these languages. Somehow, I felt and knew from my heart that she needed a listening ear. It did not matter whether I

26

understood what she was saying; it seemed so important to her to just say it. She talked with a lot of gestures and I listened and let her speak. Her emotional pain was so obvious that compassion overcame me. As she calmed down after her outpouring, she put both hands over her heart. Then she dug her hands into her chest, making a gesture of grabbing and pulling her heart out. I did not say anything. I was not afraid, but full of empathy, of love for this human being who was in such distress. To my surprise, she then moved her hands-curved in the shape of a cup, as if she was holding her heart in her palms-and gently deposited 'her heart' on mine. I was overcome by deep emotions. I opened my arms and held her. She cried on my shoulder then left without a word.

I stayed still for a few minutes to register what had just happened, not quite comprehending the full significance of this event. I did not know her name or where she was from, I just sensed her sorrow, which would have been so profound, and sent her my love. I promised myself to carry with me whatever pain she had to Santiago de Compostela. Out of respect for this woman, I did not share my experience with Claude and Monique and, deep in my thoughts, I continued to explore the inside of the basilica.

As I was discovering this beautiful basilica, I went to the crypt of Saint Mary Magdalene. Two women were deep in prayer kneeling on the cold stones. Behind two very heavy metal doors there is a magnificent wrought-iron casket that is painted gold and contains the remains of Saint Mary Magdalene in a small, red, cylindrical glass. In the crypt there was a feeling of peace, but strangely enough I could feel sorrow as well. While I was praying, I saw two young women lying on the cold stony floor with their arms in the shape of the cross. It was quite moving. I felt so much respect for these ladies and sensed their suffering. Later, Claude, Monique and I went to our lodging in the refuge of Saint Mary Magdalene, which was run by Franciscan friars. I had heard that it was here in Vezelay that Saint Francis of Assisi had opened the first French monastic community for friars in 1217. The building was imposing; it was made of huge stones and constructed so long ago, yet it was still providing respite and shelter to pilgrims. In the dining room I met ex-pilgrims from different pilgrims' organisations. The three of us shared the substantial dinner that Monique had prepared for us in Reims, and I saw for the first time what my life was going to be like for the next few months. It would be about sharing and being respectful towards everyone and everything. We sat on wooden benches in front of a long wooden table and shared the dinner using the cutlery and plates provided. Before bed, we had lovely hot showers, which I savoured after my day's walk. The individual showers were used by everyone, males and females. They were small, so small in fact that I had trouble finding a place to put my travelling documents and my clothes without getting them wet. I put my shoes outside the door to inform other pilgrims that I was using the shower. I would have to get used to this and say goodbye to comfort. I was advised that from now on I would have to learn to carry everything with me wherever I was going, even when taking my shower. It was going to be a hard lesson. I was in this frame of mind when I suddenly remembered that when my sister and I were young we used to go to the 'Thermes', the communal baths in Aix-les-Bains, to have our weekly shower. We had to sit on a bench outside the cubicle and wait for our turn. There was always a long queue, as in those days very few families had a bathroom. Life has changed so much. I was back in the 'good old days' and it made me realise how we take so many things for granted today.

Privacy was going to be quite a challenge for me. During the night I did not sleep very well; sharing a bedroom with other people was hard. I did not dare to undress or put on my pyjamas in front of everyone, as I am quite self-conscious. Realising how sheltered I had been, I crawled into my sleeping bag fully dressed and waited for everyone to fall asleep, then, still in my sleeping bag, I undressed. It was quite a challenge, but I managed to put on my pyjamas, still feeling quite uncomfortable. Today I was among friends, but what about tomorrow? Suddenly, from Monique and Claude's corner came the sound of snoring. At least they are sleeping well, I thought. Good on them. After a while, I fell asleep, but was woken by music and singing around midnight. There was some festivity outside in front of the basilica as it was Easter Sunday. I stirred in my bunk, but Monique and Claude were still asleep, oblivious to the noise. Soon I fell back to sleep and managed a few more hours' rest.

We got up early to assist at the Lauds and afterwards the benediction of the pilgrims at the basilica. The Lauds is a religious celebration with psalms and songs after the Matins. The Matins are the first part of a religious ceremony that is performed before daylight for the monks and nuns. The Franciscan nuns' glorious voices and songs lifted my soul. The mass was said in the nave where on 23

June 1976 at exactly 2.27pm, Father Hugues Delautre, a Franciscan monk serving in Vezelay at the time, discovered the secret of the basilica. At midday on the summer solstice, when the sun is in the middle of the sky, the rays that shine through the southern windows fill the entire length of the nave so perfectly that it looks as though a tunnel of light is streaming through the very centre of the basilica. Father Delautre ascertained that the basilica had been measured and built so precisely for this very purpose. This glorious event can be seen every year on 23 June, the summer solstice, which is also Saint John the Baptist's feast day.

I was listening to the beautiful voices of the Franciscan nuns when a complete peace entered my soul. When the nuns sang 'Christ is resurrected', a little bird flew inside the basilica and landed on one of the columns above the altar and started to sing at the top of its voice, joining in the chorus. It was divine. This little body could express such high notes. It stopped as the song finished and flew away. I felt the hand of God over all of us. Was it a message? I did not know, but whatever it was, it was magic and a great present for my 64th birthday.

After the Lauds we had the blessing of the pilgrims; there were emotions galore. My name was mentioned as well as where I came from and where I was going to finish. Two other pilgrims were mentioned, and of course Monique, who was just going to walk a few days. A Franciscan nun gave me a little booklet; it was the gospel of Saint John. Another nun agreed to have a photograph taken with me, close to the altar. Usually, this is never allowed and I felt blessed. As we reached the entrance of the basilica, a young Frenchwoman approached me and asked me if she could speak to me for a few minutes. I followed her and she told me that she had come to the Lauds hoping that I would be there, as she had noticed me in the basilica the day before. She asked me if I could hold her. I did and she cried in my arms, her sobs making her small body shake vigorously. She was suffering so much and I saw the pain of all of us in her. After a while her cries lessened and eventually stopped. She confided in me the reason for her distress and I gave her words of comfort. We walked together up to my lodging. For the last time, I hugged her and said goodbye before going inside the Saint Mary Magdalene refuge. I told her that I would pray for her along the path and in the Cathedral of Santiago. As she left, Claude said, cheekily, 'You cannot do that all the time otherwise you will never arrive in Santiago de Compostela!' I smiled. He understood that I would keep on doing this hugging and I realised that he would have seen me on the previous day with the other woman in the basilica. At that very moment, and as a result of these two incidents, I realised that my pilgrimage might be somewhat different, special, and might become for me a 'pilgrimage of the heart'. I would need to stay very attentive in all my meetings along the path.

I had been doing some volunteer work back in Brisbane and hugging is part of my nature. My volunteer work takes me to people in oncology and palliative care wards. All human beings need to feel they are special. Hugging is a way for me to show love to another being. We like to stroke a baby because its skin feels so lovely and smooth, but I have noticed in the hospitals that some people stop stroking their family members when they are all wrinkly and old, or perhaps they are too afraid to show their emotions. I believe that a time like this, however, should be a time to re-connect with people's loved ones. I have been blessed with the ability to hug freely, as I find it easy to connect with other people in their times of distress.

Back in our lodging we collected our bags. Mine felt somewhat lighter, the reason being that it was so cold that I was wearing two jumpers, one fleece jacket, a thick water-proof jacket and a warm scarf that had belonged to my Maman. As we were saying our goodbyes, an ex-pilgrim gave me his address in case I needed a place to sleep, as his house was not far from the path. I thanked him. Another kindness; I was going to be alright.

Claude took us back to where we had stopped the day before at Pierre-Perthuis. We were going to meet him again for lunch after a few hours' walking. I texted my children, who were probably sleeping back in Australia, to let them know that I had started. Monique and I waved goodbye to Claude and started our walk to Charpuis, some 22 kilometres away. I was thrilled and excited. We went along the Roman road after Pierre-Perthuis and my joy soon faded, as we had to walk through such muddy paths for at least 10 kilometres, up and down hills, through forests and fields with the rain, wind and cold as companions. I had to be alert at all times. I could not walk on the edge of the tracks as they were so wet and slippery that my feet would sink into the ground, which was soft and wet thanks to the rain and the melted snow. I tried to look at the gorgeous scenery and take some photographs, but was too afraid to do so in case I lost my balance. My backpack was uncomfortable as it leaned towards the right side of my body. After a few hours of this awful walk, Monique and I reached a bitumen road. We travelled through villages and saw beautiful countryside. It was so green. I saw my first 'perce-neige' ('snowdrop'): spring was here, but I could not feel it. In French, 'perce-neige' is very expressive and poetic: it means 'piercing through the snow'. Bonjour to spring, au revoir to winter.

We passed close to the 12th century Chateau de Bazoches, built over three centuries, as well as the 17th century Castle of Vauban. After crossing another forest we walked through green fields again. Suddenly, at the edge of a forest, the Chapel of Saint Roch, which was a refuge for pilgrims in the Middle Ages, appeared as if from nowhere. Unfortunately, the doors were closed, so we could not see inside. After walking more kilometres in the mud, my mobile rang. My children and their partners wished me happy birthday and sent me their love. Instantly, I forgot the difficulty of the path and the pain, and shared the joy of these precious calls: a beacon for the spirit.

As we arrived at Neuffontaines, we saw Claude sitting on a bench in a chapel courtyard waiting for us. He had prepared a lunch of sandwiches and fruit. As the doors of the chapel were open, my curiosity got the better of me and I went in. I found the vault of Marshal Vauban and his family. Sebastien Le Prestre de Vauban was a soldier, engineer, economist and scientist of his time. He changed the way of warfare and during his lifetime built almost 160 fortifications. At the left of the altar is a painting of Joan of Arc, beside her, Saint Philippe, and at his right the 'warrior', Archangel Michael. Joan of Arc is said to have heard the Archangel Michael's voice at Domremy, telling her to deliver France from the English.

I re-joined Monique and Claude, and after sitting with

them for a little while I could not get up again. I was in such pain: it seemed that all my joints had seized! I saw Claude and Monique's worried looks, but I did not say anything and started walking again like an old woman. After a while the pain eased, then it was more mud, more climbs and more descents.

Monique was teaching me about the symbols that I had to look for, which would indicate the pilgrims' way. The symbol is a yellow shell or a yellow triangle on a blue background. The direction in which the shell or triangle is pointing informs you which way to go: left, right, or straight ahead. You have to always be alert, as you can find them anywhere: on a sign-post, on a tree, even on a fence. I still tried to look at the scenery, but could not stop to admire it as we had to keep on walking. At times, the symbols were difficult to find or were missing and I was grateful to be walking with Monique. I was getting more and more tired. The huge distance that I was planning on covering was slowly sinking in. Every metre felt like a kilometre and I longed to arrive at our destination.

My sister, Michele, and her partner, Bernard, had decided to come down from Orleans to wish me happy birthday and to see me off. Monique and I were so tired and I wished that a car would come and pick us up. Michele rang saying that she could not find the lodging. Oh dear, if my sister could not find the lodging, what hope was there for us? I was imagining more kilometres to cover when I saw my sister's car coming our way. When she saw the state I was in, she begged me to get in the car as I was so pale, even my lips were white and she said that I looked like a ghost. I told her that I could not accept the lift as I had to walk into Charpuis to our lodging.

Monique intervened and said that Claude would bring us back to this point the next morning. I was so relieved not to have to walk another metre! Seeing the state I was in, Bernard smiled teasingly and said that he was sure that in two weeks' time, I would call and ask them to come and pick me up. Moreover, to be sure to hear my call, he promised to keep his mobile phone under the pillow! I smiled, but inside I was fuming and it made me more determined. I would have to make sure that I would show him and my workmates back home who I really was and what I was capable of.

We arrived at l'Herminiere and our hosts, Mireille and Jean-Claude, welcomed us with open arms. Their names can be found in Mme Chassain's pilgrims' guide- book. They receive pilgrims at their little farm as their contribution to society. They felt sorry for me when they saw the state I was in. They had prepared tea, coffee and cake for all of us. Their place was warmed not only by the heating of the house, but also with their kindness. Michele and Bernard did not stay for dinner as they had to go back to Orleans; it was Easter Sunday and they had to see their family. I tried to get up to say goodbye, but could not: my joints were locked and painful. With great effort and will I managed it, and once up I felt a bit better. I hugged Michele with all my love. I could see how worried she was. Bernard reminded me that he would see me in two weeks or perhaps before. With a smile, I told him not to bother. After a beautiful dinner in their marvellous renovated farm, Jean-Claude opened a bottle of champagne for my birthday. It was not every day that they had a pilgrim arriving at their farm house on her birthday and from Australia. I was touched.

After dinner we went to bed, but thanks to my lopsided backpack, my right shoulder was extremely painful and red. I did not sleep well as the pain woke me often. Mireille had left some gel to massage into it and I spent most of the night doing so. By morning I felt better, but I had very little sleep. After a good breakfast, Monique and I left. I could barely walk. I was so stiff and I was not looking forward to the day ahead. It would be a hard one again.

For an hour or more, the pain in my joints was excruciating, but eventually it left my body as I warmed up. We climbed up and down hills and our friend 'the mud' was still our constant companion. The two of us got lost and we had to trace our way back to the last symbol we had seen. We had planned to cover 26 kilometres, but had to add extra kilometres to the walk that day. Being on the road all day, you dread the thought of adding extra kilometres. We crossed forests and fields and saw strange trees without leaves that looked like ghosts. I took some photos of the first wildflowers I saw that day. They had been able to blossom because they were protected by fallen branches. What a contrast: the forests with their leafless trees represented death, while the spring flowers represented life.

We saw a tiling factory, the Tuilerie de la Chapelle, which dated back to the 18th century and it was still producing roof tiles for the old houses in the area, using the original production methods. A bit further on, the yellow shell symbols of the Saint James' Way disappeared and were replaced by symbols of bronze scallop shells which appeared on the pavement, indicating the direction to follow.

We arrived at Guipy and met Claude who was waiting patiently for us, smiling as usual. Again, he had prepared lunch for us. I was concerned for him as he had to wait for us. I thought, '30 kilometres by car is nothing, but on foot it takes all day'. He was not bored, however, as he always managed to talk to the locals. It was so nice to see him again. After our 45-minute lunch break, Monique and I started again and crossed a forest with the trees still stripped of their leaves. I wondered what the forest would look like in summer with the trees covered with leaves of vibrant green. It must be wonderful to walk in the forest at that time. Between Corbigny and Chitry-les-Mines we passed in front of Jules Renard's childhood home. Jules Renard was a French writer who was born in 1864 and died in 1910. He was elected to the honourable 'Academie Goncourt' (Goncourt Literary Academy). The Academy was founded by Edmond Goncourt in opposition to the 'Academie Francaise', as he did not like their policies. The Academy Goncourt promotes and encourages works in literature in French and was not limited to only citizens of France. It took me back to my youth when I read some of his works and here I was looking at the house where he spent his early childhood.

We crossed the bridge over the Nivernais Canal and arrived at the village of Le Bouquin. Behind us we saw a beautiful view of the Morvan region and walked along a lane of linden trees. Still tired, but surrounded by the beauty of this region, I forgot my fatigue for a while.

After Breches, we took another path, but it was muddy and slippery. The water from the rain had created a track along the path and I suggested walking where the rain had cleared the track, as it seemed safer. I did not care about my boots getting wet as they were water-proof. The muddy section of the path was too dangerous. After walking for a while along a stream, we arrived at the bottom of a very steep hill with more mud, fast running water and wet, dead leaves everywhere: very tricky. A cold wind from the north was causing havoc with my body as well. It was piercing through all my clothes and reaching my bones: horrid. My backpack was so heavy. I felt my tiredness coming back. Every step triggered pain all over my body, in all my joints, hips, back and feet. It felt as though every part of me was hurting and we still had to climb up and up in such bad conditions. At one stage, I felt I could not go on any further. Even the beautiful scenery could not take my pain away. I wondered what the pain would have been if I had not taken some analgesic tablets. Monique was tired too. She was walking a few metres in front and was encouraging me to carry on. At one point, my right leg did not want to listen to my brain anymore and I could not control it. I was afraid. Would I make it? I decided to push aside my fear and I made a huge effort to keep my mind on the climb, trying to forget the pain and the fact that my leg did not listen to me anymore. I had no choice: I had to be strong and finish the climb. I was trying with all my might to focus on the task at hand when I heard Monique shouting a message of encouragement, for after two more bends and a little climb, there was a sealed road. I gritted my teeth and eventually, I made it. After reaching the summit at a height of 382 metres, we arrived at 6.30pm in Saint-Reverien where we found Claude sitting on the stairs in front of the town hall, chatting with the locals. They were waiting for us in front of the communal lodging of Saint-

Reverien. We had walked more than eight hours that day in bad conditions. My thoughts went back to the young girl who brought us some water when we had arrived at Pierre-Perthuis and I understood the pain she would have endured during the first day of her pilgrimage after walking 36 kilometres.

Saint-Reverien is situated in the north-west of Burgundy and 204 kilometres from Paris. In the centre of the main square there is a beautiful Romanesque church, huge for such a small community of 241 inhabitants. In the year 200, Saint Revezianus (Saint Reverien), a missionary bishop, was beheaded and became a martyr in that village. A small chapel was built above his tomb and the village and the church took the name of Saint-Reverien. Later, a Benedictine monastery was built and in 1055 it was affiliated with the great Cluny Abbey. The church was finished during the 12th century. Due to its affiliation with Cluny, the village of Saint-Reverien became a common stop for the pilgrims on their way to Santiago de Compostela. At that time, the village would have been a vibrant community. Nowadays, the village is dying as its youth have left to find work in bigger cities. There is not one shop open, only a mobile butcher, baker and greengrocer who come once or twice a week. To this day, Monsieur Thionnet, a member of the local community, takes great pride in receiving the pilgrims who pass through the village, just as they had done in the Middle Ages. We found a nice, small and clean municipal refuge with a few bunks and everything we needed for the night and we prepared our meal. Thanks to the dedication of M. Thionnet towards pilgrims, the village still lives.

After standing still for a little while my body felt like ice;

even a hot shower did not fix this. M. Thionnet kindly brought a heater and told us to switch it off before we went to bed. We had our dinner with what Claude had bought along the way and M. Thionnet joined us for a chat. When we went to bed I was still in pain. A few minutes later, I could hear some snoring coming from Claude's bunk.

The next morning it was minus two degrees and we had to go outside as the toilets were in the square in a public area. My body was still stiff and aching. From the previous day's experience, I knew that after walking for one or two hours the pain would go away. I learnt to be patient and tried to forget the pain, but that was easier said than done. We crossed Saint-Reverien and started our walk by taking an ancient Roman track, then we started to climb again. The day was cold, but sunny. I found the path was not as difficult as the previous day, though my backpack was feeling heavier and heavier and was giving me trouble. We went through beautiful scenery and were taken in by the beauty of nature. Later, we met Claude and had our lunch in a bus shelter as it was starting to rain. We did not cover much ground that day: only 19 kilometres.

We arrived at Premery quite early and stopped for the night in a small lodging. Premery had been badly affected by the global financial crisis. Firms had closed down and a lot of people had lost their jobs. At the dinner table, Claude asked me to stop drinking water and to drink beer instead, but I declined and told him I would never drink beer! He then lectured me about the healthy ingredients in beer for a pilgrim who spends so much energy on walking, as well as the need to replenish the minerals in the body. I was still not convinced and stuck to my water.

As a pilgrim, I had to follow certain routines every single day and this had to be done religiously. One of them was that as soon as I arrived at my refuge, I would have to unpack, have a shower and wash my day-clothes, hoping that they would be dry by the morning. There was no heating in our lodging, so I tried to dry them in a towel and extract as much of the water as possible. When I woke up I would put on the clothes that I had washed the evening before, even if they were damp, and put the dry ones back in my backpack.

After a typical French breakfast, we left. It was cold, dull and there were a lot of clouds and wind about. The cold wind was still reaching my bones, despite the fact that I was wearing two special winter jumpers that I had bought in a special shop back in Brisbane. At the time, I had been dubious about their capability to keep me warm and I was right. I had the one fleecy jumper and my heavy jacket, but I was still feeling the cold, even while walking. I felt a shooting pain through my buttock and down the back of the leg. My sciatic nerve started to give me trouble and my body begged me to give it a break. After walking four kilometres, the pain lessened and then disappeared, thankfully! My bag still felt heavy, but by re-organising the way I packed it, it no longer hurt my right shoulder. I was learning. On that day, an event occurred that triggered one of my greatest fears. While we were going through a suburb, two dogs escaped from their yard and followed us, barking ferociously. Oh dear: dogs! I was frightened of them and always had been ever since I was tiny. I told Monique of my extreme fear of dogs, as I had been bitten as a child and I still had the marks on the back of my leg to prove it. Monique told me not to be frightened, as the

41

dogs would smell my fear. I knew this, but how do you control that fear? She told me to use my trekking poles and showed me how to draw a half circle with them behind my back and to keep on walking in a way that ensured my legs were always guarded by the poles. I had to keep one trekking pole close to my left foot and the other one close to my right foot, and continually move the poles in a half circle as my feet kept on walking. Apparently, the trick is to have your trekking poles at ground level at all times, otherwise the dogs will think that you want to attack them and you can guess the result. Monique was hopeful that the dogs would get tired of the game and would go back to their home and leave us alone. I was somewhat dubious of this method, but I did not have any other choice. I listened and tried to do my best, but I was still not convinced and I was scared. To my amazement, however, the dogs left. My legs were like cotton wool, but I kept on walking, doing this half circle for a little while longer, too afraid that the dogs would return. They did not. I could relax and pull myself together.

As usual, Claude was waiting for us for lunch with his lovely smile and cheekiness, this time at the little village of Mauvron. I realised that tomorrow I would be walking by myself for the first time. Claude and Monique would go to Nevers by car and wait for me there and I knew I would miss Monique, with her advice, the chats we had and her kind concern. Tomorrow would be my big start and I realised how much I had relied on these two friends. Claude was always there for us with lunch prepared and he had looked at the map and judged how many kilometres we could cover on the day, taking into consideration where the lodgings were and making sure we were safe. Monique taught me the ropes, what to look for with the symbols and to walk back to the last symbol if I did not see any after walking 500 metres. Monique had been such a great companion and pillar of strength. I would miss her. From tomorrow, I would have only myself to rely on. Each night, I would have to look at the next day's walk and work out how many kilometres I would cover. This would depend on where I could find lodgings and the difficulty of the track. I would have to deal with my insecurity and fear, and I would have to learn to trust God and my intuition. It would be the beginning of my solo pilgrimage, come what may.

That last day, we walked about 19 kilometres and stayed in Guerigny at a hotel with special prices for pilgrims. It was cold in the hotel as the heating had been turned off after 1 April. I managed to wash my clothes and with extra towels I dried them for the next day. Suddenly, I remembered that about 36 years ago in France, my ex-husband and I had had the idea of walking all around France when we retired. And here I was. I was the one who was going to walk across France and Spain, but by myself! How strange is life? He was the sporty one, I was not.

Claude, Monique and I went to our rooms before going out again to wander around the lovely town, which is full of naval history. I bought some food for the next day's lunch: a little packet of nuts, some bread, cheese and a tiny box of lollies just in case, and went back to the hotel.

My feet were painful and when I took my boots off I saw that my toes were blue due to the pounding from going down the side of the mountains, and my little toe was showing signs of a blister. Blisters are dreaded by all pilgrims as they can be quite debilitating. I tended to the blister, promising myself to be more aware and to take good care of my feet from now on. One week before the beginning of my pilgrimage, I had massaged my feet twice a day with the juice of a lemon to harden them, but my feet had obviously not been prepared fully for the tough conditions of the walk.

The next morning it was very cold and gloomy again. I covered my little toe with bandages and put lambs wool around all of the toes to prevent blisters. The oil from the wool protects the skin by absorbing sweat and stopping friction between the toes. I checked and re-checked everything, making sure that I did not forget anything. I packed my guide-book, the maps and the things that I would need most at the top of my backpack. We had an early breakfast and I said my goodbyes to Monique and Claude for the day. Claude repeated what he had taught me. My throat was so tight that I could not speak, but I kept on smiling. I was taking my first step alone, like a baby, though I took great comfort from the thought that I would meet them again in Nevers. I received some text messages from Australia, wishing me good luck and courage for the task ahead and lots of love. I started this part of my pilgrimage with heaviness in my heart and I questioned my reasons for doing this walk, wondering if I was not mad after all. It was a bit late for those types of thoughts.

I crossed bridges and villages and the noise of the cars was already driving me crazy. I saw a horse farm, castles, a disused railway station at Urzy and the Castle of Bordes, which was built between the 11th and 17th centuries. At each intersection, my insecurity came flowing back like running water. After walking some kilometres through woods and fields I arrived at an intersection in the middle of a forest. I could not see any symbols, even though I looked everywhere. I was gripped by fear and I did not know what to do. After some hesitation, I decided to turn to my right. I was very tense for the following few kilometres, wondering if I had made the right decision, but I kept on walking just the same. After a while, I saw the symbol of the shell: I was safe. Tears welled up in my eyes and I started to relax a bit.

I crossed more fields and I bathed in the solitude and learnt to relax more, telling myself to trust my own judgment. As I calmed down, I began to enjoy walking alone more and more, appreciating the beautiful scenery that this region has to offer and taking time for photographs. It was such a wonderful feeling until, again, I could not find any more symbols. Fear took over even faster than before. I started to pray when suddenly I saw some little birds singing with joy along the track in front of me. I noticed a few on my right and only one on my left. The one on my left was singing higher notes than the others. The quick flapping of its wings and its high-pitched notes attracted my attention. The other birds flew away after a few minutes. Then the little bird from the left side started to fly from left to right, right to left. Its voice was getting stronger and louder, as if it wanted to give me a message of courage and trust. It was just magical and I started to walk again following the little bird. It did this dance until I arrived at another intersection where there was a symbol. Upon reaching the symbol, the little bird flew away. It reminded me of the little bird that had flown into the basilica at Vezelay to sing during the Lauds. Was it another sign? I had been told that strange things happen on the path and although I was quite sceptical of this, I kept an open mind. I felt as if nature or God was sending me a message. I rested against a tree and tried to make sense of what had just happened, and as I did peace, came upon me and enveloped me. It was unreal.

I continued walking in this peaceful state, enjoying the beautiful scenery. I reached a sealed road with houses on the left and right as far as the eye could see, when suddenly I got cramps in my stomach. Oh dear! I could not see any area where I could be safe, hidden away from everyone. I panicked. I was alone with no more Monique to protect me and a new challenge ahead. I had not given much thought to this predicament before leaving Australia, thinking that I would be able to find toilets everywhere along the path. How naïve of me! I grumbled about why my body was giving me such a difficult time when simply finding my way was hard enough. I kept on walking until I could go no further because of the pain. Not too far from me I could see high walls and some bushes and trees beside them. Perfect. I took my courage in both hands and reached the spot, holding onto my stomach. I was so very afraid that someone would see me, but when nature calls! It was another challenge to deal with. I checked everything, making sure that I would be sheltered from view, when I saw that someone had cut a tree with a branch protruding. It had been cut in such a way that it was at the height of my backpack. I could not believe my luck. Taking off my backpack, dropping it on the ground and lifting it back onto my shoulders again was quite a difficult task because of the weight, and as I had to do this many times a day, my back was getting a real pounding. I thanked the person who had the idea to cut the branch in such a way, however, my thankfulness did not last long, for I was still terrified that someone would see me. Luckily for me, no one came past. Afterwards, as I was walking back to the road, I noticed that the walls were those of a cemetery! I asked God and the inhabitants of the cemetery to forgive me, but in that situation there had been no other choice!

I resumed my walk in the direction of Varennes. I could see the 17th century Chateau des Eveques de Nevers, the castle belonging to the Bishop of Nevers. On the left there was a very small village road with a sign-post indicating 'Pont Saint-Ours'. My heart started beating fast. I was in the Nievre in Burgundy and my mother had been born in a small village in Savoy called Saint-Ours, hundreds and hundreds of kilometres from here. I kept on walking a few metres further when I arrived at a little hamlet called Le Vivier. Imagine my surprise, as my father had grown up in a village called Le Viviers in Savoy. This was too much and it took my breath away. Was it a coincidence that I passed through these places? Were they the same coincidences that had occurred at the beginning that directed me towards this pilgrimage? It felt like a sense of belonging and from then on I knew I would be ok as the sign-posts reminded me that my Maman and Papa would protect me all along my journey and that they would walk it with me. I was not alone. It was such a beautiful feeling.

I had a very small break for lunch, just a few minutes, as I wanted to keep on walking, not knowing how long it would take me to reach Nevers. I crossed the village of Luanges and asked for directions: one can never be too sure! The old farmer on his tractor told me that he did not see many pilgrims going through his village and wished me good luck, but I was on the right track. Thankfully! I had not met a soul that day until then.

I went through a dirt track and walked up and up on a very rocky path when out of the blue, in the middle of a forest and fields, I saw a long lane leading to a well-kept castle: Le Chateau de Luanges. It was hidden behind some tall trees. I was stunned, wondering who would have had the idea of building a castle so deep in the wilderness and what its history was, but there was no one around to ask. I walked for a long time without any problems until I arrived close to Coulanges-les-Nevers. The roads indicated on my map had disappeared as well as the Saint James' Way symbols. From the top of the hill I could see the cathedral of Nevers in the distance, and I asked an old man in his garden for directions. He indicated the direction to me with his hands, but I got lost in his explanation. 'Turn left in the street so and so, then right in the street so and so'. Could he not tell that I was not from the area? I thanked him and left, still confused. I asked some workers, but they were not from the neighbourhood. As I could see Nevers, I thought to myself that it should not be too far and I could manage, until I got completely lost walking in circles. I asked another worker further on, who suggested a road and I followed it for a while, but it took me in the opposite direction. I remembered Monique's advice to be careful when asking someone for directions, as for them it is never far because they use their car and I was on foot. There is a big difference. Sometimes, people did not know the way and would point me in the opposite direction. In the wilderness I was getting lost and there was no one to help me, and in towns there are people, but they do not know the right way or they send me in the opposite direction! I smiled to myself: what else could I do? After a while, I approached a young man who kindly looked in his street directory. I was saved! I arrived at the outskirts of Nevers quite early. I was in pain and my backpack was heavy, though I was trying to push all of this to the back of my mind because I had arrived and I was proud of myself. At the top of the street I saw two familiar shapes: Monique and Claude. I started shouting their names, not caring that the people around were looking at me strangely. I had passed my test with flying colours. I had seen the two of them as soon as I entered the centre of Nevers, and I did not even have to find our designated meeting spot. Hearing me, Monique and Claude turned their heads and saw a 'wild' woman swinging her trekking poles above her head and making quite a racket. They waved at me, huge smiles on their faces. Monique and Claude took me to their car and we went sightseeing in the beautiful town of Nevers. It would be the last time I would be using a car to visit a city. From now on, everything would have to be done on foot.

Nevers is part of the Nievre region in Burgundy in the heart of France. It is located 260 kilometres to the south of Paris and is on the bank of the Loire River. Even though this city was bombed during World War II, it still retains a lot of beauty and character, with its small, winding streets and gorgeous houses. Nevers is well known for its porcelain, which was introduced by the Duke of Nevers during the 17th century. As we drove past the beautiful stone houses, I noticed that a lot of them were for sale. I was told that the global financial crisis had hit Nevers very hard and that people's needs had changed and they did not use porcelain the way they used to. This meant that the porcelain factories were closed down and many people lost their jobs. Heating costs for these houses were too great and people had no choice but to sell. I felt sad when I thought about the consequences of the global financial crisis and about the porcelain disappearing from our dinner tables. Are we going to lose this art form? Only the future can tell, but hopefully we will not. Plastic is so much part of our lives now; it is cheap, light, convenient and unbreakable, but it will never replace the beauty of porcelain.

Nevers is the official site of Saint Bernadette Soubirous, known as Saint Bernadette of Lourdes. She was born on 7 January 1844 at Lourdes and died in Nevers on 16 April 1879 at the age of 35 after contracting tuberculosis in the knee. She learnt to read and write at a hospice school in Lourdes run by the Sisters of Charity. In 1866, at the age of 22, she joined the convent of the Sisters of Charity in Nevers. Monique, Claude and I decided to visit the shrine of Saint Bernadette, each in our own way. As I arrived at the grounds of the convent I saw a grotto on my left, a replica of the one in Lourdes. It took me back to many years ago, when I went with my little family to Lourdes before migrating to Australia. Here I was now, in front of the same grotto, but in Nevers. I was starting something new; walking by myself across France and Spain, not knowing what lay ahead of me, just as I had done 30 years ago when I set off to Australia. Was it another coincidence?

I walked around the convent along the path Saint Bernadette used to walk every day so many years ago. I joined my footsteps to hers as thousands of other pilgrims before me had done. I reached a little chapel, but the door was closed. I tried to open it and with a bit of effort it gave way and I went in. Saint Bernadette used to come and pray here and it was beautiful in its simplicity. I stayed a little while, as I felt at peace, when suddenly I was overwhelmed by a strange emotion and I started to cry. I could not control myself. I could not comprehend what was happening to me. After a while, I noticed that I was standing on the top of Saint Bernadette's original tomb. I was experiencing the same sensations I felt when I was in Lourdes so many years ago. I moved from the top of the tomb and prayed in a corner of the chapel and gradually the peaceful feeling returned to me. On 22 September 1909, 30 years after her death, Saint Bernadette's tomb was opened so that her body could be exhumed. As the story goes, when the tomb was opened for the first time, a pleasant smell came from it and Saint Bernadette's body was discovered to be still perfectly intact. Her skin was smooth and her body had not decomposed at all. Ten years later, her tomb was opened for a second time. Again, her body was still perfectly preserved and there was no trace of decay. There is no natural explanation for these facts, for human beings start to decay soon after death. After much study, and under oath, doctors and lawyers swore that nothing had been done to keep the body in a preserved state. It must have been the hand of God.

Saint Bernadette's body is in a golden, crystal casket inside the chapel. A wax cast has been made to cover her face and hands to protect them. I was so surprised to see how small she was. There is also a museum on the premises dedicated to her life. Every year, many pilgrims stop in Nevers and visit the shrine of Saint Bernadette on their way to Santiago de Compostela. I found Monique and Claude in the little gift shop. Monique took me aside and gave me a Saint Bernadette medal. I wondered if she had noticed my emotion in the little chapel, but I did not ask. I was so touched. I thanked her and gave her a hug. I wore that medal for the rest of my pilgrimage. As Nevers is a major city, I thought there might be an internet café, as I wanted to e-mail my children, but I could not find one. Eventually, I found an 'Auberge de Jeunesse' ('youth hostel') where people could use the computer for free, if available. For the first time since the beginning of my journey, I contacted my children by e-mail. It felt so good. I had walked my first 105 kilometres (according to the map) in five days and I was feeling so proud that I wanted to share it with them.

The three of us left Nevers for Coulanges-les-Nevers, the same area that I had crossed a few hours before. It was so much easier to do it by car! We arrived at Mariele and Jean-Pierre's home. They were ex-pilgrims and had started their pilgrimage in 2008 from their house. Now they welcomed pilgrims into their home, preparing their meals and attending to their medical needs as they could. They welcomed us with open hearts. Their kindness was very evident and they did not ask anything in return; the joy of meeting other pilgrims was enough for them. Jean-Pierre was a 'baliseur', someone who checks all the symbols along the Saint James' Way. He gives his time freely to ensure that all the symbols are still in their right places in the surrounding area. Jean-Pierre informed us that he would leave early the next morning with some other volunteers and planned to cover 60 kilometres in a few days. Such volunteering is vital for the pilgrims, as it helps them to find their way and allows them to keep going forward.

At Mariele and Jean-Pierre's house, we met a young Dutch woman, Brigitte, who was also staying the night. Brigitte had started her pilgrimage from Holland and had crossed the northern part of France through Reims. For pilgrims coming from the northern countries, their paths always go through Nevers. I was stunned and full of admiration, as she would have already covered 400 to 500 kilometres by the time we met.

I laid my things out on my bed before dinner and when I took my shoes off, I could see why my feet were so painful. My toes were multi-coloured with more blisters. I had to do something about them and I decided to use a disinfected needle and thread to pierce them. As the needle went through the blisters a clear liquid came out. I cut the thread away from the blisters so the thread would stay under the skin and it would protect the re-growth of the new skin and not rub on it while walking. In a few days' time I would be able to pull the thread out. By then the skin would have healed and hopefully I would be as good as new. I still had pain in all my joints and I looked like a very old woman when I had to get up or sit down. The pain was so great I could have cried and I was incredibly stiff.

After a huge dinner in wonderful company I got up and went to my bedroom. I took the mattress out of my bag so I could give it to Claude to send back to my sister in Orleans. During the last few days I had realised how hard it was to walk with such a heavy backpack, but I could not get rid of anything else. Claude was happy and smiling. As you can guess, his cheeky eyes were saying, 'I told you so'. I smiled at him. He had won!

The next morning, we all had breakfast together except for Jean-Pierre who had left earlier. Brigitte was ready before me. She had a long staff like the ones used in the Middle Ages, a scallop shell on a very broad hat and a small backpack. I asked her where she had bought her scallop shell and she replied that she had bought it in Holland. What a pity. It would have been nice to have such a symbol of the pilgrimage to add to my outfit. Brigitte looked so much like a real pilgrim and I congratulated her, telling her how beautiful she looked. She told us how useful her big staff had been because she had been attacked by dogs. Monique and Claude showed her how to use her staff to protect herself from these attacks. My heart beat rapidly inside my chest. Dogs again! Oh dear!

I went back to my room, as we still had five more minutes before leaving, and I started a ritual that I would continue until the very end of my journey. In a little bag, I had put all my 'treasures': two Miraculous Medals of Saint Catherine Laboure: one from my Maman and one from my dear friends Charlie and Paul; a little shell from friends Elaine and Ray that they had collected on a Stradbroke Island beach in Queensland; a Saint Christopher medal from Warren; and a crystal from my darling daughter. My dear friend, Julie, from Brisbane had given me a handkerchief from Medjugorje (in the former Yugoslavia), where the Virgin Mary had appeared to three young children. A few years earlier, Julie had carried that handkerchief when she walked the Camino

54

from Porto (Oporto) in Portugal to Santiago de Compostela with her Canadian friend, Rosemary. This handkerchief was very special to her and became very important to me as well. Every day I would place a few drops of the blessed water from Lourdes over the handkerchief and place it on my chest. This blessed water was given to me by Charlie and Paul, and I also had some that had belonged to my Maman that my sister had kept and given to me before I had left Orleans. I wanted to keep all these treasures close to my heart. They represented love and would protect me along my journey. Through this ritual I would be able to connect with my friends and family and would feel their love when difficulties arose.

Why was the Miraculous Medal so important that I wanted to take it with me along the path? In 2007 when I visited my father, I went and prayed in the Chapel of our Lady of the Miraculous Medal on la Rue du Bac in Paris, in memory of my mother who was a devotee of Saint Catherine Laboure. My Maman had sent me this medal in the 1980s. In 2005, I gave it to Lenny, one of my employers, who was diagnosed with cancer. He went through treatments and this precious medal never left his side. He is still in remission. In 2007, Lenny returned my Maman's medal to me and I gave him another one. I was certain that this medal would protect me along my walk as it has protected him along his personal journey. Saint Catherine Laboure was born in Burgundy, France. Her family were devout Catholics and her father was a farmer. Catherine, the youngest child, was only nine years old when she began to look after her older siblings after her mother's death. As she had lost her mother at such a young age, she decided that from then on the Virgin Mary would be her mother. On 21 April 1830, she joined the convent of the Daughters of Charity. When Saint Catherine Laboure walked along the corridors of the Daughters of Charity convent she saw a picture of Saint Vincent de Paul hanging in the hall and recognised him, as she recalled having seen him in a dream, but did not know who he was. He was the founder of the nursing Order of Saint Vincent de Paul. On 27 November 1830, in the chapel at la Rue du Bac, the Virgin Mary appeared to Saint Catherine Laboure and told her to have a medal made according to a certain model. It was distributed far and wide. Numerous conversions, protections and healings occurred and it became known as the 'Miraculous Medal'. I mention these facts as there is a connection between Saint Catherine Laboure and Saint Bernadette, as the Miraculous Medal paved the way for the great events of Lourdes. It has been recorded that Saint Bernadette had said, 'The Lady of the Grotto appeared to me just as she is on the Miraculous Medal'. Saint Catherine Laboure's body was exhumed in 1933 and it was declared perfectly intact by the church. She lies in a glass coffin at the altar of the chapel at la Rue du Bac, just like the one of Saint Bernadette in Nevers. Brigitte wanted to visit Saint Bernadette's shrine, and so we parted ways. I wished her well and told her we might meet again as I was going to walk shorter distances from then on, because she had bad pains in her legs. We hugged and said our goodbyes.

Claude, Monique and Mariele drove me back to my departure point at the bridge over the Loire River. By then my heart was heavy with mixed feelings of excitement and fear for what was ahead of me. I was leaving wonderful ex-pilgrims, the comfort of their friendship, their care and protection. Monique and Claude had been my pillars of strength: I had relied so much on them. I had walked alone yesterday, but I had known I was going to meet them at the end of the day. From now on, however, I would be totally alone and would not see them again along the path and at the mention of this fact, we all started crying. A friendship had been forged and it was hard to separate. But I had to leave, so we waved goodbye and I started my journey with my backpack and my trekking poles as companions. They knew what was to come for me, but I did not.

It was a cold four degrees as I was leaving Coulanges-les-Nevers. Although my heart was still heavy, walking became a sort of meditation and my spirits began to lift. I started to concentrate on finding my way and to my surprise it was quite easy to find the symbols of the Saint James' Way. I saw so many trees with thousands of flowers and it seemed that nature wanted to send me a message of beauty and love. Spring was coming and had created a rainbow of colours for everyone to admire.

I crossed some villages and I noticed that the countryside had put on a green coat and the farm houses were embellished with geranium pots on their window sills. To my eyes all was perfect. After the recent long drought we had known in Queensland in Australia, the magic of the green and deep red was uplifting. My country of birth was so beautiful and it was awakening in front of me - a new season, a new life - and I was there to witness it. My heart swelled at its beauty.

I crossed the village of Yopson and I kept on walking

along the sealed roads until I reached the small village of Les Pitaux when a post van overtook me. It brought back some memories of my childhood. My parents had owned a small business and between the age of four and seven, I was sent to the countryside to stay with my father's relatives. This was very common after the war, as there were no kindergartens and people were so busy rebuilding their lives that they struggled to look after their children alone. In those days, the postman delivered the mail to the farmers either on foot or by bicycle, going from one village to the next. He used to stop at farms that received mail or simply brought the daily newspapers. For me, it was the event of the day as we did not receive many visitors: everyone was too busy working on their farms. I would wait for the postman, hoping that he would bring some mail. If there was any mail he would be invited in by the grandmother who was looking after the house, preparing meals for everyone while the other members of the household worked in the fields. She would always offer the postman a little glass of red wine, maybe to loosen his tongue! The game would start. He always refused the offer at first and the grandmother would insist. 'Oh no, Anne', he would say. 'I can't. I am on duty'. She would reply, 'Come on, Pierre. A small drop', to which he would agree, 'Ok, just this once'. It was always the same. I loved this interaction and found it very funny, as at the end he would always accept the glass of red wine and start talking. He knew all the gossip of the villages and was always eager to divulge it. He was the 'wireless', the connection between everyone. At the end of the day he would have had quite a lot of wine in his stomach and I have no idea how he found his way home at night! What a change from today as the post is now just left in people's letterboxes.

Another car overtook me again: a real traffic jam! Ah, ah! This time it was a farmer. In the old days, farmers used to walk from one field to the next, but now everyone is in a hurry, going faster and faster, and so they drive instead of walking. Are we happier with our new way of living? I really question this. Certainly, it would have been no fun to walk when it was raining or snowing, but it was a healthier life.

I was walking alone along the track, like my ancestors, in this beautiful area, and I was observing nature in all its splendour with delight. I was ready to open up to whatever might come. The birds were singing, announcing the spring. They sounded so happy and I was happy too, relating to nature, to the feeling of my very early, peaceful childhood. I still had in my mind the question of 'why do I want to walk this path and why alone?' At this point I still did not fully understand why. I would discover it in time, but for now I was just enjoying the moment.

I was crossing another small village and saw a young woman attending to her flower garden and very politely asked her if there were any toilets in the area, hoping that she would invite me in. No such luck. I checked the ones near the church, but they were closed. I was a little annoyed that the woman had not invited me into her house, but I thought about it and wondered whether I would have let a stranger into my house. I do not think so. Then how could I blame her? For a little while I felt like a homeless person and it seemed as though I was treated as such. On a daily basis, we are bombarded with fearful news through radio, television and newspapers, and we have become distrustful of others instead of being kind and caring to one another.

I arrived at Magny-Cours and in front of Saint Vincent's Church, I waited for Yves, my host, who would come and pick me up. I had read in my guide-book that Yves and his wife welcome pilgrims into their home. As soon as Yves and I met, we knew that we would have a lot in common. Yves was very spiritual and we were able to exchange so much about life in general, like old friends. This meeting was my first 'tete-a-tete' along my pilgrimage and was the first of what would be a long line of meaningful exchanges. Once we reached Yves' place at the nearby village of Saint-Parize-le-Chatel, we picked up his son from school. Thomas was of a delicate build and looked like a little angel. He had the sweetness of a gentle soul and when he sat beside me in the car, he took my hand and never let it go. With pride, Thomas showed me his village with its old 'lavoir' ('washhouse') where, in the old days, all the women used to come to wash linen and clothes as there was no running water in the individual houses. The lavoir was one of the centre points of village life for the women.

This village of Saint-Parize-le-Chatel was evangelised in the sixth century. Its church was built above a pagan temple and named after a monk of the time who became Saint Patrice. There is a crypt, but no remains of the Saint in this church. I was beginning to notice more often that many of the churches had been built on pagan temples and that there were pagan designs everywhere.

In the distance, I could hear the noise of sports cars. It was the circuit of Nevers-Magny-Cours, which is famous for its motor-racing circuit and located in the area of Magny-Cours and Saint-Parize-le-Chatel. Each year, they host the Formula One French Grand Prix and the 24-hour 'Bol d'Or' motorcycle endurance events. There was a festive air in the village and the three of us went to the 'Salle des Fetes' ('village hall') to listen to a play for children that I thoroughly enjoyed, as well as eating French chocolate made by a renowned local chocolatier. I learnt that some of the villages had had to join together to be able to survive financially and maintain their community spirit. Everyone had to learn to compromise, to broaden their thinking in some way and to understand the needs of other villages. What a good idea! Later, I met Francoise, Yves' wife. We spoke until very late in the evening and a friendship began. Not only had they opened their home to me: they opened their hearts.

I always had to get up quite early each morning to attend to my feet, massaging and dressing them. This process took me about 20 minutes, but I had to do it because my feet needed to last me until the end of my journey. I could not get new ones if these wore out! They were in pretty bad condition. Not only were they beginning to be multi-coloured, but some black or very dark green areas had appeared. I wrapped them up with the special lambs wool and bandages. Up until then, I had never cared much about my feet and always took them for granted; they were there and they had a purpose and that was it. What a lesson I was learning at the beginning of this pilgrimage, a lesson of respect for my body and that I should take nothing for granted.

At breakfast, I joined Yves and Francoise's family. Thomas was very sad to see me go. He cried and asked me to stay, never wanting to let go of my hand. I was so touched by this child's love. Then Yves drove me back to Saint Vincent's Church at Magny-Cours. The previous morning we did not know each other: now we were friends. That was the miracle of the path and this, like many others, was going to be a friendship that would last throughout my entire journey, as we both kept in touch. Once more, I had left friends, the warmth of a house, the comfort of a bed to go into the unknown. My throat tightened and my insecurity crept up on me once again. It was hard, but I had to leave and go on alone. I had to learn to trust myself and see what the day would bring.

I was still hurting everywhere: in my shoulders, in both legs and all my joints. I decided to walk fewer kilometres for a few days to give my body a rest. After walking an hour or two, the pain seemed to lessen, or it may have been a trick of the mind, but I enjoyed the relief. Are we not clever at putting aside our miseries during our lives so we do not have to face them? Now that I was facing my physical pain, however, I could not escape from my suffering.

The symbols were quite far apart and I had difficulty finding my way. I became very anxious and my five senses each seemed to grow antennae. I scrutinised every corner, tree trunk, post and stone, trying to find a sign and I became very vigilant. I knew the marking was bad in this area and with this knowledge in hand I had to be very careful, but I had no idea just how bad it was going to become further on.

I passed a splendid windmill, a beautiful building from the 18th century and I walked through meadows full of flowering dandelions as far as I could see. Nature was at its best with its bright green, yellow and blue colours. I tried to concentrate on the beauty of the landscape so that I could forget the pain that was coming back and the weight of my backpack which was wearing me down.

Every spring the dandelion flowers cover the fields and as a child I used to gather the tender dandelion leaves, as our diet was quite different in winter. In spring the dandelion leaves were used as a detox in salads as hors d'oeuvres. The leaves were bitter and my Maman used to add hard-boiled eggs to mask the taste, along with some of her home-made French dressing. This tradition of the dandelion leaves and its virtues is still alive, as I saw farmers selling them on market days as I crossed through towns or villages.

I walked along dirt tracks and the birds gave me a free concert. The winter was over and the farmers had put their cows in the paddocks. The cows loved grazing on the tender blades of grass and took time to look at me passing by, and some even walked a little way with me along the fence. With their mooing, they welcomed and encouraged me and I kept on walking in full silence. I was happy, but my peace was broken as I arrived at an intersection where there were no symbols. I flicked through my guide-book, but I had been so inattentive that I was not at all sure where I was. Deciding to follow my intuition, I turned left and had to say goodbye to peace for a while as my fears had come back at full gallop. The negative words from my sister came rushing into my mind. I could not stop these thoughts and I tried to calm myself down. Easier said than done. Suddenly I saw a sign that read 'Celine', my Maman's first name. It felt as though she was there to protect me and show me the way. My courage came back and I started to walk peacefully again, but this time along a railway track through a dirt road. Not very romantic, I might say.

I turned left and went under a railway bridge. After about 500 metres I saw an old castle, the walls of which were not too high and just at the right height for me to rest my backpack. I thought it was the perfect place to eat an apple. On the opposite side of the path there were cows in the fields chewing their cuds quite peacefully in the sun. While I was munching, I imagined a scene from the Middle Ages when the occupants would wait for the knights to come and visit, and just at that moment I saw a gentleman with a cane coming out of the beautiful manor opposite the castle. He was coming closer and I decided to approach him to ask if he knew anything about this castle, which was in great need of repair. On the front of the main gates there were signs saying: 'DANGER. DO NOT ENTER'. At first, he was not responsive to my enquiries, but told me the castle was called the Castle of Villars, and that it dated from the 14th century and had been part of his family since the 16th century. He was the Marquis of Villars. Oh dear: I had thought he was a farmer. He asked me if I wanted to visit it and then he showed me the repairs that had been done in some sections of the castle, thanks to some funding from the French Government. However, in order to receive a grant from the Government, he had to contribute financially as well and I told him his ancestors would be very proud of him, as he was undertaking such a difficult task to keep their heritage alive. He smiled and started talking on a more personal level. He had lived in New Caledonia and had come to Brisbane and the Gold Coast during his holidays. I was stunned by this coincidence. We said goodbye so that I could continue onward and he could attend to his castle. He wished me good luck for my pilgrimage and I wished him good luck for his enterprise in bringing the castle back to its former glory.

I was still deep in thought about the morning's events while walking along a lovely grassy path when I came face to face with the National Highway number 7. My guidebook said it was a very dangerous route, but that was an understatement. It was unbelievable! The traffic was horrendous: cars and enormous trucks travelling at 90 kilometres an hour and no pedestrian crossings. After a long and frustrating wait, there was a break in the traffic. I scrambled across, happy not to have been killed. I walked along the edge of this highway, which was very narrow. Every time a car passed close to me I was nearly lifted off my feet and was jolted at each passing truck. It was very dangerous, but I had no other choice. Soon a car stopped and the driver, a young woman, offered me a lift as she felt it was too dangerous for me to walk along the highway. I thanked her very much, but told her I was walking the Saint James' Way and could not accept her offer as I had to walk every metre, no matter what. I told her how grateful I was for her kindness, blew her a kiss and started walking again, fearing for her safety, as she had stopped on the embankment of this dangerous highway. A few minutes later, I saw her again. She had stopped her car on the opposite side of the highway and she beeped her horn to attract my attention. She gestured to me to accept her offer as she was still so worried about me with this traffic. I refused again and seeing my determination, she gave up, blew me a kiss and made a peace sign with her fingers. I did the same and asked God to bless her. I was so touched by the kindness of this stranger. I was walking by myself with all my possessions on my back and someone had cared for me. The other day, I felt like a homeless person and now I felt like a Queen thanks to the kindness of this young woman.

I kept on walking along this treacherous road until I reached a narrow lane named 'Biere' ('beer'). I smiled and thought about what Claude had told me a few days ago about drinking beer instead of water. I passed in front of another windmill built during the 19th century. The community was refurbishing it as they wanted to mill the grains again. Seeing this windmill, I thought about Spain and Don Quixote's story and I smiled at the thought that Spain was maybe 1,000 kilometres away. I was not there yet.

As I was getting closer to Saint-Pierre-le-Moutier, I saw a sign which read 'Le Grillet'. I could not believe it: 'Grillet' was my Maman's maiden name. Earlier that morning I had seen 'Celine' and now 'Grillet'. The day before was my Maman's birthplace and where my Papa grew up. This morning I had not dared to go to the village of Celine, as I was worried about the extra kilometres and afraid of getting lost, but this time I had to try to find out why the name 'Grillet' was there. Had any of my ancestors lived in this area? I had to know and started questioning the locals over their fences. They had guard dogs and I tried to control my fear. In my mind I was seeing these dogs jumping over the fences even though their owners were with them. Unfortunately, I could not find any connection with the name 'Grillet'. There was only a big orchard in this area and not much else. I was somewhat disappointed and went back to the road.

I arrived in Saint-Pierre-le-Moutier, which Joan of Arc had liberated on 4 November 1429. During that period, the town was an important place, but nowadays it is in decline. As I arrived early in the afternoon, I decided to walk further so I could do fewer kilometres the next day. However, before doing so, I decided to phone ahead and enquire about places for pilgrims to make sure I would find a bed for the night. Regrettably, there were no vacant bunks, so I had to stop where I had previously booked, yet after reflection, I decided that the rest would be good for my body. The next day I would have to walk about 22 kilometres to the village of Lurcy-Lévis and my lodging there was two or three kilometres off the path, adding even more distance.

Before going to the refuge, I stopped at a supermarket to buy some food, as food was not provided in the place I was staying. The owner, Simone, was an ex-pilgrim. She had broken her arm and could not cook, however, she showed me the kitchen which was at my disposal. She pointed to a note on the table and indicated that it was for me. You can imagine my surprise: who would leave a note for me? On the table was a bottle of water, the brand of which was 'Celine', as well as a scallop shell and a note from Brigitte, the young Dutch woman I had met in Nevers. Brigitte wrote in French:

Dear Claude. This morning you asked me where you could buy a Saint James' scallop shell similar to the one I had on my head Now I am happy to tell you that a Saint James' scallop shell will be waiting for you at Marciny in this charming refuge. I wish you a 'Buon Camino' and 'Ultreia!' We will meet again!

Brigitte.

After I had commented on her scallop shell the morning we left Nevers, Brigitte had bought me one, hoping that I would stop at Simone's place. If I had walked further I would not have stopped at Simone's and never known about the note and the scallop shell. What a day it had been! From that day, I put the scallop shell on the top of my backpack, carrying it with me as my protector until the end of my pilgrimage.

I contacted Mariele from Coulanges-les-Nevers to find Brigitte's details so I could thank her for her kindness. Unfortunately, she had left no address or contact details. I learnt from Mariele that Brigitte had been attacked by dogs again, but this time she had used Monique and Claude's method, which worked well and she was happy not to have been bitten. Hearing this news, the fear of dogs returned to me and I was thankful that, up until now, I had not encountered such a drama.

I re-read Brigitte's note many times that night. 'Buon Camino' and 'Ultreia'-which Brigitte had written to me in the note-are two greetings that are often used by pilgrims along the Saint James' Way. 'Buon Camino' is a modern expression for 'good walk'. The origin of 'Ultreia' is more obscure. It seemed to have been used as a common greeting on Saint James' Way many centuries ago as 'onward' or 'keep going'.

Simone returned to the kitchen, carrying with her a little basket. In it there were some eggs, pasta, butter and jam for me to use during my stay with her. Kindness kept coming my way. She stayed with me for a little while and I shared with her my uncanny and wonderful day. She told me to be very aware of the happenings that occur along the path and to stay alert. People think strange things happen on this walk and they do. These things were not mere coincidences and she told me that I had to let the magic come to me. With these words, she left and I reflected on them. I was the only pilgrim in this clean and simple lodging. I had walked all day alone and I would be alone in this dormitory away from any snoring. Joy! I could ponder Simone's words without any distraction. As an ex-pilgrim, she had had an extension built on her house so that pilgrims going through this area could find lodgings. There are very few places for them to sleep in this part of the path, apart from hotels.

I fell into a deep sleep and woke up early the next morning feeling very refreshed and curious to see what the day would bring. It was a crisp, sunny morning with a blue sky. My body and particularly my feet were still giving me pain, but I had learnt that in a few hours, the pain would go away and I would be fine. At first the track was not too difficult and I went through sealed roads, cart-tracks and small paths. I crossed a bridge over the Allier River and I entered the third region on my route and I felt really pleased; I had already crossed the Yonne and Nievre regions and now I was in Auvergne. The Auvergne region is not very populated because of its shape and geographical position. Thousands of years ago, there were volcanic eruptions in the area. The highest mountain is 1,885 metres and I would be walking through the northern end of the region, which stretches up the Loire and the Allier valleys.

As I was hiking up the road, a man who introduced himself as Jean-Marc approached me. He wanted to chat, as he was surprised to see a woman with white hair walking with a huge backpack alone through this district. Our first topic of conversation was the global financial crisis and he said that life was going to be very tough for the young generation, as the GFC had had a major impact on the area. He was worried about his son. I shared with him some of my thoughts on the matter. Today the driving force of our society is money. It is King. Big corporations and banks have become so important that most governments in the western world are under pressure from a small group of people at the top, while we, the little ants, work so hard to make them richer. I suggested that nothing has really changed since the Middle Ages. During that era, the Kings were the masters of all as well. Nowadays, the media has created greater needs and more wants in society. We welcome advertising with open arms, thinking that we cannot live without the products on display. We have to have them to make us 'happy', however, we have this all wrong. Happiness has to come from deep within our souls, not from superficial things. Through this consumerism, we have become slaves to our debts and to the banks. With consent, we give our power away and in the process we lose our freedom. Jean-Marc lifted his beret and scratched his head, saying, 'Maybe you are right'. He wanted to keep on talking, but I had to go as I had to walk about 22 kilometres that day. He repeated how surprised he was that a woman would want to walk alone and cover so many kilometres on foot just to reach Santiago de Compostela. He, like many others, could not comprehend my desire and he took off his beret in a gesture of respect. Then he told me to be careful in the forest as there was a hunt in progress. I thanked him for his advice and left.

I was still pondering as I walked. What false happiness have we taught our children to make them believe that when we have 'things' we are happy? What are we doing? How many children feel the need to have the latest gadget or outfit to be part of the group or to be accepted? The vicious circle is so ingrained that the governments of every western nation ask their citizens to spend more and more so that the economy will keep on going and the money flowing. It cannot go on forever. For example, by buying more white goods and electronics, we are increasing the pollution in the world. Where is this rubbish going? Well, I thought, we dump it in the under-developed countries and our conscience is clear, as we do not see the mess we are creating. Out of sight and out of mind. Had walking alone these past few days changed my way of thinking? No. I had had these thoughts before and I often disregarded them, but being in contact with nature I had become closer to the reality of our mistakes as citizens of this planet. Is this what I came here for? To see life from a different angle, or was it more to open my Pandora's Box? Perhaps it was both. I was so caught up in my thoughts that it seemed I reached Livry in no time, as if time had already lost its grip on me.

After Livry, I took a stony path and walked across fields. At one stage, I could see the Allier Valley and soon after that I crossed the bridge which divides the Nievre and the Allier rivers. At Le Veurdre there is a 12th century Roman church and many castles. I passed in front of the 16th century Manor of Le Coudrais. While crossing this little town of Le Veurdre I saw people playing a competition of 'Petanque'. The French are very proud of this game; it is close to their hearts and is played almost all year round. 'Petanque' is a game of bowls somewhat similar yet different from British lawn bowls. It is played with metallic balls that are a little bigger than tennis balls. There are two teams. All the players throw a ball with the aim of landing it as close as possible to the 'cochonnet', which is a very small wooden ball, while at the same time trying to move the opponents' balls away from it. It originated in the south of France, at La Ciotat near Marseille. My father came to my mind as he used to enjoy playing this game with his mates. Being a bit of a larrikin, he loved entertaining the crowd at the same time. The players saw me with my backpack and waved and shouted, 'Bonne chance!' and 'Courage!'

In the front of the houses in Le Veurdre, huge hand-painted, wooden artworks representing cows, donkeys and flowers in bright colours were on display. It was quite unusual to see such naïve works of art. I took some pictures and thought the paintings were a great idea, as they brightened the streets, especially in the grey winter days.

I got lost many times as there was a lot of distance between the symbols, and I had to walk a lot of extra kilometres. Once, I had to go back to the last symbol I had seen to make sure I was on the right track. This time, however, I was not afraid as there were villages with small farms all along the way. I arrived at an area where one large piece of a sign was missing. I could not read what was written. As I was not sure, I decided to keep on walking straight ahead. I walked for quite a while, leaving a village behind. After a few more kilometres I started to question my judgment-having still seen no symbol-and I decided to re-trace my steps. Houses soon appeared along a street, but every house had a dog. My fear was so great that I did not dare knock on any door to ask for help. Yet luck was on my side once more as a car appeared, stopping in front of a house. I called out for help. The young couple were visiting some friends, but did not know much about the area and could not point me in the right direction. They invited me to come inside the house to ask their friends, but there was a dog standing in front of the gate and I could not go in, so the couple asked their friends to come and talk to me. They did not know much about the Saint James' Way, though at times they said they had seen some pilgrims walking down the road. I decided to go back and turn left where I had seen the broken wooden sign. I tried to calm down by enjoying the scenery, as it was a perfect day and I did not want to spoil it with my fears. I crossed a forest and found myself in the middle of nowhere, with only green fields on my right and left and trees covered in flowers. I saw a fallen tree and sat down to stop for lunch. I ate the hard-boiled eggs cooked the day before, a bit of goats cheese and bread: a frugal meal in a divine environment. There was music from the birds and the bumble bees were going from one flower to the next, busily collecting their nectar. My eyes could see the beautiful colours of nature with its deep green, blue sky and yellow sun at its zenith. I was far away from any civilisation; there was not one farm around and not a single noise from a car, truck or dog. I felt peace enveloping me. I was so happy and connected with the surroundings. I did not need anything else, though I missed my children and their families. I wished that they could be with me to enjoy the beauty of their ancestral country. My thoughts went to my Papa who had loved

73

nature so much, and I felt his arms around me. It was beautiful. I enjoyed the moment, not thinking about anything else, and emptied my mind. I was in paradise, taking in with full breaths what God had created.

Eventually, I had to leave and continued along more stony and grassy paths and crossed little streams that were flowing rapidly. I had to be careful where I put my feet so that I would not fall down into the mud or into the water. In the end I found my way and I arrived at my designated destination, which was the town of Lurcy-Levis where there is a beautiful church, but its doors were closed.

Lurcy-Levis is a lovely town in Auvergne and it is built around the Abbey of the Plein Pied, which owns the Priory, and which is the most important in the region of the Allier. From now on, I would be crossing towns and villages where there would be no lodging for pilgrims. My only choice was to stay in hotels. Consequently, in this part of France, the distances I had to cover on a daily basis would depend totally on the availability of lodgings. As a pilgrim, I received quite a substantial discount, but it was still expensive at 25 euro a night, which, at that stage, was around 40 Australian dollars.

The Auvergne is still quite cold at this time of year, but there was no heating inside the hotel where I was staying. As I got to my room, I took off my shoes and removed the bandages from my feet. When I saw my toenails I realised that I would lose them all, as they had turned black. After a hot shower, I washed my clothes, hoping they would be dry by the next morning. I texted my sister as promised, and every day she would ring me back. It was nice to hear her voice and share my day with her. Through our exchanges we became closer. I had not met a single pilgrim since I had left Nevers three days ago, but this did not bother me. I had been walking for one week and had covered about 160 kilometres on the map, without counting the extra kilometres I had walked because of wrong turns. I was still in pain and could not sit for long as my body would stiffen and getting up was still quite painful. During this first week I had been challenged in more ways than one, but I had grown stronger within myself and I was proud of my achievement. I looked forward to and was ready to face the next challenge.

'Learning to trust'

I woke up on 12 April 2010 to a sunny, yet very cold morning of about three degrees. I was staying in a lodging that had been built in the 16th century and which had been used as a stage-post. What a feeling. I wondered how many thousands of travellers would have stopped, rested and refreshed themselves here while their horses were changed over, before continuing their journey in carriages or buggies. If walls could talk over the centuries, how much could they have told me! I took my time over breakfast as I had to walk only a short distance because of the limited accommodation available. I was hoping for an easy walk, but I was informed by the owners of the hotel that the symbols in this area were hard to find and I had to be very careful.

Before leaving, I encountered a problem with the zip of my heavy jacket and had to find someone who could repair it. I was annoyed, as this was an expensive jacket from Australia and I had a warranty, however, I was in the centre of France. What good would the warranty do me so far away? The zip was found to be irreparable and my annoyance turned to frustration. If I wanted to wear it I would have to slip it on and make sure not to drag the zip too far down, otherwise I would not be able to zip it up again. I was going to be walking through quite a lot of extreme weather from now on, yet putting my frustration aside, I collected my backpack and left.

Walking alone can be quite challenging at the

beginning of a new day, both physically and mentally, because there is no one to give you encouragement if you do not feel like taking to the road. Sometimes a little push would be welcome. Indeed, it can be quite easy to just stop, as your body is in so much pain. But as you take to the road, very soon you forget these feelings and walk along happily, enjoying the moment.

The symbols were few and far between and I was constantly worried. My only companions were the birds and they were chirpy, for spring had arrived. I enjoyed their concert tremendously. At times, I felt as though they were encouraging me because I walked for so long without seeing an indication of the Saint James' Way and then my worry would return. My mind was playing tricks, as at times I thought I could see a symbol, but when I got close to it I realised it was only the reflection of the sun on a leaf. How could I be so mistaken?

I walked through routes where the cars were driven by mad drivers without any respect for walkers. I remembered Claude's advice, 'This is not Australia. People do not respect the rules of the road'. As cars overtook me I was pushed aside and was very happy to finally arrive at the edge of a wood away from the noise and traffic, even though there were only muddy tracks. My inner peace did not last long as I could not find any symbols at all. At each intersection I did not know what to do or which way to go. It was a gamble: left, right or straight ahead. I got lost, so lost. There was no one around as I was in the middle of a forest. Walking in a forest was another new experience, especially because there were no visible symbols. I lost my sense of distance and my insecurity grew and grew. I thought about my children and their families; I was missing them so very much. I had tried to ring them, so that I could hear their voices, but with the era of mobile phones not many people use public telephones. So, when the public telephone stops working, the private phone company does not bother to come and repair it as the cost is too high and it could be vandalised again. In many villages and towns, I saw the broken glass of some of the phone-boxes, shattered pieces simply left there. I stopped at many phone-boxes where the receiver was broken and full of rust. I was baffled that a big company would leave its equipment to deteriorate. To me the waste was incomprehensible. To ring Australia, I had to take in the considerable time difference and the best time to ring was when I was walking, which meant I could be anywhere. I had crossed many villages and towns with no public telephone in working order. It was quite a problem for me and I got so exasperated.

I was in the middle of a forest deciding what to do next and my fear got the better of me. I sat on a log, calmed myself down and visualised all my different options and put my trust in God. The thought of my workmates and my sister's partner crossed my mind again and I promised myself that I would not be defeated, when suddenly I heard a dog barking. Oh dear! Amazingly, I did not freeze with fright at this sound. Instead, hope came back: maybe there was a farm not too far away. A farm means people and life. I concentrated on the direction from where I had heard the barking and started walking. The path was very muddy and slippery. I hoped I was heading in the right direction and at the same time prayed that I would meet someone. I had not met one pilgrim that day, like the other days, and I had to be brave; there was not much choice really.

After a while, I saw the roof of a house or farm. My heart pounded so hard: I was safe. But as I got nearer, I realised it was an abandoned one and I felt a huge heaviness in my shoulders. I had to think very hard and not let myself feel despondent. I looked around and there was not another house in sight. I was sure I had not dreamt that I had heard a dog barking and that my mind had not played a trick on me. My eyes slowly got used to the bright sunlight as I scanned the landscape around me, and there at the top of another small hill I could distinguish a grey patch. Could it be a road? I did not know, but I felt relieved and walked faster following the path that led to the grey area. I reached the top of a hill and shouted in relief. Yes, it was a road, but as far as the eye could see there were only fields in this beautiful landscape, not a house or a roof. I stayed positive; it was a road at least. I turned right in the direction of another hill, but this time I was walking on a sealed road. I remembered that not long ago, a few hours before in fact, I said to myself that I hated walking on sealed roads with cars passing me. Now, I would have loved to see one, but none appeared. Soon, in the distance, and like a mirage, I saw the roof of a farm and hoped this one was not abandoned. I had to stay positive and trusting. As I got closer to the property I heard a dog barking. In my wildest dreams I would not have thought that one day I would be 'saved' by a barking dog! I was grateful, but scared and prayed that someone would come out of the farm house. I did not know whether I would be brave enough to ring the bell or call out to someone. Fear can be so debilitating and my fear of dogs was extreme. I kept on saying, 'Please

God, please God'. My prayers were obviously heard as I arrived at the corner of the farm and saw a man coming out of the barn. Phew! The farmer had seen me and waved with his beret and I waved back with a gesture that I was worried about his dog. He told me not to be concerned and went to tie it up. I was informed that a lot of pilgrims got lost in this area; the symbols were there in the forest, but it seemed that somehow the pilgrims missed them. The farmer gave me the direction to follow. It turned out that after just a few extra kilometres I would be back on the right track. I thanked him and he wished me good luck. I had been really scared in the woods and realised that I would have to learn to trust more, to be more vigilant and that at the end all would be well.

I received a call from Yves and Francoise, my hosts from Saint-Parize-le-Chatel, who were worried about me. It was amazing timing and I told them of my trials. They had talked about me to a friend and about the conversations we had had. His friend commented, 'This lady is special. You have been very lucky to have met her'. I was bewildered and told them I was just like everyone else. Apparently their son, Thomas, was still talking about me. They wished me luck and said they would call again. I was touched by their kindness.

As I was passing in front of a house at the top of another hill, an old man, Raymond, called me over for a chat. He informed me that two days ago a young woman with a long staff had got lost, just like me. I wondered if it could be Brigitte, and thought, 'I am not so bad after all as I was not the only one to lose my way'. Hearing this gave me a real burst of confidence and I had to admit it was very good for my ego. Raymond told me he liked to help the pilgrims passing in front of his house as it took away the monotony of his days since he had stopped working.

Later, I saw another old man in his garden. Somehow he reminded me of my Papa who loved gardening. I could see my father bending over his vegetables, taking care of them, watching them grow with so much love. My father was so proud of his garden and he had a deep connection with plants. Papa used to be another man when he was working with the earth. I remembered how happy he was when he let the soil run through his fingers. In these moments, I saw the real man coming out of his shell. My father had planted so many fruit trees on his plot of land for his children and his grandchildren. The irony was that the three of us had left our place of birth to spread our wings somewhere else. My father has passed on, but his fruit trees are still there producing fruit for someone else's pleasure. His loving work has not been wasted, however, as it has created joy for others. Is the circle of life not a wonderful thing? Doing something for others and not knowing where your love and care will end up. We are just like one big family, after all.

I arrived in Valigny just after 1.00pm. It is a small village and part of the Troncais county. In the main square there is an old priory and the 12th century Church of Notre Dame. As I got closer to the square I noticed a phone-box and I ran straight towards it to see if it was in working order. Yes! In a few hours I would be able to ring my children and I felt on top of the world.

My lodging was at the 'Relais de la Foret', which was an ancient relay house for horses that was built many centuries ago. There, I met Josette, the owner, who was a very active and busy woman. Josette did the cleaning, cooking and attended to the guests at the restaurant and the adjoining corner shop. Her husband was behind the bar, letting his wife manage the business. She was a 'maitresse femme', a female manager, with a strong character. I was surprised by the way she dealt with her customers, but I liked her. She was very direct when she had something to say and she was quite entertaining.

Brigitte, the Dutch pilgrim I had met in Nevers, had left another message for me. She had rested at 'Relais de la Foret' for two days, as her leg was still quite painful, and had hoped I would have caught up with her. She had left that same morning. Sadness overcame me as I wanted so much to thank her for the scallop shell, but it was not meant to be. In life sometimes we run after a dream yet never realise it. Why? We never know. I was sure that Brigitte was the woman who had got lost in the same area as me and who Raymond had also helped two days ago.

Josette let me use her washing machine and I hung my clothes over the boiler so they would be dry by the next morning. I was delighted. Every day I washed my clothes by hand, but what a luxury to have a washing machine at your disposal. I washed everything I had in my backpack: my day-clothes and my 'cleaner' clothes to refresh them. I did enjoy the mod cons, even though I knew that a washing machine was no luxury.

I stayed in the upper part of the hotel with a shared bathroom. Josette told me she was looking after an old man as his health had deteriorated and he was very sick. He had been working with her in the kitchen for many years. She made me aware that sometimes he would make funny noises during the night as his head was not quite right, but told me not to be worried. His room was just beside mine. In the middle of the night I was awakened by weird sounds coming from the next room, but I went back to sleep quite quickly. Josette told me that he had helped her so much and she could not bear the thought of him ending up in a hospice, as he had no family. She had decided to look after him. Behind her grumpiness and her iron fist, Josette had a gentle and loving heart.

Later, I went to the phone-box and rang my children. I was so happy to hear their voices and they mine. They were eager to hear of my progress. I did not tell them of my fears and about the number of times I had got lost, but instead, I reminded them of my daily contact with my sister so they should not be worried about me. Hearing about their daily life back in Australia was so nice. My grandson, still, could not quite comprehend what his grandmother was doing, walking alone through France. Would I have understood such a thing at the age of 10? Probably not. After putting the receiver down, I felt as though I missed them even more. Before leaving Australia, I had given them a detailed plan of my trip and told them that I would be the one who would get in touch with them, because neither of us would know where I would be sleeping each night. I deeply regretted my decision to tell them not to contact me because at the time, I had no idea how much I would need to hear their voices for my inner strength.

From now on, the symbols would be almost non-existent along the path and I would have to study my maps and rely more on local guides, so I decided to take two days to cover the next 30 kilometres. I had a lovely French breakfast and bought a baguette for lunch as I still had some cheese in my backpack. It was a crisp and cold morning. My sister had told me that rain was on the way, but seeing the sky so blue, I had doubts.

The phone rang when I was leaving. It was Chantal, with whom I was going to stay the night. She told me she would not be there to welcome me and gave me instructions on how to get into her house. I told her that I would prefer to wait outside until she arrived as I would feel uncomfortable going inside without her being there, but she did not want to hear anything about it. She told me where I would find a bedroom with four beds and I could choose any bed as I would be the only one sleeping there that night. I was amazed, because I could have missed her call if I had left a few seconds earlier. I felt the protection of my Maman and Papa and a sense of serenity.

I spent another day alone on the path. I had wanted to be alone, and there I was. Be careful what you ask for, as you will receive it! My trust and confidence were challenged every time I got lost and every time I would think about how much I missed my little family in Australia, but somehow I enjoyed walking alone and being by myself, listening to the birds, watching nature come out of hibernation and putting on her coat of various colours. Every day, I witnessed nature's transformation, as if by magic. The wildness of this region is perfect for lovers of nature. In the past, it was an impossible task to industrialise this area because of its remotenessand difficult accessibility, but it was God's blessing in disguise. Its natural and beautiful landscape and spectacular unspoilt hills are here for us to enjoy in the 21st century-just the way God had created them-in such magnificent perfection.

I became so humble walking this track, making sure I did not disturb anything, not even a blade of grass. I felt so blessed to be here and appreciated every single moment to its fullest. I thought about the damage done to nature by us human beings in the name of industrialisation and greed and realised that we are fully responsible for its destruction. I have always respected nature, but when you walk through it day after day, a deeper respect grows in you for the Creator of this universe. Walking in the midst of nature, it seemed that I could touch my inner self fully and be totally at peace. Life was becoming so simple. I wondered if the feeling of my closeness to nature was due to the fact that my ancestors were farmers or because I spent my very early childhood on a farm. Back then I had no one to play with, not even a doll, and therefore, I had to learn to create my own games, watching nature and working with the adults of the household. As I was going back to my early childhood and its simplicity, I wondered if we could go back and put straight the mess we have created. Indeed, I feel as if a change of ideas is coming into the world, as we seem to feel more responsible about the environment nowadays. All of us have to be more aware of what we are doing to the world. Maybe now is the time. Was I ageing or simply yearning for a better environment for the children of this earth? I did not know. Perhaps I would find out along the way and so I kept on walking through forests and fields nearly all day.

Along the path in the countryside, away from everyone, the birds would sing and keep me company. They would jump from one branch to the next as if they were showing me the way. I thought back to the little bird from a few days ago. It was quite strange as they would fly off when I reached a sealed road to join me again a bit later. That day I had to stay very alert to all road signs from the areas I was crossing so I would not get lost. I thought I had been very careful, but once more I got lost. You would think that I would have learnt by now. Well, I had not, and as such, I was forced to add many kilometres to my daily walk. I did not know where I was, but I kept on the sealed road, as the signs in the area were quite confusing. It was hot. It is always hotter when you walk on a sealed road. I could not find any sign on my map indicating where I was. I had no clue and kept on walking, hoping I was still on the right track. Time was passing. It was getting even hotter. My watch was inside my backpack so I looked at the position of the sun in the sky to guess the time. It was past midday. I wondered more and more about what to do. I started to pray and asked the 'one above' to help me. I knew He would not let me down.

A few minutes later, a red car appeared. I waved to it. The car stopped. As always, the first thing I said was that I was a pilgrim, then I asked the gentleman if he could show me on my map where I was, telling him where I wanted to go. He put his hands on his head and said, 'Oh my poor lady you are so far out of your way, you should have turned right there', and he pointed to a spot on the map. I told him there was no sign-post to be seen and that I had looked everywhere and even re-traced my steps. He offered to drive me back to where I had taken the wrong direction and I happily accepted. He was amazed at what I wanted to achieve alone and said that he himself was surprised to be here as he had not planned to drive this way. He was from Paris and had bought a house in the region a while back. That very morning, he had decided to give his old car a bit of a run. He could not comprehend why he had driven along this road, as he never normally used it. I smiled, as I knew someone was protecting me. I was not even surprised. He left me at the intersection and showed me on my map the direction to Ainay-le-Chateau.

I was walking along the main road after the sign for Chandon when I was stopped by a lady in her garden. She informed me that the day before, a lady from Holland had been attacked by a dog a few doors down and I had to be wary because some owners did not close their gates, as they were afraid of pilgrims. I thanked her and kept on walking towards Ainay-le-Chateau, wondering how people could be scared of pilgrims! Are we, as human beings, scared of the unknown, of people behaving differently from us, people who do not conform to the mould of what society has decided we all should be? Now I was part of that minority, walking with all my possessions in a backpack through France. I was one of the 'weird ones' and society had to be wary. I did not conform to what society thinks is proper! How privileged I had been up until now along the path, as I had met only nice - very nice - people. Had I been lucky? Had I been protected? Had I really been called on this path to do something a little bit out of the ordinary? I thought about what the lady had said about the dogs. Had I been safeguarded from a dog's attack up until now? In Australia, I had thought about this danger, but felt I would be ok. Until now I had never been attacked. Every time I had walked past farms or private houses, any dogs were either tied up or the gates were closed. I was more certain than ever that I was protected. I had to do this walk no matter what. All these were messages, I was sure. I had to trust and all would be well. Nothing would happen to me. There was something bigger than me at work here and for that I thanked God. My thoughts returned to Brigitte. She must have been the one who had been attacked while walking yesterday. Poor girl, how many times had she been attacked since she left Holland? The lady in the garden had said that she protected herself with a big staff and did some weird movements with it on the road and I was certain it was Brigitte. Monique and Claude's method had worked again and I would have to remember this.

I arrived at Ainay-le-Chateau, which was a small fortified town during the Middle Ages and even though it was not very big, it was a town of some importance. Some of the ramparts, as well as the 12th century Saint Etienne medieval church, are still well-preserved and there are many 16th and 17th century monuments in the town. There are also many castles in this area. I was advised to follow the main road and not go through the countryside as it would be too difficult and I would get lost. I took some money out of an ATM in the village when I noticed a young man watching all my movements. He looked scruffy and was talking to himself. I smiled at him and he started to mumble some words that I could not comprehend and I left. I found out later that this small town receives people with psychiatric problems. Instead of being institutionalised, the patients live with a family who look after them and the family receives a salary from the French Government. There are hospitals as well for in- and out-patients just outside the town. I thought it was wonderful what this little town was doing for people with psychiatric problems and how much compassion there must be from the inhabitants towards these patients. Maybe a lesson for us all.

I left Ainay-le-Chateau using the national road which was not very large as it was the same road that had been built during the Middle Ages. I passed under the 12th century arch 'La Porte de l'Horloge' ('the door of the clock'). On each side of it there were some medieval streets. As I was walking down the ancient road people would wave at me, shouting, 'Bravo! Bon courage!' Some even wound down their car windows and wished me luck. I was touched and waved back.

I reached a bridge and crossed the Sologne River. On my right, I saw the Saint Roch Chapel from the 16th and 17th centuries and decided to go through the countryside as indicated in my guide-book. I thought it would be beautiful and peaceful, since many spring flowers had come out. Somehow I did not care about getting lost again; I just wanted to be with nature.

The birds welcomed me again and gave me another private concert. I saw some little wild rabbits crossing the forest. I felt so happy and serene; paradise must surely be like this.

There was a big change within me while I was in the wilderness: I felt so at peace. However, this beautiful state would leave me as soon as I saw a roof, as fear would enter my mind with regard to dogs. I tried to learn to control my fear, but this was not easy. I would repeat the following mantra to myself, 'You will be ok, kid. You have been ok up until now. They are inside an enclosure, they cannot get you'. Just say that to someone who feels extreme fear. It was not easy, but I had to do it. I had to overcome my fear. I would shake when I passed in front of any property with guard dogs. Sometimes, I would cross and walk on the other side of the road or the path and I would not look at the dogs, but keep on walking at the same pace, all the while shaking like a leaf. At times, I felt as though they were going to jump over the fence as their barking was so powerful, but it never happened. I was just so scared. I promised myself that I would overcome that fear sooner rather than later.

I was leaving the Allier region for the Cher, which would be the fourth region I had entered. I arrived at Charenton-du-Cher. This is a beautiful small town, situated on the banks of the Canal du Berry and the Marmande River and is surrounded by farms and forests. It has small streets and very old buildings that pre-date the Middle Ages. As I walked along the narrow streets, I felt history surrounding me. Some of the many villages and towns I had passed through had played a very significant part in the history of France, and this history has given soul to these places. Unfortunately, however, this soul is all that remains for some of these towns and villages, which have been so badly affected by the global financial crisis. I wished I could stay longer to learn more about this part of France and its history, but I had to take to the road the next day.

In the centre of the village is the Roman Church of Saint Martin from the 12th century. In the 'Vieux Charenton', a small area of the town, I found a chapel called Notre Dame de Grace. It occupied the nave of the old Benedictine convent for women, which was dedicated to Saint Columbian in 620. It used to be a pilgrimage place as some miracles had happened here. The doors of the chapel were open and I went inside. As I went under the entrance, I sensed a lot of energy coming from the chapel. I sat on a pew and prayed, thanking God for protecting me since the beginning of my pilgrimage. Tears started to roll down my cheeks; they had appeared from nowhere and I could not stop them. Was I in this privileged place to let go of some of my fears? I did not know, but it seemed something was happening inside me. I was disturbed by the barking of a dog on the other side of the chapel where the old convent was. From the sound of its bark, I felt it was a German shepherd: my worst enemy. I felt safe in the chapel, however.

After a while, I left and went to look for my lodging. As I could not find it in these small streets, I asked for directions. I was told to go to the chateau. A castle? I had never asked to stay in a castle. Fortunately, I had been told of the cost for the night and food beforehand, otherwise I would have really started to worry. I arrived at the address and looked at the place: I was relieved to see it was not a castle. I was not sure it had ever been one. It would have been an impressive house in its time, but now it was a very faded old lady and needed a lot of repair work and refurbishing, plus a lot of tender, loving care. I tried to remember what I had been told about accessing the property. I found the stairs outside the main entrance at the back. The section on the left was crumbling down. I arrived at the door and opened it. It opened onto an entrance and a staircase. I went up the staircase, then along a corridor. At the end I found a room with four beds. Each bed had one sheet covering the mattress and a pillow. There was a small bathroom next door and the toilets were along the corridor under the stairs. The bedroom door would not close properly and so I decided to put a chair behind it to keep it closed and if anybody tried to enter, it would make such a noise that I would hear it and wake up. I had been there a little while when Chantal, my host, arrived. Chantal was a lovely lady. Her husband had passed away and she was trying to keep her 'demeure' ('family home') which had been in her husband's family since the 16th century. It was a heavy burden for her. She had financial difficulties and could only barely maintain one section of the house and do very few repairs. In France, taxes to keep this type of property are very high. Chantal also told me that a pilgrim had once stolen her money and this made me feel so sad for her, but it was also a reminder and a warning for me that on the path I would meet the same people that we find in the 'real world', and that not all are genuine pilgrims.

Chantal was carrying a heavy burden and she was sad, but I managed to make her laugh. We went into the kitchen to prepare a meal. Chantal's life had changed a lot. Originally from a well-to-do family, she married a landowner, but the huge taxes had eroded their assets and then her husband had died. She has to take in pilgrims to help her survive and pay some of her bills. Through my life I had to work hard and make do with what I had. I had to learn to cope and keep on going, whatever the circumstance. Chantal had to learn this hard lesson of life at nearly the end of her journey. She had a big house, but was full of insecurities. I told her that I would pray for a lot of pilgrims to stop at her place and give her their business. We ate in the kitchen and laughed a lot. While we were washing the plates from our dinner the phone rang. She answered it and as the person on the phone was speaking English, Chantal gave the phone to me. It was someone wanting four beds for the next night in her 'castle'. Chantal jumped and clapped her hands and said, 'Claude, you brought me good luck'. I answered, laughing, 'It was not hard work!' In my heart I thanked God. She was so happy. It was nice to see that the extra money would help to pay some of her bills.

In the bedroom there was a 'Livre d'Or' ('guest-book') in which pilgrims write about their stay or their pilgrimage. I always wrote something every time I found one in a refuge, private lodgings or churches. That night, I put pen to paper and wrote something along the lines of, 'Thank you for the exchanges and the laughs. I hope that from now on a lot of pilgrims will stop here and enjoy your hospitality'.

It was 14 April 2010 and I had covered nearly 200 kilometres according to the map. I was proud of myself, but I knew I had many more kilometres in front of me. I slept well that night and when I went down for breakfast the next morning, I found Chantal all excited. She had received another phone call after I had gone to bed and one more that same morning. Now, she had six more pilgrims coming for the same night and did not know where she would put them all. I laughed. She had to give up her bed for a night and sleep in her reading room. I hugged her and said goodbye to a lovely lady.

Outside it was cold and overcast and I hoped that it would not rain. I still felt pain in my body, but not as much as before. Maybe the tablets that I was taking every day were starting to work or I was getting used to the efforts I asked of my body. I did not know. My backpack still felt heavy. Very heavy, in fact, even though I had not added anything else to it. It was exactly the same weight, but it felt so much heavier. If I could compare my backpack to our pain and our sorrows, it would seem that at times we carry burdens that we feel we cannot deal with. At other times it seems we can deal with them much better and they do not seem to weigh down on us quite so much.

The tracks were quite good that morning. The symbols of the path were placed at regular intervals, making the walk easier, or perhaps I was getting used to noticing them more easily. Maybe there was a similarity with life as we go through our ups and downs. We learn to accept our pain and wait patiently for the 'sun' to shine again, getting stronger along the way. Was I doing the same thing here? I was still walking through villages and hamlets and in beautiful farming areas. The birds still accompanied me with their songs. In the fields, the cows were grazing. They lifted their heads when I passed and looked at me with blank stares, as though I was an extra-terrestrial being or as though I was disturbing them with the noise of my footsteps on the track. I laughed. At one stage, there were cows on one side and on the other side there were sheep, with some of the females showing their big bellies. Very soon they would give birth and little ones would be running in the paddock. I could just imagine how beautiful it would be.

The walk was quite easy that day. Some people beeped their horns, wished me good luck, or clapped their hands when I walked near them. It was so lovely to feel such warmth coming from strangers. But others did not dare to look at me and ignored me.

The sun was back and it was not going to rain. Great, I

thought to myself. As I was walking, my thoughts turned to Brigitte. Our paths had crossed, but we had not had the chance to exchange very much. A feeling of sadness overcame me as I had learnt that she had a lot of challenges in her life. I wondered if I could have helped her and questioned why our paths did not cross again. Did I miss an opportunity to help? I felt sad at this thought. Perhaps it was not meant to be and I asked God to protect her.

I was still walking through a farming area when I arrived at a bridge which crossed the Canal du Berry. The Canal du Berry links three canals and is 261 kilometres long, however, it is no longer used after being closed in 1995. I arrived in Saint-Pierre-les-Etieux with its Roman church from the 12th century. It was a majestic walk along the Canal du Berry with its rows of trees on each bank. The grass was so green and lush. Nature seemed at its best. I saw ducks with stunning colours paddling in the canal and birds everywhere, all chirpy as the sun was out. Then I saw an animal on the bank of the canal. It was as big as a cat and was feasting on the lush grass. Seeing me, he jumped into the canal and I realised it was a raccoon. It was my first encounter with one.

I loved being in this lovely flat area along the canal. After the difficult walks through the mountains and hills, I appreciated the respite it gave my body. I could visualise French families walking during the weekend with their children in this safe and relaxed environment.

I reached Saint-Amand-Montrond around lunch time. The establishment of this little town dates from prehistoric times and there is evidence of Roman settlement as well. The layout of the town has barely changed since the

Middle Ages and, as such, it is steeped in history. I saw the importance of Saint James' Way in this town, as the symbol of the shell was sculpted in the gates on some of the houses. I visited the Saint Amand Church, which dates from the 12th and 13th centuries. After exploring the church, which I felt had Benedictine and Byzantine influences, I sat on one of the benches in the little square opposite the church. A woman sat beside me and we began a conversation. She was a teacher and shared her concern about the education system in France. She felt the system was failing the children and that all the young ones had lost their sense of direction. I shared her concern, as this problem is the same everywhere. She left after finishing her sandwich, wishing me good fortune on my walk.

I crossed this beautiful little town, which was filled with placards in the streets for tourists to read about its history and the important people who were born in Saint-Amand-Montrond, as well as well-known people who had lived here. What a good idea. As I was crossing the town, people would stop me to wish me luck. I met a couple who had walked the pilgrimage a few years ago and they shared with me their experiences. They had not finished the walk, but they were planning to cover more kilometres in the years to come. I had not met a pilgrim since Nevers-seven days ago-yet I had met ex-pilgrims. It was so special.

The town with its clean streets and squares gave off a sense of order and it felt so nice to be in such a well-organised place. I could not enter the Chapel of Saint Roch, as the doors were closed, but on a stone above the main door I read the following inscription: 'AB ABA AD

ASTRA THS' ('altar of the stars') and I wondered if it was a reference to the Milky Way and the Saint James' Way. I decided to buy some postcards and food for the next day's lunch, but all the shops were closed. It frustrated me that the shops closed between 1.00pm and 3.00pm. I tried not to carry too much food, especially if I read on the guide that I would find some shops along the way. I was engrossed in the history of this town and had forgotten all about the time and there was very little food left in my backpack. As a pilgrim, I could not wait for the shops to open: I had to keep on walking as I did not know the condition of the track. Despite my hunger I had no choice but to continue on through the township and other villages in the direction of Bouzais where I arrived before 4.00pm, which was the time when the doors of the refuge opened.

Bouzais is a village of less than 300 inhabitants. In the centre of the village, I found the Saint Roch Church with its Maltese cross on a gable and the Saint Roch statue. The inhabitants take great care of their village and I could feel the pride of its residents. The community had built a small shelter for pilgrims in an old farm house and the doors were closed. There was a chair outside close to the door and I sat and waited. A dog was barking like mad on the other side of the street. I decided not to be frightened and stayed put. It was going to be my challenge for the day. While I was waiting, my sister rang and I shared with her my feelings about Saint-Amand-Montrond. There was a dead silence on the other end of the line, then her voice said, shyly, 'You know I want to finish my life in that town'. I was surprised, yet told her, 'You could not have chosen a better place. You will be alright here, I feel it'.

At 4.00pm, I met Anne and Jean-Pierre. Once again, I was the only pilgrim to stay in the shelter, which had a few bunks and had been very well refurbished and perfectly cleaned. Anne and Jean-Pierre were ex-pilgrims from Belgium and Anne cooked a wonderful meal. To give back what they had received during their pilgrimage, they had decided to volunteer for two weeks in the refuge and attend to pilgrims. What a lovely gesture! As unbelievable as it is, Anne and I were born on the same day in the same year and at the exact time-she in Belgium and I in France. In a way, she could have been my twin sister. She did volunteer work in a hospital looking after premature babies, and I volunteered in Brisbane in palliative care and oncology for adults. Between the two of us we were covering the circle of life. My unborn child would have been born the same year as their son, and Jean-Pierre was born on Saint Claude's feast day. It was baffling. My mind was working at high speed. Was it just a coincidence that I had decided to keep on walking until Bouzais, such a small, but beautiful village, so that I could meet Anne and Jean-Pierre? I do not think so. We meet people on our life journeys. We might not know why at the time, but I feel there is always a reason. There may have been something I had to learn from them or perhaps they needed to learn something from me. Now it was Jean-Pierre's turn to quiz me about my pilgrimage. He asked me why I wanted to do the Saint James' Way by myself. I told them that I was not quite sure why, but I knew that there was a purpose and that I would find out the reason along the way. Anne and Jean-Pierre were worried for me as walking alone was not safe and I had a backpack that was too heavy. I told them I would be protected and would be ok and that they should not worry. 14 April 2010 had been quite a special day and I went to bed happy and waiting to know what would happen next. I left in the morning with many emotions and as always, it was hard to leave, as I had felt another great connection with my hosts. We hugged and waved goodbye. It seemed we had known each other forever and had so much in common. I will never forget them.

It was another cold morning-four degrees-and the sky was overcast. Despite the weather, I had to walk. The tracks became more difficult. From then on, hills and mountains were on the agenda. They were not as kind to my body as the previous two days. The altitude was greater and the trees had not started to put on their green coats: they still looked like ghosts. At Charron, I saw a huge barn which was the former stronghold of the Noirlac Abbey. I crossed forests and did not see any symbols in the woods or maybe there were none. Who knows? I had to rely totally on my intuition. I noticed more changes within me. I was starting to trust myself a little bit more and was not as fearful. It was amazing what just one extra day can do to improve your confidence. This quiet did not last long, for while I was crossing a forest, I saw a truck parked on the side of the track. My heart started to beat like mad as I was alone in the forest. All of my sister's warnings to me flashed through my mind at the speed of light. I tried to control my thoughts and kept on walking towards it and saying, like a mantra, 'Breathe in, breathe out. Relax Claude, you will be alright. You know you will be protected'. If someone had seen me they would have thought that I was walking calmly, but it was quite the opposite: I was shaking like a leaf. Someone once asked me how it was that I always looked so calm and I answered that they should not be mistaken by the easy appearance, as it takes years of practice. I compared myself to a billabong, which seems calm from a distance, but when one comes close, one will see the ripples under the quiet surface. When I got closer to the truck I realised that it had simply been abandoned there and was starting to fall apart. Relieved, I kept on walking and promised myself that I would stop behaving like a baby. I had received so much proof up until now that I would be alright and I told myself again that I must learn to trust!

In the forests you lose your sense of distance and it was quite difficult for me to follow the guide-book accurately. I decided to keep on walking straight ahead and after a long while I saw a sign for the Saint James' Way. I lifted my trekking poles in the air. I had been right and I shouted with joy. The symbols of Saint James' Way are paramount for pilgrims and they rely so much on them. I could compare them with the arteries of my body. When I know I am on the right track, everything functions as it should, my mind is free and I can enjoy the walk in nature. It allows me to be more connected with my soul. I walked through lovely countryside, but after many hours in the wilderness I was always happy to see the roofs of a farm or the steeple of a church, as it meant people were about. With that, however, another feeling would invade me: the fear of dogs. Today I was lucky as all the dogs were tied up. I paced myself so I could arrive at Le Chatelet around 4.00pm.

Since early in the morning, I had been dying for an apple. I had not had an apple for quite a while and I really felt like eating one. Have you ever felt in your life the desire for something that you could not get? I was experiencing that feeling about an apple and I was dying for one, hoping that a shop would be open in Le Chatelet. I reached Loye-sur-Arnon at about lunch time. In front of the 12th century Saint Martin's Church there was a little square and I saw a couple sitting and eating. I could not believe it: they had a backpack. I thought they must be pilgrims. I approached them and asked them if I could sit on the same bench. Yvette and Michel were not pilgrims, but walkers, and therefore to me they were sort of pilgrims. They were the first other 'pilgrims' that I had met while walking along the path since Nevers, but when I thought further about it, I realised they were the first other walkers I had seen since the beginning of my pilgrimage in Vezelay 11 days before. Yvette and Michel lived in a small village close to Grenoble near Savoy. They were walking 30 kilometres each day. Michel's feet were covered with blisters and I felt sorry for him as I knew how painful they could be. As I was eating my bread, which was three days old, with cheese and some nuts, Yvette put her hand into her backpack and offered me an apple - yes an apple. She had no idea of my craving and just imagine how surprised I was. They left and I stayed eating the apple, savouring every little morsel. I had asked and I had received. Before my departure from Brisbane, I used to write down what I needed to buy for my pilgrimage - not big things, just little things - and within a few days someone would give me a present of something that was on my list without me having to ask for it. I had been so surprised then and now it had happened again. How blessed I was! Back on the road I thanked God for his care.

I crossed another forest, but could not see the oak tree which, according to the guide-book, should have indicated the direction, so I followed my intuition. I arrived at the edge of the forest and I could see in the distance the steeple of a church. What a relief! There was a lot of vegetation in this area with beautiful wild flowers, but I did not know any of their names. I crossed some foot bridges over little streams before I reached Puy Ferrand with its church and abbey from the 11th and 12th centuries, and after that I came to the lovely little town of Le Chatelet where I would be staying for the night. As I ventured through it, I sensed unhappiness and saw a lot of shops closed, even the chemist and the doctor's surgery. My heart ached as I felt this little town was dying. I stopped at a bakery and shared my feelings with the assistant. I was right; there had been only one factory in this little community which had employed 400 people. The factory had to shut down following the global financial crisis and this closure affected not only the workers and their families, but all the surrounding farms. The farmers had already gone into debt to modernise their equipment so they could provide more poultry to the factory. After the factory closed, the workers lost their jobs and the farmers went broke. There was a real snow-ball effect which resulted in the death of this lovely little town. There were two bakeries still open, but one had to deliver bread to all the little villages and hamlets around Le Chatelet just to survive. I left saddened by this news. Money and the idea of profit were destroying everything in their paths.

I paced myself and reached my lodging. There was no shelter in Le Chatelet and so I stayed in a small hotel

which took in pilgrims at a discount price. I had a room
with a shared shower upstairs. It was in this hotel that I
met Michel and Yvette again, however, they were lodging
in the 'high society' section, rather than in the section for
pilgrims. The evening meal was simple, but excellent. I
have to say, it was cheap overnight accommodation, as
dinner and breakfast were included. At breakfast I learnt
that there had been a volcanic eruption in Iceland
creating an ash cloud and causing enormous disruption to
flights everywhere and affecting Europe ecologically. I was
shocked by this big news and realised that I had started to
leave behind the problems of the world, as I was just living
in my daily walk and in the moment.

The owner of the hotel was quite a larrikin and was
extremely funny. He took a photograph of Michel, Yvette
and me for his 'Livre d'Or' as a souvenir of our stay.
Before I left the next day, guess what happened? The
owner gave me an apple, even though I had not shared
my story from the day before. I thanked him for his
kindness, gave him a big smile and left.

As I was walking through Le Chatelet, my thoughts
went to all the small villages I had crossed up until that
moment where I had seen no one walking along the little
streets and all the shutters of the houses had been closed.
Even the small 'epicerie' ('corner shop') and bar - the life
blood of any village - had gone from these places. The
villages had lost their identity. My eyes saw the beautiful
huge stone houses, which had been built with love so
many centuries ago to protect a family, and were now
empty and left abandoned. The youth had left for a new
life to find work and had taken their families with them.
This exodus had been the death of so many villages I

passed through. This feeling was overwhelming. My heart felt so heavy and I started to cry as I myself had left the small village where my little family and I had lived before I migrated to Australia. I had been part of the problem and to a certain extent I felt a sense of responsibility for what was happening in these small French villages, even though I knew that the global financial crisis was most likely the culprit. It had hurt the small communities in France so much and elsewhere in the world. In a way, we are also responsible. Are we not all a link in the scheme of things? Through greed or inaction we have let things happen in the world and acted like ostriches, burying our heads in the sand. I was seeing the results in front of me and it was very sad.

I walked around a castle and at its base a little grotto for the Virgin Mary had been built. Soon after that, I reached the Church of Notre Dame, which was built during the 12th century. A little while later I was back in the countryside. Flowers were everywhere and the fields had joined the party by putting on their spring coats of yellow and white flowers. It was magical. Calmness entered my soul once more and my spirit lifted as I listened to the birds' beautiful, private concert. The climbs were becoming a bit more difficult and I remembered that I was in the Massif Central. I crossed more forests with trees still stripped of their leaves. This time I did not get lost and went over a bridge to cross the small stream called 'Portefeuille', the French word for purse. I longed for the rocky path, as I was walking a lot on roads. Suddenly, I felt a few drops of rain. I looked for a shelter, but there was not one in sight. Fortunately, as soon as the rain had started, it stopped again. I crossed a hamlet and saw a sculpture of a man made out of empty terracotta flower pots in a house window. There were dogs everywhere. I tried to control my fear again, which was not easy, and kept on walking. To my amazement, some barked like mad and others did not even care about seeing me passing in front of their property. It was very early when I crossed Archers, the small village of potters, and as I peered in through the windows along the main street, I glimpsed the sight of potters already working in their little shops. In comparison, this little village was alive and I felt so good now; all was not lost. I sat in front of a gate and enjoyed the moment.

I arrived at Saint-Jeanvrin and met Andre, a very nice young man, soon to be a father. He was the village gardener and told me that in this part of the Berry region, the community was trying to bring the young ones back to the village by creating work. The work involved looking after the environment in some way. One objective was to re-open the school to attract young families to the quality of life and peaceful environment so that they could bring up their family away from the troublesome cities. To do so, the community of Berry was part of the concept of the 'Green area' in France. As a keen gardener, Andre was making sure that this little village looked its best and he was making flower beds everywhere. He had great pride in what he was doing, as he had left the city for the countryside to perform such work. His little village had received an emblem from 'Villes et Villages Fleuris', which was a flower painted on a post that you saw when you entered the village. 'Villes et Villages Fleuris' is an organisation that was created by the French tourism industry in 1959 to develop green spaces in villages or towns. There are stringent rules which specify that only biological and ecological products can be used in order to respect the environment. We walked a few metres together and he showed me a pilgrim made out of wood, which was sitting in the main square and holding two Saint James' shells. I asked Andre about the village of Archers with all its potters. He explained to me that there are 40 'ateliers d'art' (craftsmen shops). The shops are leased to craftsmen for a two-year period and then they have to leave their little shops to make way for 40 new potters who then take up the new leases in the shops. The craftsmen can come from everywhere in Europe and have to create their art on the premises. Once a year, the village organises a huge exhibition, during which all the artists display their works, bringing up to 40,000 visitors from all over Europe to the little village. This idea has brought life back into Archers. I noticed how vibrant this part of the Berry was and how different it was from the villages I had crossed up until that point. The saying 'Help yourself and God will help you' was so true in this part of France.

I went to the town hall and had a stamp put in my pilgrims' credential. I met Delphine there and she allowed me to use a computer, so I sent an e-mail to my family in Australia, still wishing that they could see the beauty of France with me. This feeling was to overcome me again and again all along my journey.

I left in the direction of my next stop: Chateaumeillant. I visited the beautiful 12th century Abbey Church of Saint Genes and passed through an area of wineries, farming and forests, which was a real delight for the eye. I left the Cher region for the Indre and in doing so I was entering the sixth region of my journey. To reach Neret I had to climb quite a steep route, but the beauty of the scenery was breath-taking and made me forget my pain and struggles. When I reached the top I walked along a very grassy path, which was a nice change from the bitumen roads I had walked on earlier that day.

At the top of the hill stands the 15th century Saint Martin Church, and when I reached it I turned around and looked out: scenic landscapes stretched as far as the eye could see. I was staying in a camping ground owned by a Dutch couple and they welcomed me with open arms. It was not every day they had a woman walking alone to Santiago de Compostela with backpack and all.

It was a sunny day, but the wind was going through to my bones and I could not warm up. I was offered a cup of piping hot chamomile tea. My room was in a refurbished barn adjacent to the farm house - very simple and clean. To access it I had to climb a ladder! I was scared of heights, but I managed my fear very well, as no one realised I was shaking with fright. It was still sunny when I finished my chores and I went to sit on the lawn. Francois, the owner, seemed a bit wary of me, but somehow we talked and had some lovely exchanges. At the end of our conversation he complimented me by saying he liked me. They had some friends from the Netherlands staying with them at the same time, and Wilhelmina, his wife, invited me to share their meal. They were a jolly party and tried their best to include me using the bit of English they knew. I felt very special; it was a wonderful feeling. I was to leave early the next morning and Wilhelmina woke up before the others to prepare my breakfast. She told me she was missing Holland. My heart went out to her as I had known the feeling of isolation in my life. She felt comfortable enough to share with me some of her personal worries. I felt so privileged to be part of her life for a little while and to be able to help her along the way. I had to leave and we hugged tightly. I told her that a meeting, even a brief one, can change someone's life and I would carry her sorrows with me to Santiago de Compostela.

Wilhelmina had explained to me how to get back on the track from her camping ground, but somehow I got lost. Good start. Hmm! I met a farmer walking with his dog. It was another German shepherd: my nemesis! I had no choice; I did not know when I would see another human being who could put me back on the right track. The only solution was to stay calm and I approached the farmer and his dog. The dog did not move and stayed beside his master and I learnt to trust a bit more. The farmer pointed me in the right direction and I had no problems with the dog. What an improvement on my part. I crossed dirt and grassy tracks following the Roman route through more villages. As I was walking along a bitumen road, a dog jumped through a farm gate and came towards me. I walked calmly to the other side of the road and used Claude's method with my poles. The dog did not stop barking, but did not cross the road and I kept on walking, making the half-moon circle with my poles. It worked and I carried on. That day, I had built my confidence, though I was shaking like crazy.

Later, I met an old man riding his bicycle while his little French Poodle, Melba, walked by his side. I told him the origin of the Australian dessert, Peach Melba. From then on, I assumed that Melba would remind him of his encounter with an Australian-French woman along the pilgrimage. He had lost his wife and was missing her more and more every day. He noticed my backpack and said it was far too heavy. I replied that I could not get rid of anything as I was too worried in case I might need it. On the path, I was behaving the same way I behaved in my normal life, keeping things just in case I might need them at some point in the future. Many of us do, indeed, live so much in the past, not letting things or possessions go, but keeping them like a security blanket. Maybe some did not have enough possessions in their earlier years and are scared to be without again.

I carried on through fields and flat ground. It felt good. I was in a valley and all around me I could see small, bare hills with just a top line of trees without leaves. They looked like soldiers checking the surroundings for any intruders. I reached the village of Les Lacs when I saw a sign for 'Circuit George Sands'. I wondered and wanted to find out more about it. I waved at a man who just ignored me, but 30 metres further down the road, I met a well-educated man, Dominique, who was quite willing to answer all my questions. Not far from Les Lacs was the house of the well-known French writer Amandine Aurore Lucile Dupin. She wrote under the pseudonym 'George Sand' and lived most of her life in a village called Nohant. There she wrote the novels La Mare au diable, Le Meunier d'Angibault and Consuelo, most of which are set in the countryside of Berry around her village. Chopin lived in her house and composed some of his masterpieces there, including the Sonate Funebre, the Nocturnes from Opus 37 and the Mazurkas from Opus 41. George Sand died on 8 June 1876 and is buried on her property. These days people can visit her garden. Dominique talked to me on a more personal level. Like a lot of French people, he was concerned about the financial crisis and he was also concerned for the youth of France. His daughter had to go to England to try her luck in the cooking industry as this was dominated by men in France and she would not have had a chance.

I reached La Chatre by crossing the old Roman bridge called 'Pont aux Laies' with its two arches. Underneath, flows the Indre River and I wondered how many pilgrims of Saint James' Way would have walked across that bridge to reach La Chatre, an old Gallo-Roman town built on a hill. While walking through the town, I saw many traditional shops with medieval architecture. It was Saturday and market day. The locals were sipping the traditional drink of 'Kir Berrichone' (cream of black-currant with red wine) on the terraces of the cafés. I decided to sit at one of the cafés with a hot chocolate and to admire the medieval houses and the cobblestones covering the main square. An elderly lady asked me what I was doing with my huge backpack and she advised me to visit the village where George Sand had lived. Nohant was just six kilometres down the road or five minutes by car. She was disappointed because I refused. She could not comprehend how I could not walk just 12 kilometres extra that day to see George Sand's house. I realised at that point that if someone has not walked with a backpack for many days, it is difficult to comprehend what the body goes through and just how challenging 12 kilometres can be.

I decided to look for my lodging. In the square there was a fair with much activity. The owner of the hotel I found put me at the back so that I would not hear the noise during the night. The room had a private bathroom and television at no extra charge. I felt like a queen. I was not interested in switching on the television, for life away from the path had lost its grip on me. As I wanted to visit the museum of George Sand, I dropped my backpack at the hotel and decided to go straight away, changing my routine for the first time.

I passed in front of the 12th century Saint Germain de La Chatre Church. A surprise was in front of me as I saw a couple with backpacks on who were leaving the square. They were pilgrims who I had noticed were carrying Madame Chassain's guide-book. Can you imagine my excitement? I had to talk to them! As I was asking if they were pilgrims, the man, Michel, asked me my name. I answered 'Claude' and he enquired whether I was 'Claude the Australian'. I could not believe my ears. Who would know me? Michel introduced me to Josette, his wife. Michel had two messages for me: one from M. Thionnet of Saint-Reverien and one from Anne and Jean-Pierre from Bouzais. I was speechless and I could not believe what was happening. They gave me the messages and we talked for a while. Before we departed, they informed me that the walk from now on through the Massif Central would be difficult and I should preserve my strength. I was warned. After leaving Josette and Michel, I went inside the Saint Germain de La Chatre Church to have my credential stamped, still astounded by the events of the afternoon. Your life can change in a second, believe me, it is true. So much love and friendship had come from the messages these two strangers had passed on to me, and I was thankful to have listened to my intuition. From now on, I would have to become more aware of my insight. How many times in our lives do we listen to our intuition? Sometimes, we are too scared to act right away, not grabbing the moment. God was sending me messages. To me there was no coincidence.

I visited George Sand's museum which was situated at the 'Donjons de Sauvigny' ('Sauvigny dungeons'), which were built during the 15th century and had walls 20 metres high and two metres thick. It was used as a prison during the 18th and 19th centuries until Jean Despruneaux bought the building and gave it to the town before his death, but not before he added his 'collection' to it. About 3,000 stuffed birds are displayed, some from the 18th and 19th centuries. I wandered and walked on the cobblestone streets of La Chatre and was able to send an e-mail to my children from the 'Syndicat d'Initiative' ('tourist centre'). What a day!

The next morning as I left, I passed in front of the half-timbered, red house described in George Sand's novel Andre and F. Chopin Street. Both Sand and Chopin are intertwined in this town. It was often difficult to get out of town, as sometimes there was no symbol and I got lost one more time. Once I was outside the town, I calmed down and found myself again. The walk was a little more difficult, but I still went through beautiful scenery. Everywhere, I saw colza fields with their yellow flowers in bloom. The green and yellow colours were everywhere and with a blue sky as background, nature was displaying its beauty in front of me.

After La Coudraie, I crossed a wood and saw a symbol of Saint James' Way on the top of a tree, but I could not judge clearly which direction it was pointing and I decided to turn left, passing in front of farms with dogs tied up in their enclosure. I felt that I was getting calmer when I heard dogs barking. What an improvement! After walking a while, I noticed that I had not seen another symbol. I kept on walking and grumbling. I decided to turn right and I arrived at an intersection when I saw four Dutch women with backpacks coming along a footpath. One of them, surprised at seeing me coming from another direction, asked me if I was walking Saint James' Way and which route I was following. I started to laugh as I told them about my own stupidity and my tendency to get lost. As usual, I had made a mess of taking the wrong track and I apologised to Mme Chassain for all my whingeing, as I had initially blamed her for not giving the right information in her guide-book. The Dutch women asked me if I wanted to have a coffee with them, but I declined. I left these ladies and kept on walking until I arrived at another beautiful spot. There was a stream and some stones where I could drop my backpack and sit down. It was idyllic and I had lunch with my little friends, the birds. I thought about my Papa and guessed that he would have loved to share this special time with me and I remembered as a child how I was proud to go with my father to the market with his truck, the two of us in the cabin watching the birth of a new day. We did not talk much, but were in communion and these memories are still very dear to me. I felt him close by. I left this special place and I arrived in front of the old Cistercian Abbey of Varennes from the 12th century. At Fougerolles, I again bumped into the four Dutch women I had met that morning. We all laughed, as we seemed to bump into each other quite easily, even though they had followed a different track, which was indicated in their Dutch guide-book.

As I entered Neuvy-Saint-Sepulchre, I met the four Dutch women who were on the terrace of a café, enjoying a beer. It was the third time that day that we had met! They called out to me and this time I joined them, not for a beer, but for a mineral water. It was a good chance to replenish the minerals in our bodies that we had lost after walking for so many hours. Their English vocabulary was limited, but somehow we understood each other. They were a very jolly group and I told them I was staying in a shelter for pilgrims.

Afterwards, I went to visit Saint Etienne Basilica, which was dedicated to Saint James during the 11th and 12th centuries. I was amazed, as the church has a style quite different from the churches I had seen up until that point. It has a rotunda resembling the grotto of the Saint Sepulchre in Jerusalem. It is a monument with a circular hall which is unique in France. It was built during the 11th century by Eudes de Deols after his return from his pilgrimage to the Holy Land. The basilica is very similar to the church that was built in Jerusalem in 326 AD on the site of Christ's burial place. On the ground floor in the vaults of the rotunda, there are eleven columns which represent the eleven apostles. Judas, the twelfth and missing apostle, is not represented due to his betrayal of Christ. As I visited the church, I noticed a chapel called Chapel of the Relics where I found three golden caskets. One contains drops of the blood of Christ, another, a fragment of Christ's tomb and the last one, a copy of one of the crucifixion nails. Pilgrims who were unable to go all the way to Jerusalem would finish their pilgrimage at this basilica before returning to their homes, and as such, it is an important point along the path. Saint James' pilgrims would have been stopping at Saint Etienne for centuries on their way to Santiago.

I left the church and looked for my lodgings. After I arrived, I began unpacking straight away when I heard a commotion and saw the four Dutch women entering by the kitchen door. I was surprised to see them, as they had planned to stay at a hotel. For the first time since Nevers, I shared my meal with pilgrims and it was a very nice change. The four of them would walk part of the pilgrimage each year, leaving their families behind, in the hope of reaching Santiago de Compostela at some stage. This year they would stop at Limoges. I found out that it was one of these women who I had talked to when I answered the phone for Chantal at Charenton-du-Cher. How strange.

On that night of 18 April 2010, after two weeks of walking, I had covered about 280 kilometres. It felt good.

'How I met Saint Peter'

The next morning on 19 April 2010, the four Dutch women and I had breakfast together. I had not slept well, as one of them had been snoring through the night. It did not seem to have bothered the others as they all looked well-rested. We would walk our separate ways and meet again in Gargilesse.

It was a lovely sunny day, a good sign, for a long and hilly walk was in front of me. Climbing up and down was quite challenging and I decided to use the 'Savoyard's pace', that is to say, you always walk with a regular and steady pace. It may seem like you are walking in slow motion, but this is not the case. Your body gets used to the steady rhythm and you go further without feeling too tired at the end. In one area the grass was very thick; it was a delight to walk on and Heaven for my feet. I had to rely on the G.R. symbols to find my way. The G.R. is a French hikers' association and they have their own symbols. In Mme Chassain's guide-book, there was information about their significance, but I could not remember any of it as I had discarded the page, thinking I would never need it! To make sure I was on the right track, I asked everyone I met. At one stage, I had been walking for a while without seeing any symbols, but saw yellow stickers flickering in the sun. I thought I was doing well and congratulated myself. As I got closer to them I realised that they were the markings of a construction site! Luck was on my side, however, as I met someone and I was told that I was on the right track.

I reached Cluis-Dessous with its medieval fortress from the 12th and 15th centuries built on a raised hill. I crossed hamlets with English names such as 'Priest', as this region had been part of the Duchy of Aquitaine which came under the dominion of the English when Eleanor of Aquitaine married Henri Duke of Normandy who became King Henri II of England. The Duchy of Aquitaine was annexed by France at the end of the Hundred Years' War of religion. I reached Cluis and went to visit the Saint Etienne and Saint Paxen Church from the 12th and 15th centuries, which was built in granite according to Roman and Gothic styles. Opposite, there was a corner shop and I stopped to buy some fruit, bread and cheese and a packet of dry soup for my dinner. The owner, Mohamed, was from Morocco and as he was not too busy we started a conversation about religion. We got along just fine - he the Islamic and I the Christian. We concluded that we are all one and that the philosophy of any religion is good, but the way people interpret it can, at times, make it a dangerous tool. He wanted to offer me some tea, but I had to keep on walking. The hike was long that day and I could not talk any longer, as I still had to walk 18 kilometres and the weight of my backpack was still a problem. I wished I could stop a bit longer, but I could not as there were lodgings to find and the condition of the track was unknown. Before leaving, Mohamed gave me a kiss on the cheek and a mandarin from Morocco and said to me, 'As Allah taught in the Quran, "give a bit and you will gain a lot"'. I was really touched by his gesture.

While I was crossing the village and pondering how easy it would be for all the world to get along if only human beings would respect others' views and open their hearts, I heard the voices of my four Dutch friends behind me. We waved and kept on walking our own ways. I arrived at a viaduct named 'Cluis' which goes over the Auzon River. It used to form part of a railway line that is no longer used, and it is 499 metres long and has 20 arches. At the top I could enjoy a breath-taking view of the surrounding countryside. My day had started so well; I was feeling happy and I did not care how many kilometres I still had to cover.

I kept on crossing little hamlets with no worry at all until I got lost in a forest and could not work out where I was. There were no symbols about and Mme Chassain's guide-book could not help me. I walked and walked and walked until I came face to face with a castle and decided to follow its contours when I saw a road. I stopped a car. The occupants, an older English couple, told me to jump in their car as I was so far from Gargilesse that I would not be able to make the town by nightfall. I declined, for I was doing every bit of the pilgrimage on foot, and they told me bluntly that I was completely mad and doing a pilgrimage on foot was a stupid idea! I had heard that comment before. They left and I smiled.

I kept on walking in the direction that they gave me, but was on edge when I saw two council men working on the road and they informed me that four Dutch women had also got lost this afternoon. I was not so bad after all. They had eight eyes between them: I had only two! To go back I had to cross a forest again for kilometre after kilometre. I felt a lot of different emotions - frustration, annoyance and fear - and I was cross with myself. Maybe I should have looked more carefully for the symbols.

Suddenly, my mobile rang. My son and his wife wanted to find out if I was ok. That was incredible! I was in a mess, but I did not let them know and hearing their voices at that moment was just a blessing, and courage came back. It was so good to hear from them. I was missing my little family back in Australia so much. Later that afternoon, Yves, my host from Saint-Parize-le-Chatel, rang me as well. I could not lie or pretend and told him how I was feeling lost and how I did not have the heart to tell my children the truth in case they became worried. Through these phone calls, someone from 'above' was sending me words of courage and trust.

I kept on walking and I repeated the directions in my head, non-stop, so as not to forget them. I was in a forest. It was hot and for the first time since the beginning of my pilgrimage, I took off one jumper, making my bag heavier. At one point, I climbed up a hill in an attempt to see a village, a roof, a church, but there was nothing. Then I heard the sound of cars. Somehow I climbed down and turned left, when suddenly I saw a village at the bottom of a very steep road. It was Gargilesse. I could not believe it! I had arrived. I would have walked more than 30 kilometres that day. Fortunately it had been a sunny one.

Gargilesse is a charming village of 300 inhabitants. Its houses with their brown, tiled roofs are built all around its castle, which was formerly a fortress and dates as far back as the eighth century. I was taken by its beauty and peaceful energy. It felt like I was back in time. Many artists live and work in Gargilesse. It is considered the most beautiful village in France by an association which endorses small and picturesque French villages. In the chapel of the sandstone Notre Dame Church there is a wooden statue of the Virgin Mary dating from the 12th century and the crypt is decorated with frescoes from the 12th and 16th centuries. A beautiful church. I climbed the very worn granite stairs and wondered how many pilgrims and people would have climbed these steps and I felt very humble to be adding mine.

As I walked down the main lane in the middle of the village, I saw a plaque indicating 'George Sand's House' and I went to have a look. I was amazed by the tiny two-roomed house, adjacent to other houses, where she lived for a few years. I found it hard to believe that she came here, at the age of fifty-three, to live in such a modest environment, as she had known only luxury since birth. Perhaps she had come to a point in her life where she realised that the simple things in life make you really happy. She loved Gargilesse and referred to it as 'a little Switzerland'. I had to agree. I took to the road again, as my lodging for that night was in a caravan park about two kilometres from Gargilesse. I was expecting to meet my four Dutch friends there. As I walked along the Gargilesse River, I saw the field that had been voted the most beautiful field in France. I was tired, but it was so very beautiful that all annoyance left me and I felt peaceful.

A while later, I met my four Dutch friends who had also had a difficult day. We slept in a little chalet just like the one in Savoy. At the end of a frustrating walk, all was well as I arrived safely at my destination. My feet were so painful and red and I did not have a restful night, as it felt like they were burning. The next morning I wore thicker woollen socks in the hope that their thickness would better absorb the perspiration and create some cushioning for my toes and feet.

At Gargilesse, the two branches of the path of Saint James' Way from Vezelay re-join. That is, the northern branch through Bourges and the southern branch through Nevers, which was the one I had taken. From now on, I imagined that I would meet a lot more pilgrims along the way and I was informed that getting lodgings could become a problem.

We left early and, as usual, I was the last one to leave, taking time to do my dressings. My body was still sore, but I had learnt to deal with it and I knew that l would forget all about it once I was on the road. It had rained during the night, but the sun was out now.

I walked along the Gargilesse River again, absorbing its beauty and its surroundings. The cherry trees were in full bloom with their colourful flowers; a real delight to the eye and the soul. Soon after I left Gargilesse, I was reminded that I was in the Massif Central for the mountains were higher in this region. I walked along the sealed roads, went up and down mountains, followed stony and grassy paths through green fields with dandelion flowers that added splashes of yellow to their green carpet, and passed through hedges and vineyards. I saw the first Limousin cows grazing in paddocks and enjoying the sunshine. The vegetation was dense and the birds were singing. I was again in harmony with nature, enjoying each moment and it was so good for the heart. After a while, I had to climb another mountain. It was hot and my backpack felt so heavy, as though it was damaging my back. I was really struggling and I could not see the end of the climb. At one point, I looked up and felt disheartened by the challenge ahead and made up my mind not to look up again. I put my cap just above my eyes and took one

121

step at a time. I could feel my Maman and Papa around, encouraging me. I was not alone. I lost track of time and without any problem, I arrived at the top of the mountain. I was getting stronger and it felt so good. The training I had done in Brisbane had started to pay off.

I reached a small village called Cuzion with its little Church of Saint Etienne. It contained the tomb of Francois de Montmorency, Marshall of France, who died in 1657. As I was resting in the shade of a building, Janine, a retired woman, came up to me for a chat. She was amazed by what I was tackling and could not stop congratulating me. She was a farmer's wife and when she retired, she told her husband she did not want to hear the verb 'work' ever again, or the expression 'come on, hurry up'. We had a good laugh and I connected with her delightful sense of humour.

From Cuzion, I went through more forests. Birds and wild flowers were all over the place and I regretted not being a botanist, because I did not know anything about the flowers and only my eyes could enjoy their beauty. I had to climb down very treacherous, steep and narrow, rocky tracks towards the Creuse River. My backpack was making matters worse and I nearly fell. I had drunk all my water so as to lighten the weight. Slowly and surely, however, I arrived at the bridge Pont-des-Piles. My mind was still baffled at what I had achieved that day and at the beauty of the Massif Central region.

I could not find my track as a huge storm had crossed this area, tearing down trees and signs. I asked two cyclists, Sebastian and Sylvain, for directions. They were sitting outside their weekender, waiting for their wives, as they had forgotten to leave them the keys. They had a bit of water left in their bottles and shared it with me. I felt privileged as I had received so much from strangers: apples, a mandarin, water, help and many signs of encouragement. Everyone had been so kind. I knew I was in physical pain, but I had received so much from my fellow human beings.

I had to cross another forest where a lot of trees had been uprooted and were now blocking the path. I had to climb over their trunks so I could keep on going. Every obstacle I met challenged me. However, with each challenge, I gained more confidence and felt I could do it no matter what. I was crossing the little town of Eguzon when I heard my name being called. Sylvain and Sebastian were coming out of a restaurant with their wives. The men had wanted to see me again as their wives also wished to meet me. They were so surprised that we happened to run into each other again. They were amazed by my courage, for as cyclists, they had an understanding of my challenges. We hugged and I left with their kindness and good wishes in my heart.

I crossed more beautiful villages and hamlets with houses made of stone walls. Gorgeous red and yellow tulips were planted in their gardens or front yards. I had to climb down more difficult and dangerous tracks and up and down sealed roads as well. That day, I crossed another region: La Creuse, leaving behind L'Indre. Because my feet were pounding so much on the path, I started to feel pain under my toes, like electric shocks. I was afraid, as I had to walk so many more kilometres to arrive in Santiago de Compostela.

The road passed through the forest and I could enjoy the shade while going down towards Crozant. Between the branches of the leafless trees, I could enjoy the scenery and I noticed the ruins of Crozant's fortress. I crossed the bridge on La Sedelle and arrived in front of the ruins of the huge fortress built by the Lords of De La Marche during the 10th to the 13th centuries. Nowadays, the ruins are privately owned.

That day it took me nine hours to cover 19 kilometres and I could not feel my feet. My lodging was two or more kilometres away from the track, but before that I had to reach the Romanesque Church of Saint Etienne. I was left with two solutions for getting to it: either by following the sealed road or by climbing up a very steep hill that would take me directly to the church. I decided on the latter. The climb was very hard and at one stage, I thought my backpack was going to pull me backwards, but once again I made it. When I reached the top I saw two men on a bench speaking English, one with a French accent and the other one with a strong Yorkshire accent. Hoping for another chat, I approached them. The Frenchman was an artist. His girlfriend was doing permaculture according to the Australian system created by the Australian ecologists Bill Mollison and David Holmgren. Australia, one way or another, was never far from me. Then our conversation steered towards religion. The Frenchman was open to anything and believed in something bigger than us, the man from Yorkshire was an atheist, and I am a Catholic, a Universalist and really a bit of everything. It was an exciting and enjoyable debate, but unfortunately I had to go. Before leaving I asked their names. The Frenchman was Jean-Marc and the Yorkshire man answered 'Saint Peter'. I laughed and told him that when I arrived at the Heavenly Gates, he should remember that we had met in

Crozant and open the doors of Heaven for me. 'Saint Peter' assured me he would not forget me and wished me good luck for the walk. Jean-Marc offered to drive me to my lodging and this time I did not refuse. My four Dutch friends were already there. I had a private bedroom, but did not sleep well at all. No pills were able to alleviate the excruciating pain I was feeling.

The next morning, I left my four friends, not knowing if we would ever meet again. I had to go back to the church where the track starts and again I climbed a steep hill. The difficult track was covered with small stones and the slope was almost perpendicular. My backpack was pulling me down and again, at times, I felt I was going to fall backwards. I had to go up and up and up and I remained brave, even though I knew that what goes up has to come down. At times I climbed down backwards, but it was not easy. I walked very slowly, being attentive to where and how I was placing my feet and trying to forget the electric sensations I had under my toes. Then I came to a cliff that was maybe 50 metres straight down. I could not panic; I had to go down no matter what. I had no other choice. I could see a lot of trees down the slope and I thought if I fell, the branches would catch me and perhaps this was similar to what I would have to expect in Spain, so courageously I kept on going forwards. I descended the cliff cautiously. I had to crawl at times and when I reached the end, the sense of achievement was overwhelming. I had never felt such excitement. I had succeeded and was so proud to have overcome one of my fears: the fear of heights.

I reached the Valley of La Sedelle and I crossed the forest called 'La solitude'. I walked along La Sedelle River and came to a mill named 'Le Moulin de la Folie' ('the watermill of madness'). Quite an apt name, considering my sister's opinion of what I was doing. I wanted to take a photograph of the watermill, but I could not get my camera to work. I panicked, as the previous day I had dropped it. The camera was a present from my friends Charlie and Paul and was going to be the visual witness of where I had been on my pilgrimage. I was devastated and at a loss, when out of the blue a couple of horse riders appeared. Isabelle and Denis had seen me walking along the track in the early morning and wondered how a mature woman could cross these forests by herself. They had thought that either I was brave or maybe a bit mad! Denis checked my camera; there was nothing wrong with it, but the memory card was damaged. Fortunately I had another one and replaced it. Amazingly, I had received help again and I was so thankful that people would come along at just the right time. I would have to remember to trust more instead of panicking as I usually do. As I checked my watch I realised that I had covered only 2.7 kilometres in one and a half hours with still 22 kilometres to go before I would reach my destination. I kept walking along La Sedelle River with its forests on both banks. It was picturesque scenery, a real marvel of nature. I crossed the famous bridge Pont du Chauraud dating from 1603. Leaving the bridge, I kept on walking in this magnificent area until I came to a little stone cross. Some small stones had been deposited at its base, by pilgrims presumably, and I decided to look for a heart-shaped stone so that I could leave it in memory of my family.

At La Chapelle-Baloue, I stopped at a café owned by a Scottish woman who had fallen in love with a Frenchman and did not want to go back to Scotland. She informed me that my four Dutch friends had stopped there as well and were about 10 minutes in front of me. I was surprised that they were not further ahead and assumed that they must have encountered the same difficulties as I had. While I was drinking my coffee, a young Frenchman approached me. He was living in the village, in the same house as his ancestors. For 230 years, the property had been passed on from father to son and he was happy that, nowadays, the English had decided to live in the area as they had saved his village from oblivion.

I had to walk a while along the sealed roads. My feet were getting hotter and the electric shocks under my toes were worsening. I was trailing the Roman route since I was not able to walk on the grassy edges of the road. The thick grass could have hidden uneven ground causing me to twist my ankle. Occasionally, I went through paths overgrown with knee-high nettle grass and I was glad to be wearing long trousers. Spring was really awakening in this area with its wild blue, white and yellow flowers; it was like paradise on earth. As I crossed more villages, people would cheer and wave at me and I was on cloud nine with all this attention.

I reached Saint-Germain-Beaupre with its castle and dungeons dating back to 1182. They had been destroyed and then rebuilt during the 16th century and now the castle is privately owned. After the 12th century Saint-Germain Church I was happy to find myself walking through farm tracks again. My eyes were attracted by a wooden letterbox that was nailed onto the trunk of a tree. There was a Saint James' scallop shell with the word 'Ultreia' written on it on the front of the letterbox. My curiosity got the better of me and I opened it.

Inside, there was an exercise book in which pilgrims had left messages for other pilgrims. What a beautiful thought! On the open page I could see that there were three messages for me: one from Michel and Yvette, whom I met in Le Chatelet, and two from my four Dutch girlfriends. I was overwhelmed and tears of happiness rolled down my face. The more I walked, the softer my heart became. I felt so very blessed and lucky to have seen the letterbox. I left a message for them, knowing that they would never see it, but it did not matter and I signed it 'Claude the Australian'. Inside the letterbox, there was a card for a pilgrim lodging. I rang the number and found out that the owners were English. I was relieved as they would be waiting for me for dinner and I would not have to sleep on the streets!

At Saint-Agnant-de-Versillat I found a boundary stone for the three regions of Poitou, Limousin and La Marche. I went through fields with easy trails, but also some muddy ones. I was in the middle of nowhere and amazingly at peace, just happy to know that I had a bed for the night. When I arrived at La Souterraine, I had some trouble finding my lodging. I asked a few locals who had never heard of it. Eventually, I found it. I was welcomed by the Englishman who showed me the way to my room. I had to climb up three flights of stairs and I was dead tired. Each step was so painful. I could not put one foot in front of the other as I had walked for more than nine hours with difficult climbs to cover approximately 25 kilometres. I was shown to a bedroom with only two beds: one was empty and in the other one there was a man resting. I was perplexed and asked if this was where I had to sleep and the owner enquired if I was a pilgrim. I was surprised by his question and after confirming it, he stated that there should be no problem then. I did not answer back and the Englishman left. I introduced myself to Yves from Canada, who was the man who had been resting on the other bed in the room, and then I put my backpack on the floor and went for a shower and washed my clothes. When I returned to the bedroom, I told Yves not to be offended, but I could not share the bedroom with him, as I had never shared a bedroom with a man other than my husband. Yves very politely told me that a pilgrim is always a pilgrim and that pilgrims have to respect one another. If I did not feel comfortable, all I needed to do was to ask the owners if they had another room available for pilgrims. Yves informed me that I should not forget that I would meet this situation time and time again on the path, however, I was free to do what I wished. I sighed, relieved, as Yves did not seem to be hurt by my reserve. Later on as we talked, I found out that he had been a director of human resources in Canada and had been an educator all his working life. It was his third Saint James' pilgrimage, yet each time he had taken a different route. He was walking to help others and he was sponsored to help two different associations: an orphanage in Haiti and an association to help children in India and Canada.

I received a frantic call from my sister; we had lost contact for more than 24 hours as I was crossing areas where her mobile phone could not reach me. I told her not to worry. I was walking not only for me, but for all our families and I could feel the presence of our Maman and Papa. They were accompanying me and protecting me

129

along the path. I laughingly told her that I was not mad, though I had passed in front of a watermill called 'La Folie'. We both laughed and my sister realised after all that I was not mad and she was proud of what I was doing.

After a good night's sleep in a separate room, I left behind the beautiful town of La Souterraine with its lovely cottages that were embellished by the colours of the spring flowers. I went through 'La-Porte-Saint-Jean' ('Saint John's door') from the 13th century, which was one of the entrances of the ancient walls surrounding the town. I passed the Church of Notre Dame built by the monks of Saint Martial during the 11th and 12th centuries with its imposing, high steeple from the 13th century. I cut across La Souterraine without any problem when suddenly I heard some shouting. I turned my head and saw two women waving at me. I was taking the wrong turn. In La Souterraine, the bronze shells of Saint James are placed on the pavements and indicate the direction to follow. I must have failed to spot one, yet sure enough, I was helped again. The track was not as difficult as the previous days. Higher in the mountains, there were still no leaves on the trees. Nevertheless, the fields and tracks were covered with wild flowers with colours of different shades of blue, red, rose, yellow and white. The buttercup and primrose flowers were announcing springtime to everyone in the area. In the valley, the cherry trees, apricot trees and walnut trees were all in bloom and I had the impression that I was walking in a mystical land. Seeing such beauty made my heart swell.

After so many days in nature my eyes were noticing the awakening of spring at a different level and any insect movement would catch my attention. I marvelled at what God had created. Everything was in front of me, I just had to look. It was free for me and everyone to enjoy, but most of us do not look at these simple pleasures, which are placed in front of us every single day. Most of us are often too preoccupied with worries, too busy accumulating wealth or just surviving in this modern world. We have to take time, although only a few do. Many of us walk like blind people through this paradise. Some have lost the habit of looking and enjoying the simple things in life as they walk in too much of a hurry. Maybe there is still time for us to wake up and do something about it and change our habits. Suddenly and to my astonishment, a pilgrim overtook me while I was deep in my thoughts. He was nearly running! Was he running after his life, his worries, or was he in a competition? I was surprised. For me the pilgrimage was not a competition, but a chance to connect with my soul at a very profound level and to do so I had to walk at a gentle pace.

The scenery of the Massif Central was magnificent. From time to time I could spot the Monts d'Ambazac that I would climb in a few days' time. It was a hot day and at Chamborand I stopped in the cemetery to look for a water tap. I had been told that I could always find drinking water in a cemetery, but that day it was not to be; not a tap was in sight. Disappointed, I went inside the 15th century Saint Martial Church to cool down and there I met a pilgrim, Alain, who was having a rest. He too was feeling the heat. Five years ago, Alain had walked to Santiago, then to Jerusalem, as he had taken a sabbatical year. This time he was taking two and a half years off from his very demanding work and was going to Santiago de Compostela. From there he was going to go to Fisterra, then to Fatima in Portugal, through Lourdes in France and he would cross Italy, Turkey, Syria, Lebanon and Israel through Bethlehem and he wanted to finish in Tibet. I was stunned and could not comprehend how someone would want to do the walk again after what I had been through up until now. You have to be a masochist I thought, but I kept my opinion to myself. Alain was the first pilgrim I would hike with since I left Nevers some nineteen days ago. We crossed a lovely village and a woman gave me some water. Later, we were stopped by a man working in his garden and he invited us to meet his wife. Roselyn and Patrick, from England, had decided to live in this little French paradise. They offered us some tea and were amazed by our endeavours and bravery. Roselyn took some photographs of us as we left. We had a lovely time in their charming company. It had provided us with a beautiful rest from the heat and we were ready to climb whatever came our way.

Coincidence or not, Alain, who was from Nantes in Brittany, had worked for one year in my birth town, Aix-les-Bains. It was a very nice change to be able to walk with someone, however, Alain was walking faster than me. I tried to keep up with him and in no time I felt pain in my groin and my sciatic nerve started to hurt. Noticing my limping, Alain reduced his pace, but the damage was done and I promised myself not to repeat the experience. Even if I had to miss out on having company, I would have to go at my own pace, no matter what.

I shared with Alain what had happened at La Souterraine with Yves the Canadian, and when I rang the private refuge at Benevent l'Abbaye where I was planning on staying that night, I was told that there was only one room left with two beds and a gentleman would be sleeping in one bed and I would be in the other. The owner added that the gentleman was a very nice person. I asked if his name was Yves from Canada. The surprised voice on the phone confirmed it. I was stunned. It could not be. Another repeat of yesterday? I queried if four Dutch women had also booked a room. Yes, was the reply and relieved I asked her if I could sleep in their bedroom. There was no free bed, but she said that a mattress could be put on the floor for me. As I was talking, I saw a cheeky smile appearing on the corner of Alain's mouth. He was quite amused by my shyness.

At Benevent l'Abbaye the church doors were open and we took this opportunity to visit it. It was built with granite during the 11th century and was dedicated to Saint Bartholomew as his relics had been brought from Benevento in Italy to this village in 1028. It has a magnificent dome and the portal has Arabic influences. A huge shell of Saint James had been placed on the pavement, and this reminded visitors and pilgrims of the importance of Benevent l'Abbaye during the Middle Ages.

Benevent l'Abbaye is a lovely village with medieval houses. As I was crossing a street to look for my lodging, a lady approached me asking me if I was a pilgrim. I noticed that her eyes were without light, as though dead, but she could not stop looking at me in awe as if I came from another planet. I sensed Edith was a human being in distress. I hugged her and tears rolled down her cheeks. She thought I was an angel, but I told her I was simply a pilgrim. As I left her, she was still smiling and kept looking at me walking down the street. As I was going to turn into another street I looked back and saw Edith still standing at the same spot, following me with her eyes. I waved goodbye. She was still smiling. It was the miracle of a hug. Such a small gesture of kindness, indeed.

As I continued walking along, the image of Edith's eyes, without light, reminded me of an incident with my Maman. In February 2002, my son, David, and I went to France. At that time my Maman had Alzheimer's, but was still able to recognise me. At the end of my stay I had to inform her of our return to Australia and she queried why I was leaving her. At her question, a dagger dug into my heart. I tried to give a simple and clear explanation while holding her hands very tightly. She did not comprehend why I had to leave and where Australia was and very patiently I explained again, which seemed to hit home and she suddenly became silent, lost in her thoughts, just staring at the table in front of her. She seemed so far away and looked so very sad. It might have lasted a few seconds, but to me it felt more like a century. Eventually, she came out of her mental torpor and said the following words that have stayed engraved forever in my mind: 'My little one, you have to do what you have to do'. After these final words, the light in her eyes disappeared again as my Maman retreated back into herself. From that day on, I still carry the pain I felt when I left her to return to Australia. Through her words, her wisdom had shown me the incredible love a mother could have towards her child so that I could return without guilt, yet despite this, I still felt guilty.

I looked for the town hall of Benevent l'Abbaye so that my credential could be stamped, but it was closed. Out of another office came two ladies, Monique and Annie, who were working at the Treasury and could stamp my credential. I wondered how many pilgrims had a stamp from the Treasury on their credential and then I thought to myself, 'I suppose I will have no financial problems on the path, as I will carry the stamp from the Treasury and it is never bankrupt!' They shared with me some part of their lives and I gave them some caring advice. I left them on the steps of the town hall, both of them with tears in their eyes. They told me how happy they were to have met me, wishing me courage mixed with words of thanks.

At my lodging, I found Yves and my four Dutch friends busy cooking and I went for a very quick shower as there was no hot water. The shower was icy and far from pleasant, but as a pilgrim I accepted it and I learnt to become more humble and thankful to have some water to clean my tired body. My Dutch friends went to visit the town and I stayed with Yves in the kitchen and like, all pilgrims, we talked and a friendship was created. Later, we all shared our dinner around the table.

The next morning, I left the refuge after a good night's sleep. I had not heard the snoring! I knew that the day ahead was going to be quite physical. I was starting to meet more pilgrims and thought that I probably would have to expect more cold showers.

The altitude of Benevent l'Abbaye is 485 metres and the tracks through the forests were somewhat difficult. I arrived at Marsac where I saw a sign for a post office and sent back 400 grams of excess baggage to my sister. My backpack felt lighter, but not for long as I had to buy some food and water, for after Marsac there were no shops for 15 kilometres.

As I was crossing Marsac, a 70-year-old woman,

Jacqueline, stopped me. She had done the Saint James' Way a few years ago and was going to do it again, but this time from Le Puy-en-Velay with a young female friend. I was full of admiration for her enthusiasm. Over the course of our conversation she told me that by the time I had finished the walk I would be totally changed and I would see things differently. I shared with her what had happened with Edith the day before, and then she said that I already had the knowledge of the change in me and I would know more after the walk. I told her that I started my pilgrimage on Easter Sunday, which had also been my birthday, and she replied that it was a sign that I had to stay aware of all coincidences and to always have my heart open. We hugged and I told her that I would think about her on 13 May 2010, which was the day she would start her second pilgrimage.

As I was in a mountainous area, I was going up and down all the time. I began another climb and it felt as if it was never going to end. The climb had lasted a long time and it had taken its toll on me. My heavy backpack did not help and I was not sure if I could make it. At times the narrow path was stony and treacherous. The sun was on me all the time and it felt hotter than ever as it reflected off the mountain. Once I thought of going back, but as I looked behind and I saw the difficulty of the track, I could not face the climb down the steep side of the mountain I gathered all my willpower and using my Savoyard pace I kept on going up and finally I reached the top and saw what was ahead of me: more climbs up and down. I sighed and took my courage in both hands. The only choice was to go forward. As I was going down, suddenly I lost my balance and my right leg gave way. I felt a sharp pain all along it. I did not fall, however, and I tried to put the pain out of my mind. I climbed down very slowly and the best I could do was to tell myself that I had felt pain before. 'Come on girl, keep on going'. I was trying to psych myself; mind over matter. I went through coniferous forests where there were birds and flowers, but I did not stop to look at the roses or smell them, as I had to reach my destination and I was in so much pain.

As I crossed Arrenes I saw a shell on the lintel of a walled-up door of a house that dated from the 13th century. It was a reminder of the passage of the pilgrims on their way to Santiago de Compostela.

In the Monts d'Ambazac, the highest peak is Puy de Jouer at 694 metres and from the peak of Saint-Goussaud (660 metres) there was a lovely view of the valley below. A narrow monument, about six metres high, attracted my attention. It was called 'Lanterne des morts' ('lantern of the dead') from the 12th century and it had an altar. I wondered if it was used to inform the population that someone had passed away, or for the spirits to know where their bodies were buried, but there was no one around to give me an answer.

The village's Gallo-Roman church, which dates from the 12th century, was dedicated to Saint Goussaud who lived in the seventh century as a hermit and became a shepherd. Inside the church, some of Mother Teresa's words were written down and I copied the ones that resonated with me. *Joy, generosity, small words of kindness, humility and patience, a simple thought to others, our ways to be quiet, to listen, to look, to forgive, to speak. Here are the true drops of Love'.*

I met two old women sitting on an outdoor bench,

enjoying the warmth of the first rays of sunshine and they informed me that I was the ninth pilgrim to pass in front of their house that day, but the first pilgrim from Australia that they had ever met. It was difficult for them to comprehend that someone living at the other end of this earth could have heard about Saint James' Way.

A little later on, I placed a heart-shaped stone at the foot of a cross for the people I had known in my life. From then on, every time I saw a cross, I would deposit a heart-shaped stone for someone at its base.

The paths had been difficult as I had to go down and up mountains all day, and besides, I did not rest as I worried about not reaching my destination before dark. I was also in a lot of pain. Some of the woods in this area were coniferous and dense and with my previous experiences of getting lost, I was cautious. It was the real wilderness and there was no village in sight. Eventually, as I was going down a road, I spotted a small, picturesque village through the trees down below. It was a relief to see Chatelus-le-Marcheix as my leg was hurting badly and my feet felt as though they had been through a blender. I stayed at the municipal refuge and met Sarah from Leeds who was looking after it. Kindly, Sarah had left some tins of food for my dinner with the price of the tin marked with a felt pen. I left the money in a tin with my donation for the night's accommodation, as all is done in trust.

My mobile phone rang. It was Yves from Canada who wanted to find out how I was coping, as the track had been challenging. He informed me that further ahead through the forests, the trees that would normally indicate the route to follow had been cut down. He advised me to be alert, as it would be very easy to miss the very little path on my left and I could get lost. I was very moved by his gentle attention. My Dutch friends rang me as well. They had walked as far as Les Billanges, covering nearly 30 kilometres that day. They were concerned that I was walking alone through the Massif Central's wilderness. I felt the spirit of the path descending on me as I sat alone in this little refuge after I had walked for more than seven hard hours.

I went to the lovely 'auberge' at Chatelus-le-Marcheix, as all shops had closed, and I was hoping that I would be able to buy some bread for the next day. The next village would be Le Chatelet-en-Dognon at 20 kilometres from Chatelus-le-Marcheix. As I entered the hotel I could only hear English and thought, 'I must be in England'. The patrons and owners were all English. As soon as the owners heard that I was a pilgrim, they prepared a French breakfast for me for the next morning, adding an apple for the day, free of charge. I was blessed again.

This part of France had a close connection with England when Eleanor of Aquitaine married Henri II. Nowadays, the English are helping the village to survive, as a number have settled in this part of France.

Upon my arrival back at the lodging, I took some analgesic tablets. Consequently, I slept well, even with my swollen and painful leg. Before the start of the new day, I would swallow more analgesics together with my daily dose of homeopathic tablets for pain and put my faith in God. It was 23 April 2010.

The following morning, I started off with a steep, heavily wooded hill, which suggested a hard day ahead. On a milestone I read that I was leaving La Creuse and entering La Haute-Vienne region. Like the previous day, I went through mountains from 300 metres to 650 metres high, as well as through pastures and fields. My leg was hurting and I tried to control the pain by putting it out of my mind. This required a huge effort, but somehow I did it. I am sure that someone from 'above' was helping me. I had to fill up my container with water and this extra weight would pose a real challenge. There were a lot of streams in the area, yet nonetheless, I was not sure if the water was safe to drink. I became more and more conscious of what I was putting in my mouth.

My desire to reach Santiago de Compostela was getting stronger and stronger by the day. The hike was not an easy one and I remembered Alain's suggestion to walk along the roads instead of the pilgrims' tracks when it was too hard. I had simply rejected such a recommendation, as my aim was to cover the Saint James' Way in its entirety along the ancient path. He added that God would forgive me if I took the roads. I had laughed at his remark as for me this walk was based on the discovery of why I was sent to do this walk. Was it to challenge my body, to put my feet where so many millions of pilgrims had marched over the centuries all the way to Santiago de Compostela, no matter how long it would take me? My aim was to arrive using the pilgrims' path. Yes, I was huffing, puffing and in pain, but I was fulfilled and no one would have changed my mind. I would do the track in its entirety and I would be able to look into the eyes of my children and everyone else and say, 'I did it all'.

The first 10 kilometres of that day were hard, not only because of the difficulty of the climbs, but also because the paths were full of unstable stones, and I had to be constantly on alert mode so I would not twist my ankles.

The pain in my right leg was a constant reminder of how quickly things could go wrong. It became a daily preoccupation after the jolt I had experienced the day before. I arrived at Les Billanges and crossed over the bridge of Dognon. As I journeyed along the Taurion River, the panorama was breath-taking with fir trees on both sides of its banks. I could just imagine what it would look like when all the trees of the forests would be covered in green leaves. Through a forest, I stumbled on a tree's roots in the shape of a goose's foot. It was amazing to see, as during the Middle Ages, this was the emblem that pilgrims had sewn onto their hoods after their return from Santiago de Compostela.

Every day brought its beauty, its discoveries, its challenges, and its pain, but it was all worthwhile. My connection with nature was getting stronger and stronger with each passing day. As I was walking slowly, I could observe every little insect and see them climbing stones with all their might and with a constant, regular speed. I learnt to respect them so much. I was watching the way the ants were working and they taught me a lot about perseverance, determination, continued efforts and never fearing any challenges. Nature was my teacher and I thought I had better be a good student. On higher peaks, nature was waking up later and patiently waiting for the warmer weather of spring, in contrast to the valleys where all the trees had already bloomed. My heart would lift at the sight of the dandelions and their flowers covering the fields. It felt like spring was always behind me and trying to catch up with me or even playing hide and seek.

I had put the apple that was given to me the previous day at the top of my backpack, but it was hurting my neck. I resolved the problem by eating it: less weight in my backpack. I learnt that even an apple not placed properly can make your walk a misery. Yes, one single apple! I had a bit of a rest before climbing again and was pacing myself, focussing on what I was doing.

In this peaceful environment, I wondered again about the journey of the human being who had become a slave to society. A balance would have to be found so the human being could find their true spirit again and live their life fully in harmony with the world and nature. I was deep in these thoughts as I walked along the winding road, and then round a bend there was a dog just outside the gates to a property. Yes, a dog - a German shepherd - the same breed that had a taste of my leg when I was ten years old. I held my breath and walked back very quietly. I was shaking and stopped to think. I did not have the courage to walk past that dog, even though it was asleep. I had to have a plan or a strategy to do something about it. From where I was, I could see the shape of a head inside the house. Perhaps someone was watching television. I thought to myself that if I shouted I could attract the attention of the owner, but that might also mean that the dog would wake up and come for me. I froze at the idea and pondered my dilemma for a few more minutes and thought about my next step. Having no choice, I bravely decided to walk forward, but on the other side of the road, away from the dog. I took a deep breath and walked straight ahead without glancing at the creature that was still sleeping in front of the gates. But how could I really trust a sleeping dog? It could jump in a second and have a bite of me! I did not want to share part of my flesh with a dog again! I courageously passed the dog, praying like mad and hoping that the ones 'above' would not forget about me. To my astonishment, the dog did not even move and stayed in its sleeping position. I was so relieved. When I was far away from it I relaxed and congratulated myself on my big achievement. On that specific day I really started to conquer my fear of dogs.

I crossed another forest with difficult footpaths and arrived at Le Chatelet-en-Dognon after nearly eight hours of walking. I stayed in a hotel that welcomed pilgrims in a separate lodging. Martine, the owner, allowed me to use her computer, but sadly I could not access my e-mail account. I found out that Anne, my 'twin sister', and Jean-Pierre from the refuge of Bouzais had stayed there two days earlier.

As I was visiting the village, I passed Saint Mary's Church from the 11th century. Above the main portal, I found a stained-glass window with the name of God in Hebrew characters and alpha and omega symbols in a triangle, which signified the beginning and the end of a human being. At the centre of the altar there was a beautiful painting from 1844 by V. Zier of Christ in his tomb. I had seen a lot of beautiful paintings along the way, but this one was special, as it was a present from the Emperor Napoleon III in 1869. I was amazed at what I could find in such a small church and village.

I was finishing my third week of walking on 24 April 2010, having covered 400 kilometres on the map.

'Going forward no matter what'

The next morning on 25 April 2010, while I was having my breakfast, I noticed some small packets of sugar on the table with the name 'Gilbert' printed on them. I sensed I was going to have a good day ahead, for Gilbert was my father's name. I felt he was sending me a message through this little packet, as if to say, 'I am with you. Have courage'.

As I crossed the village, I was astonished to see that nearly all the houses had lilac trees in bloom. In all their glory, the flowers were hanging like grapes over the fences and their smell intoxicated my senses. Spring is such a magnificent season. I was happy to have decided to walk at this time of the year, even though I had been discouraged from doing it because of the cold. My chest had been painful for a while and I was coughing, but it seemed that I was feeling better today, which made my climbing a little bit easier. For the first time since the beginning of my pilgrimage I did not wear my special compression tights. I had cut them to enlarge the opening, as I found they restricted the blood flow around my ankles and leg, which were swollen, and I was hoping I had made the right decision.

I went over mountain after mountain and at times the paths were very steep. Nonetheless, nature was at its best and beaming. Now, at this altitude, the trees in the forest were starting to cover themselves in green. I traversed more meadows full of dandelions with their majestic yellow flowers and in the woods I saw the first wild strawberry bushes in flower. Very soon their fruit would delight someone's palate. The Limousin cows were grazing in their paddocks and looking so peaceful with not a worry in the world.

In this part of France the panorama changed all the time, from forests, to meadows, to corn fields, tomountains and streams. I reached the end of a forestwhen out of the blue a picturesque house appeared. On one side against the wall stood an old watermill and a few metres from this gorgeous dwelling the La Galamache stream was running quietly. In front of the residence there was a pet rabbit eating some grass. It saw me, but, to my surprise, it did not move. I had never seen this in France as usually rabbits end up in a pot! This one was special: it was the homeowner's pet.

Every single day I had challenges thrown at me, then strangely enough, fear gradually left me bit by bit. When I got lost, I was still frightened, but my level of nervousness had lessened. From these paths where millions of pilgrims had walked over the centuries, an energy was radiating. It was enveloping me, giving me strength. I was beginning to really trust and the strong desire to achieve the almost unthinkable grew in me. It was so powerful that I knew no one or nothing would ever stop me. This progression of will had evolved little by little as I progressed along the path, and at that moment, I felt as though doubt had left me. Now I was even more convinced that I would reach Santiago de Compostela. On a deeper level there was a change in me too and I promised myself to listen to my intuition more, as my awareness had been allowed to develop and to fly freely in its fullness. All went well until I reached Lussac where I missed a road. I had hiked for quite a while before I realised my mistake. I was so mad with myself that I decided to rest on a log when my eyes caught my Maman's name - 'Celine' - on a letterbox. Like my Papa at Le Chatelet-en-Dognon, she was sending me a message of courage and trust. I smiled and carried on, but at each step, I was still livid and fuming at how stupid I had been, for I had to march along bitumenroads. As I reached a very busy national highway I saw a woman standing in front of a tombstone on the corner of a road at a place called Le Trianon. I went towards her to ask for help, but she had no knowledge of the Saint James' Way. I would have to keep on going along this busy highway, as it led to Saint-Leonard-de-Noblat. Then, my eyes caught sight of the inscription on the stone that the woman had been looking at, and I read:

'Le 17 Novembre 1943, Louis et Paul Dessagne ont ete arretes par la Milice et la Gestapo. Ils sont morts en deportation'.

This place was very important to Sylviane, the woman visiting the tombstone. The inscription read that her brother and father had been caught by the Gestapo on 17 November 1943 and both had died in a concentration camp in Germany. Sylviane would have been very young when this tragedy happened, however, I could see that it was still very raw in the deepest part of her being. I felt her pain and sorrow and gave her a hug. She said, 'It is what I needed today. You are a very kind person. Thank you'. I had given her so little, just a bit of love, compassion and shared her sadness only for a short time. I understood why it was that I had missed the track that morning. In everyone's life, things happen for a reason and sometimes we do not know why, but eventually we find out. My frustration had disappeared as if by magic. This was another lesson for me: to learn to be patient and not get frustrated so easily, as maybe someone would be in need of my help. But would I remember this in times of distress? That remained to be seen.

It was a hot day and I had to go up a steep climb to reach Saint-Leonard-de-Noblat, which is a small medieval town, situated on a hill above the Vienne River. The town was named after a hermit, Leonard de Noblat, who died in 556. The town grew around his tomb. It was Sunday and my footsteps took me to the centre of this lively little place. I had heard that it is a UNESCO World Heritage town, and as I walked along its charming medieval side streets and houses, I was in awe of everything my eyes could see and discover.

Finally, I arrived in a square in front of the Collegial Church of Saint-Leonard-de-Noblat and I heard a brass band coming from a corner and saw Sylviane, who was part of the procession, waving at me. A group of seniors approached me, as they were puzzled at seeing a mature-aged woman with a backpack and trekking poles in the middle of the square. They asked quite a few questions and took some notes in order to write an article in their local paper about their strange meeting in Saint-Leonard-de-Noblat with 'Claude the Australian' from French origins, who wanted to walk alone to Santiago de Compostela, crossing part of France and Spain. They were baffled, but wished me luck.

I entered the 11th century Collegial Romanesque church, built above Saint Leonard de Noblat's tomb. The church has a very tall bell tower, which has become a landmark for pilgrims walking the Saint James' Way. Inside this magnificent church there are seven chapels. The rotunda and cupola of the christening chapel were built on the same model as the one in Neuvy-Saint-Sepulchre where I had stopped a week earlier. In one section of the church I found some enormous chains that had been worn by prisoners. They were placed there in honour of Saint Leonard who had helped them. I was astonished at their weight and size and pondered for a while about how a human being could have lived in a cell with such chains torturing their body. What suffering the prisoner must have endured. I wondered how any human being could become an executioner in the name of punishment and justice. Would they be able to sleep peacefully in the dark of the night? Do we have the right to kill in the name of justice? With these thoughts, I left the church and headed out of Saint-Leonard-de-Noblat, passing in front of a 13th century hospital that had originally been built for pilgrims and nowadays is used as a hotel.

I took the ancient Roman road which passed under a granite viaduct that was 407 metres long. On my way to Noblat I crossed a 13th century Roman bridge over the Vienne River. Both sides of its banks held picturesque houses from the 16th and 17th centuries and I took in the beauty of this ancient place. As I walked along the Vienne River, I passed a porcelain factory and then I scrambled up a steep, rocky slope. If that was going to be an indication of what the end of the day was going to be like - steeper hills and downward climbs - then poor me! It became apparent that my training had not been sufficient to keep on walking day in, day out. It came to a point where my mind was focussing only on the pain I was experiencing. My feet felt as if they had been put in an oven and my leg was aching so much. At last, I noticed the sign-post with the direction of Auriel and my heart lifted, as very soon it was going to be the end of my day's trip. After a while, however, I gasped in sheer horror! The church was at the top of a steep hill! I did not want to walk one more step. The path continuously passed in front of churches and I usually visited them without annoyance like all pilgrims, but today I grumbled. Why did some priests and monks have to build their churches at the peak of a hill? Maybe they wanted to be closer to Heaven, but why so high? Everyone would have to take their time to reach it. I was so tired and in so much pain. I knew I would have to ascend these 400 or 500 metres uphill, but I was disgruntled and my willpower was weakening. However, after deep breathing to release my nervousness I started the climb with my Savoyard's step. I was still amazed at the power of my mind and body, as I had decided not to be defeated, and with sheer strength of will I made it to the top. I took refuge inside Saint John the Evangelist's Church for a rest and to cool down. Inside this church, I found the relics of Saint Gaucher and Saint Faucher. Saint Gaucher was born around 1060. He became a hermit and founded a priory near Auriel. He believed in celibacy and sharing all assets among the community.

At the church, I met two French women and found out that my lodging was about two kilometres away from the path. Seeing my poor state, Blanche and Sylvie drove me to my host. I did not refuse as I was dead tired. When I arrived, I met Angeline, who welcomed the pilgrims. Her son, a priest, had walked the Saint James' Way and realised how few shelters there were in this area. He and the young community of Auriel had decided to refurbish a barn and create a shelter for the joy of all pilgrims. The word 'barn' did not mean tin shed as it might in Australia, as the walls were one-metre thick. It was divided into sleeping quarters, bathrooms, toilets, a lounge room and a kitchen. I was so grateful to have found this respite and I was alone, once more. Angeline, an elderly woman with a big heart, lit the stove in the dining room with dry wood and left me ample logs to burn during the night, so I would not feel cold, as she told me that the temperature would drop significantly after dark. She brought me a rustic hot meal that I left simmering on the side of the stove and the smell filled the barn, reminding me of my youth. The barn was separate from Angeline's private lodging. In fact, there were fields on both sides of the barn where Limousin cows were grazing, enjoying the rest of the day. The main road was not far away, but somehow, I did not hear the cars. It was very peaceful and a nice place to rest my poor body. As I relaxed in the barn, I thought about the coming day. Claude, Monique and the few pilgrims I had met along the way had advised me to skip Limoges since it was such a big town. During the Middle Ages, Limoges played a significant part in the Saint James' Way. I could not comprehend why I should avoid it, except for the problems that I had already encountered when I had crossed a big city. I decided to ignore all the advice given to me and visit Limoges the following day.

I started early. The sky was blue and the cows were still grazing in the paddock, the dew on their coats glittering like diamonds in the sunlight. It was a wonderful start to the day! Angeline had prepared a lovely breakfast and we shared it in her kitchen. She told me that her family was struggling to keep the property. The 'rich' people of yesteryear were gone and all battled to keep afloat so their properties could stay intact. It was an eye opener and I reminded myself that it was not the first time that I had encountered such a situation along the path.

Angeline kindly drove me back to the path and I went forward, eager to know what the day would bring. The pretty countryside with its new festive colours accompanied me all the time and I went through a lot of hamlets, climbing up and down, when all of a sudden disaster struck. While I was climbing down, I twisted my right knee. It was so painful. Droplets of perspiration appeared on my forehead, but I could not stop. I had to keep going, no matter what, and I was in the middle of nowhere. I was thankful to have decided to do a short trek.

I crossed little bridges, passed rows of imposing oak trees, but I had to stop constantly as each step was so painful. Finally I found a log to sit on. After some rest, my knee was still hurting, but the ache was bearable and I set off again, but at a slower pace. It did become a laborious task and the slow motion of my pace allowed me to reflect on the reactions of some of us when life sends us challenges. Every human being has to face them during their lifetime, and how we confront these obstacles is the way we walk our journey. One could feel very sorry for oneself, or one could do the opposite and accept what comes along, analysing it, learning from it and with the learning, hopefully becoming a better person. Some of us love to stay in the frame of mind of 'poor me, poor me', as it is always so easy to blame someone else for our own problems. If one looks at situations in this way, one does not have to look too much inside oneself. I thought about it and came to the conclusion that these mishaps did not happen to me without reason: there was a purpose to them. I would have to wait and remain open, aware and patient.

At Feytiat I passed in front of the 12th century Saint Leger and Saint Clair's Romanesque Church which was refurbished during the 19th century. I passed a chateau used now as a town hall. A bit further on, down below, the city of Limoges emerged. As the crow flies it was not too far, but walking, it was another matter! Outside Limoges, I reached a big shopping centre. I went in as I knew I would always find an ATM in these centres. In a town, banks were often hard to find, adding more kilometres to my daily walk. I was taking my money out of the ATM when my mobile rang. It was a friend from my birth town, Roger, who had called me by mistake, but fortunately this call was going to be important to me and him in the future, though unknown to both of us at that time. We talked about my journey and his family. The two of us were happy about this strange mistake and timing, as I knew that if my mobile had rung while I was on the busy road I would probably never have heard it.

The traffic along this highway was horrendous. I walked past big stores, car yards, and factories: not a pleasant experience. I started to comprehend why pilgrims by-passed Limoges, capital of the Haute-Vienne. Limoges was founded by the Romans around 10 BC and was a flourishing city and used as a market place. In 1960, one of the largest Gallo-Roman amphitheatres was discovered in Limoges. Saint Martial with his two disciples came to evangelise Limoges around 250 AD and Saint Martial became Limoges's patron saint. In the 11th century, Limoges was renowned for its school of music and unique type of porcelain, which became famous and highly sought after all over Europe during the 19th century. In addition, Limoges is also famous for its oak-tree barrels that are used for the production of cognac.

The map of the city was confusing and the signage was so bad. I had to cross the motorway. After taking a wrong turn and getting lost I became despondent. Frustration flared again. I managed to trace my way back towards Limoges when I noticed a Saint James' shell placed on the pavement. It was directing me to a park with lovely lawns and I rejoiced at the quietness of the place, away from the commotion of traffic. The Vienne River runs along the path and ducks and wild birds were enjoying a swim. I calmed down upon viewing this peaceful scene. I traversed the river across the famous Roman Saint Etienne Bridge with its eight arches and cobblestones. It was built in 1210 and was used by the pilgrims of the Saint James' Way who came from the northern parts of Europe to enter Limoges on their way to Santiago de Compostela. It is called the 'Via Lemovicensis' and is also known as the Vezelay route. High above some rows of trees, I saw the Saint Etienne Cathedral looming over the bridge. The bridge links the city and the right-bank quarter of washhouses, where I was standing. In order to reach the centre of the city, I crossed the bridge and found myself at the bottom of a very steep and winding cobblestone hill. The excruciating pain was back along my tibia and knee. Every step was a challenge, but at last I made it to the top and tried my best not to show too much of my discomfort to the passers-by. A few steps before the top of the hill I found a patisserie and bought some cakes for my lunch, hoping that this extravagance would soothe my physical pains. It was wishful thinking, yet I ate them all the same in the park in front of Saint Etienne Cathedral. The building of this Roman-Gothic cathedral had started during the 12th century and was finished during the 19th century. On my visit to Limoges, the cathedral was getting a facelift and so there was scaffolding everywhere. I could not fully appreciate its beauty. I did not visit it as the visiting hours started at 2.30pm and I had to continue onwards. I was disappointed, for I would have liked to have a stamp in my credential as proof of my passing through Limoges.

I went through the old part of Limoges with its half-timbered houses and reached a square with an old fountain in the centre. The square was lined with cafés, old houses, shops and a church, in front of which stood two huge stone Celtic lions. It was the Church of Saint-Michel-des-Lions from the 14th century, and as its doors were open, I entered. Originally, it had been a chapel dedicated to the Archangel Michael, hence the church's name. It is a remarkable Gothic, granite church with an elegant spire that is 70 metres high. On the very top of the spire there is a copper globe which I thought could act as a beacon for pilgrims arriving in Limoges. The church has marvellous stained-glass windows from the 15th and 19th century. The Church of Saint-Michel-des-Lions holds the relics of Saint Martial, Saint Loup and Saint Valerie. I approached a woman inside the church and asked her where I could find the priest who could stamp my credential, and she took me to the vicarage. The priest was not there. However, we met Denise who was volunteering at the office. My face must have shown my suffering as Denise asked me what I had done and then asked where I was sleeping that night. I had not booked anything so she invited me to stay at her place. The woman who had accompanied me to the vicarage happened to be a nun and said she would have taken me to the convent if Denise had not suggested it first. Tears came to my eyes at such generosity. Both suggested to me that I should go and see a doctor at the hospital. I declined, too scared to hear the following diagnosis: 'You have to finish'. I could not imagine being told to stop. Something or someone was pushing me and I knew I would not listen, but I agreed to see a chemist. Denise suggested that I visit the 'Boucherie' Lane and Saint Aurelien's Chapel on my way to the chemist. I went along cobblestone alleys, the uneven stones making my walk very difficult and painful.

The 'Boucherie' Lane, or 'butchers' quarter', dates from the 14th and 15th centuries. In those times, the street was lined with old, colourful, timber-framed houses and traditional butchers' shops and lamp posts. Nowadays, the shop number 36 had been preserved and can be visited, but I could not pay a visit as it is not open all year round. Apparently 180 butchers' shops used to be in this passageway during the Middle Ages. I felt the wonderful sensation of being back in the Middle Ages, as it seemed nothing had changed since it had been built, and it felt as though things here were moving at a slower pace. It was wonderful and I loved it. To experience the real feeling of the place I closed my eyes so as not to see the modern placards placed on some of the shops. I walked on towards Saint Aurelian's Chapel, which was built in 1475. As Saint Aurelian is patron saint of the butcher, the butchers' guild is responsible for the maintenance of this chapel.

On my way back, I stopped at a chemist who advised me to see a doctor. This advice fell on deaf ears again, so he gave me the strongest medication he could prescribe. Afterwards, I walked into the city to find my way out of Limoges for the next day. As I arrived close to the Church of Saint-Michel-des-Lions, I saw some 'Trompe l'oeil' paintings on buildings. 'Trompe l'oeil' paintings are ones which deceive the eyes and make something look real and almost three-dimensional, even though it is only a painting. The fronts of the buildings were painted as flats with windows with people looking out of them, just as they would in real life. The two sculpted lions in front of Saint-Michel-des-Lions were used to mark the entrance to the market during the Middle Ages. I went back to the vicarage and as it was catechism day, Denise asked me if I would be willing to talk to a group of eight and nine-year-old boys and girls about the Saint James' Way. I spoke for the whole lesson and the children were captivated, listening with so much attention that you could have heard a fly buzzing. Their questions were very inquisitive and we all had a very lovely time. They asked me to keep in touch and to pray for them and their families when I arrived in Santiago de Compostela. Some made drawings that I carried with me all the way. The person in charge told me that the planned lesson for the day was about 'Emmaus'. Emmaus was an ancient town about 11 kilometres from Jerusalem where Jesus appeared three days after his crucifixion to two of his disciples who were walking along the road. She was surprised about the coincidence; the disciples had been walking towards Emmaus and I was walking towards Santiago de Compostela!

Later on, Denise took me to her lovely flat. After nights in a sleeping bag, finding a bed with clean sheets, a bath and the warmth of a real home was such a luxury. Denise lent me her computer. It was a delight to have the opportunity to read the e-mails from my children and friends and for me to send some back. In my e-mail inbox, a prayer to Saint Anthony of Padua was waiting for me from my friend Dominique. Saint Anthony would be able to help me find my way when I got lost; I really needed it! I was in so much pain that I told my children about my incident, though I did not tell them the full story. Denise spoilt me and I was so touched by her kindness. She had a friend's daughter who lived in Perth and was hoping that if her friend's daughter needed help, someone with a kind heart would help her as well in Australia. I told her how generous and helpful Australians are and that she need not be worried: if her friend's daughter needed help, someone would give it to her. She felt too that it was not a coincidence that we had met.

The next morning after a substantial breakfast, Denise took me back to the path. We parted as friends for eternity and she kept in touch with me along my walk. I thanked her and let her know how grateful I was for her kindness. I was always touched by the generosity and love of another human being. When we allow our heart to open to someone else without judgment and prejudice, the simple beauty of love will flourish and happiness will grow in us. I was leaving Limoges behind, but I took with me beautiful memories, hoping that one day I would return.

My pain had not lessened, but bravely I started walking. The roads were as dangerous as the previous day and I will not mention the traffic. At an intersection I got lost again. This time, I did not get mad. It was part of my journey and who knew who I would meet along the way and what would happen. After a while I found my way and it did not take long for me to meet someone. A man was walking his dog along a hospital fence and he started a conversation. In his youth, he had done a lot of walks, but he had damaged his knees and had to end his passion for health reasons. He was waiting for his wife, who was having a knee operation. Were these messages for me, the stubborn Savoyard? We kept walking and talking for a little while longer when, to my surprise, I realised that I was not afraid of his dog. It was an unbelievable change! I thought if my children could see me they would think they were dreaming or I was a stranger, not their Maman! Before leaving, I asked the gentleman his name. Gilbert, he said. Oh dear! Was this a message from my Papa, concerning my knee? My heart started to beat more rapidly and my mind was racing. Fear came to me, but as quickly as it had come, I brushed it away. No way, nothing would ever stop me.

At a major roundabout, I was puzzled about which road to take. I took one, but after a while I gathered that I had taken the wrong one and walked back. As I arrived back at the roundabout, I saw a couple with backpacks and I felt they were pilgrims. I waved at them and they waved back. I was saved. Michel from France and Marie from Belgium had met along the path and had decided to travel together for a little while. Marie asked me my name and when I told her she asked if I was 'the Australian?' Surprised, I replied, 'Yes'. Then Marie went on, 'I have a message for you from Anne and her husband'. Just imagine the shock of this meeting and its coincidences! I was stunned. Marie had met Anne and Jean-Pierre on the path after they had finished volunteering at the refuge of Bouzais and when they had started to walk their own pilgrimage. What a chance in a million that both they and I had met Marie. I had to get lost so that our paths could cross. I thanked her and gave her a hug.

Because of my injuries, I could not walk fast. Marie and Michel kindly reduced their pace as we all had planned to sleep at Flavignac. It was nice to have some company. The first time I had met a pilgrim while walking was on the way to Benevent l'Abbaye five days ago when I crossed paths with Alain. Marie was a botanist and knew about all the flowers along the edge of the road. I wished I had a memory like an elephant to remember all their names as I did not have time to write them down. We climbed up and down hills, went through meadows and tortuous tracks in this green Limousin with its springs, rivers and ponds. As we were walking along a bitumen road, a doe jumped out of a thicket in front of me. It happened so fast that I thought I had dreamt it. Like kangaroos, they cross without thinking. It stopped suddenly behind another thicket and to my amusement we looked at each other for a minute. It had lovely, soft eyes, with gigantic eye-lashes. What a thrill! At one point we lost our way and were advised to go through a steep path called 'Le Chemin des Cles du Ciel' ('path to the keys of Heaven'). I giggled when I saw the sign and thought to myself: never an easy way to get there.

At Aixe-sur-Vienne, we crossed over the Vienne River. The inhabitants of the town are called the 'Aixois', as in my home town of Aix-les-Bains. I stopped at the 13th century Gothic church, Sainte-Croix, which had apparently been built to protect a fragment of the cross which was brought by a pilgrim from the Holy Land. On one of the pillars there were some sculpted shells of Saint James, still quite visible. In the Middle Ages, this town on the 'Via Lemovicensis' had its 'maladerie' ('leper hospital') and a shelter for pilgrims. After the sign-post indicating 'David Mill', we had a rest and we shared our frugal lunch. Michel and Marie were surprised to find out that I was born in Aix-les-Bains, as Michel's wife's family had a farm in Chindrieux, a small village on the edge of Lake du Bourget. Marie was surprised too, as she had spent quite a few summer holidays there. Strangely enough, Michel's and Marie's paths had crossed on their way to Santiago de Compostela, but never in the small village of Chindrieux.

After a bit of a rest, Michel decided to continue going forward, as the refuge was opening late in the afternoon and it had only four bunks. We had to be present by 5.00pm to get the keys. I advised Marie to go ahead with Michel, but she refused. Marie rested a little while longer under the shade of a tree. She would catch me later as she walked faster than I did. I set off again, gathering all my courage because the medication was wearing off and walking was becoming more difficult. Close to Mardaloux, I passed a farm house when an elderly woman, Anne-Marie, with her snow-white apron, came out of her house and brought me some water. Seeing the pain on my face she suggested that I stay with her and her family overnight so she could take care of my leg. I could feel the warmth of this woman's heart and her real concern. I had to decline as I had organised everything with Marie and Michel. Anne-Marie was astounded that I came from Australia as her grandson was in Sydney doing a thesis on sharks. She repeated her offer, but I declined it again. We hugged and I left. Another blessing from a stranger along the path. If there was still any small doubt in my mind, I knew at that moment that there was definitely no coincidence for what was happening to me on this pilgrimage and that no matter what, I would be protected. Marie had caught up with me and we had been walking for five minutes when we heard someone shouting behind us. It was Anne-Marie who, at the age of 79, was running, waving and trying to catch up with us as she wanted to take a photo of us. Then we wrote a few words in her 'Livre d'Or'.

I was walking at a slower pace as I was hurting so much and only sheer determination kept me going. At one point I told Marie to go ahead, as I felt I was a burden. Marie did not want to hear about it. We passed in front of the majestic Chateau de la Judie and had covered about 21 kilometres when we reached Saint-Martin-le-Vieux with seven kilometres to go to reach our destination.

We arrived at Flavignac at 6.30pm and a surprise was waiting for me at the refuge. Alain, who I had met on my way to Benevent l'Abbaye, was also at our refuge. It was nice to see him again. Alain had had to stop for a rest in Limoges and consequently I felt pretty proud of myself. A bit of ego was good for the spirit! I informed him of my strange coincidental meeting with Josette and Michel at La Chatre and Marie who had a message for me from pilgrims. He told me, 'Now you are a real pilgrim and pilgrims have heard about you along the path'. This occurrence was called the 'pilgrims' radio', when messages are passed along the path from pilgrim to pilgrim. It was only the beginning and this would follow me all the way to Santiago de Compostela. I was baffled and I had quite a lot to absorb. Me, the little Claude, known on the path! I went to visit the 15th century Assumption of the Virgin Church across from the refuge. This church was full of treasures placed behind electrified windows to prevent any theft. It contained jewellery and religious objects from the 13th century and paintings from the 16th and 18th centuries.

At the refuge, everyone was taking care of me, putting ice packs on my leg and knee. My knee was the size of a football. They checked to see if they could find a doctor. I was so lucky and touched by everyone's care. We barely knew each other, but there was a community of sympathy and genuine love for one another, as well as a sense of belonging and understanding.

As she did every day, my sister rang me. She was following my progress on a map with the help of her computer and had noticed that I had not walked as many kilometres in the last few days. She had received a copy of my last e-mail, sent to my children, confirming her suspicion. The cat was out of the bag and I tried to the best of my ability to reassure her that everything was alright. Easier said than done!

The next morning I was the last to leave, the reason being that Alain, Marie and Michel had drummed into me that my backpack was as heavy as a man's backpack. They told me, 'You will not make it. Look at your leg and your knee. There is a post office in this village. Send something back home and see a doctor. You can't keep on going like that. You have to learn to be wise'. In private, I cried. Nothing would stand in my way. But gradually, the inevitable sank in. My leg and knee were very swollen and painful. I thought I might have to give up and come to some reality check, but I could see my workmates with their doubting faces and was spurred on. 'No', I thought to myself. 'I will make it. Even if it takes me until the end of my life on this earth, I will finish it'.

Alain had left with a message for me to take the bitumen road, rather than the track. He said it would be better for my leg and knee, even in Spain. After he gave me the names of areas where I would have to be extra careful because of their difficulties, he added, 'I can't say any more. I know your stubbornness'.

Alone in the refuge, I was fighting with myself about what I should send back home. I had plenty of time to make a choice as the post office did not open until 8.30am and, I can assure you, it was not an easy task. I arrived in front of the post office, yet to my surprise, it was closed on Wednesdays. I laughed. It had been so hard for me to make a decision. I had made it meticulously and now the post office was closed. On the door there was a small sign saying: 'Open at Les Cars'. I had to pass through the village of Les Cars that same morning and as I had carried these clothes for so long up until that point, a little bit longer would not make much difference.

I went to the doctor's surgery, but the doctor could not see me before 12.00pm: too late for me. I thought to myself, 'You have no choice, my darling. Keep on walking'. I reached Les Cars and looked for the post office. The doors were closed as well. It was to open at 2.00pm. Again, too late for me. I laughed at the succession of events. Was it a message? I saw the ruins of the 14th century castle with its unusual architecture. It would have been a splendid castle during the Renaissance. The ruins showed that one section would have been used to shoot at enemies.

I left Les Cars and took to the road. Walking on the side of bitumen roads was quite hot and I appreciated the shade of the trees. I was dying to be back on a track in the middle of nowhere, when at last the path took me across meadows and woods with muddy lanes due to the recent rain. The mountains were quite high and I was regularly going up and down. When I was climbing down, it was just torture, as with each step it felt like an electric shock was passing through my entire leg and knee. I regretted not having been patient at Flavignac. I should have waited for the doctor's appointment. All my life, I had never listened to physical pains and it was no different this time. I had to be tough, resilient and keep on going, no matter what. I recalled my promise to my son, to listen to my body and not to become a martyr, but I could not obey. I prayed and prayed for help and amazingly, the pain lessened.

I got lost again in a wood while climbing uphill. I was wondering where I was when I met a couple, Lydie and Jacques, who were collecting small branches of oak trees to make barrels for wine. Jacques was a 'feuillardier', a person who makes wooden barrels the old-fashioned way. It is a disappearing trade in France. His company has four firms in France, two in the USA and one in Australia, which he longed to visit. He was the person in charge of the walkers' association in the area and he put me back on the right track. Now, was that luck or what?

I was walking on the edge of another forest when I came across two lovely elderly women walking arm in arm. They wanted to talk and informed me that they had had a 'battle' on their hands for a long time. They had wanted a seat along the lane so they could rest when they were doing their daily walk. Their tenacity finally won and the seat had been put in place just a few days ago and I was quite welcome to sit on it when I came to it. They considered it as theirs, with good reason. I smiled and enjoyed the spirit of these two 80-year-old women and thanked them. They showed me that perseverance was the way to go. I did look for the bench and eventually found it. It was made from the trunk of a tree, divided into two large, round pieces with a simple plank nailed across them. Nothing grand, but for them it was the win that had counted and for me a message: never surrender.

I entered Chalus, my destination for the day, through the route of Richard Coeur de Lion. I breathed a sigh of relief. It felt as though I had been walking on an electric mine for a long time with my leg and knee. I had to cross Chalus to go to the convent where I had booked a bunk for the night and I passed in front of the ruins of the Chalus Maulmont Chateau. To my surprise, the nun, Marie-Jo, and the other nuns did not remember my phone call. Nowadays, the nuns of this convent do not receive pilgrims any more as only a few of them are left and they are getting older. I repeated that I had rung the previous day, showing them the phone number and that a woman had said, 'We will be waiting for you'. They were as surprised as I was. The nuns offered me a glass of cold juice and I enjoyed a rest in their cool kitchen. When I was leaving they kindly handed me a packet of biscuits.

On my way to find a hotel, I stopped at a tobacconist and asked if there was a chiropractor in this little town. There was one, but his practice was on the other side of the town from where I had entered. I grumbled, as I had passed just in front of it. At each step the electric shock was back in my leg and knee. Something had to be done. My heart was broken, but a decision had to be made. I arrived at the chiropractor's and sat patiently in the waiting room. After a while, the chiropractor came out and I asked him if he could have a look at my leg and that I was prepared to see him at whatever time. This was to no avail, as he was too busy and he did not want to budge from his decision. I left feeling very sorry for myself. I could not walk anymore and so I stayed at a hotel called 'Richard Coeur de Lion' that was 200 metres from the chiropractor's.

My sister rang and she was not feeling well. I felt a lot of compassion for her and prayed that she would be feeling better soon. Then Denise from Limoges and Marie from Belgium rang; it seemed that everyone was worrying about me. My bedroom was on the first floor and I had great difficulty climbing up the stairs. I was washing my clothes when my son and his wife rang. After my e-mail, all my family in Australia were worried. Oh dear! My son reminded me of our last conversation. 'Mum, you are just like me. You never listen to your body and always push yourself too far. You promised me that you would stop if you got hurt. I am sure you remember our conversation and your promise'. I asked him not to worry, but David did not want to let it go. He knew he would not change my mind and he said, 'Please be careful, Mum, we love you'. I assured him I would be ok and that he should trust me. I could feel all the love from my little family and everyone I met on the path; it was so overwhelming. All my life, I made sure to always keep my promises, regardless of how much it would cost me on the emotional level. A promise is a promise, no matter what, but this time I could not keep it. Deep down I knew I had to walk the pilgrimage no matter what the challenges or the pain. In this case the challenges and pain were only physical and so they were nothing in comparison with the emotional pain some of us go through in life.

I did not sleep very well and when it was time to go down for my breakfast, I was not able to climb down the stairs as the pain was so great. The hotel owner came to my rescue and advised me to see the chiropractor just down the road. I shared with her what happened the previous afternoon when I went to his practice and she said, 'Leave it to me'. While she was phoning, I noticed a frame with some French script writings which said that Richard Coeur de Lion had been mortally wounded by a crossbow during a game at the Chalus Maulmont Chateau. He was shot by Pierre Basile and died on 6 April 1199 in the arms of his mother, Eleanor of Aquitaine. Before his death, he asked her to lay his body at Fontevraud, his heart at Rouen and his intestines at Chalus and I remembered that the day before I had just passed in front of the chateau, not knowing the importance of this piece of history. The owner of the hotel spoke to the chiropractor who agreed to see me before his first patient. I left and waited outside his practice, not believing my luck. When he saw my leg, his words were,

'You have to stop. You can't walk with a leg like that'. He noticed that I did not have any feeling under my heel and explained that my tibia was displaced and there was a lot of inflammation around the knee and the ligaments. 'You have to stop,' he repeated. Did he know to whom he was speaking? I did not answer. Before he did the three manipulations to put my tibia in its place, I prayed with all my strength, putting all my energy into the prayer and all my pain in the hands of God. My concentration was such that I did not feel a lot of pain, much to the chiropractor's surprise. Then, with a gentle voice, he said again, 'You know you have to stop. It is not wise what you are doing to your body'. I answered, 'I feel better already. I will keep on going. Thank you for seeing me this morning. I appreciate your kindness'. He could not believe his ears and with a softer voice he told me to be careful. He had changed. He was not the serious, grumpy man that I met the day before. I understood why I had decided not to wait for the doctor at Flavignac; he would have only given me medication to alleviate the pain. There is always a reason for everything and I was happy to have followed my intuition.

At the chemist I bought some medication as well as a lot of homeopathic tablets. I did not care about the extra weight; at least I would have them to help the pain and keep me going forwards. I stopped at a grocery store where I met Sister Marie-Jo who told me that all the Sisters had prayed for me when they were at church that same morning. I replied, 'Sister Marie-Jo, your prayers have been answered. Thank the Sisters'. Then I shared with her what had happened at the chiropractor's. She was bewildered, unsure whether the Sisters had been responsible for this little miracle. Then we hugged.

The post office was open and I sent back the few items I had packed the previous morning. My bag was lighter by 1.2 kilograms, but as I had added some food and the medication, there was very little change in the weight.

I was leaving Chalus in the Monts de Chalus, which was part of the National Park of the Perigord and Limousin. It was full of rolling hills, some very steep ones, chestnut forests and meadows. I was so happy that my leg had received some attention thanks to God's help. I was able to admire with more intensity this beautiful area. The trees had put on their green coats and the birds were singing.

At Monchaty, I left the Haute-Vienne region and entered the Dordogne. The weather was perfect, however, some of the tracks were really muddy. I had been so lucky up until now, as for the last few weeks the rain had not been my companion, even though my sister was saying every day, 'Rain is on the way'. Nonetheless, up until now it had missed me. I could not imagine what it would be like walking in the rain, day after day with my leg in such a condition. It was bad enough to have muddy tracks and I thanked my lucky stars that I had missed it so far.

I was walking along a field towards a wooded area when I was overtaken by two male pilgrims. They said 'hello' and kept on walking fast. I was certainly meeting more pilgrims now, but what were they heading towards so fast? Later on, I met Jacques from Reims along the way. He told me it was his second pilgrimage and he would stop at Saint-Jean-Pied-de-Port. He also said, 'Once a pilgrim, always a pilgrim, Claude'. I still did not comprehend how someone could punish his body twice like that. I still had a lot to learn about the reasons behind these pilgrimages. It did not take long for Jacques to realise that I was in dire straits, especially when climbing down. Indeed, it felt as though my knee was not staying in its place, but shifting from left to right at every step. It was uncomfortable, but it was a pain I could handle.

At an intersection we saw a sign for Perigord Vert. The Perigord province, part of the Aquitaine region, is divided into four different sections. Each one is characterised by a separate colour: green, white, black and purple, corresponding to the colour of its soil, fields, forests and vineyards. I was crossing Perigord Vert ('green') which describes the light-coloured green of the chestnut and beech forests. Jacques went to his refuge at Saint-Pierre-de-Frugie while I kept on walking towards La Coquille. He was sure that we would see each other again. I passed in front a Buddhist temple entrance with a cross beside it and an oratory to the Virgin Mary. I loved seeing Buddhism and Christianity side by side, as I think we should respect religions other than our own.

I arrived at La Coquille and saw two men sitting outside a café in a square called Place de Saint-Jacques de Compostelle. To my surprise, they were calling out my name and clapping my achievement. I thought, 'They knew what I went through to reach La Coquille. How nice!' Jules and Frank were from Holland and had heard about me through the pilgrims' radio. They wanted, as good pilgrims, to offer me a beer, but I declined very politely. However, I had to drink my first bottle of Coca-Cola for the sugar and for the fact that it would kill all the bugs I had gathered along the way. I said to myself, 'If Coca-Cola kills all the bugs, it might kill me too'.

Alexandra, my daughter-in-law, would not have believed her eyes if she had seen me drinking it, and she would have thought, 'Someone is changing!'

La Coquille is a small town between Limoges and Perigueux dating from the Roman times. It was in this parish that for the first time a 'coquille Saint-Jacques' ('Saint James scallop shell'), now the symbol of the Saint James' Way, was given to the pilgrims on their way to Santiago de Compostela. I went to my refuge where I was welcomed by Annie, an ex-pilgrim, who had been informed by the pilgrims' radio that I was having trouble with my leg. I found another Dutchman, Yan, who was the other pilgrim who had overtaken me that same morning, walking so fast. Annie took care of my leg and knee with a pack of ice, making sure I was as comfortable as possible. I went to the chemist and bought a gel pack weighing 750 milligrams. Bye-bye to a lighter bag! I laughed at the irony of it all. Annie cooked a beautiful meal; she was a real delight. I received a lot of phone calls: one from Marie, Alain, Annie, Michel and Yves. They were still concerned about me. I also had a call from Yves from Saint-Parize-le-Chatel, who had advised me to stop even for just a few days, but they had all forgotten they were talking to a Savoyard named Claude! As usual, my sister rang and begged me to stop, asking me what it was that I wanted to prove. My brother told me to be careful. I tried to appease everyone, telling them nothing would stop me and I would keep on walking. I was thankful that they did not know the real truth! Nevertheless, I was very touched by their concern, but all advice fell on deaf ears. I could not make them understand that I had to do this pilgrimage, that there was such a powerful push within me. It was not stubbornness. It was something deep inside that made me want to do it, something more powerful, stronger than I had ever felt in my entire life and I had to listen to those feelings for whatever reasons.

In the dining room area there was a big map of France hanging on one of the walls with the four different routes of the pilgrimage highlighted. For the first time, I saw what I had covered since my first day in Vezelay. When I saw how far I had travelled already, I could not believe it and I looked at it, amazed. It was a real revelation. I had walked every day without any concept of what I had covered. As we say in France, 'Small streams make big rivers', and I must also add that, 'Small hikes make long walks'. In this refuge there was another challenge as for the first time I had to sleep in a room with four bunks, three occupied by men and obviously the fourth one by me. I recalled the events at La Souterraine with Yves from Canada. Here I was, sharing the same room with three Dutch men. I could see Yves having a good laugh and I smiled too.

After a rest, I left La Coquille quite late at 9.45am in the rain. My leg was still painful, but bearable. My knee was still moving from side to side with each step. It was enormously inflamed, but I had to keep on walking. I made sure I took all my medication and homeopathic tablets, massaging my knee with the emu cream made by native Australian Aborigines, which I treasured and advertised along the way.

This region is heavily wooded, with meadows surrounded by charming and peaceful villages. It was just exquisite. I walked alone all day and enjoyed it. The tracks were muddy - that is the least I could say - and slippery. I had to concentrate on the task, making sure of where I was putting my feet, it was but nothing compared with what I had lived through at the beginning of my pilgrimage after Vezelay. I thought how fortunate I was not to have any backache, as my backpack always gave me problems, particularly when I was going downhill. The scenery was misty, but the mountains had to be climbed. They did not seem as high or as difficult. Eventually, to my delight, the rain stopped.

The vegetation was very dense and I went my own way along the grassy paths with my friends, the birds. After the village of Les Rivailles, I took a dirt road south called Route Napoleon. I was joining my footsteps, not only with all the pilgrims over the millennia, but with those of Napoleon's army. It felt somewhat bizarre and ironic: one type of footsteps represented peace, the other, conquest. I crossed typical hamlets and forests and from the top of the hills I could distinguish five or six different shades of green amongst the trees, the meadows and the corn fields. It was so beautiful to the eyes and so peaceful. Life felt so simple in this environment and I was so blessed to be witness to such simple beauty. My heart was full of love for God who had created it all.

This time I did not get lost. I thought, 'I will have to put a star in my diary!' The only down side was my leg and knee, which were quite sore, but this did not make me want to end the pilgrimage; I had to go forward no matter what. I took the sealed Route Napoleon in the direction of Thiviers. At an intersection a sign-post was placed with the writing 'Le petit Claud' and the spelling attracted my eyes. It did not have the 'e' at the end of 'Claude'. At the age of 21, I went to England and I lived with a family as an 'au pair', and the head of the family used to write my Christian name that way. Maybe it was a reminder of the English history in this part of France. Back then, I was so shy that I never dared to say anything to them regarding the mis-spelling of my Christian name.

The Route Napoleon was a straight and busy road over a few kilometres leading directly to Thiviers. At the entrance to this town, I followed the scallop shells placed on the pavements, which would lead me to the church. It is a pretty medieval town and to get to the square where the church is, I had to walk along a steep street lined on both sides with beautiful medieval houses and shops. As I arrived in the square I heard someone calling my name. It was Frank and we went to visit the 12th century Church of Notre Dame together. It was partially destroyed after the religious wars. The statue dedicated to the pilgrims and to welcome them on their arrival at the entrance of Thiviers had been moved into the church. On the columns, I noticed carved male - human monsters and I was informed that they were similar to the ones in the Church of Saint Isidoro at Leon in Spain. During its history, Thiviers had been under the control of either the French or the English, depending on which one was in power during the Hundred Years' War of religion. Therefore, the people had to learn to adapt to the different reigns. Behind the church there was the Castle of Vaucourt, which was privately owned. Frank and I joined Jules and Yan who were drinking a beer on the terrace of a café. I ordered a Vichy mineral water - the experience of one Coca-Cola had been enough - and I went to buy some cakes for everyone. As we were staying at different refuges, we said goodbye to each other, since we did not know if we would see each other again.

I was leaving the café when I heard my name again. This time it was Jacques from Reims who had just arrived in Thiviers. Amazingly we were staying in the same house and we visited the little town together. As we arrived at our guest house we were welcomed by a very nice Dutch couple, Janine and Jos. We took possession of our individual bedrooms and were able to wash our clothes in a washing machine, a luxury much appreciated. In the garden at the back of the house we were introduced to Papa black duck, Mama black duck and three baby black ducklings. I must tell you that we were in the capital of the 'Foie Gras'. Fortunately, this duck family would never finish in a pate tin.

The next morning as we arrived back at the church square, there was a market with a variety of vegetables, fruit, pate and cheeses fresh from the farms. It was like going back to my early childhood, when I used to go with my Papa to sell our produce at the market in Lower Savoy and Upper Savoy. Within a second I was back there, as if my mind had frozen in time for a little while.

We were leaving Thiviers, one of the five 'doors' to the Perigord-Limousin National Park and the place where the famous philosopher and writer Jean Sartre had spent his childhood. We walked through scenery that was similar to the previous days. Jacques and I talked about spirituality and life after death. Our exchanges were honest, profound and both of us enjoyed this interaction. Away from the hustle of the modern world I noticed that, in general, people opened up without shame or fear of judgment. It was so beautiful. During our lifetime, we do not take enough time for the most important person in our lives:

ourselves. We are too busy looking after others or our position in the world. I wondered whether Jacques was walking the path again for this reason or if there was something else, but I did not ask as I respected his wish for privacy. Was it the communion of words that pilgrims were looking for, as back in their daily lives they were missing this simple connection with others so much that they had to walk it again and again? Was there something special on these paths that made people shed their skin and allow the light to enter their soul? Are human beings looking to find on this path something that they have lost in our modern world? We are so absorbed by our day-to-day lives that we do not see the person beside us. We are becoming invisible to each other, and all our energy is taken up by either the accumulation of wealth or survival in our daily lives. Few of us are prepared to approach someone who seems to be in emotional pain. Many close their eyes and pass by, ignoring a human being in distress. What have we become? I have been rebuked by people that I have approached upon seeing their distress, but even this has never stopped me. The gift of a smile to someone else is very simple and it is only a sign of acknowledgement, of hope, and of recognition.

It was nice to walk with Jacques and my mind was taken away from the physical pain, which was becoming unbearable. We passed in front of a field and on a tree was a sign: 'Truffiere Protegee. Passage interdit' ('Protected truffle field. Do not enter'). We crossed more green fields and forests; it was so peaceful. Our footsteps on the path were the only noise we could hear in this magic place.

At Sorges, the 12th century Roman-Renaissance

Church of Saint Germain d'Auxerre was open. It has a very old holy water basin in the shape of a scallop shell and modern stained-glass windows, which are surprising to see in such a small church.

On the square of this neat little village, we again met Frank from Holland, who kindly had bought food and water for all of us to share. We also met Christian, a 27 year old from Germany, who did not drink coffee or alcohol. Christian had left from his home on the boundary of Luxembourg and Germany to walk to Saint-Jean-Pied-de-Port, and now he was walking back home. For him, this walk was in preparation for the one he was planning to do in 2012. He was planning on crossing part of America, which would be a distance of 3,000 kilometres. He had to be back at his home town by a certain date and was covering 50 to 55 kilometres a day, minimum. He was not carrying much. I was astounded by the distance he was covering every day. Oh dear!

Jacques accompanied us to the pilgrims' refuge of Sorges. I could barely walk and Jacques went to his lodging. The refuge was to open at 4.00pm and we were welcomed by our hosts Christiane and Marcel, who were ex-pilgrims. The smell of Christiane's cooking was a delight to our hungry stomachs. I was in so much pain that I could barely stand on my leg and the painkillers were running out. Frank made sure I did not have to carry my backpack up the stairs to the sleeping area. I felt he could relate to my pain and besides that he was a real gentleman. I did not complain, but Christiane and Marcel saw the state I was in and drove me to a chemist to get more medication. Unfortunately, the chemist did not have what I needed. We went around to a few different villages, but the chemist shops were closed because it was late Saturday afternoon. Despite these problems, I still met genuine friendship and care.

Together, we ate the delicious dinner prepared by Christiane. The atmosphere was divine and we sang some folklore songs. Annie, my host from La Coquille phoned as she was still worried about me.

On 1 May 2010, I had been on the track for four weeks and had covered 530 kilometres on the map. I wondered how many more kilometres I had actually done!

WEEK FIVE

'A door opens'

The following morning, Frank and I left under a grey sky. The pain in my leg was bearable, but I had little sleep as I was constantly woken by the pain and had to put ice on it. As I put on my backpack the pain came back with a vengeance. The weight was becoming a real issue again. Frank, a very caring man, was always making sure I was ok and I was so grateful for his kindness. Somehow, underneath his gentle manner, I sensed some anger deep within him. I found out that Frank had started his pilgrimage from Holland and about fifteen days into the walk he had a problem with one of his legs, which was so painful that he had to take the train and return home to rest for two weeks before starting again. He told me when one part of our body is not functioning well, it is because we have to deal with some anger about something or someone. It is a reaction by our body to make us think or act differently or change our way of life. The physical pain starts to take over our minds so we have to let go of our emotional pain. He used the pilgrimage to let go of his anger and told me I should let go of my emotional pain too. I knew about the connection between body and mind, but it was the first time that someone had mentioned this on the pilgrimage. With a gentle voice, I allowed myself to let him know that I had felt he still had some anger to deal with and maybe he could use the rest of his walk to let go of it completely before re-joining his little family in Perigueux. As I was saying these words, Frank suddenly left me, wishing me luck for my pilgrimage. I was surprised at how abruptly he had left and I will always wonder if I had said something too challenging for him. Perhaps it could have been one of those moments when one hurts another without realising, or maybe he just needed time to be alone to deal with what was left of his anger. We all used the pilgrimage for different reasons; each pilgrim had their own journey.

I was walking alone along a path and pondering whether I had been too honest with Frank and about what he said to me. Come to think of it, our legs and feet support the whole structure of our body and without them we would not be able to stand or move forward. I did not have time to go deeper into my thoughts, however, as Jacques from Reims caught up with me. I informed him that I would stop at La Cornille and that I was cutting down the number of kilometres to 12 a day for a few days so my leg might mend. He welcomed my decision, saying, 'It is good to hear you have made the decision to stop being the obstinate Savoyard you are!'

It was lovely to walk with Jacques, not only for his company, but because I did not have to be worried about finding the track. In fact, it was like a weight had lifted from my shoulders. It started to rain at La Cornille and after lunch, Jacques went his own way and I looked for my lodging. Luckily, I found my host at the market while I was asking about the lodging. She was busy and would be ready in a while so I seized the opportunity to visit the lovely village. As I was walking around the 12th century Saint Eumache Church, I noticed that on the north section of the church in a little niche, there was a statue covered with a black cloth. After asking about it, I found out that it was a statue of Saint James that had been restored by volunteers and would be unveiled on Saint James' feast day on 25 July 2010.

My host, Camille, took me to her place, which was in the middle of a forest. It was a great home in need of some repair, but the surroundings were splendid. It was an enchanting place and once more I was going to be alone. I was exploring my lodging when I opened a door. To my surprise, it opened to reveal a stony staircase leading to a dungeon. As there was no key to lock it, I took a chair to block the door. I asked Camille if she knew whether there was an acupuncture clinic in Perigueux, where I would arrive the following day. Straight away, she told me that she did not believe in acupuncture, but had a friend who did and who knew an acupuncturist.

When I was alone, my thinking went back to the problems people face in our modern society where money is the only driving force and where big firms now ask their employees to achieve more and more, no matter what. Day after day, year after year, the employer will squeeze everything out of the individual until there is no more to give. Sometimes, the employees will put their family in second position, so they can achieve what is requested. Young men age and suddenly they are of no more value to the firm. Without any respect for the work done over the years the firm will drop them like an old sock, not caring at all about the consequences of the dismissal. Employees that are 50 years old are too old for the firm. It has a domino effect. The employee is reduced to nothing and it is not only that one person who is affected, but all their family. When this drama happens in the lives of men and women, they face a huge challenge. They have lost their position, not only in their firm, but often they feel they have lost their position in the family and society. They used to be someone of importance and now they are nothing. This cannot go on. Things must change in the future and we have to think about what we are doing to our society. The young will become old someday too. Society has to re-think its actions for the lives of its individuals. Are we becoming too cynical and materialistic, with no heart, all for the sake of progress? Are we progressing or going backwards? Maybe some take the road of the pilgrimage and surround themselves with the peacefulness of nature, hoping that they will be able to make sense of what has happened. With the challenges of the tracks, they can re-think their lives and the steps to tackle for their future and that of their family.

The next morning, Camille brought my breakfast of one orange, jam, bread, butter and coffee. I had not heard from her since the previous afternoon. In the top-left corner of the tray there was a cup and in it were some beautiful, freshly cut flowers: one small bunch of white flowers with very small petals and a black rose. I was so touched that tears came to my eyes. I had never seen a black rose before. The rose bush had belonged to her family for a very long time and Camille had always taken great care of it and treasured it. Camille asked if she could stay and have a bit of a chat with me while I had my breakfast. She was a wonderful woman and like all of us, she carried sorrow, pain and sickness. Our exchanges were honest, profound and emotional. My heart went out to her. I could feel her pain and I would have loved to lift it from her, but if there was one thing I could not do, it was that. It was something that I had learnt through my life: someone else cannot carry another person's emotional or physical pain or sorrow. I could only be compassionate. I felt so blessed that I was there for her at this delicate time in her life and thanked God for allowing it even for a brief moment. I would remember her in Santiago de Compostela. Camille then left to phone the acupuncturist. She returned to me with an appointment for 1.30pm. It was nearly 10.00am, therefore, I had to leave straight away, as I would have to cover 12 kilometres to reach Perigueux and also I had to find where the acupuncturist was. It was going to be tight timing, especially with my leg. I would have to walk fast. We hugged like old friends and I left.

As I started walking, I wondered whether I could in fact make it to Perigueux on time. I had to cross a forest to reach the main road and started praying to God to help me as I was afraid of getting lost and missing my appointment, which was vital for me to continue my journey. It was very hard to get an appointment straight away; it was more likely to be months than hours anywhere else in France. I had to keep on trusting. I asked God the Almighty to send me someone who could show me the way, as lately I had been running into a few pilgrims. It should not be too hard for Him to do so, I thought. I had walked about four kilometres when a pilgrim overtook me. Dear me, it was Yan, one of the Dutch pilgrims I had met at the refuge of La Coquille. I looked at the Heavens and said, 'Thank you'. He was the one sent to me. Yan was known to walk very fast; he was the one I needed. He had left his lodging fairly early that same morning and after walking many kilometres, he had realised that he had left his Dictaphone behind and had to go back to get it. Coincidence? Was I surprised? No, not anymore.

Yan knew about my leg. I informed him of my appointment in Perigueux and told him I would try my best to follow him so that I would arrive on time. Yan was a man of few words. I tried to keep up with him, but he was walking too fast. Walking fast made my pain worse. I was trying my best to block it from my mind, but it was very hard. Yan showed me what type of person he was, for at each intersection, he would either wait for me or check to see that I was not too far behind him so that I would see which track or street he was taking. At the entrance to Perigueux-the capital of the Dordogne in the northern part of the Aquitaine region - he waited for me with a can of fruit juice and we arrived in front of the acupuncturist's consulting room at 1.25pm, just five minutes before my appointment. I was really touched by his kindness. Behind a rough facade, he was a very caring man. We exchanged our mobile phone numbers as Yan was going to book a bunk for me. As I entered the acupuncture surgery, the doctor said, 'Madame, you are a very lucky lady. 10 or 15 minutes before you rang someone had cancelled an appointment. If they had not, I would not have been able to see you'. To her disbelief, I answered, 'I am not surprised. This was planned. It is the way things have happened to me on the pilgrimage. Doors open at the right time. It is incredible, but that is the way things occur'. The doctor was quite puzzled by my answer, then looking at my leg, she said, sternly, 'You cannot keep on walking. You have to stop. Have you seen the state of your leg and knee?' I thought to myself, 'I have heard that before', and I answered that I would rest tonight and be on the road tomorrow morning. She added that she would not be able to do much in one session and I replied that I was sorry, but I asked her to do the best she was able to. She could not believe her ears and shrugged her shoulders; another one who thought I was mad. I probably had enough of them to create a fan club now! Before leaving her consulting room, she gave me a long list of medication. Oh dear, was my first thought. More weight to carry.

Outside the surgery, I received a devastating text message from Yan: there was no bunk available in the refuge. Disaster! I felt frustration invading me. I would have to look for another lodging, but where? I had to calm down, but first things first, I went to find a chemist. As I came out of the chemist, I started to look for a map of Perigueux. I must have looked completely lost, as I heard a female voice coming from behind. 'Are you a pilgrim? Are you looking for something? Can we help?' It was an elderly couple: Martine and Jean. Martine was in a wheelchair and I shared with them my dilemma. Martine could not believe that I could not find a place at La Residence Diocesaine. With a brisk movement, she took her mobile out of her bag and immediately rang someone and within two minutes, I had a room for the night at La Residence Diocesaine. As the cafeteria of the hostel was closed, Martine sent Jean to buy some food for me. I pleaded with them not to spend their money, but to no avail. Martine was not the person to whom you could easily say 'no'. I pleaded more, as they had already done so much for me, but they would not listen. I had asked for only two or three tomatoes, one cucumber and one banana, but Jean came back with a bag full of food: fruit, tomatoes, cucumber, cheese, salami, bread and small packets of salt and pepper. Martine and Jean had always wanted to do this pilgrimage, but due to ill health they had not been able to realise their dreams. I would do it for them as well. We parted and I thanked them, adding that I would take them in my heart to Santiago de Compostela.

To reach my lodging, I had to climb a very steep hill and to give me some courage, I thought to myself, 'It will be easier tomorrow: you will go down'. I was climbing the stairs of La Residence Diocesaine when a man asked me if I was doing the Saint James' Way. I was introduced to Lucien and his wife, Jacqueline. Lucien was a 'baliseur' like Jean-Pierre from Coulanges-les-Nevers: a person who puts the symbol of Saint James at intersections and on trees so pilgrims can find their way on the path. I thanked him for his work with all my heart, as without the volunteers' devotion in checking the markings on the path, the pilgrims' walk would be very difficult. I shared with him how, after walking kilometre after kilometre in the wilderness, I felt lifted with joy at the sight of the symbols and that my smile could have gone all the way around my head. The symbols brought such a feeling of reassurance. Lucien laughed and said he was happy that his work was appreciated.

As I entered the lodging, I saw a computer. My heart leapt and I asked if I could use it, but it was not possible. They advised me to go to 'L'Office du Tourisme', which was quite a distance away. There was no way I could go because I needed to rest my leg, so my joy was short-lived. Fortunately, Lucien and his wife had overheard the conversation and invited me to use their computer at their home. Somehow, I was not able to connect to my e-mail account once again.

Jacqueline and Lucien drove me to Saint Front's Cathedral and Jacqueline explained its origin. It was built on the ruins of an abbey which had burnt down in 1120. Its shape is quite unique in France with its Greek cross and five Byzantine domes. I learnt that Saint Vincent de Paul was ordained in this cathedral and on Charlemagne's feast day on 28 June a special celebration is held here. Jacqueline also showed me the chapel dedicated to Saint James, which had been refurbished thanks to the pilgrims' donations.

We were in the middle of this cathedral when a woman in black approached me, as she had noticed my limping and asked about it. Jacqueline explained my situation to her and then the woman said to me, sternly, 'Lift your trousers'. I looked at Jacqueline, puzzled. Believe it or not, the woman was a doctor. She did not believe much in acupuncture and she wanted to see if my tibia had been put back properly. She noticed my patella going left to right and once more I was told to stop. I replied, 'Everybody is saying that to me, but I have to keep on going. I am compelled to do it. Something is pushing me, though I do not understand it myself. The only thing I know is that I have to keep going, that's all'. Taking my knee, she showed me how to put the patella back in its right position. Seeing this, Jacqueline said, 'Claude, you have to be wise. The doctor does not think it is safe for you to go on. She is worried about you and I am too. I myself have a problem with my knee and suffer every day with it. Please think twice about the advice given to you'. Feeling hopeless, I responded, 'I know, but I can't'. I hugged Jacqueline and left with the doctor who took me back to La Residence Diocesaine. It turned out that the doctor's husband was an orthopaedic specialist and she knew a lot about bones. While we were alone, she emphasised, 'Your tendons are all inflamed. You should rest, you really need a rest. I don't know how you have been able to make it up until now'. She confided in me that she had lost her mother a week ago and was shattered. I consoled her as best I could and opened my heart to her pain. In her car she had a CD playing and the nun who was singing had an angelic and healing voice so we listened and let ourselves be healed. I left her, but I was in turmoil following the sequence of the day's events. I had received so much love. It was more than I could take and I went up to my room. What a day!

La Residence Diocesaine is situated near the top of a very steep hill and from one of the corridors on the upper floor I had a magnificent view of Perigueux. Perigueux is a UNESCO World Heritage site and is well known for its many prehistoric sites as well as the famous paintings of Lascaux, which date from 17,300 BC. My sister rang me, worried, as there was no mobile connection in the areas I was passing through. She was frantic and so concerned that something had happened to me. I comforted her as much as I could. She had to trust because for the next few days there would be very little reception in the isolated places I would be traversing. To reassure her, I emphasised that on the track there were now more pilgrims. I received six phones calls and many text messages from pilgrims that night. Everyone was worried for me, including my family in Australia. I was hoping to find a phone-box in working order and ring to reassure them.

It was cold. 'Les Saintes Glaces' was on its way, maybe a bit earlier than normal. Every year on the 11, 12 and 13 May, which are the dates of 'Les Saintes Glaces', the weather pattern could change drastically and quickly and the French gardener avoided putting seedlings in the garden at this time of year. I felt as though snow was on its way. I went down to the refectory the next morning, hoping to find Yan so I could thank him for his kindness, but he had just left with Jules the other Dutchman. He had fulfilled his purpose; our paths would never cross again.

On my way out of the city, I walked down to the town with its alleys lined with boutiques and Renaissance houses. The section called 'Venusa' is the historical heart of the city and contains the remains of large Gallo-Roman residences, which have been beautifully preserved. I left the old Roman and medieval section of the town for the west section called the 'modern town'. Car drivers were beeping at me, wishing me 'good luck', 'courage' and 'bravo'. I was carried along by all these good wishes from strangers. It was heart-warming.

I was so cold that I was wearing most of my clothes and my backpack felt lighter. I stopped at a fruit shop to buy some nuts and packet soup for my evening meal. The shopkeeper, a very lively person, informed me that two years ago, an Aussie girl from Brisbane had lived next door for a year. She could not stop talking about this Brissie girl who would send her cards and a Christmas calendar every year as well. Unfortunately, she could not remember her name at the time I was passing through.

I was passing in front of a college for young men and

189

women and at the entrance I saw that three couples of six young students were kissing. When they saw me, they started to grin. I could understand. At 17 years of age, if you saw a mature-aged lady with white hair walking down the streets and carrying a backpack, it would be quite funny. For some reason, I decided to talk to them and crossed the street. At first they answered me with a grin and smart-alec remarks, such as, 'I would use a car' and 'weird'. I wanted to teach them something and told them about the dream I had. This dream had been to walk from Vezelay in France to Santiago de Compostela in Spain. I also told them that I had covered, up until now, more than 600 kilometres through mud, forests, rivers, tracks and mountains and so on, and that I would have to cover nearly four times more than that to reach my final destination of Muxia. I stressed again that I had a dream and that I was bound to realise it, no matter what. I continued and told them that I was sure each one of them had a dream. I gave them the following advice, 'Do not let anyone shatter your dream. Follow your desires and you will have no regrets in your life, no matter how old you are. Age has no relevance. Every one of us has a dream, big or small. You must know that you can be the creator of your dream'. Unexpectedly, as I was talking I saw the young men's facial expressions changing. They became serious. I saw the transformation of boys suddenly developing into men and their faces showed respect. My message had knocked at their doors. We talked a little bit more. All of a sudden, they had no more disrespect and their questions were constructive. Within a few minutes, the children had left and in their eyes I saw the men they would become. The girls shyly kept on smiling, a little bit more embarrassed, but I understood their shyness. As I was leaving, all the boys thanked me for taking the time to talk to them. They were happy and I was too. That day, they had grown a little bit more. Maybe they would remember that on 4 May 2010, a mature-aged woman with white hair and a backpack on her way to Spain took the time to speak with them about what life could be and told them to follow their dreams. They wished me good luck and courage, all of them shouting at the same time, 'We won't forget you. Thanks'. I waved goodbye and left.

I travelled to beautiful areas with lots of vegetation, forests, rivers and small vineyards with difficult tracks at times and at other times not so challenging. I was surprised at some of the street names such as 'Saint Angel'. There was a lake called 'Lac de Claude'. Oh dear, I thought. I would have to be careful of my ego! I went along a dirt track and read a sign for 'Abbaye Saint-Jacques et un banc pour les pelerins' ('Abbey of Saint James and a bench for the pilgrims'). I sat on the wooden bench for a few minutes and enjoyed this little rest. It was a treat and replaced the usual rough, dead tree trunk that I always looked for so that I could rest or eat my frugal meal. The more I travelled in this region, the more I could feel the importance that the Saint James' Way had played in this part of France.

It was bitterly cold when I arrived in Chancelade, west of Perigueux. In this small, prehistoric village, a skeleton of Cro-Magnon dating from 15,000 to 9,000 BC had been found. There is a Roman abbey, which was founded in 1128 by monks and dedicated to the Virgin Mary, as well as a small chapel dedicated to Mary Magdalene. I saw a phone-box and my heart started beating with happiness, but only for a short while, as my phone card was rejected.

I traversed more beautiful hilly areas with cows in the paddocks, but the cold was piercing me like sharp knives. After only 10 kilometres, my leg and knee started to give me trouble, however, it was a big improvement on the pain from a few days earlier. As I was walking along the bitumen road, I noticed a house made of small bricks and a design on the outside wall, which looked like the rays of the sun. Then a little bit further, I saw a wooden letterbox with the inscription: 'Halte gourmande pelerin, ouvrez s'il vous plait' ('a sweet stop for pilgrims, open please') on the lid. My curiosity took over and I opened it. Inside there were tins of nuts and dried fruit left for weary and hungry pilgrims. I was so touched by this kindness. It was left there so that pilgrims could rest a few minutes in this peaceful environment and eat some nourishing food before starting to walk again. I wrote a few words of thanks for this beautiful gesture, as a kind heart had been thinking about us pilgrims marching through cold, heat, snow and rain, with no shop around.

When I entered the little village of La Chapelle-Gonaguet, the pain came back like a monster. My host's lodging was far away and it was difficult to find. As such, Margaret decided to come and pick me up. I did not refuse and I waited patiently for her in front of a 'Lavoir' ('washhouse'), even though I was freezing. Margaret told me that it was snowing two kilometres away. She had a big dog called Topaze and with all the courage I could muster I patted it. I could imagine the faces of my children and my friends back in Australia and their disbelief if they had seen me. What a transformation! I used Margaret's phone with my card, which worked and I rang my children. It

192

was nice to hear their voices and to hear about what was going on in their lives in Australia. I reassured them about myself and when I hung up, tears rolled down my cheeks. I then called my sister. I had a lovely time that night, and with Margaret, I was there once more for another human being and I hoped to have brought comfort and some peace to her.

The next morning it was still bitterly cold when I left. Margaret had begged me to stay another day to rest my leg, but to no avail. In my mind I knew I had to keep going. The weather was horrendous, but I had to go on and I wondered what the state of the track would be if I stayed on an extra day. It would have been harder to walk the following day, for with the heavy rain that was predicted, the tracks would become harder to walk. Margaret drove me back to the 'Lavoir' and sadness filled my heart. Once more, I was leaving the comfort of a home for more adventures.

As I climbed a hill, I passed beside a house with two huge dogs. When they saw me, they started barking like mad, so much so that a man came out of the house, asking whether I had upset his dogs. Me? Certainly not! Then his wife came out and she picked some Lily of the Valley that was growing in their front yard and gave them to me. In France, on the first of May, a bunch of Lily of the Valley is given for good luck. I smiled and thanked them. It was a small gesture of kindness, but one that I cherished all the same.

I crossed a huge and dense forest, the tracks of which were muddy and full of water. The light-green colour of the trees' leaves was divine. To find my way in the middle of this forest, I had to follow the symbols of the French hikers' association. The tracks took me up more steep hills and then I had a bit of a respite as I walked along the Isle River, crossing hamlets and forests. After passing a watermill, I saw a sign that read: 'Saint-Jacques de Compostelle 1,107 km'. Laughing, I said to myself, 'Oh, just next door!'

While the medication was working I felt so much better, but when it wore off, it was another matter. By lunch time, the weather was very bad and it started to pour down just like our sub-tropical summer rain in Brisbane; the only difference was that the rain here was icy cold. I was wet through. My boots were filled and I felt as though I was walking on water. I was coming out of a very grassy path along the canal to enter the small town of Annesse when I saw Margaret in her car. She beeped and waved. I was surprised to see her. I presumed she was concerned and wanted to see if I was ok. I waved back, telling her everything was fine, though I was feeling overwhelmed by the heavy rain. It was really pouring down and I was soaked.

At last, I noticed a sign for Saint-Astier and reached a very busy national road. The embankment had not been mowed for a while and the grass was as high as my shoulders. I could not see the ground, but my boots felt heavy and I could hear the 'flop-flop' sounds of my feet inside them. There was no chance of walking on the bitumen road as the cars were going so fast and there was only poor visibility. I would probably end up in hospital pretty soon if I tried. Frustration and doubt started to build inside me and I wondered if I had turned at the correct intersection. Not one soul was walking; there were only cars on the road splashing me as they drove quickly through the huge puddles. I was at the end of my tether when I saw a car turning left into what looked like the entrance to a cave. I thought to myself, 'Help on site'. I managed to cross the busy highway in the direction of the cave. Inside it was very dark and I could see electric lights further down and huge gates with two big trucks in front of them. I called out when, suddenly, a very imposing man appeared and shouted, 'What are you doing here?' I let him know that I needed directions to Saint-Astier, as I thought I had taken the wrong turn. He started to laugh and laugh. I was getting annoyed. He may have found my question funny, but I did not. He told me I was going in the opposition direction. Annoyed with myself, my next question was, 'How far is it?' He replied that it was 20 kilometres away! I was going over the track in my mind and wondered where I could have made such a mistake. The man was still laughing while I was fuming. Then, composing himself, he said, 'It is just down the road, straight ahead. Five minutes down the road'. He had pulled my leg and I was quite relieved, yet fuming at the same time, thinking he probably meant it was only five minutes by car. Still, that was much better than 20 kilometres! Then he continued, 'By the way, you know you are not allowed in here? You are on military ground'. I had not seen the sign at the entrance. Later on, I learnt it was a training base and that American and French soldiers were practising there at that time. Trust me!

Finally, I reached Saint-Astier and a woman stopped me to tell me she had some rooms for pilgrims. The place seemed rather dirty. I declined as I had booked at the Chateau de Puyferrat at a cheaper rate. I searched for a tobacconist to buy some newspapers, as I remembered that my Maman used to put sheets of newspaper in our wet boots at the end of the day when we were children. By the next morning, the paper would have absorbed nearly all the water and we would go to school in dry boots. I needed quite a few newspapers considering the state of my boots.

Saint Astier was born during the sixth century and became a hermit who performed a lot of miracles in this area. A monastery was built in his honour during the eighth century. After many invasions, a fortified church was built and the village of Saint-Astier grew around this church. In the crypt of the church is Saint Astier's tomb. It was there in this church that I met Solange who invited me to her place for a cup of coffee and a bit of warmth. I had to turn down her offer. My lodging was about two kilometres out of Saint-Astier and it was still raining heavily. She walked with me for a while and showed me the way. She needed a listening ear and I was happy to be there for her. Once I was on the right track, she went back and I arrived at the 16th century Chateau de Puyferrat without any problem. I was amazed at the good state of this castle and was welcomed by its young owner, Etienne, who gallantly took my backpack and carried it to the pilgrims' room. As I was climbing the stony stairs, I could not believe my eyes when I saw how well-kept the castle was. I started to wonder if I had correctly understood the price for one night when a strange noise came from down below. In a flash, I asked myself where I had ended up. Etienne, seeing my startled face and sensing my confusion, informed me that there was a filming company below in the underground cave and not to be worried. At that moment, the 'film stars' walked up the stairs in their medieval costumes.

I would be sleeping in an area for pilgrims with shared bathrooms and bedrooms and I would be alone once more as the only pilgrim in the whole place. My sister, Michele, rang and begged me to stop. I surrendered and promised I would stop somewhere for a day, but I was not quite sure where; it would depend on the lodging. Francoise and Jean-Paul, who came from my birthplace and who had done the Saint James' Way after starting out from their home in Aix-les-Bains, rang me and advised me to rest. For them, the bad weather was the grace of God sent to me and I promised to stop.

After having a hot shower and washing my clothes, I went downstairs to the vast reading room where enormous logs were burning in a huge fireplace, sparkling with thousands of yellow, blue and red stars. In the centre of the room there was a large table with Renaissance chairs, as well as elaborate tapestries covering the walls. The actors in their medieval costumes were in front of the fireplace. They were sitting in massive armchairs from the Middle Ages while resting and warming their cold bodies. It was surreal: I was walking a medieval pilgrimage and here I was in a castle with artists in medieval costumes, as though I was back in 1200. I placed my boots that I had filled with newspapers close to the fire in the hope that they would be dry by the next morning. In one of the chairs was a guest, Michele, whose retired husband was the group's camera man. The film was to promote a game called 'Jeu de Rondes', taken from the Middle Ages, in which performers went from village to village making impromptu speeches in front of a crowd in a square, or at a castle in front of nobles. Nowadays, the participants in the game find out about their roles just a few seconds before starting their performance and, using their imagination, they create a scene and quick rebuttals for the other participants. The actors were from all over Europe and I was fortunate to be at the Chateau de Puyferrat at that very time to have the pleasure of meeting this European crew.

Michele was pretty impressed when she found out I was from Brisbane, as her daughter loved the band 'Savage Garden' and she revealed that her daughter had plastered every wall in her bedroom with their posters. Her dream was to come to Brisbane and meet them. Michele's husband, Jean-Claude the camera man, was also a writer. His current project was a futuristic science-fiction book about a story which is set in Australia in 50 years' time. Along with his research on Australia, he was convinced that there was life on other planets and that some stars had the same temperature as earth, with water as well. Why not? Everything is possible. He was full of knowledge and shared the complexity of his project as he had to imagine and foresee what life would be like in 50 years in a world moving so fast. Another day, another meeting, another adventure!

The next morning, I walked through the park of the castle, which was nestled among trees, and I enjoyed the breath-taking, panoramic views. I paid my dues at the Chateau de Puyferrat, relieved that there was no extra charge!

I left on a cold and windy morning, later than usual. I had studied the map very carefully in the evening and I had decided to take the roads. Indeed, with the amount of rain we had had and the state of my leg, it was not wise to walk along the tracks, which would have been so slippery and muddy with rain and snow. I did not really like the road, but it was easier on my leg. Somehow I ended up on a busy highway with the cars travelling at 110 kilometres an hour. I walked for quite a few kilometres along the embankment with high grass before I realised my error. I was walking on a toll road where no walker was allowed. How lucky I was that there was no 'gendarme' in sight!

I walked back and arrived at Neuvic-sur-l'Isle, which is in the heart of the Isle Valley in the Perigord Blanc between forests and rivers. From afar, I saw a lot of castles, but I had no time to visit them. The Dordogne is an area where there are more than a thousand medieval or Renaissance castles; plenty to visit, if you have the time. Typically, my lodging was about one and a half kilometres off the track and I was welcomed by Agnes. As no meal was provided, she drove me to the centre of Neuvic for my evening meal. On the corner of a street, I spotted a shop-front which contained painted figurines. It was a bakery and I decided to go in and buy some croissants for my breakfast. As I went in, I noticed a certain kindness in the owner's eyes. I ordered my croissants, then he said, 'You are a pilgrim, aren't you? Here are some croissants, petits pains au chocolat, brioches and cakes for you. I do not want a cent from you. My wish was to do the pilgrimage too, but with my business I can't and I feel you are a very kind lady'. I did not know how it happened, but he started to talk about his sadness, his sorrows and his life. I knew when I came into his bakery that he was a very sensitive man. Once more, I was the listening ear. I let him talk and when he had finished, I spoke to him with compassion. Hearing my words, tears rolled down his cheeks. As I left, he thanked me, but I had done so little. I felt so privileged and thanked God for the opportunity to have someone put in front of me who needed help. I was blessed to have been able to give aid in a very small way. One more person to take with me to Santiago de Compostela.

Back in my bedroom, I wrote down the events of the day in my diary. Even if I was tired, I would never miss a day to put pen to paper. Back in Brisbane, my friend, Dominique, had learnt about my leg and knee problems and had contacted her friends, Cristele and Bruno, who live in south-west France at Casseneuil, which is about two or three hours from where I was. Dominique said to them, 'If we don't stop her, she will never stop. I think she is near where you live. Do you think you could stop her and help her?' I was astounded when they rang me. They wanted me to rest at their house for a few days. I agreed on one condition: that they would bring me back to the same spot where they picked me up. We agreed to meet in two days' time. I was going to meet two angels on the path. This succession of events was baffling, that was the least I could say. Yesterday, I had just agreed to stop and today I was contacted by two unknown angels who were going to welcome me into their house.

The following day, I went back to the track to find my way out of the small town of Neuvic-sur-l'Isle. Having no reference, I approached a woman, Bernadette. After giving me all the information that I needed, Bernadette asked me if I could hug her. This was exactly what I had encountered in Vezelay. Without question, naturally, I did as I had done so many times before. Then she said, 'I am astonished at your courage and bravery. Please protect yourself and be careful. You are such a beautiful person'. When I left her, tears rolled down my face as I was so touched by the kind words of a stranger. I had been walking for a while when I saw Bernadette again in her car at an intersection, waiting and making sure I took the correct turn. Then she followed me in her car until she was sure that I was on the right track. I might repeat myself, but I felt so protected everywhere I went, as though the hands of God, as well as those of my Maman and Papa, were protecting me,

I passed in front of a large area that was like a park. There was a dam and a reproduction of a traditional village with 16th century houses made of wood, dirt and stones. The atmosphere and the simplicity of the habitat gave me a sense of harmony between human beings and their environment. Both were part of the same world and living in common accord and I wondered if that was not the solution to save our planet. Animals, human beings and nature could live in full harmony, instead of humans destroying the soil with the overuse of chemicals to produce more and satisfy our never-ending need. We could still live in a modern environment, but with respect and no over-consumption of any sort. God gave us a pristine, natural world and what have we done to it?

I cut across big forests and the birds were singing even despite the cold. Their songs warmed my body, my mind and my soul. Such simple peace was in me; I was blissfully happy. I was experiencing such humility in front of God's creation and the kindness of other human beings. I was convinced that if humans were put in the right environment, we would be good and loving. The walk along the Saint James' Way was showing me this simple fact every single day. I was blessed to have witnessed it. In this silent communion with nature, my soul was singing, life was serene and another beautiful door was opening.

There were more vineyards now, as I was in the wine country. I entered Douzillac with its fortified Roman Saint Vincent's Church of the 12th century, where I found another scallop shell, which indicated the church's importance to the Saint James' Way pilgrimage during the Middle Ages. Then there was Sourzac with its 11th century Church of Saint Peter.

In a forest, I saw my first wild strawberries and there were millions of them. They would be ripe in just a few days, but this was bad luck and bad timing for me. I was too early for 'la cueillette' ('the picking'). Luckily, I found three ripe ones and ate them very, very slowly. They left a delightful taste in my mouth. It had been more than 30 years since I had enjoyed the pleasure of this delicacy and I wanted to savour every little bit.

While I was looking for my lodging at Mussidan, a young woman, Fleur, approached me with her dog and asked if I was going to Santiago de Compostela. I said, 'Yes' and she asked me to pray for her inside the cathedral there. I noticed despair in her eyes and informed her that I had some spare time if she wanted to talk. There was so much hopelessness in her eyes. Fleur had to make decisions that day and was not strong enough to do it. My heart went out to her. Her partner's addiction was creating havoc in their relationship and her security was at risk. Fleur knew what she had to do, but she was too scared. She was like a little bird with a broken wing and wanted someone to take care of her. I held her and she cried in my arms. I said that I would pray for her so she would find the courage and strength to do what she thought was best.

We live in the 21st century, yet many women are still living in prisons with fear still in their psyche. This fear paralyses them so much that they are unable to make the right decision for their protection. That afternoon, I met total despair and I was powerless to help someone in such complete distress. I prayed to God to send me someone who could help her. I left with a heavy heart, promising that if I could help, I would. At certain times in our lives, many human beings need to make decisions, hard decisions, that will change their lives forever, but fear stops them. Fear for their future, fear of not having a roof over their head, fear of the unknown. These insecurities paralyse us and we stay in relationships longer than we should. When an addiction means that someone's safety is at risk, the hard decision to leave has to be made. However, many will choose distress and fear over freedom.

I arrived at the refuge for pilgrims and in front of its doors I saw two men exchanging some words. I could hear one saying, 'Yes, yes, you have' and the other one answering, 'No, no, I have not'. They did not stop arguing, then I heard, 'But you are Claude, aren't you and your name is written on my register'. I walked towards them and said, 'Excuse me, gentlemen, my name is Claude and I made a booking yesterday. All is well', and cheekily, addressing myself directly to Claude, I said, 'Bonjour Claude', and we all laughed! As I went in, I met Paul from Denmark. Paul was doing the pilgrimage for the third time. His face showed melancholy and so much unhappiness; all these emotions were coming from his whole body. I saw a lonely man with a heavy burden to carry. He was walking at times alone or at times with a 70-year-old woman, a friend, who had managed to convince all her children and grandchildren to walk part of the pilgrimage with her. Each one of them was walking a section at a time. What a wonderful present this family had given to this woman and what a lovely idea to connect or re-connect with her family, one at a time, away from the 'mad crowd' and world. I am sure that all of them would remember and cherish these beautiful memories. Paul was walking with her only when none of her family could make it. Claude, who I had met when I first arrived at the lodging of Mussidan under amusing circumstances, simply wanted to do the pilgrimage. Claude had the most awful blisters: his feet were raw and bleeding. I had never seen so many blisters or a pair of feet in such a state and I wondered how he had managed to walk this far. Paul and Claude had met previously along the way. Paul was amazed that Claude could have made it so far and he was sure that with such determination, Claude would reach Santiago de Compostela. I thought, 'He is a Claude. Maybe all the Claudes are the same: as mad as can be'.

We were the only three pilgrims in the refuge and shared our meal of pasta, cheese, eggs and vegetables. I stayed behind in the kitchen to write my daily journal when Paul joined me. He sat on a chair and for a while he stayed deep in thought. I did not engage in any conversation and there was a quiet, pleasant atmosphere about us. After a while, Paul asked me why I was doing the pilgrimage and, in particular, why I was doing it alone. I was answering him when, to my astonishment, words poured out of his mouth and he talked and talked. His life's burden was lifted for that moment and he cried freely, then suddenly, he left the room as if he could not handle what I presumed he saw as a weakness. Maybe he felt weak to have shared his burden with someone. He was too raw; he had to leave the room to hide his emotions. A little while later, he came back and asked me to hug him, which I did. Through this simple hug I gave him all the love any human being could give in a compassionate way. It was a very simple gesture. God had given me this ability to share love through hugging. I was the first person Paul had been able to talk to for a very long time, that is, heart to heart. Then he left and went for a walk, as he needed to be alone, though not before saying, 'I am so thankful to have met you'. I had known the power that a simple hug could have on a person during my volunteering and it was my message of love through the pilgrimage. With a hug, someone does not feel alone anymore, as they feel connected to someone who is not judging them. After walking for so long, alone, you leave your protective shell. You face yourself, your life and at some time you need to release all the emotional pain and sorrow buried deep in your heart. There are so many different scenarios that people try to overcome along the pilgrimage. Perhaps someone had their dreams shattered, or someone else was unable to overcome the results of their actions or was stuck in a life of frustration, anger and despair. But as you walk every day on the path, slowly, and without realising it, changes happen, and one day the emotions that are bottled up will come out just like the steam of a pressure cooker. It needs to be released and this is one of the miracles of the pilgrimage.

The next morning, Paul was the first to leave, and with tears in his eyes he thanked me again, adding that it had been a privilege to have met me. He told me to keep safe and we hugged goodbye. There was hope in his eyes; he was a different man. Whatever I had voiced had triggered something in him.

Claude and I left Mussidan together, in the rain. As we crossed the square, we saw a market and went to do our shopping. It was the beginning of the strawberry season and I just looked at them, too delicate to put in my backpack. I would probably have ended up with mashed strawberries! We took the road, as the paths were in a terrible condition due to the rain. With the state of his feet, Claude could not run the risk of hiking along dirty, muddy paths and the road would give my leg a break too.

We just got out of Mussidan when rain started pelting down. I put a raincoat over my water-proof jacket, but the rain seeped through it and I was soaked in no time. We walked at our own pace, not disturbing one another, as we wanted to be alone with our own thoughts. At an intersection we met two walkers: Ruddy from Holland and Ferdinand from Belgium who had used the track. They informed us that the tracks were almost impassable at times and quite dangerous. Claude and I were relieved to have made the right decision. Ruddy had been in Australia on business in Sydney and Melbourne. He told me that he was amazed at our work ethic and said that our 'laid-back' attitude was just a façade. He was astonished at how hard we worked. He commented on the cleanliness of the big cities and the countryside.

As we entered Fraisse, we met Raymonde who was coming back from a ceremony in commemoration of 8 May. On that day in 1945, the end of the Second World War was announced. Raymonde was carrying a tray with nuts, olives and nibbles that she offered us. Over the years, she had lodged pilgrims in her house. She told us that she helped a Dutch woman and recently a Canadian man who had arrived at night, looking for lodging. From her description it seemed that the two people were Brigitte from Holland and Yves from Canada. Raymonde could connect with the pilgrims as her sister-in-law walked some section of the route every year. But she was also stunned at how anyone could walk so many kilometres and for so long.

As the rain had stopped, Claude and I shared our lunch in front of the church and when we reached the area of Cabane, he kept going, while I looked for my lodging. I was welcomed by Andre, Noelle and their dog. Somehow, my fear of dogs seemed to lessen more and more. Later on, another pilgrim arrived at the lodging: Thomas from Holland. As we were having our dinner in the cosy kitchen, Thomas talked about his youth and the decisions he was forced to make at the early age of 18 for all his family because of his father's addiction. Even after 40 years, the turn of events was still a sensitive subject in his family. I was listening very silently, not saying one word. It was the same addiction that Fleur's partner had. I was deep in my thoughts when Andre said he and Noelle had helped people with this type of addiction for more than 20 years. Shocked at the coincidence, I was glued to my seat and did not say anything. God had answered my prayers and I knew why I was doing the pilgrimage. Later, I received a call from Marie from Belgium. She, Michel and Alain had reached Saint-Jean-Pied-de-Port.

That night, on 8 May 2010, I had finished my fifth week, after covering 634 kilometres on the map.

WEEK SIX

'Angels on the path'

I could not sleep because I had too much on my mind. The next morning on 9 May 2010, Thomas left first and I stayed back as I wanted to talk privately to Andre and Noelle. I was so worried that I had not said the right things to Fleur the previous day, and I confided in them about her situation. I was hoping Andre and Noelle could help her. I gave them the details that I had obtained from her and put my heart at ease as they informed me that I had said the right words to Fleur. I left with a lighter heart, for I knew they would be doing everything in their power to help her and I thanked God for directing me to their lodging. Andre and Noelle had told me to look for a huge oak, which had been planted by a pilgrim hundreds of years ago. It was called 'the pilgrims' oak tree' and they told me I should pass it on my way out of the village. Unfortunately, I must have passed by without seeing it as I was too much in my thoughts about what had happened in the last 24 hours. I was also thinking about how violence has created fear in individuals and made them submissive and paralysed so that they are unable to make the right and sensible decision for themselves.

When I had left Fleur she had given me a smile, but there was so much distress behind it. I started to analyse her smile, as we women often hide underneath it to protect ourselves. For Fleur, there was so much fear in her eyes. I did not know anything about her life, but fear had entered into her psyche. It could have happened when she was a child or a teenager, I did not know, but fear had stopped her from being strong and it was still controlling her. She could not see freedom on the other side. I prayed that Noelle and Andre would be able to help her to see the beautiful being she was, so that one day she would be strong enough to do the right thing for herself and flourish into a confident woman and become what she was born to be. Because of the 'macho' world we are living in, I think that men who have gentle hearts or souls often bury them deep down for fear that they will not fit into this world or they will become outsiders. Only a few are brave enough to show that they are different. In fact, all that men and women need is courage and trust. During the previous night when I could not sleep, I wished that I had met Andre and Noelle before meeting Fleur, but as I was walking I realised that everything had happened the way it was supposed to.

I crossed Monfaucon with its unusual church. There was no bell tower and the bell was placed in a wooden box above the roof outside. The style was very peculiar and was different from anything I had seen since I had started my pilgrimage. I would have liked to have met someone who could have given me some explanation of its origin, but it was not meant to be and I kept on walking. I crossed forests and vineyards which were bigger now and more frequent. I got lost once more and had to walk back to find my way again. After the rain of the last few days, the track was hazardous and slippery, demanding all my attention. I got lost a second time that day, but this time I needed more help. I was in the middle of nowhere and with the difficulty of the tracks, I had put so much pressure on my leg that the pain had come back with a vengeance. I decided to pray and ask for help from 'above' and three minutes later a car appeared with a young woman in it. I could barely stand up and she noticed how much I was suffering and suggested I should stay at her humble place for the night so that I could rest. I had to decline, as Cristele and Bruno were travelling from Casseneuil to Sainte-Foy-la-Grande, about two and a half hours away, to take me back to their home for a rest. I felt so blessed. It was a message that, no matter what, I would be protected and I would meet people along the way who could help me. I just had to learn to trust. In our lives, trust can be challenged so quickly, as it often flies off the second any obstacle is put in front of us.

I crossed a lovely medieval village, Le Fleix, on the Dordogne River. This area had had a lot of flooding and to regulate the flood waters, dams had been built with the result that the highest flood of 1723 was never repeated. On a poster, I read the following words from Leonardo da Vinci: *'Water eats mountains and covers valleys. If it could, it would reduce the world to a perfect sphere'*.

Noelle had kindly packed a lunch for me and I ate it next to this magnificent river while watching swans paddling along and looking at the beautiful trees with their various shades of green.

I reached my destination, Sainte-Foy-la-Grande, and left behind the Dordogne for the Gironde region. Sainte-Foy-la-Grande is a 'bastide', built in 1255 over the Dordogne River. A 'bastide' is the name given to a medieval town which was very powerful and of a certain importance in the western part of France. The 750th anniversary of La Bastide Sainte-Foy-la-Grande was celebrated in 2005. I strolled along its narrow streets with its medieval houses. I sat under the arches of the main square to wait for Cristele and I watched a very thin teenager playing alone with his skate board. I decided to buy some cakes at a baker's shop so I could share some with him. Who could refuse French cakes? At first he did not want any - maybe he was wary - so I started to talk to him by asking what he wanted to be in his life. He said he would love to be part of a guild as a carpenter or a stonemason. This type of apprenticeship was resurging in France. The guild sends apprentices to different towns in France and even to other countries throughout Europe so they can learn the trade of refurbishing churches or other buildings the way it was done during the Middle Ages. I thought this was a terrific way for the young ones to learn their trades. Unfortunately, this young man would not be able to do it as he did not want to leave his mother; she would be too worried for him. When he left, he agreed to take the rest of the cakes with him.

I was still waiting for Cristele when a woman approached me - another pilgrim - and asked my name and whether I was a pilgrim. I answered that I was one and gave my name. She recognised me as 'the Australian' and asked me to keep on doing the good work I was doing along the Saint James' Way. I was becoming known on the path! I did not have a chance to ask her more as a car stopped in front of us and I met one of my angels for the first time: Cristele. She was of small stature and had such a lovely smile. Before leaving, I hugged my fellow pilgrim who renewed her advice and wished me 'good luck' in my endeavour.

Cristele and Bruno had a little 'guinguette'. This is a place where people from 30 years old and onwards (the eldest probably around 90) come and dance all night long. I found that quite interesting. Their little 'guinguette' was called 'La Grange', the name of a suburb in Brisbane. I spent three days with Cristele and Bruno. This was no coincidence: we had to meet because we had so much in common on a spiritual level. Not only did they open their home to me, but also the most precious thing they had to give: they opened their hearts.

The next day, they took me to see a chiropractor. As a twist of fate, he had visited Queensland a few years earlier and had given free treatment to rugby players and others along the way, but could not remember exactly where in Queensland. His diagnosis was that my pelvis was displaced, my foot twisted and, as we all knew by now, I had a very inflamed knee and tendons, but thankfully the tibia was alright. After a few manipulations, I left his surgery with my heart full of hope that from now on I would be alright until the end of my pilgrimage. The chiropractor suggested that I have some rest and reduce the weight of my backpack. This time I promised to rest a few days, but to reduce the weight of my backpack was another matter. I was such a stubborn girl!

Cristele massaged my leg a few times a day and bathed my foot in iced water. Both gave me so much love through their kindness and care. The three of us talked every night until late about the world, religion and the progress of the human spirit. I bathed in their warmth and love during my stay. On 13 May 2010, we had to say our goodbyes. Our deep friendship would remain forever. My heart was heavy, as once more I was leaving two beautiful angels, a roof above my head, a warm bed, beautiful meals, wonderful company and I was going forward into the unknown. Before leaving, Bruno put something on my leg and stuck it there with sticky tape. He told me to remove it only when I was completely healed and not to open it until that time. I was curious, but I agreed. We had weighed my backpack: 12 kilograms without water or food. We left their house, which had been a little nest for me, but not before Bruno put on a CD and the song 'Waltzing Matilda' circulated throughout the whole house. Tears flowed down my cheeks as I was so touched by their gentleness and kind attention. They took me back to Sainte-Foy-la-Grande in front of the church where Cristele had picked me up a few days earlier. Our goodbyes were emotional, but we knew we would meet again somehow, somewhere, though we did not know when. We waved goodbye and I started walking ahead, waiting for new adventures and meetings.

I had a new challenge in the Gironde region, as there were no symbols for pilgrims who had come from the direction of Vezelay. Therefore, I had to rely purely on my guide-book, maps and the signs of the G.R. walking association. I was in a state of uncertainty, when, one kilometre into my walk, an elderly gentleman stopped me and showed me the way. I had not asked for anything; the kindness of strangers was back with me. My spirit lifted and I felt protected again. Yes, I was back on the track and I thanked God for all the blessings He was sending me.

I was not going to walk too far that day. I planned to stop after Les-Leves-et-Thoumeyragues, about seven kilometres from Sainte-Foy-la-Grande, so I could get myself back into the routine of walking every day and to see how my leg was going to react after the rest. The weather was wonderful and the walk quite easy through some hills and marvellous countryside. There was vineyard after vineyard as I was in the Bergerac region.

This region had been mentioned in the classical play 'Cyrano de Bergerac', but it is mostly well known for its wines, especially Cabernet and Merlot and many more. I heard that there were about 1,000 growers in this area, so there was lots of competition.

The track was quite muddy and I still had to climb some hills before I reached the small village of Saint-Andre-et-Appelles. An elderly woman working in her vegetable patch waved at me. Yvette, 81, was still very active and invited me in and as I had plenty of time, I accepted. Yvette had been to Portugal to the Lady of Fatima's shrine and recalled her stay there. She had lost two husbands through very tragic circumstances and was still wondering why. As the years passed by she felt more and more lonely. After I signed her 'Livre d'Or', Yvette decided to walk with me for a little while. She gave me all the directions and I reached the next village without any problem. We hugged and she asked me to be careful. Everybody was worried about my well-being except me, and all these blessings were God-sent. They gave me confidence and trust.

As I was walking along a main road, I was stopped by a very distressed young man in his car who was looking for his dog, a German shepherd. I had indeed seen one a little bit earlier and, at that time, my fear had reappeared, but I was relieved when the dog went across a field away from me. I pointed out where the dog had gone to the man in the car. I passed a huge wine cooperative and learnt that the largest group of wine producers of the Bordeaux region was based in Les-Leves-et-Thoumeyragues village. As I came out of the village church, I noticed the young man who had been looking for his dog and went towards him to ask him if he had found it. He had indeed and thanked me; I was happy for him. He and his family wanted to offer me a drink, but it was getting a bit late and I had to keep on walking, especially as my knee was starting to ache badly. They asked me why I was walking by myself on the road and I gave them some reasons. They were of Algerian descent and were concerned for me because the roads were dangerous and you never know who you might meet along the way. I thanked them and told them, 'Do not be worried. I am protected'. They were really dubious about the word 'protected' and I could understand why, in a way, and I left with their renewed advice. I had heard these messages so many times. Fear was everywhere, except within me, though I had to confront it when I was lost, but I had never felt fear when it came to people.

I was going along a steep road when another car stopped. It was my host, Gerard, who offered to drive me to his place. Though I was feeling pain in my knee, I declined, as I had to fully complete the daily walk. He was on his way to do some errands and he would pick me up on his way back. His house was two kilometres away from the path and I agreed on the condition that I would have to reach the intersection where the path left the road. Eventually, he met me again one kilometre from his house. I was welcomed by Yvette, his wife, who was very worried, as two other pilgrims should have arrived and she was wondering if they had got lost while trying to find their house. Kindly, Gerard decided to go back to Les-

Leves-et-Thoumeyragues to try to find them, but to no avail. These other pilgrims arrived early in the evening, oblivious to the commotion they had created in the household. In fact, they were not pilgrims at all, only tourists who were passing through this area. We all laughed and had a lovely time together, exchanging family stories. I went to bed while Yvette and Gerard talked among themselves.

The next morning, they told me that I should not carry such a heavy backpack and that they were concerned about the state of my knee, which was so swollen. It was as big as a balloon by that stage. Both of them were so concerned and they had come up with a solution for the day. The strategy was that I would walk with no backpack and when I reached my destination, I would give them a call, then Gerard would bring my backpack. I was really touched, but wondered if I should do it, as I did not want to abuse their kindness, and I went back to my room. After some soul searching about whether I was trying to make things easy for myself, I decided to go ahead with the idea. On a cold, but sunny day, I left from their place with a small bag containing only water and my warm and supposedly water-proof jacket. The bag was so light that I felt my body had grown wings. I was no longer walking: I was flying. At that moment, I realised what hard punishment I had put my body through by carrying such a weight. It was a real eye opener. I was experiencing such freedom and thought more about my fellow human beings and myself. All of us were carrying millstones around our necks, maybe for our whole lives until our deaths, in the same way that I was dragging my heavy backpack day after day. And like me, we hold onto our possessions, come what may. I was still part of that world, even after 42 days of walking in solitude. I could not let go, too scared that I might need one of the things I left behind. I did not have the heart to disregard even one single item and consequently, I was putting my body through a lot of punishment.

All day I walked along row after row of vineyards and through forests with birds as companions; I was flying like them. Nature was at its best with flowers blooming everywhere on the trees and on the edge of the path. I did not care that at times the track was muddy and slippery. I was in Heaven; that was all that mattered. As I was crossing a forest with its very dense vegetation, I nearly fell over a small root that had grown over the path. Someone had started to cut it, but did not finish the job properly. I decided to use my Swiss-Army knife, a very important tool when you walk a pilgrimage. The roots were so hard to cut that I got blisters on my fingers, but I was happy, as it would no longer be dangerous to anyone.

Later, I arrived in the small, very picturesque village of Pellegrue with its cobblestone streets. In the square, there was a little café with tables and chairs out the front and I decided to ask for directions. There I met Jean-Charles and Natalie, the owners, who offered me a mint cordial and water and they informed me that about 10 days ago, a Canadian by the name of Yves had stopped at their little café. Oh dear, I was 10 days behind him. That was not a very good track record and I laughed at the thought. In one cobbled street, I noticed a very old, weathered stone in the shape of a scallop shell above a door. On each side there was a cornucopia with fruit and fish flowing out of it. I looked for a chemist to buy more medication, but it was lunch time and everything was closed. Bad timing again! Every day, I was taking small granules of arnica in homeopathic form. The homeopathic granules were subsidised by the French Government and, as such, they were at a very reasonable price and I could find them at any chemist. However, I needed extra painkillers to keep on going. No luck!

There were more forests, vineyards and meadows before I reached Saint-Ferme where I spotted the bronze shell of the Saint James' Way. I breathed a sigh of relief upon seeing it: the symbol was back on the track. I would be ok from now on.

I called Yvette and Gerard and while waiting for Gerard to drop off my bag, I decided to visit the Abbey of Saint-Ferme. The monastery was founded during the sixth and the eighth centuries by the 'Moines Noirs' ('Black Monks') from the Order of Saint John of Jerusalem. They protected and took care of the pilgrims who stopped in their hospitals. During the 11th century, the 'Moines Noirs' were driven out and the Benedictine monks took over. Saint-Ferme's Abbey became an important place for pilgrims who worshipped Saint Mary Magdalene along the way to Santiago de Compostela.

Once Gerard arrived with my bag in his car, he insisted on driving me back to Pellegrue, as the chemist had been closed when I had passed though there and he knew that I would not be able to find another for quite a while. Yvette and Gerard cared so much and once again I felt humbled by the thoughtfulness of the human spirit. After Gerard dropped me off again at Saint-Ferme, I went to my lodging, which the little community there reserved for pilgrims. I met Guy and Michel who were also walking the

Saint James' Way. Guy had been to Sydney to install medical equipment for the 2000 Olympic Games.

After a good night's sleep I took to the road again. It was a sunny day, but very cold. The weight of my backpack really wore me down and it felt as though I was pulling a car after the freedom I had known the previous day. My thoughts went back again to all of us, carrying burdens during our lifetimes. The track was not so hard, but my knee and my leg were giving me trouble. I decided not to walk too far for one more day. I marvelled at how beautiful my country of birth was. I had a stunning view of the Dropt Valley and the tranquil scenery of horses grazing in their paddocks in the sunshine. I was feeling such peace and contentment; I was really happy and in harmony with the world. I loved being in nature so much. This feeling was warming and fulfilling. My needs were very simple: I did not want much and I could live forever like this.

As I was walking along the road, I saw a sign carrying my maternal grandmother's name, but what intrigued me was a large, yellow arrow painted on it. I had seen the same painted arrow and a Saint James' shell on an electricity pole the day before and I had wondered about its significance, as it was an unusual symbol and new to me. I noticed that my grandmother's name was quite common in these areas. It was a confirmation, for me, that all my family and my ancestors were doing the pilgrimage with me. These were signs and my pilgrimage took on another dimension. At this thought, I sensed a warm feeling enveloping me and it was probably for these reasons that I never felt alone, even in the wildest areas that I had crossed up until then. They were all with me.

Certainly, it was another reason for me to have chosen the Vezelay route.

I crossed over the Dropt River, which cut through the little village of Coutures-sur-Dropt near a regional national park. On a hill stood the ruins of the Chateau de Caze built in 1202 and I noticed on a sign-post 'La Miche', which was the nickname that my father had given to my sister, and I was even more convinced that I was walking with all my family.

That night, I shared these coincidences with my sister, but she was not swayed and not ready to accept my views, though she had informed me that she was always bumping into things relating to the Saint James' Way. Since I had started my pilgrimage, wherever she went, she had found signs or symbols about Saint James' Way, even when she was on a walk during her holidays. I told her there was something she had to learn about the path, that maybe she should do some of the walk, but she could not contemplate it. I ended the conversation by saying, 'Maybe it is enough to have one mad person in our family!'

At the picturesque village of Roquebrune, I sat on one of the seats beside the Church of Saint John the Baptist to eat my lunch. It was freezing. There were no more symbols, and once again, I had to rely solely on maps, my guide-book and the G.R. walking association signs. I got lost and ended up kilometres off track, having covered double the distance I should have. In my favour, however, the weather was good and the scenery a delight. I had tried to ring my children, but without any luck, as most of the phone-boxes were only for local calls or were not working, as usual. At times, I was boiling inside with frustration, but I could not change anything and I had to learn to accept the situation.

I arrived at Saint-Hilaire-de-la-Noaille and looked for the farm house where I was going to spend the night. It was freezing and I was welcomed by Bernadette with cake and herbal tea. Her warmth and her herbal tea helped thaw my body and my mind. Once more I would be the only pilgrim. Bernadette and her husband were farmers and wine makers and welcomed pilgrims to their farm. The three of us sat in their kitchen beside a wood fire. They shared their experiences and how much they had learnt and grown personally over the years by being in contact with pilgrims from all over the world. Through the pilgrim community, their horizons had broadened. They had not seen many Australian pilgrims and were thrilled to have one in their lodging. With the wood burning in the fire place, I revisited my childhood on the farm in Savoy, where my aunt, uncle, cousins and my family would talk endlessly around a wood-stove. Soon afterwards, Bernadette left and she reappeared all dressed up in a beautiful outfit. As she came down the stairs we clapped her entrance and she was delighted by the attention. She and her husband were going to a dinner dance and I stayed with their daughter, Aurelie. Prior to leaving, Bernadette informed me that tomorrow she would take me to La Reole by car. This would mean about two kilometres less for me to walk. Her reasoning was that I would have a hard day of climbs and she could not believe that I was walking with such a swollen knee and leg. I thanked her, but my answer was, as usual, 'Thanks, but no thanks'. She left, saying, 'We shall see about that tomorrow morning'. I had a good evening with

221

Aurelie. It was nice to talk to a young person and hear her views about the world and her aspirations. We can learn a lot by listening to the youth of today.

I did not sleep well that night as I was thinking about Bernadette's last words. I knew I had walked more kilometres than what was written on the guide-book as I got lost so many times, but my conscience was worrying me. The next morning, as I went into the kitchen, I was caught by Bernadette's tirade, 'I have decided, I will take upon myself the responsibility of driving you to La Reole, which is two kilometres less than what you have to walk. You got lost many times. Tell me, how many extra kilometres have you walked since Vezelay? How many more kilometres to go until Santiago de Compostela? Today will be a hard and long track, so no ifs or buts!' I had no chance of answering, as she and her husband started laughing upon seeing my face. My eyes must have jumped out of their sockets, but to be honest, I was happy that the decision had been taken from me, even though I experienced some guilt. Bernadette would take the blame: I was off the hook! Ah ah ah!

Bernadette dropped me in the centre of La Reole, which is approximately 61 kilometres south-east of Bordeaux. In this region, La Reole is the second biggest town after Bordeaux and is situated on the right bank of the Garonne River. It is a lovely town, with its origins dating back to the Roman times. In the monastery there was a scallop shell indicating that the town had been part of the road to Saint James' Way since the Middle Ages.

I arrived at a magnificent suspended bridge called the Rouergue Bridge, which crosses the Garonne River. I was surprised to find out that its designer was the well-known architect who had created one of the most famous monuments in Paris: the Eiffel Tower. The architect was Gustave Eiffel who had drawn the plans of the bridge when he was just a little-known public servant.

I was leaving the right bank for the left bank of the Garonne River and along this side I found houses covered with stunning rose bushes. I was admiring them when Michel and Guy, the two pilgrims I had met in Saint-Ferme, caught up with me. I was somehow surprised to see them, as I always thought that I would not bump into someone I had met previously. Most of the pilgrims walked faster than I did and I assumed that they would be kilometres ahead of me. When this happened, it was a nice feeling for my ego.

Each of us was walking at our own pace when, just after La Reole, a dozen hunters with their dogs came out of a huge plantation of poplars. To my horror, they were hunting foxes that were close to the road, which was their way of dealing with the problem of foxes in the area. My heart sank when I saw them force the animal into a corner with the help of their dogs. It had no way to escape. What fear this animal would have felt, and my thoughts went to Fleur as she too felt trapped in a corner.

The track was steep at times, but after what I had already covered it was not that bad. My body was getting used to the ups and downs of the path. It would have been alright if only my patella did not move from left to right when I was climbing down. I was hurting and I have to admit I was afraid of damaging it more. I came up with a very simple idea, which was to climb down backwards very slowly, like a snail with its home on its back. Going up was less worrying as the pressure on my knee was different.

223

I crossed a canal over the Garonne River after Floudes and reached Puybarban, which means 'Barbarians' Hills'. This village had its origin in the Gallo-Roman times. Later, I arrived with Michel and Guy at Pondaurat with its fortified church, founded by the 13th century Order of Saint Antonin. On the coat of arms of the church, I noticed a 'T' still there, which was the symbol of the Antonin. Beside the church there is a 13th century toll bridge over the Bassane River. In the Middle Ages, people had to pay to cross bridges. Sounds similar to our toll roads! We went into the church and Michel asked me if I knew the pilgrims' song. As I did not know it, he sang it for me. The depth of his voice resonated not only throughout the church, but in my heart. I experienced quite an emotional moment. It was the magic of the pilgrimage.

At Auros, Michel, Guy and I went our separate ways. From the top of the road, I could see so many different forests with varying shades of green. It felt as though I was walking in a watercolour painting. These beautiful green tones were lifting my heart even more and I wanted to carry them with me to the other side of the world. Halfway down the road on an embankment, I saw an old boot left by a pilgrim. The sole was nearly coming off; it would have been of no more use to its owner and I wondered if he or she had had to walk barefoot until the next town. It was a reminder of what a pilgrim might have to go through along their journey nowadays, or what they would have gone through in the Middle Ages. I pondered how many would have had to walk barefoot to finish their pilgrimage through the years.

I crossed plantations of hazelnut and walnut trees and

arrived earlier than planned at the intersection which would direct me to my lodging. I was staying at a privately owned castle, Chateau du Mirail, where one quarter was kept exclusively for pilgrims. I decided to ring the owners to find out about direction and distances. A cold, abrupt and rather annoyed female voice answered the phone and I was informed not to arrive before 4.00pm, as she had some guests. I was quite taken aback, as no one, up until now, had been rude to me on the phone or otherwise. I rested my backpack on the wall of a bridge and thought about what my next move should be. I had two solutions: either I could go on to the next town which was about seven kilometres away, or I could reach the castle which was quite a few kilometres away from the path, with a very steep hill ahead. I was very tempted to keep on going, as I could reach the next town before dark. One part of me was saying, 'Go ahead, keep on going', and the other said, 'Put up with it and stick to your plan'. Eventually, I decided on the latter and I started to walk in the direction of Brouqueyran. As I arrived at the top of the steep hill, it was cold and windy and I sat at the foot of a cross and waited patiently until 4.00pm. I mused over what had happened earlier. A lot of emotions arose within me: one was a sense of rejection. This emotion, or what I perceived as rejection, had occurred quite a lot during the course of my life, but it was the first time since I had begun this pilgrimage that this had happened. I felt unsure and I wondered how I would be received. To keep myself busy, I decided to write in my diary and while I was waiting I received phone calls from my sister, my brother and my two angels, Cristele and Bruno. These phone calls where like a balm to me.

At 4.00pm, with my body feeling like ice, I took the small road leading to the castle. As I arrived, I realised how big the castle was. It had a few different entrances and I was not sure which one to take. I did not want to do the wrong thing again and I opted to go through the main entrance when a woman appeared with a dog. Blimey! A dog! I met Charlotte, the lady of the house. She was embarrassed and very apologetic for being rude to me on the phone. Seeing her distress, I gave her a big smile and told her not to worry, and that all was forgotten. My anger and frustration had gone and my heart was filled with compassion when I saw her anguish. After all, everyone can have a bad day. She showed me my room and told me to use her computer as much as I wanted. I was thrilled and was able to send e-mails to my little family in Australia and read theirs and the ones from my friends. They sent me not only their love, but told me how proud they were of my achievement. Tears of joy poured down my cheeks as I was missing them so much. I would have loved to share with them the life on the path.

I had my dinner with Charlotte and her husband, Jacques, who was a very reserved and sombre man. When the phone rang, Jacques got up to answer it. I said to Charlotte that her husband looked like a very worried man. These words came out of my mouth without me realising it and I was shocked by what I had just said. When Jacques came back, he was more hunched up, as if all the sadness of the world had fallen on his shoulders and I was concerned by his pain. Later on I learnt that one of their sons had died in an accident and the other one now wanted to go overseas to an unstable part of the world. As parents, they were very worried, as they had lost one child and were fearful for the safety of their surviving son. As a mother, my heart went out to them both when I learnt about their sad loss. Parents always expect to die before their children, not vice versa, even though I believe that death is only a passage and that we go to another world.

Charlotte and Jacques came from a long line of nobles, but today, nobles are not like the nobles of yesterday. Along my journey, I had been welcomed by people living in quite big properties, manors and castles and learnt about their struggles to keep their inheritances, which had been held for generations. As outsiders, we think that they are rich because they have a large building with a lot of land around them, but it is not the case as many of them struggle to keep afloat. Taxes and the cost of repairs are astronomical and weigh on their shoulders. Charlotte and Jacques were in this same boat. Jacques' passion had been his vineyards and with the arrival of competing wines from various countries and the regulations and restrictions of the EU and the global financial crisis, the prices had dropped. Consequently, he had to make the hard decision of pulling out three quarters of his vineyards and laying off an employee. His heart had been broken in doing this and he was worried about his future and that of his family. After being in contact with your employee, as Jacques would have been, a relationship is created and any laying off is very hard. In big companies, when a person is laid off, there is often no love lost because the employee is just a number. I could understand what Jacques would have gone through, probably due to the fact that my ancestors were farmers and my father had also loved the land so much.

At the end of my sixth week on the road on 16 May

2010, I had walked approximately 700 kilometres according to the map, but I had covered much more than this. Somehow, it did not seem to be as important now. It had become just a number.

WEEK SEVEN

'Anger, tears and love'

Early in the morning of 17 May 2010, I was woken by a dream. I had visualised putting some Elastoplast strips in the shape of a hexagon around my knee, like the footballers do when they hurt their knees or have trouble with them. I had read and had been told that we dream every night. If we do so, I rarely remember any of my dreams, but this one was different. I was able to recall it and then fell back to sleep.

The next morning, I took some Elastoplast strips from my little first-aid kit and placed them as I remembered they had been placed in my dream. Was this another help from beyond? I was curious to see if it would work. I went to have my breakfast where Charlotte joined me. She sat at the kitchen table and eventually opened up to me. She too was worried for the future of her family and humanity and I saw the real Charlotte. She had found solace through prayer and by volunteering with diverse associations. After sharing her story with me, she said, 'Claude you have such a beautiful smile and gentle face. I feel such peace all around you. Such calmness comes from you. Through your kindness, you are projecting peace and protection. I could open up to you without reservation. Your face and movements seem to channel peace and I am so happy that you have stopped here'. I felt so humble at hearing such kind words. I thanked her and then gave her a hug. I was grateful to God for having given me the awareness to stop at Brouqueyran, as I had been able to help another human being in a very small way. I was blessed once again. Before going to bed the previous night, unaware of the events to come, I had written in her 'Livre d'Or' that I would pray for the two of them during my pilgrimage and at Santiago de Compostela. I had sensed their pain and hoped they could find some peace.

Before I left, Charlotte showed me the chapel in the castle grounds, which had been restored recently with some help from the French Government. It was a real privilege to be able to see it. A very fine rain started when I left the chateau. Charlotte had pointed out to me another road to follow, which I decided to take. Not far into my walk, I stopped at the 11th and 12th century Saint-Peter-Es-Liens Church, a UNESCO World Heritage building. In 2004, two new bells had been cast at the foot of the church by a 'Maitre Saintier' from Strasbourg, and this master had used the same tradition of bell making as had existed in the Middle Ages. The medieval trade of bell making is disappearing, as now there are only three masters involved in this craft in France.

After quite a few kilometres, I could not find my way. This path was easier than previously, but I was lost and decided to wave down a car. Eventually, one came into view and I met Fabienne who brought me back to the intersection where I had left the path the day before to go in the direction of Brouqueyran. In the paddocks I saw some Bazardais cows grazing. Their coats were of a greyish colour, similar to the colour of donkeys, and were quite unusual colours, in fact. The Bazardais cows are pure-bred and found only in this area. I watched them, as they looked so calm and in harmony with their natural environment, doing what their instinct told them to do. There was a lesson for all of us to learn. Nature gives us big lessons on a daily basis, one of which is to take time to smell the roses because the world will still be here tomorrow. How many of us do it in this mad world of ours? Fields of maize, corn and wheat were more prominent, however, I still saw many vineyards. Amazingly, I noticed that the strips placed around my knee were giving some relief and support to my patella. When I went downhill, I always heard and felt my patella clicking in the knee, but with the Elastoplast it was staying more or less in its position. I did wonder if my mind was playing games with me, but it was true. It was amazing what some simple Elastoplast strips could do. I realised how my dream would be vital for my pilgrimage.

Again, people beeped, shouted words of encouragement and waved with big smiles. It happened often, but each time it warmed my heart. As I neared Bazas, from the top of a hill I caught sight of the impressive Saint John the Baptist's Cathedral, a UNESCO monument, and I entered the city through a very narrow and somewhat steep, cobblestone alley. Bazas is a fortified city, about 2,000 years old, situated above the Beuve Valley. Inside the cathedral I was surprised by its long and narrow naves with no transept. Above the apse, I saw many paintings donated by King Louis XVIII. The cathedral dominates the town and stands on a very large square on the 'Via Lemovicensis' leading to Santiago de Compostela.

As I was coming out of the cathedral, I met a group of French tourists who were grumbling about not being able to find a public toilet, or if they did find one, it was usually closed. I agreed with them and one of them, a writer, said,

'I will write a book about the toilets in France'. We all laughed. I could have told him some of my experiences regarding such a delicate subject! As usual, they were astounded that I was doing the pilgrimage alone and that I was not scared. I told them that I was protected and they wished me good luck. Maybe they too thought I was mad.

As it was a Monday, there were very few people on the streets and nearly all the shops were closed. In France, shops have to close one day a week and most of the shops are closed on Mondays, though some, like the chemist, take turns and so I was able to buy some more analgesics. I crossed Bazas without too much trouble, as the few inhabitants I met were eager to help or would stop me for a bit of a chat. After leaving the city, I found myself back amongst nature where I was happiest.

It was very cold for the season - only four degrees. Nevertheless, a lot of birds gave me a concert, which kept my heart warm. I stopped for lunch and while I was eating I heard the song of a bird. It had quite a specific sound: it was the song of a cuckoo. I had heard it the last few days and felt as though it was following me. I kept on climbing up and down nearly all day with the strips around my knee working perfectly. I was on a high. With less pain, I was of the opinion that I could walk hundreds of kilometres in a day. It was as though I was a new person.

After crossing a forest I was lost again and ended up in a private property. I got lost quite a few times that day and arrived late at Bernos, as I had taken yet another wrong turn before at last finding the youth hostel where I was going to stay overnight. It was situated at the edge of the Bernos-Beaulac village, an idyllic environment in a

232

large park with a forest on one side and a brook along the edge of the property on the other side. Quite a few young men who were working on the new Bordeaux-Toulouse toll road were away from their families and were staying at the hostel as well. A large kitchen was at our disposal, as no meal was provided and I was informed that I could go and buy some food in a supermarket about two kilometres away. But first things first, I had to have my credential signed at the town hall and pay for my lodging, as the offices would be closing at 5.00pm. After a 20-minute walk - as I got lost again - I reached the centre of the village and I heard magical voices coming from the church close to the town hall. I almost ran to have my credential signed and paid for my lodging, and then I rushed to the Church of Notre Dame where a choir was rehearsing. Their voices were like angels and I sat on a pew and listened in awe. At the end of their rehearsal, I clapped and they clapped back. It was just so lovely.

On my way back to the youth hostel, I decided not to go to the supermarket. I had an old piece of bread at the bottom of my backpack and a packet of dried soup that Monique and Claude from Reims had given me before I left Nevers. They had said, 'One day you might need it'. I had carried it until now and today was the day for me to use it. I always kept some bread in my backpack, as I never knew when I would be so hungry that I would eat it. Even if it was as hard as a rock, it could be quite filling. At the youth hostel, I dined with two of the young men working on the toll road. They were working one week on, one week off. One was a rugby player and was from the west of France where this game was king. The other one was a soccer player from Rennes where soccer was king.

233

Cheekily, I started a conversation about which sport was best. I was delighted by the exchange of ideas and found it really funny. At the end, we all laughed and they shook hands.

The next day I started early. It was cold, but sunny. I crossed over a foot bridge of the Ciron River to cut across a forest, when a man, Michel, appeared from a footpath. He and his wife had moved from Paris to live in this area a year ago and every day he would enjoy his morning walk in the forest. He was quite surprised to meet me walking in the middle of the forest with a backpack. I was the first pilgrim he had ever encountered.

Every day I loathed walking along roads more and more, and Beaulac, the next village I had to go through, was on a national road. I tried to advance as fast as I could in order to reach the countryside as quickly as possible. I just wanted to be away from the noise and the fumes. After some kilometres, I walked for the first time in the Landes Forest with all its pines. The soil was sandy and at times my feet would sink into the sand. I had to be very careful as I was following an old railway track and some of the sleepers, bolts and some pieces of metal had not been removed and were covered with sand. As I walked, some would get dislodged and come out. At times it was dangerous and I did not want to fall. Around 2.00pm, it started to get very hot and I could not get any shade from the pines. I remembered reading that, in Spain, I would have to cross a flat area called La Meseta - which is about 250 kilometres long - without shade or water, and I wondered how I would cope with the heat under the Spanish sun.

Eventually, I arrived at the entrance of Captieux, which

was marked in Mme Chassain's guide-book for its sculpted, wooden mascot and emblem of a magic squirrel holding a fir cone and announcing the 'Gate of the Upper Lands'. I had seen some squirrels in the middle of the pine forest, but they were so agile and fast that I did not have a chance to photograph them.

Captieux is a small town situated east of the region's national park of Landes and of Gascogne in the Gironde region. Its castle, built during the Middle Ages, had belonged to the Comte of Harcourt whose granddaughter, Marie de Lorraine, had married Antonio II, Prince of Monaco. Marie de Lorraine and Antonio II were ancestors of the current Albert II of Monaco. I stopped to buy some food when I met another pilgrim: Hans from Holland. I had not met a pilgrim for a few days and it was nice to come across one. We ate on the terrace of a café and he informed me that he had run into another pilgrim who knew me and who had given him a message, but he could not remember the pilgrim's name, as he did not expect we would ever meet up. However, that pilgrim had told him that I had a problem with my leg and my knee and he was sure that Hans would catch up with me! I was still surprised by these coincidences and it was so nice to be remembered. Hans' wife had started the pilgrimage with him, but became injured and left him at Perigueux to go back home. Though we were stopping at the same lodging, we decided to walk separately, each at our own pace.

I went into Saint Martin's Church, the same church where King Francois I married Eleanor of Austria, Charles V's sister, on 4 July 1530. I was approached by a woman, Veronique, who I had smiled at in the square a few minutes earlier. She asked me why I was walking with a big backpack and where I was going. I gave her my explanation and, as always, she was surprised, although she could understand my desires and I told her the pilgrimage was different for everyone. I had found out along the way that for me it was the meetings and the sharing with others without judgment, just compassion, which made this pilgrimage special. For me it was being able to give empathy with an open heart to someone unknown to me and who I would probably never meet again. My role was just to be there when that person needed a shoulder or a listening ear. She asked me if I was aware of the effects I had on people, but before I had time to answer, she kept on saying, 'Do you know that you have such a sweet and peaceful face? You must have attracted others like you have attracted me'. Humbly, I replied to Veronique that though I had heard that many times along the path, I was not naturally aware of the impression I made on others. In fact, I went on to explain to her that when I was talking to people, sometimes I had no recollection of what I had said; it was almost as if someone was speaking through me. I had the belief that there was something much bigger than me happening within me. I felt privileged to be part of the sharing and I sent love from the bottom of my heart, for I could sense the fear and pain that others were experiencing. I felt I was connecting with people on a deeper level. At the special time when I shared people's feelings, we were not strangers: we were one. I thanked God for giving me the ability to help others in a simple way when our footsteps crossed at the right time on the path. I was receiving much more than I was giving.

I continued telling Veronique that, as I was walking, I was growing in my inner self and I wished I could share with everyone the beauty of life and what is really important. We have to learn how to listen to the little voice inside us. If we listen, we will find out that we are all blessed by the little miracles we receive on a daily basis, and we can then feel that we are part of the one community. It is so simple. It is in front of us all the time: every second of our lives. We just have to look around at the beauty of a flower, a leaf, a big or small animal, an insect, a smile. It is not difficult to give a bit of love to others, as we know we are all equal. We need to look at every human being as a loving being with their faults and qualities, without judgment. Through these simple facts, life could become so much simpler. On the path, I found that most of the pilgrims I met were open to this spirit of community, though some did not exchange right away, maybe for fear of being judged. Veronique was very silent. I hugged her. She was shaking and I held her for a while longer and left. Later on, I met her again in front of her house and she was crying and asked me to pray for her. This was another sad heart to take with me along the path to Santiago de Compostela. This was no coincidence.

As I was crossing the Landes Forest, the monotony started to bear down on me. The track was flat, flat, flat and it had been like this most of the day. It was easy to hike along, but it was so boring and I was already missing the mountains, the picturesque scenery, the climbs, the fields full of different flowers with their striking colours, the cows and the birds. I had to turn left after a certain number of intersections. At first, I concentrated very well in counting them and then I was overcome by boredom as there were too many and my wandering mind took over. I lost count and got lost. There was no hill or contour to help me find my way. It all looked the same to me and I rang my host who did not have the faintest idea where I was. From afar, I could hear a lot of traffic noise. I decided to go towards that direction and I ended up on an extremely busy main road with trucks and cars going at 100 kilometres an hour. Due to the building of the toll road, there was a detour and traffic was mayhem. When huge trucks came towards me I was lifted from the ground and many times I thought I was going to end up under their wheels. My backpack was heavier with the extra food and water, it was hot and the bitumen was scorching under my feet. As there were no sign-posts, I did not know where I was. I was angry with myself. It was hot and I was bothered. Losing my cool, I started screaming for a few seconds. With all the traffic, no one would have heard me anyway! Finally, I calmed myself down and wondered what all this anger was about. It was like the raging current of a river. At last, I reached an intersection with a sign and rang my host again for directions, only to find that I was well off the track. She told me that after about six kilometres on the main road I should see a post and turn left in the direction of their farm, which was about four kilometres from there. My feet were burning more than ever. I was hot and getting even more bothered by the minute, and, believe it or not, I was missing the cold weather and even the rain and the mud. Like lightning, thoughts about my life with its joy, pain, sorrows and betrayals revisited me. Tears rolled down my cheeks. I could not stop them: it was uncontrollable. I could not comprehend why now, why such despair? I could not shake my sadness. In a deserted, area I found part of a tree trunk and sat on it at the edge of the road and let my heart cry out. After a while, I could not cry anymore. It was as if all the tears had left my body and I took to the road again with a feeling of peace and release.

As I passed through this area, I noticed the destruction of the forest so that the toll road could be built. There were many piles of pine trees in the forest. Because I had walked for so long in the wilderness, I had been more conscious of what we individuals were doing to nature through greed. I knew that we needed wood to build or make things, but this was different: we were destroying huge forests to make way for a toll road. In this ever-fast world of ours, we barely stop to take time to admire nature anymore, and for our selfish wants, we are wiping out thousands of pines so that we can arrive one hour earlier. But what are we leaving to future generations? This area is the lungs of France and it was being destroyed bit by bit.

Finally, I made it to Le Billon where I met Yvette and Joseph who had been welcoming pilgrims to their farm for more than twenty years. Hans, who had arrived earlier, informed me that he had waited for me at one of the intersections and took to the road again when I did not arrive. I thanked him for his thoughtfulness and in case anything like that happened again, Hans took my mobile number. The care of another pilgrim on the road was so warming to the heart.

As I took off my boots and socks, my feet appeared covered with white foam and my poor black toes were more fragile than ever with nails that looked as though they would fall off if I touched them. I could see I was going to lose some of them quite soon after being in such a 'sauna', so I took care of them right away.

Later, I was with Yvette in her kitchen when she whispered to me that today, 18 May 2010, was her 84th birthday and that she was going out, but she would tell me a 'secret' on her return. While Yvette was away, Joseph commented that his wife was very stubborn. I smiled and was sure that their married life would have been quite interesting from time to time! On her return, Hans and I sang 'Happy Birthday' to Yvette to her surprise and enjoyment. Later on, she confided in me her secret that she had been going to yoga for years. I was full of admiration for her and wondered if Joseph knew or suspected it. It was quite obvious he would not have agreed to it, as yoga is a strange and exotic form of sport for his generation. He probably would have thought his wife was mad. What a wonderful woman. Indeed, she was well before her time. Her determination was a lesson and I recalled my meeting with the two elderly ladies who had fought for the bench along their walking track. What courage the women of that generation had!

After a good night's sleep, we left Yvette and Joseph's farm. Joseph had given Hans the instructions to find our track back to the path, as things had changed with the building of the toll road and it was more difficult for pilgrims to find their way. With my track record, I decided to walk with Hans. Before leaving, Yvette whispered in my ear, 'I will miss you'. I, too, would miss her.

Five kilometres into the walk, we left the Gironde to return to the Landes. I was so thankful to be walking with Hans, as I was crossing part of the 108 kilometres of flat land with pine forest after pine forest, which was quite boring, but at least I was able to keep pace with Hans. It was, in fact, very pleasant to hike through the forests in the morning and the path was quite wide from time to time. We passed through Bourriot-Bergonce and a little further on a sign caught our eyes. It read: 'Chapel of Lugaut, 100 metres'. We were stunned: a chapel around here? It was hard to believe and we decided to see what it was all about. Discovery was, after all, part of the path. There was a beautiful ancient forest close to this disused Romanesque chapel and I noticed that the trees had been planted in a circular shape around it. To our disappointment, the doors were closed, but there were enough information boards to find out all about the history of this chapel, which had been built over the Bourriot Creek. In 1960, some walkers found the chapel, which had been overtaken by brambles, and they discovered a treasure of medieval art with mural frescoes that represented a variety of scenes. It was fortuitous that these walkers had found the frescoes, as in 1760 the walls had been covered with plaster and then whitewashed.

After leaving this wonderful place, we walked the last 13 kilometres without any problem at all. I was still enjoying walking with someone, as I did not have the worry of checking where I was going. After walking 27 kilometres that day, my leg was feeling good - probably due to the fact that the walk was mostly flat. We stopped at Roquefort-des-Landes for a glass of Perrier water and while we were there, we were asked to fill in the café's 'Livre d'Or'. To my surprise, I recognised Brigitte's handwriting on one of the pages, but to my disappointment I could not decipher the address she had written down. She had passed through this area one week earlier and I felt regret at missing her again. The scallop shell that she had given me was always at the top of my backpack and had been the witness of my efforts, my strength, my weakness, my doubts, my joy, my sorrows, my difficult climbs, my relief at finding my way and my meetings.

We crossed the bridge 'Grand Pont' over La Doulouze River to enter Roquefort-des-Landes where we saw the impressive Notre Dame de L'Assomption Church on a headland. Halfway through the 12th century, the Benedictines, dependent on the Abbey of Saint-Sever, settled there and built the impressive Notre Dame de L'Assomption Church. Then, Roquefort-des-Landes became important for pilgrims on their way to Santiago de Compostela on the 'Via Lemovicensis'. Roquefort-des-Landes is not the well-known town, Roquefort, where one of the world's best-known blue cheeses of the same name is produced.

Part of the front of Notre Dame de L'Assomption was covered by scaffolding and I decided to stroll into its courtyard when my eyes caught sight of a small chapel and I went in. Natural light and whitewashed walls brightened this plain chapel dedicated to Saint James, the pilgrimage's Saint and patron saint of Roquefort-des-Landes. It was a real contrast to the larger Notre Dame de L'Assomption Church, which was so dark with its small, stained-glass windows and only one rose window. The church had an olden-day smell. Its walls and arches were painted and decorated with both complex and simple frills and marvellous religious paintings.

Through the ancient pagan times, temples used to be built above streams and rivers, then churches and chapels

242

were built above the pagan temples that had the water flowing under them. Temples were placed under the protection of their gods and the churches were placed under the protection of a saint. It felt like pagans and Christians were united in this way. In the Landes area, there are still customs which revolve around the healing powers of water. There are about 200 different sites in this region which are still visited nowadays and where the healing properties of the water are celebrated. In all of France, you will find 2,000 sites are listed for the power of their healing water. Beside an old cemetery, there is a miraculous spring named after Sainte Radegonde and its water is supposed to ease rheumatism pain.

At the municipal library, I sent e-mails to my family and friends and read their words of encouragement. Back at the refuge, we meet Yan, our 'hospitalier', as well as Eileen and John from England. My meeting with these two was my first encounter with people who were doing the pilgrimage on bikes. They were covering approximately 80 kilometres per day and cycling on bitumen roads only. It would have taken me three days to cover that much. All round the table, as pilgrims, we shared a lovely meal and sang.

It was a nice, crisp morning when Hans and I left in the direction of Sarbazan. We then visited Bostens with its Church of Saint Marie, which had been modified during the 12th century. The walk was easy, with only a slight gradient, and we stopped at Gailleres for coffee. We saw some bread in a basket and we asked if we could buy some. To our surprise, all the bread had been ordered by other people and we received a blunt, 'No, all sold'. Although surprised by the owner's reply, I did not mind

243

too much, as my guide-book indicated that there was a shop in the next village.

Hans and I had lovely conversations along the way. He was a scientist doing research on the function of the brain, while I was more on the spiritual side of life, but very respectful of science too, as I think both can go hand in hand. We valued each other's view withouttrying to change the other's opinions. Hans thanked me for our exchanges and for having the courage to challenge his observations.

We arrived at the picturesque village of Bougue where we separated. Hans had to be back in Holland by 9 June 2010 and he had planned to finish his walk that year in Pamplona in Spain. Bougue is situated south of Mont-Marsan at the edge of the Landes Forest, which contains the biggest maritime pines and oak trees in Western Europe. At the 11th century Saint Candide Church I saw four magnificent carved, wooden pillars holding up the porch and in front of the churchyard was a stone landmark with a Saint James scallop shell with the following words carved into it: '970 kilometres to Santiago'. Hmm, a walk in the park! I looked for some food as I was staying at the local refuge. Unfortunately, the only shop in the village was closed. Apart from some small, dry pieces of bread, there was nothing else in my backpack, as I had relied on the information in the guide. Too bad. I went to collect the keys of the lodging and asked the lady who gave them to me, Jeanette, where I could buy one or two eggs. She could not give me an answer. Oh well, it would be a lean meal for that night and for breakfast the next day. I was a pilgrim. It was part of the journey and I was sure that, over the ages, pilgrims did not always have a full tummy!

The refuge was very clean and I was going to be alone. This would mean no snoring, which would be a delight, though I would miss the conversations. I looked in the kitchen cupboard. Miraculously, I found about 50 grams of pasta in a packet, as well as some dried bread that was maybe a month old and hard as stone, but it would do. I was so grateful and thankful to the pilgrims who had left this food behind. I would not starve! While I was contemplating my 'gigantic' meal, I heard a knock. At the door was Jeanette and she had two eggs in her hand. I was over the moon and I ended up with a lovely meal of pasta, eggs, dry bread, plus a tablespoon of grated cheese that had been left in the fridge. I thanked Jeanette and whoever had left these treasures in the refuge. I counted my blessings, as blessings come in all shapes and forms.

After a good night's sleep, I took the road to Mont-Marsan, but not before writing a little note to the Mayor of the village, asking him to leave one or two cans of food to save pilgrims from starvation, and to leave a money box so that the food could be paid for.

The 21 May 2010 was a beautifully cold, yet sunny day. I walked along a wonderful area called Voie Verte du Marsan and de l'Armagnac, which was for walkers, cyclists and horses, and all along there were benches, tables and fountains. This road followed the old train tracks linking Agen to Mont-Marsan. Everyone was welcoming me by waving and saying, 'Bonjour'. I felt I was back in Brisbane where everyone is so friendly. My walk would be short that day, as I wanted to ring my children and with luck, I would find a phone-box in working order in the next city. I was happy, as I was going to hear my children's voices.

Nature, too, was at its best and my mind was totally free. I did not have to worry as the road was straight until Mont-Marsan. I was enjoying this serenity to the fullest when some very tiny birds started to give me a concert with their exquisite voices and I heard a cuckoo joining their chorus. It was such a perfect moment that I ended up taping their songs on my Dictaphone. I was in Heaven until I heard the noise of the French Air Force planes based in Mont-Marsan. It was a reminder that away from the track there was another life that would never leave me, no matter what. This other world would stick to my bones forever, much as I wanted to leave it behind. There was always something to remind me of its existence. After the planes flew over, it was back to the quietness and I felt so blessed to be able to live this beautiful experience, enjoying the moment and wishing that this time would freeze forever. It was so powerful that I did not even care what happened in the future, as I felt so fortunate to be able to experience this walk, with its silence, and the occurrences it brought along the way. I knew I had pain in my leg, my knee, my joints, my feet and that my bag was too heavy, but it was a small hindrance in comparison to what I was living at that moment. Our ancestors from many years ago would have known this communion with nature.

I arrived on the outskirts of Mont-Marsan and sat on a bench to eat the first cherries, strawberries and peaches of the season. I had been craving fresh, seasonal fruit for a while. While I was eating, I wondered how I could cross this town to find my lodging, when a woman, Marie-Martine, approached me. She had visited Melbourne and

Tasmania and we chatted for a while. It was a simple, yet profound dialogue, but it was no coincidence. She gave me advice for the climb of the Pyrenees, having done it with her husband previously, and she knew where the refuge of Mont-Marsan was and came along with me to show the way. As we parted, she said, 'Claude, I will never forget you'. One more friend that I would carry in my heart to Santiago de Compostela.

Mont-Marsan was also known as the 'City of the Three Rivers'. The Douze and Midou rivers merge with a third one called Midouze River in the centre of the town. To access the town, 25 bridges have been built over the rivers. It is the capital of the Landes in the south-west of France. As I had seen previously, this region had a strong connection with England through Eleanor of Aquitaine and her husband, Henri of Plantagenet, who became the future King Henri II of England. Mont-Marsan was under the control of the English for approximately 300 years until 1441.

I was not far into the town when I saw an exhibition of toilet bowls in the middle of a square and thought to myself, 'I wish I could have found some of them on my walk!' Then I noticed two phone-boxes. I thought I could be lucky and nearly ran towards them. My joy was short-lived, as they were not in working order and council workers were using a drill and making such a racket that I would not have heard my children's voices anyway. I recalled that during my youth, in France, there were phone-boxes inside or outside any post office and I tried my luck by walking through the city to find a post office. Upon finding one, I went inside and asked if there was a phone-box in the hall. The receptionist looked at me as if

247

I was a prehistoric being! With a blank look, she said, 'That was so long ago'. I smiled and thought, 'Thanks for reminding me that I am not a young chick!' She informed me where I could find other phone-boxes in the city and I went to look for them, but they were all out of order. I was sad, very sad, but I could not change the fact, so I gave up and tried to find a place where I could send some e-mails. Better that, than nothing.

Later, I met Claire and Michel who looked after the refuge. Michel gave me more advice regarding the climb of the Pyrenees and the challenges I would meet, plus he also gave me a second credential card, as the one I had first received in Vezelay was full. He informed me that Hans had tried to contact me the day before, but in vain: there was no connection.

They left and when I was alone in the refuge, I realised that the key had been bent and I would not be able to close the entrance door, which opened out onto a garden where there was a gate. I began to feel afraid, even knowing that the entrance gate was locked, and decided to sleep in the smallest bedroom with four bunks after making sure that the door was closed with the help of a chair. It took me a while to fall asleep, but in the end no one tried to enter the lodging.

The next morning I left very early as I wanted to get to Saint-Sever. The well-known market of Saint Roch was on and I bought some food for lunch, then I started on some new adventures. As I was crossing Mont-Marsan, people started beeping their horns, shouting words of encouragement and best wishes.

I reached the small village of Saint-Pierre-du-Mont. I was in south-west France. It was hot during the day and I went through sandy tracks as well as difficult stony paths. My backpack was heavier, for I had to carry the extra clothes that I usually wore on me. It was amazing how one garment or two could make such a difference. Passing through the picturesque village of Benquet with its beautiful paths full of spring flowers, such as daisies, red and yellow poppies, cornflowers and buttercups, and its lovely castle, I stopped at the Church of Saint Jean Baptiste with its stunning stained-glass windows to cool down. I wrote my thoughts and feelings of the day in the 'Livre d'Or' that had been left on a table. Outside Benquet in front of a house, a tree branch was decorated with paper, flowers and garlands of various colours, and underneath there was a sign with the inscription 'Heureuse retraite' ('happy retirement'). I saw more of them along the way, informing the passer-by of the birth of a child, a birthday or a special event in that household. I thought it was quite a cute tradition, a bit like in Australia when we put balloons on the gate of a house or in a park for birthdays and parties.

As I was walking along a bitumen road, a woman stopped me for a chat. Her reaction was the same as everyone else's: she was so taken by my enthusiasm that she left hoping to walk part of the pilgrimage one day. Soon after, a cyclist, Jean-Claude, stopped. He had done the pilgrimage a bit at a time over two years. He was from Besançon and he knew my birthplace and was also a pilot in the Air Force. Before migrating to Australia, I had worked for the airline company, Air Alpes. The French Air Force and the airline shared the same airport. Life on the path was full of surprises!

In the village of Saint-Christau, the little church was

closed and I wandered into the cemetery, and surprisingly, I found a grave where one of King Louis XVI's bodyguards was buried. His name was Bertrand Petit-Loussetau, but the date of his death was illegible. This would have been such an important fact in the 16th century for this small village to have one of their own working for Louis XVI.

I witnessed the destruction caused to the Landes Forest when in January 2009, fierce winds of 180 kilometres per hour came from the Atlantic Coast and swept the area, flattening hundreds of thousands of trees. Huge earth-moving equipment had been used on the track to go back and forth to clear the fallen trees, and their enormous tyres had left craters 40 centimetres deep or more on the wet, sandy tracks. No one had come back to level the surface when the tracks had dried out, so it was quite an experience for me to keep my balance, as with each step I could have fallen down or twisted my ankles. I understood why Hans had said to me that he was going to avoid that area and take the road. However, I emerged safe and sound from this very precarious stretch of the path. Each different experience was teaching me to be more and more confident about my physical abilities.

I took the Pere Bridge to cross the treacherous L'Adour River, which had cost so many pilgrims their lives over the ages, when I was hailed by two men, Jose and Michel, who were father and son. They asked me if I was doing the pilgrimage of 'what's-its-name'. Jose told me that he did not understand why I was doing the walk. He did not belong to any religion and was dubious about the existence of a higher being. I told him that I respected his views, but for me there was a creator, God, and that at the end, God would not differentiate between believers and non-believers, as we are all His children. What is important is the way we lead our lives. Michel asked my age and where I was from and when we separated, both men said, 'Please be careful and I hope whoever will protect you, always'. They were surprised when I told them that I was already protected.

I had to climb a very steep hill along a stony pathway, passing in front of the remains of the former hospital of Saint Michael. Pilgrims in the Middle Ages used to have a break here and probably a wash before climbing the same steep hill called 'Brille' to arrive at the Benedictine Abbey of Saint-Sever. The town of Saint-Sever was a centre of strong religious and spiritual life during the Middle Ages and was the most important city in the Landes. The abbey became very important and its control reached as far as Pamplona in Spain, as well as an important section of the 'Via Lemovicensis'. This route was used by the pilgrims who came from Vezelay to honour Saint Sever on their way to Santiago de Compostela. In 1998, Saint-Sever and the abbey became part of the UNESCO World Heritage list.

The Romanesque abbey is imposing. I was staying in the cloisters of the Jacobins, not far from the abbey, and was going to be alone again. In 1280, this Dominican cloister, made of small, red bricks, was founded by Eleanor of Castile, wife of Edward I, King of England. In the refectory there was a fresco dating back to 1335. I could sense the past and imagined the monks walking along the corridors and staircases. Since the French Revolution, the cloister had been made available to the general population and a section was reserved for

251

pilgrims. It was Saturday. There was a wedding at the cloister and the party lasted well into the night or, should I say, early into the morning.

Next to this Dominican cloister, there was a museum which exhibited archaeological Gallo-Roman remains, and in a small room there was a display of 105 slides showing the Apocalypse of Saint John. The parchments had been painted by the monks in the scriptorium of the Abbey of Saint-Sever during the second half of the 11th century using Beatus of Liebana's notes. It is the only work of art of the Apocalypse of Saint John in France.

On Saint John the Baptist's feast day in 1457, a tradition started in Saint-Sever. Some bulls were sent running through the streets and this was the origin of the running of the bulls called 'course Landaise', which is so well known in this part of France. These bulls were never killed during this celebration.

The 22 May 2010 saw the end of my seventh week. I had been on the road for 47 days, including my resting days, and on the map I had covered about 810 kilometres.

WEEK EIGHT

'The first time I saw the Pyrenees'

The refuge at Saint-Sever was free of charge, but unfortunately there was no stove. Therefore, my evening meal consisted of a sandwich and fruit.

The following morning I had a late start around 8.00am so I could buy a coffee from a local café. I could never start my day without a black coffee; I could say it was my addiction. It was 23 May 2010. I had forgotten that it was a Sunday. On top of that, it was Pentecost Sunday and every shop was closed. I was in big, big trouble, as I needed my coffee! Every day, I was so focussed on not getting lost and on arriving at my destination that I had stopped thinking about the days of the week. Days had become blurred and non-existent. They were one morning here, one night there and a walk in between. Somehow, they did not mean anything to me anymore. Maybe this is what it was like to live as a hermit in seclusion with days rolling into nights and nights into days. Even when I met someone, I was there just for that specific moment or interaction. Only my diary kept me in check, yet even so, I recorded dates, not days. Anyhow, I needed the world to help me find a coffee and I stopped a woman, the only visible soul crossing a square. Aline could not believe that there was nothing open and decided to show me where I could find an open bar. We walked through Saint-Sever and, to her surprise, they were all closed. This little episode made me realise that everyone lives so much in their own little corner of the world with their own routine and rhythm without seeing the needs of others. The same way that some walk through life as if they are blindfolded. However, there is always a good side to every story, as I had the pleasure of walking through the lovely, narrow and winding deserted streets of Saint-Sever, only hearing the cadence of my trekking poles beating against the pavement. It was enchanting, despite the lack of coffee. We then returned to the abbey and found a tea-room that was open, which had a great display of mouth-watering cakes to make any 'greedy' person like me envious, but I had to be wise and let the temptation go, to my disappointment. Nevertheless, I was spoilt by the owners who gave me a large, strong coffee with some scrumptious home-made biscuits, all on the house. It was a good start to the day after all.

After I had been hiking a few kilometres in the beautiful environment, the mountains returned. I could enjoy the undulations of the scenery that I had missed so much lately when, suddenly, I was overcome by an incredible tiredness and sadness. I could not comprehend what was happening to me; I felt so lonely, so very lonely, and I could not figure out why. I was doing what I wanted, so I did not know where this sadness and loneliness had come from. Over the last few days I had not met any pilgrims on the road or in the refuges. Maybe I was missing the sharing, the company and, more than ever, I was missing my children. Was my tired body playing tricks on my mind? Since the beginning of my pilgrimage, I had walked days and weeks without meeting any other pilgrims. I never minded. I would focus only on the task ahead: to arrive at the refuge before dark every night. I had experienced excruciating pain and fear, but I always had to continue forward, and gradually, my body got stronger, and the pain - relieved by analgesics and treatments - had become bearable. I learnt to trust bit by bit.

Along the pilgrimage, one goes back into one's life. It is unavoidable, for, in the wilderness, without the distraction and the noise from the modern world, you face yourself and your life. You cannot escape. I had met pilgrims who had confided in me and for a brief moment I had shared their worries, their secrets, their regrets and their hopes. I had listened and counselled. Today, in this deserted area, it was my turn. I was receiving a reality check. Sad thoughts engulfed me, such as the solitude of life, the abandonment, the betrayal, the pretence and fear of judgment, which are feelings experienced by me and most people, in fact, I should say, by all of us, during the course of our lives. This loneliness I had just experienced was at a very deep level. It was the feeling of profound abandonment. I stopped on the bank of a small stream and sat on a pile of wood. I was shaking. But, bit by bit, the soothing noise of the water brought peace into my heart and my sadness lifted. It was as if the Spirit of Pentecost was entering my heart and from far away I heard my cuckoo. It seemed that he knew about my sadness and he was sending me a song of encouragement. From a very early age, I knew that we were never totally alone, as God was always with us. But how many times have we felt alone in the course of our normal daily lives? Sometimes, we have to deal with difficult situations or have to make decisions that only we, alone, can make. Due to our uncertainty and fear, we feel so lonely, and many scenarios with all their consequences turn over and over in our minds and our burden appears heavier and heavier. We have to rely totally on ourselves and we feel so alone, carrying this load every single day. Deep down, we know that if we do not deal with the problems arising in front of us, we will drown and fear will become the winner.

Along the pilgrimage I had met fear, but I had been forced to deal with it then and there, as I could not ignore it. There would have been no way to postpone it and, upon reflection, maybe it is the way we should react to many of our problems so that we can walk more freely into the future as quickly as possible. All of us have had to learn to conform to what the world expects from us and, fearful of judgment, we have become robots. The freedom of the individual's spirit has been squashed, along with their creativity. We have deluded ourselves as to who we really are, then months, years pass and one day the real person could come alive again. As we are re-discovering ourselves, we will feel more alone than ever, as we are still frightened to move the dust, the sand and the stones that have covered us. We need courage if we want to be what we are supposed to be in this lifetime. My thoughts flew to Fleur in Mussidan.

One day, we all have to face ourselves, like a reflection in a mirror, and we will have to feel the pain of our mistakes or what has been done to us. This is so that forgiveness can enter and allow the real person to grow and live the path of life freely and be at peace as God has intended it for all. If you look around in the streets, how many of us are ready to approach someone if they see despair in their eyes? We prefer to look in the other direction instead of helping our fellow human beings, too frightened to be judged, misunderstood or rebuked. We all have the modern conveniences, but most of us are living on our own island like Robinson Crusoe.

Later, I met two elderly men, Claude and Roger, who were riding their bicycles and had stopped at the intersection of a lane which was lined with cherry trees on both sides. It was hot and the cherries were very tempting. They were all red on the branches and it seemed they were looking at me and I could have so easily quenched my thirst with them. Roger, who was 80, must have read my mind and told me to eat some. I declined, as I did not want to have the owner running after me. Roger started to laugh, as it turned out that he was the owner. Roger shared with me part of his life. With his beret, he reminded me of my father who, like him, had planted fruit trees on his property for his children and grandchildren, but they had left to find work or walk their life journey. I told him that, as a very little girl, I used to go to my uncle's property and eat the cherries on the cherry tree that my father had planted when he was young, and I would sit on a branch and eat kilo after kilo of them until I could not move any more. I relished the juicy and sweet fruit of my youth.

I arrived in the little village of Audignon, which had its origin in the Palaeolithic times. Many English nobles used to come and hunt in the nearby forests. I passed in front of one of the many medieval hospitals that can be found along the path. In the Middle Ages, pilgrims were able to attend these hospitals, whereas today the modern pilgrim has to reach a town to obtain care from a doctor or chemist. I wondered who was the most civilised! I stopped at the 11th century Roman Notre-Dame de l'Epiphanie Church to cool down. After a few minutes' rest in this cool and peaceful environment, I was back on the track in the scorching heat.

At Horsarrieu, I passed in front of another medieval hospital and stopped to look for water at the 15th century Gothic Saint Martin Church. Later, on the side of the road, I saw a monolithic cross and looked on the ground for a small heart-shaped stone to lay at its foot, asking God to look after the person I was thinking about. I trusted my heart to bring to me the name or names of the people for whom this stone should be laid, and it did.

I went across a wonderful green area with the embankment full of beautiful wild flowers. I had been walking for many days where the fauna and flora were protected, but I had to leave this magic area to follow a long, main road. It was hot, I was tired emotionally and physically and my body was really starting to give me trouble again. Each step took a lot of energy out of me. At the top of a little hill I noticed the town of Hagetmau down below, and far ahead I could distinguish a chain of snowy mountains.

For the first time, I was seeing the famous mountainous ranges of the Pyrenees, which stretch from the Mediterranean Sea to the Bay of Biscay: a natural barrier between Spain and the rest of Europe to the north. Although they were still far away, the Pyrenees were there and I could not believe it. Tears started rolling down my cheeks. Words would be difficult to find to transfer onto paper the feelings that overcame me when I saw them, but I have tried my best. I had been walking for seven weeks through different terrains, paths and pain, and each step took me closer to the Pyrenees. I had many conversations about these mountains with pilgrims along the way, and here they were, finally in front of me. I did not know when I would climb them, as they were far away in the background, but it did not matter as I could see them. I was overwhelmed. These mountains were going to be my next challenge and Spain would be on the other side. I was blown away. It was 23 May 2010: Pentecost Sunday. My emotions were so great that it was almost unbelievable. Still crying, I sent the following text message to my children and friends in Australia: 'Here I am at the entrance of Hagetmau and far, far away I see, for the first time, the snowy, mountainous ranges of the Pyrenees. So emotional, seeing them. I am crying. Love. Maman'. I was so shaken that I forgot my tiredness and I also forgot to buy some food for my evening meal.

When I arrived at Pierrette's farm, I was welcomed by her daughter, Marie-Jo, and I told her I had to go back to Hagetmau to buy some food. She asked me to stay put until her mother's return. I was in the French Basque Country and was going to experience, for the first time in my life, the warmth and welcome of the Basque people. Later, Pierrette and her husband arrived and informed me that their daughter-in-law was having a family reunion and I was more than welcome to share their meal. The tables were set in the farm courtyard and we enjoyed each other's company. I felt as though I was a member of their family. What a beautiful end to this special day.

The next morning, I was up at the crack of dawn. Pierrette had breakfast ready for me in her dining room and she sat with me and opened her heart. I thanked God for the privilege of that meeting and gradually, more and more, I understood why I had such a strong desire to do the pilgrimage. In a very humble way it was to help my fellow human beings. I was blessed to be a listening ear and I was opening my heart to them. I went to fetch my backpack and when I returned to say goodbye to Pierrette and Marie-Jo, a cyclist, Dominique, had just arrived at the farm. Dominique had stayed at Pierrette's previously on his way to Santiago de Compostela, and because the welcome had been so warm, he decided to pop in on his return journey. He was riding back from Santiago de Compostela to Deols in the Indre region of France, and along the way he was collecting money for a charity called 'Maison Margaux'. The money collected would be used to buy two special chairs for two disabled children, and each chair cost about 3,000 euros. He was hoping to get one euro per kilometre. What a beautiful man, I thought. Dominique told me that he had been to Australia a few years earlier and had crossed it by bike from Adelaide to Darwin. He had also been to New Zealand as well as the Andes in Peru, and he was planning to cross New Zealand again by bike in 2011 before the rugby World Cup, God willing. As I said goodbye to Pierrette, she handed me a packed lunch and, with tears in her eyes, she said she would never forget me. All around us the emotions were tangible. Once more, I was leaving behind a beautiful family.

The sky was blue and the air was already hot. I would have loved to walk through forest, but it was not to be; as far as my eye could see, there were fields of maize. As I continued to walk in nature, my eyes and ears had developed a seventh sense and I noticed some tissues on the embankments of the track. I thought maybe they had been dropped by pilgrims. It was pollution, as Claude had said to me in Nevers when he instructed me to burn all used tissues. To me, however, these tissues were a saving grace, as they helped me trace the path when I began to feel insecure and unsure of the way.

Far away, I heard a cow's bell just like the ones we have in Savoy. The farmers put a bell around the neck of the dominant cow so that when it is time to bring the herd back to the barn, the farmer follows the lovely sound of the bell and knows where to find his cattle. Upon hearing the bell in this part of France, I had a special feeling, as though my ancestors and family were around me.

I was walking along the road near Momuy when a car stopped. Serge, an artist, wanted to have a chat. Serge was a very spiritual man and we exchanged views on humanity's behaviour. We discussed how so many people, like myself, have gone through difficult times as children. I suggested that their behaviour is shaped from this hurt early on, and they learn to protect themselves by gradually building a wall between them and the rest of the world. Through the years, this wall can become so thick that no one is allowed in and they make sure that no one ever breaks it down. It becomes their castle, which they have to protect at all costs. They are so scared of any invasion that they sever all connections with their real self. They are too frightened to show the world their own insecurities and the terrified child within. Some have become so clever at ignoring who they are that their 'pretend self' can keep on walking the path of life, always with their mask glued to their face. No matter how many times the frightened child resurfaces, crying and begging to be let out, they do not listen, as they are never ready to face reality. They wait for their internal storm to pass so that peace can creep in again, and with the mask still on, they leave the sad, little child in a corner of their heart. They repeat this process so many times during their life that the amount of sadness in their heart compounds until, one day, they almost suffocate. The pretence has to end, however, and the result is very scary. They do not want to see the walls of the castle crumbling and they will fight until they can fight no more. How many are walking this way of life?

Serge was stupefied by my thoughts and we kept on conversing for a long time. He said that I had given him such happiness through our conversation, and he wished that the same happiness and knowledge could be carried to all those who I would meet along the path of the Saint James' Way. With that said, he started his car again and left. I was so moved by Serge's words. I thanked God and I asked Him to open my heart and to put the right words in my mouth so I could help, with humility, anyone in need. I had been so blessed already, as people could open up so easily to me, but talks on the path were easy because most of us dropped our barriers. It might not happen right away, but at times, through talk, just a crack can appear. Even a tiny fissure as thin as a hair is enough to make a wall weaker, as each droplet of consciousness passing through it will open the fissure more, until one day, an uncontrollable river will flow through. If we learnt to deal with our emotions properly, we would be able to find freedom.

A few kilometres further on, I saw Serge again. His final words to me were, 'I have thought about what you said. I wish that the universe protects and blesses you for you are such a special person'. As he left he blew me a kiss. I was so touched and felt humbled by his heart-felt words of kindness. Yesterday morning I had been crying, overwhelmed by the emotion of sadness along the path, and now I was crying again, but they were tears of joy and happiness because of the love I was receiving from strangers. Lifting my eyes to the sky, I thanked God for these beautiful blessings.

Later, I stopped at the Miraculous Fountain of Saint Peter, which was on the side of the road, behind some shrubs. During the Middle Ages, this fountain was renowned for its miraculous medicinal properties, and people used to bring children here who had walking problems. The fountain was built during the 12th century by a family of stonemasons called Cazenave from Momuy. On a large, ancient stone, there was an effigy of Saint Peter carrying a key with the Papal tiara on his head. On their way to Santiago de Compostela, the pilgrims in the Middle Ages used to stop at this fountain to rest and wash themselves and their feet, so I did the same. I filled up my water container with this miraculous water, hoping with all my heart that it would help my leg and feet, as I did not have any more feeling under my right heel and none under my left toes.

After a rest, I started again and I passed in front of a statue of the Archangel Michael. I was surprised to find such a beautiful sculpture on the side of the road. I felt attracted to it and became very emotional when I looked at it. While I was admiring the statue, I was overtaken by four pilgrims and was very surprised to see them walking so fast. It almost looked as though they were running. After a while, I caught up with them, as they had stopped for lunch. They were Dutch and they planned to cover about 100 kilometres before going back home. Each year they covered a certain amount of kilometres so that they would finish their pilgrimage in more or less eight years' time.

I passed Labastide-Chalosee and with no symbols or sign-posts at all in this area, I asked a farmer who directed me to climb down a very steep hill. I went down slowly, still fearful of hurting myself again, but gradually I made it, relieved that I did not fall.

It was still very hot and I had to walk along bitumen roads, which were throwing the heat back at me and it was a real challenge. I went through Argelos with its hospital from the Middle Ages. I was relieved, for in that little village, I found some shade in a woody area and had my lunch before starting again towards the village of Beyries.

Some of my workmates had been sceptical about my ability to do the walk. I wondered why. Why do people have to be so sceptical about others? Is it because they feel weak in themselves? Human beings through the ages have become cunning and clever, and it seems that their trust in other human beings has disappeared, allowing the fox to grow in them. From a very early age, I have always trusted and believed in people. In my early childhood I did not care if someone did not trust me, as I always relied on God and talked to Him, as He knew the truth and that was enough for me. During my teenage years I rebelled, and when people did not believe me I became frustrated, as I could not bear the hurt of not being trusted. I still managed to hide my feelings from the outside world and usually gave a big smile as though nothing mattered, even though I was really hurting inside. I got angry at God, too. However, I kept on trusting people and my trust has been challenged many times over. My trust in others never diminished, as I always found an excuse for the person who had broken it, and I kept the hurt locked away in a little part of my heart. Somehow, I felt a shift in myself and today was going to be the day when I would have to start to let go of some of the hurt and the sorrows of my life. Along this path, on which so many millions of feet have trodden, I could feel such a powerful energy. This was an experience in itself. I supposed a lot of pilgrims would have analysed their lives and cried in this area like me, and I joined my sorrows to theirs and released some of the pain.

I crossed fields of wheat and a beautiful thick forest. I heard my cuckoo again as if he was sending me a message of courage and trust. I had the impression that my cuckoo could always sense my emotions and would sing in my times of need. Only once or twice did I enjoy the cool of the forest instead of the bitumen roads that day. As I reached the top of a hill, I spotted the Pyrenees in the distance and my heart started to beat fast again, as each step was bringing me closer to my next challenge: the crossing of those mountains and my journey through Spain.

After Beyries, I entered the Atlantic Pyrenees region. Walking along the Luy-de-Bearn River, I arrived at Sault-de-Navailles, which had had a troubled past and was the ancient historical frontier of the Gascogne and Bearn regions. Its castle was built upstream on a hill overlooking the village, yet all that remains of it is the tower. There was an ancient hospital still intact. I went to the only café-hotel that was open and I bought a Perrier mineral water. Bruno, my 'angel' from Casseneuil, has a brother, Frank, who lives in Dax, a spa town about 40 kilometres from

Sault-de-Navailles. Frank wanted to meet me and I had agreed to visit him in Dax. I would be able to have a night's sleep in a comfortable bed and Frank would bring me back to Sault-de-Navailles after a day of rest.

I had been in the café for quite a while waiting for Frank, yet he was nowhere in sight. I ordered a sorbet made from the wild berries of this area, regretting not having insisted on getting Frank's mobile number. I was so absorbed in studying the map for the next walk that I had not seen the man go inside the café and I jumped out of my chair when I heard a familiar voice, asking, 'Have you seen a pilgrim today? She should be waiting for us here'. To my disbelief, Bruno and Cristele - my two angels - were in front of me. I was overjoyed to see them again. They told me that when I left them in Sainte-Foy-la-Grande, they could not bear the thought of not seeing me once more, and with the complicity of Bruno's brother, they had organised to stay at his place on the same day as my visit. They had hoped that I would say yes to their suggestion to meet Bruno's family. I have to admit that they had had some convincing to do before I agreed.

Australia was never far away from me, for at the entrance to Dax, Bruno and Cristele showed me the exterior wall of a café where the map of Australia was drawn and over it the words 'Byron Bay Australian Café' were written in large, black letters. I met Frank and Natalie's family, had a barbecue at their home and was spoiled rotten again. Cristele attended to my leg. I was so very touched by everyone's kindness and, as always, I thanked God for putting such kind-hearted souls and this delightful experience in front of me.

The next morning we were up very early as Bruno and

Cristele had to take me back to Sault-de-Navailles. They had decided to drop my backpack in the village where I would stay that night and there were no buts allowed. My heart was a little heavy, as I was leaving behind the warmth of such wonderful friends, but this time I felt ready and stronger within myself for my next challenge. I was getting more powerful physically and mentally through my wonderful experiences, and I had more faith in my ability to handle what God put in front of me. I knew He would always help me and never leave me, but at the same time I was well aware of the task ahead regarding my personal growth.

My walk was lightened because I only had my day pack. It was great. As I walked along the Luy River, I spotted a poster telling visitors that in 1492, the Lord Nompar embarked on the 'Via Lemovicensis' in the direction of Santiago de Compostela. Since then, millions of pilgrims have crossed the small town of Sault-de-Navailles situated at the foot of Bicat Hill, and I joined my footsteps to theirs. Someone I met informed me that within one hour I would reach a plateau and would enter the Bearn region. My day trip took me through small valleys and up and down over woody hills and through dense forests where there were a lot of chestnuts, oaks, maritime pines, alders, willows and hazelnut trees, as well as shady dirt tracks. In some stretches I could see the magnificent Pyrenees still in front of me.

Along the path, I read a sign left by protesters about the building of an overpass: *'Pilgrims and sportsmen and women pass through this area, but the overpass will not'*. It was nice to be part of the community, even if the pilgrims were just passing through. On a poster, I read about the possibility of seeing the last endangered tortoises called the 'Tortues d'Europe' and I took a 'variant track' that might lead me to them, but I did not see any tortoises, to my regret. A variant track is a route that differs from the original path of the pilgrimage, but will eventually link back to the original medieval track, thereby, adding more kilometres to your day trip.

In these areas, foxes, birds, squirrels and grass snakes were in abundance, and I had to remind myself to check under any stone or piece of wood before taking a rest. I then followed an ancient dirt track and went through Sallespisse before entering Orthez, passing by the convent of the Trinitaires and what is left of the Chateau de Moncade. In the Middle Ages, Orthez was the ancient capital of Bearn. I walked down the main street where I was startled by the very imposing and sturdy doors of the houses dating from the 15th and 17th centuries.

The municipal refuge was in a stately 15th century medieval residence called 'Hotel de la Lune' and had been refurbished to welcome pilgrims. Orthez has always been a very important place along the Saint James' Way, which is demonstrated by the six medieval hospitals still there. I decided to visit the 13th century Saint Peter's Church, which is seen as a very daring structure for the Bearn region. As I was leaving Orthez in the direction of the small village of Sainte-Suzanne, which was also important during the Middle Ages thanks to the Saint James' Way, I got lost and with no sign or symbols around, I prayed to God to send me someone to help. Within a minute or so, an elderly woman appeared. As I came closer to her, I thought I was seeing double as she looked like my godmother who had passed away a long time ago. They

268

both shared the same Christian names, I found out. I was stunned by these coincidences, but this lady had always disliked her name, contrary to my godmother. I told her about her resemblance to my godmother - whom I had loved very much - and that they both had the same name. She said, 'We always have a double. I have one walking stick: you have two. You must go twice as fast as me!' We both laughed. She gave me the directions and we went our separate ways. I knew then that someone else was walking with me: my godmother.

I arrived in Sainte-Suzanne where, during the Second World War, the inhabitants and religious groups of this small community had risked their lives by hiding Jewish children that were fleeing persecution. After Sainte-Suzanne, I crossed small valleys, woods and meandering streams, and cut across private properties, making sure I closed the gates behind me as cattle were grazing in their paddocks. At Trescoigt, I was welcomed by Mireille who had opened her house to pilgrims just a fortnight before. She asked me to sit in a comfortable chair on the terrace and within minutes, she came back with a container of hot water and washed my feet, just like the monks used to do to the pilgrims. It was so soothing for my tortured feet and a very special experience. Mireille washed the feet of every pilgrim who stayed in her home. She put ice on my sore knee as well. We had long, heart-felt talks; there was a gentle being filtering through Mireille.

The next morning, I left Mireille's peaceful and welcoming home. As I got closer to the Pyrenees, the landscape changed; there were more picturesque mountains and obviously, more up and down climbs to come. A long time ago in these mountainous areas, the shepherds and farmers of the small village Aas used to communicate by whistling from one part of the mountainside to the other. It was a complex language passed down from generation to generation. Sadly, it has all but disappeared. The sense of belonging that I felt in this part of France could have come from my ancestors, who used to blow into the dry horn of a cow to communicate too.

Every day, I prayed for my knee and leg to hold until Santiago de Compostela, and every day I kept on putting Elastoplast strips around my knee, as it helped so much. At the entrance to the village of L'Hopital d'Orion, there was a statue of a pilgrim. I was informed that Gaston Phebus, a feudal lord, had died in this village from a stroke during a bear hunt and I remembered a pilgrim's advice. 'Be careful of the bears when you cross the Pyrenees'. Well, maybe I would not have to wait so long for this meeting, as I would be crossing forests all day, every day, for the next few days. I had to trust my lucky stars that I would not have an encounter with any bears.

All day, I went through mountains up to 230 metres, which is not very high, but steep just the same, as well as through forests and fields with muddy tracks. It was difficult to hike here as the tractors had left craters with their wheels. But I was in the thick of nature, and therefore happy. The birds and my cuckoo were my escorts. It was dangerous at times, but it did not matter. At the top of a peak I saw the snowy Pyrenees forming a cradle with the other mountains. My heart swelled at seeing such beauty. I was passing through a farming area when a farmer who was ploughing his field stopped and decided to have a chat with me. We talked about life on the farms, children, the global financial crisis and its effects on the world as well as in France and in Australia. We also talked about the insecurity of the world we live in because we are at the mercy of the big corporations and banks. It was great and before I left, I asked him his name, which was 'Claude'. I voiced my surprise that there were so few pilgrims along these parts. He laughed and said, 'Ma Petite Dame, you are following the pilgrim's way, going through the forests, the fields and so on. The others don't: they take the roads. It is shorter and not so difficult. You are a true pilgrim; I admire you'. That was good for my ego! I thought to myself, however, 'To each their own pilgrimage'.

I arrived at the village of Andrein. As some of my relatives' names had appeared in different areas, I had started to visit cemeteries, just to see if anyone carrying their names was buried there. I went into the cemetery of this little village and noticed a tombstone with a modern sculpture made of metal. It represented a human face divided in two, with one section higher than the other, and it made me think about human beings and our own duality: the face we show to the world and our real faces. When we meet our maker, we will not be able to escape and the truth will be revealed.

I was climbing down a short, steep hill when I heard a young voice behind me joking about my speed. Laughing, and without turning my head, I told him I was a snail on the path. This was my introduction to Mario, a young German who had started his pilgrimage from Cologne in Germany. Mario had decided to walk Saint James' Way on the spur of the moment to try to put some sense into his life, as he was not sure about his future in this

271

uncertain world. He then revealed to me that he had just seen the Pyrenees and was still overwhelmed by emotions after seeing them for the first time. He had stayed sitting in a field for 45 minutes to admire them. Like me, he had been walking for so long, day after day, week after week, in the direction of the Pyrenees, and when he finally saw them for the first time it had been an unbelievable moment. As he was describing his emotions I thought I was hearing myself, as his impressions and feelings were so similar. The age difference had disappeared and we were just two people who had lived the same emotions, but at different stages in our lives. The barrier between young and old had vanished. It had been an incredible exchange.

Before entering Sauveterre-de-Bearn, we had two options: we could either go up a steep hill or climb up the stairs along the 33 metre high Monreal tower, which had been built during the 12th century and had been used as a look-out to keep an eye on any raids from the Spanish or Basques. We went up the stairs. I could not envisage one more climb, as I still had to make it to Osserain-Rivareyte some kilometres further down the track. We visited the Monreal tower and before we parted I gave Mario a little heart-shaped stone that I had collected while he was talking. I said to him that every time he was feeling sad, lonely or had problems or worries, he should just take out this little heart and remember that he had met a friend along the way and that friend would be with him always. It was the first time that I had given a heart-shaped stone to someone. Mario was very touched by this simple gesture. We hugged and each went our own way, but not before Mario said that he wished we would meet again.

From the top of the hill, I saw the old bridge which was

used by pilgrims in the Middle Ages and which had created the wealth of this picturesque medieval village on the way to Santiago de Compostela. While looking around Sauveterre-de-Bearn, I was approached by a French couple who informed me of their meeting with a penniless Spanish pilgrim on his way to Rome who had shown them his blisters and they had given him some money. I was warmed by their kindness until I met the pilgrim in question. He stopped me and requested some money. I refused, as he smelt of wine and he was not quite stable on his legs, but I was prepared to buy him some food. It was not quite what he had in mind and he threw a very nasty look at me. If looks could kill, I would not be here now. Though I knew that alcohol could change someone's personality, this Spaniard really scared me as he was looking at me so angrily and swearing. It felt as if he was putting a nasty spell on me. I walked away all shaken, carrying within me his demonic glance and his threatening words, 'I will find you again'.

I got lost and arrived late at my lodging where Helen, an English woman, welcomed me with a bubble bath. As she had done some of the pilgrimage, she could relate to a pilgrim's needs. Once more, I was to be the only pilgrim in the lodging that night, and I was sure to sleep like a log. I closed my eyes and counted my blessings. My feeling of contentment, however, was short-lived. I slept like a log for the first three hours, but then I could not get back to sleep, as I kept reliving my encounter with the Spaniard and his evil eyes. The look in his eyes had really scared me and all the warnings I had received along the way came flashing back. Fear overcame me. As I was restless, I left my lodging quite early for a hard day of hiking ahead.

I was crossing some dense woods which were the bandits' refuges in the Middle Ages, and I prayed for protection, as the Spaniard's look and his words, 'I will find you again' were constantly in my mind. Amazingly, I could not shake them off and to make matters worse, I had read the legend of this area, which says that the spirit of the chief of the bandits, Olhainia, still roams these forests. It was not very comforting, I might say! The crossing of this forest was quite difficult due to the recent rain. The uphill paths were steep, muddy and slippery and I tried to walk as fast as I could, as the black and green sky on the horizon looked threatening. Rain in this part of the world could create havoc on the track. At the top of a hill at Paussassac, I noticed some ancient stone landmarks. They were boundary stones and I was standing at the entrance to the old Kingdom of Navarre where quite a few disputes between shepherds and cattle farmers had been settled. On 15 April 1395, Charles the Noble, King of Navarre, had a boundary stone raised where the regions of Bearn, Soule and Navarre meet.

After leaving the woods I felt a sense of relief, as I had crossed the dense forest without any problem. I did not care about the challenge of the rocky and muddy paths and the up and down climbs, even though in some parts I had to go down backwards, as the descents were so steep and dangerous. I was just enjoying the majestic scenery with the red roofs, red shutters and white walls of the Basque houses, the farms with their background of green, rolling hills, the forests and the pastures where pigs, sheep, cattle and ducks were roaming in freedom. This would be Heaven for the animal kingdom. I compared the lives of these animals to other animals that live in certain parts of the world with little room or no place to romp, such as in cages, in cattle-yards and feed-lots, so that our ever-hungry population can be fed.

A vibrant and lovely energy came from this area and I felt happy. My body was working hard and my mind had to be aware of the difficulties of the track. But gradually, these difficulties had become such a part of me that I forgot about them and simply got on with the job ahead. Mentally and physically, I was really cut off from the world: I did not know what was going on in our mad world and I did not want to know anything about it either. I just wanted to live in the moment and my only wish was for my children to be beside me and enjoy with me what I was living.

Close to Suhast, wild strawberries were growing everywhere on the embankment of the road, and I made a glutton of myself. Nature was such a good provider. The cold rain arrived as I had predicted and it was bucketing down, but fortunately not for too long.

I crossed a metal bridge over the Bidouze River and at one point noticed the church tower of Aicirits. Before arriving at the town of Saint-Palais ('Donapalu' in Basque), I was greeted by a large statue of a pilgrim. The statue looked as though it was welcoming us modern-day pilgrims to this medieval town, which used to be the capital of Navarre and was founded thanks to the passing of pilgrims on their way to Santiago de Compostela. As I was tramping along the straight medieval street, a man who was collecting his mail invited me in for a nice cup of hot coffee and cakes. Claude and his wife, Marie-Ange, had travelled all around the world, but had never been to Australia as Marie-Ange was worried about the snakes.

Fortunately, she was not aware of the spiders! I left a while later with a warm tummy and a bag of goodies for my lunch. Later, I stopped at the Franciscan convent for a break. There was a lovely energy of peace and calm in this place. I was asked to stay by the head of the convent, but I declined as at that stage I had covered only 12 kilometres in five hours and I still had to cover that amount again in unknown conditions.

Outside Saint-Palais at Saint-Sauveur, I spotted the Stele of Gibraltar, which is otherwise called the 'Crossroads of Gibraltar'. It is the point where the three roads of Saint James' Way meet: the route from Vezelay ('Via Lemovicensis'), from Tours ('Via Turonensis') and from Le Puy-en-Velay ('Via Podiensis'). From now on they would join and become a single track. As I was in the western part of France, the stele - this monolithic monument - would appear everywhere in cemeteries and along the road. This Stele of Gibraltar, however, should not be mistaken for the Rock of Gibraltar.

At the pass of Saint-Sauveur and Soyarce, I came upon a steep, rocky path going up to the Soyarce Chapel. It was worth the effort to walk it because there was a 360-degree view of the Pyrenees and the surrounding mountains, which were breath-taking with the mist and the dark clouds in the background. At the top of the path, the stele of the pilgrims and the Basque cross were engraved on a stone. After a bit of a rest, it was time to climb down the hill. I went along rocky paths, still absorbing the various landscapes, when I noticed a few houses in a gap. Four houses, in fact. It was the 12th century village of Harambeltz and it was here that Saint Nicholas was venerated as the patron saint of travellers and protector of

276

the pilgrims. Reaching Harambeltz would have been such a relief for the pilgrims of that time after crossing the harsh environment with the dense forests full of brigands and bears. Luckily, I did not encounter any brigands or bears when I crossed the same forests! At Harambeltz, the pilgrims' needs for food and shelter in full security would have been taken care of; it would have been a true respite. I could identify with their feelings, as every day I was always relieved to arrive at my destination and to rest in shelters or other lodgings in full safety, the safety being more important than the comfort.

There was a lot of activity in the little church at Harambeltz, as workers were putting up scaffolding. Its restoration would start very soon and there was a lot of excitement as some paintings, which were thought to be from the 12th century, had just been discovered behind other paintings, and the renovators were waiting for confirmation of the exact dates. For a brief moment, I joined in their exhilaration. It was a possibility that the doors of the church would be closed to the public to begin the delicate repairs. It was in this little church that the evil eyes of the Spanish pilgrim - which had been following me all day - went up in smoke, never to return. I was free and felt the protection of Saint Nicholas.

I crossed more forests full of beautiful scenic areas with wild flowers of gorgeous colours and spider webs with droplets of rain on them, which looked like blue diamonds, and I was surprised to reach the Stele of Ostabat so quickly. It was a big, long, straight piece of stone carved in very modern, straight lines with Basque patterns, not like the steles of the Basque region which were always disc-shaped. It had been designed in honour of all the travellers, the traders, the pilgrims and all people who had walked the paths during the last thousand years.

To get to Ostabat, I decided to take the ancient pilgrims' path indicated in the guide-book, even though its precarious conditions were mentioned. Indeed, it was in a dreadful condition: muddy, with large, slippery stones and small boulders and in some sections the mud was running like a stream. I nearly fell a few times, but as always I was happy to have finished it in one piece and I won another challenge. At the bottom of the village I was overwhelmed to see pilgrims coming from all directions. I knew it was the junction of the three routes, but to be confronted by such a flow of travellers took my breath away and I was really baffled. I had been on the road for nearly eight weeks - most of it entirely alone - and I grasped that my pilgrimage would be quite different from that point on.

Before entering the village, I was welcomed by a large sign which read: 'A path strewn with danger!' I was staying at a café-restaurant, as there was no room in any of the shelters, and the Basque owners of the café had let me use a bedroom in their private lodging. In the evening, I shared a typical Basque soup, cheeses from the Basque area and pasta with about 40 other pilgrims in the restaurant. I met more pilgrims that evening around the tables than over the entire journey since my departure from Vezelay over 55 days ago. Nearly all of the pilgrims were from France, but opposite me was Vince from Holland, who spoke English, but not French. After a short time, Vince opened up to me and I tried with gentle words to comfort and soothe his distress. We talked openly like brother and sister.

Ostabat owes its reputation to the merging of the three

routes of the Saint James' Way, as pilgrims used to stop here for a few days before crossing the Pyrenees. During the Middle Ages, it would have been a very busy place as fourteen hospitals had been built. Nowadays, it is quite different, nonetheless, Ostabat has kept its status and character thanks to the modern pilgrims. After a very good night's sleep, I went for my breakfast and joined some pilgrims as well as Vince. Before going our own way, we hugged and when Vince stood up from the table, I saw his size for the first time: he was more than two metres tall and built like a Canadian wood-cutter.

This was going to be my last section in France and the new stage of my journey would bring new challenges, not only physical, but linguistic challenges as well, as I did not know one word of Spanish. I had trusted my knowledge of Italian would be quite sufficient. How wrong I was! The route would take me all the way to Santiago de Compostela where Saint James the Apostle's remains are kept in a crypt in the Cathedral of Santiago. I bathed in the pure, clear air and beauty of the Basque Country, which was dotted with small green valleys. I felt a very strong connection with this land; maybe it was due to its similar configuration to Savoy. I could not comprehend exactly why, so I let myself be carried by this delightful moment. It was bliss to the eyes and the heart. I went through private properties and across small streams. In the pastures, the sheep were grazing and I could hear the sound of their bells along with the concert of the birds and my cuckoo still following me. I wished that this special moment would never end, even with the difficulties of the path.

At Utziat, there was an ancient refurbished mill for

pilgrims with two small mattresses placed above wooden crates, some wooden benches and a table: very simple and just like a monk's cell, but a blissful refuge for the tired pilgrim caught by the night, bad weather and having nowhere to sleep. I passed in front of the Galzetaburu Cross in the direction of Gamarthe. It was a resting point for pilgrims and was run by a Basque family. Some vultures were hovering above the pastures and I stopped at a farm for a cup of coffee, some cake and home-made yogurt from the fresh milk of the farm. I was resting and enjoying this God-sent manna when the grandmother came out of the farm house towards me. She took my hand and held it in such a delicate manner, which reminded me of the gentleness of my Maman, who used to do that when I was a young child. With the old lady's gentle touch, a powerful emotion came over me and I felt my Maman's love enveloping me.

Along the way, I was surprised to notice pilgrims sleeping during the middle of the day on the side of the roads, as since the beginning of my pilgrimage, I had never done this. Usually, for lunch I would take just 10 to 15 minutes' rest. I was passing some sleeping women when one of them arose and approached me. She and her friends had witnessed the moment when Vince and I hugged goodbye and they were touched by the way we held each other before leaving. They saw it as a magical moment for them and they thought it was so poignant and pure. It was something that she and her friends from Bordeaux had never seen before. I was very moved by her comments, as to me it was just natural and it was the way I always hugged. She asked me why I would always walk backwards or in zig-zag fashion when I was climbing down hills. I told her that it was to protect my knee and it was quite an effective method, as my patella did not shift or crack. By this time, her friends had woken up and they bombarded me with questions about Australia. They were enchanted because to them it sounded like a wonderful, exotic place where it was possible to live in harmony and peace. We walked together until Saint-Jean-Pied-de-Port, passing through the Door of Saint James.

Saint-Jean-Pied-de-Port or 'Saint Jean at the Foot of the Pass', is the last stopping place before the crossing of the Pyrenees. It had been founded after Saint-Jean-le-Vieux, a village three kilometres away from Saint-Jean-Pied-de-Port, had been razed by the troops of Richard Coeur de Lion in 1177. Saint-Jean-Pied-de-Port had been built by the Kings of Navarre during the 12th century. It is at the Spanish border and had been fought over by the French, Spanish and others. It is a small and charming Basque town with a busy and vibrant warmth, making it worthwhile to stay an extra day. I had been advised to do this before climbing the dreaded Pyrenees.

As I was entering the fortified citadel, I heard a voice calling out my name. It was Mario from Germany. I was astounded not only to hear someone calling my name in a foreign town, but to find Mario here, as I thought he was already well into Spain. It was nice to see him again and he told me that he was keeping the little stone I had given him in Sauveterre-de-Bearn close to his heart.

While walking along the main street, which is paved with cobblestones and has sandstone houses on each side, I collected some papers and gathered information regarding the pilgrimage that was distributed by the French Association of the Friends of Saint James' Way from the Atlantic Pyrenees. I reached my lodging to find it closed. I took this opportunity to visit the 14th century Notre Dame Church, which is situated at the end of the Rue de la Citadelle, where there is a fountain with a scallop shell. Further on, I crossed the bridge over the Nive River, which separates the oldest section on the right bank from the new section on the left bank, both with fortified ramparts. During my walk through the town, I had made the decision not to stop for an extra day, as rain was on its way and maybe more the following day, and I did not fancy climbing the 'monster' that was the Pyrenees in the rain. I went back to my lodging, hoping that it would be open.

In the room, the mattresses were placed on the bare floor and only two mattresses were free. I took the one closest to the windows. I went for a shower and had the pleasure of an icy cold one, as the other pilgrims had used all the hot water. I was already freezing and honestly I was not too happy about it, but I could not changethe situation, therefore I took it in my stride. All the other pilgrims had decided to have a meal in a restaurant, but I opted for a simple meal at the lodging and went to buy some fruit and vegetables. I needed to have some space as I was overwhelmed by the number of pilgrims around me and I really needed to be by myself. I was walking through the small town when I saw some didgeridoos on display for sale. Once more, Australia was never far from me and I was reminded of where I had journeyed from to do this pilgrimage.

On my way back, I saw Mario sitting on the steps of the Notre Dame Church, deep in thought. I felt that something was troubling him and I approached him, telling him I saw worries and troubled thoughts going through his mind. Mario was surprised that I could see and sense his troubles and we talked openly. Before we hugged, he asked me where I would stop the following day. I had been taken aback by the circumstances of our second meeting, but I knew that God had made sure we would meet again. I had to be there for Mario.

After my frugal meal, I went up to the dormitory and started to unpack my backpack so I could be ready early the following morning to climb the Pyrenees. I reflected on what had happened to me along the French pilgrimage, thinking about what I was leaving behind, and I felt scared that the meetings with pilgrims from now on would be different. I was sad, as I was closing this chapter, and I was deep in my thoughts when Ulf from Sweden came in. His mattress was just beside mine and we started a conversation. He shared with me why he wanted to do this pilgrimage and, as always, I listened with all my being. We were so engrossed in our exchanges that we did not hear the other pilgrims climbing the stairs and when they arrived in the dormitory, we were startled. As they opened the door, they said, 'We have disturbed something'. Ulf told me how my words had soothed him and thanked me. He asked me for my e-mail address and he had tears in his eyes when I gave it to him. I put my hand into my backpack and pulled out a little heart-shaped stone that I had collected at Mont-Bazac and I gave it to him. My intention had been to leave it somewhere in Spain where the two paths of France and Spain would meet, but I felt it would be better in Ulf's hands.

By 29 May 2010, I had reached Saint-Jean-Pied-de-

Port. Eight weeks after starting from Vezelay, I had covered 910 kilometres on the map, but only God knows the exact number, as I got lost so many times. Also, I often had to search for many of my lodgings, some of which had been away from the path, and on top of that, I had usually visited the churches and towns I walked through. I was proud of myself and what I had accomplished. Although I was saddened to be leaving France behind, I had met a lot of beautiful people along the way, and now I was on the verge of a new undertaking.

WEEK NINE

'A special healing and the first glimpse of Spain'

The next morning I was surprised to see Ulf still at the lodging, as he should have gone very early because he wanted to cross the Pyrenees and reach Roncesvalles in the same day. I was happy to see him again. We were having breakfast together when he told me that before he started his pilgrimage he wanted to thank me for opening his heart. We hugged, possibly for the last time. Once more, I was so touched and blessed. When I thought back on all the friends who had crossed my path along the French road, all were in my heart and always would be and I thanked God for giving me such blessings.

Saint-Jean-Pied-de-Port is the most popular starting point for the Saint James' Way. It is situated in the French Basque region at the foot of the Pyrenees.

I checked the weather on 30 May 2010, which did not look threatening, despite the forecast. There was some blue sky and a bit of sun. With my backpack and my trekking poles, I embarked upon my climb of the Pyrenees. I went down the Rue de la Citadelle, crossed Saint James' Bridge, went through the Spanish Door and started the climb, joining my steps to the others who had gone before me. In the streets, I recognised the seasoned pilgrims walking with a sturdier, slower pace and the new ones - all fresh and eager to commence - were striding.

To reach Roncesvalles, some pilgrims went through

Valcarlos as the path was easier, but the down side for me was that you had to go through sealed roads and traffic, so I had decided to go through Orisson, which was considered a more difficult walk. This hike would add more challenges because of the changeable weather in the mountains, but it was the original route via the Route Napoleon. I recalled how many times I had followed the Route Napoleon in France. I was following not only the ancient path of Saint James, but the footsteps of Napoleon's army!

For once I had listened to everyone's advice and I planned to cross the Pyrenees in two stages. I would finish stage one in Orisson at an altitude of 800 metres. I left Saint-Jean-Pied-de-Port at an altitude of 180 metres. The distance between the two points was eight kilometres, therefore, it would be quite a steep climb with a grading of 15 per cent at times: a good hike. I was ready for the challenge.

On the previous night, I had slept in the same dormitory as Mado, a scientist, who had started from Le Puy-en-Velay in France. She caught up with me after I had been walking for a short while the next day and said how moved she had been when Ulf and I had hugged. Mado had noticed a small change in herself since the beginning of her pilgrimage, but she had dismissed it as soon as it flowed into her, as her scientific mind would take over her thoughts. I felt she was terrified to dig and investigate what she was feeling, scared that it would take over everything in her soul. I told her she was not yet ready to analyse the reasons why her views about life had changed on the path. She was not the only one, however, as it could be quite confronting to see and accept the new person emerging. I told her that we are so set in our ways that if we stop to consider our transformation, it can be intimidating. We know that one day we will have to face it, but fear stops us, as deep down we know there will be a point of no return to the old you. The difficulty is returning to a normal life in which we would have to confront the world, family and the environment with our new views and perceptions, and that is a challenge in itself and an obstacle to be overcome, like the Pyrenees Mountains.

Mado was very quiet. A heaviness surrounded us and to cut the serious feeling of the moment, I shared with her some of my experiences: the so-called coincidences, the twists of fate with the different encounters and the help received when I was in disarray or lost. Mado was quite surprised, as her pilgrimage had been quite different, and I told her to open her heart and to try to be more in tune with her inner self. I told her to let go, little by little, of her scientific mind, for then she would see and accept the change in herself. She thanked me and walked forward with a quick stride.

The outlook was stunning with panoramic and majestic views at each bend. As I climbed up, I noticed the mist rising from the valleys below, but I was still able to enjoy the scenic landscape. The beauty of the surroundings was so inspiring that I wished I could be swept away by it. Higher still, I looked back and saw the cyclists struggling with their bicycles on the incline, just like those of us who were simply walking. Some walked while pushing their bicycles along the tracks and some had given up altogether. After a while I was surprised at how much I had covered as the peaks of the mountains below looked further away, smaller and smaller. To my surprise, I was not finding the climb too difficult, which confirmed how much my physical state had improved, but for someone starting their first climb from Saint-Jean-Pied-de-Port, it would have been quite a testing experience. I overtook young people who were resting in silence on the grass, exhausted by the challenge. They were quite subdued and were rubbing their sore feet and toes.

Finally, I reached Orisson and took possession of the tent that I would share with another female pilgrim who happened to be Mado, who I had met previously. I had rung the refuge quite a few days earlier, but all the bunks were already booked. I was just happy to have found somewhere to sleep so that I would not have to spend my first night in the Pyrenees out in the open under the stars! I went on to the terrace of the refuge to enjoy the stunning, panoramic views of the valleys below and to contemplate what I had climbed. A little bit of ego is good, sometimes! While I was on the terrace, I observed a man who was tending to the pilgrims with bad backs, ankle problems and so on. I noticed that some pilgrims had arrived all bent, yet after the treatment they were standing straight, seemingly without pain and ready to climb again. I approached the man and showed him my right knee and leg, thinking I had nothing to lose. Amar was a Jesuit and an ex-doctor from the Foreign Legion. He had learnt Chinese medicine and had joined the Society of Malta. He was giving his time and knowledge 'pro bono' to the pilgrims along Saint James' Way. While we were talking, he was gently touching my knee and I felt no discomfort, though he asked me if I was in pain. He told me he was shifting a little bag around my knee and that I would be ok from then on. Before I got up he asked me about the strips of Elastoplast around my knee. He told me that I could take them off as they were no longer needed. Surprised, I thought, 'I will see about that. These strips have helped me and I am not ready to get rid of them', but I did not say it. How could I take them off when they had helped me so much? I was grateful for Amar's help, but I doubted he would have been able to fix my knee, which had been giving me so many problems for weeks.

The Society of Malta is the Order of Saint John of Jerusalem and had been founded by Pope Clement V after the downfall of the Knights Templar. The Templar Order started after the first crusade of 1096. They were poor monks who cared for and protected the poor and sick pilgrims on their way to the Holy Land. They were called 'hospitaliers' and over time became quite powerful. In 1307, the Knights Templar were banished and considered heretics. However, in September 2001, an Italian palaeographer, Professor Barbara Frale, came across a document which had been filed in the wrong archive of the 17th century. This document stated that Pope Clement V had absolved the Knights Templar and on 25th October 2007, 700 years after their banishment, Pope John Paul II absolved the Knights Templar and confirmed their innocence.

As always in the mountains, the weather changed very quickly. I did not want to stay in the tent as the temperature was dropping fast. It was starting to rain and I went inside the refuge to write in my diary. I was very absorbed in writing the last events of the day and so deep in my thoughts that I jumped when I heard the owner shouting, 'Who is Claude?' No one else put their hand up, so I raised mine. The owner handed me a piece of paper and, cheekily, said, 'The person who gave it to me was a very nice-looking young man, Claude'. I smiled and went back to my seat when all the pilgrims, playfully, shouted out my name in unison. This message was in written form, unlike the other messages I had received previously, which had all been passed on by word of mouth. The note was from Mario, the young German man who I had met in Sauveterre-de-Bearn and again the previous day at Saint-Jean-Pied-de-Port, and on it were his contact details.

The rain was battering down and I wondered what it would be like the next day, as I still had to finish the second part of the Pyrenees climb and I would have to go up and down steep sections to reach Roncesvalles, the first Spanish town on my way to Santiago de Compostela. I carefully folded up Mario's note and put it in a safe place. As I turned back to my writing, Amar sat down beside me. He said he had something important to share with me. He held my hand and told me, 'You are special and you have to make sure that you do not change. Only a few have the privilege that you have received. You have a mission in life and people close to you will try to stop you from achieving it. You have to be aware of this and make sure that you follow that which you were born to be and do, no matter what'. I was so surprised by these words that tears rolled down my cheeks, uncontrollably. Amar got up and left while I tried to make sense of his words and warnings. I was baffled, but I knew this had been an important meeting and I felt I should look more closely at signs, coincidences and happenings from now on.

After the evening meal, we all sang French and Basque

folk songs and we sang my Maman's favourite folk songs from Savoy. I went to my tent to sleep. During the night, I heard the rain and the sheep that were grazing around the tent. When I woke up I discovered that my backpack and clothes were all wet. I could not believe it. I had camped for the first time and I had learnt my first camping lesson: do not put your clothes close to the ground and around the edges of the tent when it is raining. As I was feeling my wet clothes, I looked at my knee. To my surprise the swelling had gone down considerably.

I went to the refuge for my breakfast. As I entered the dining room, I noticed that Amar was tending to a Swiss pilgrim who had just fallen down on the wet tiles of the bathroom floor and had difficulty walking. Daniel was worried that he would not be able to walk anymore and I could sympathise with him on that level. He had started his pilgrimage from Geneva. Amar was helping to serve breakfast to the pilgrims while looking after Daniel at the same time. When Amar had finished his healing, Daniel got up and walked freely without any apparent pain and left to start the second part of the climb. As I was leaving, Amar asked me if I had taken off the strips of Elastoplast around my knee. I shook my head, indicating 'no', and in desperation, Amar lifted his eyes to the ceiling. Indeed, I was not game to remove these strips, as they had helped me and, to be honest, I was scared that my knee would not hold if I took them off.

As I left to begin the 19 kilometres journey that was ahead of me that day, it started to rain and to make matters worse, the fog came down on us very quickly. It became so thick that I could not see anything, not even the pilgrims in front of me. I became conscious of the seriousness of the situation, so I tried to stay close to a group of pilgrims. Mado, who I had shared the tent with the previous night and who had opened her heart to me, was part of this group. She too had been treated by Amar, but was still sceptical. Before having this treatment to her foot she had planned to stop her pilgrimage at Orisson and return home to France. When she woke up she realised that her foot was better and had made the decision to keep on going, but she was still dubious about Amar's abilities. The fog grew thicker and thicker, and I was happy that some pilgrims were wearing colourful raincoats, as from time to time I could just distinguish them in front of me and followed them. The fog was so dense that I passed in front of the Virgin de Biakorri's oratory at 1,040 metres without seeing it. Even though I could not see well, I could hear sheep's bells and hoped that I would not bump into them, as they were roaming freely. I nearly trod on a solitary yellow and black lizard that was crossing the road. The conditions did not improve and for just a few seconds, I let my concentration slip and lost sight of the other pilgrims. Fear crept into me until the fog lifted, as if by magic, for a few seconds. It was just long enough to allow me to see the Thibault Cross and the uphill mountain track on my right with the ascent going on and on and on.

As I came close to the crest of the mountains, the weather improved slightly and I marvelled at the magnificent scenery. I will always wonder, however, what that full panorama looks like, as I could not see it in its entirety, due to the weather conditions, but I was happy to have passed through the mountains safely and to have gained another new experience.

I crossed a few passes and beech forests with difficult paths. I went down a bit and then up again, with more muddy, slippery paths, thankful that I was a seasoned walker, as the fog was playing hide and seek with me all the time. To say the least, it was making my walk much more challenging.

I left France behind me and reached the Spanish border, thankful for the amount of autumn leaves on the track, which stopped me sinking into mud. While walking along, I saw a cross with a rosary attached. Someone had lost his life at that point in 2002 and this was a reminder of the difficulty of the track. Eventually, I reached the Lepoeder Pass at 1,431 metres high, and afterwards I arrived at the Izandorre's refuge, which had been built by the Navarre Government so that pilgrims could rest and take refuge in case of bad weather. Inside there was a stove and two bunks.

I caught up with other pilgrims and Mado who wanted to take the short-cut down to Roncesvalles. I decided otherwise, as the condition of the path was treacherous and I took the safer, downwards-winding road for 4.5 kilometres before reaching the pass of Roncesvalles. Here, on 15 August 778, the Basques nearly destroyed all the rear of Charlemagne's army as they went through the Pyrenees, in retaliation for the burning of their capital, Pamplona. Later on, I passed in front of Roland's Stele. Roland, Charlemagne's nephew, was killed in the Battle of Roncesvalles and his life became a French medieval classic tale called 'The Song of Roland'. I stopped at the Chapel of Ibaneta at 1,057 metres for 10 minutes before starting again in the direction of Roncesvalles, which is situated on the small Urrobi River, and where I was going to sleep in a monastery built in 1127.

I crossed the little village of Roncesvalles, home to only 27 inhabitants, in the direction of the Gothic building that was used as a hospital during the Middle Ages to care for the pilgrims who had crossed the summit of the Pyrenees. Since then it has been converted into a shelter for pilgrims with 120 bunks in one single huge nave that is 32 by 12 metres in size. Downstairs there were two bathrooms and four toilets for women and the same for men. It filled up pretty quickly, accepting only pilgrims on foot, and I was sure that I would sleep to some snoring lullabies. There was a sense of peace in this environment and everything went smoothly without any commotion, every pilgrim respecting the others.

Downstairs in the dining room, there was a computer and I took the opportunity to send an e-mail to my children. The Spanish keyboard was a challenge, but I managed the best I could, not concerning myself too much about spelling mistakes and turns of phrase. I had to do it quite quickly, as other pilgrims were queueing to use it. I then went for a walk in the village. In front of the church, I saw a female horse-rider doing her pilgrimage. Her trek would have been quite different from mine, as she had to have help from friends who were following her on the main roads with a horse-cart, which carried the food for her horse. Everyone was quite in awe of her attempt and she attracted a lot of friendly and curious pilgrims. Afterwards, I went to the pilgrims' benediction in the beautiful 13th century Gothic church dedicated to Saint James, which was also called 'the Pilgrims' Church'. The ceremony was said in many languages and was not only for Christians. I loved that. The little church was packed and at one stage, a priest called out all the names of the pilgrims, walkers and cyclists who had registered at the entrance to the village, as well as where they were from. On that day, there were 15 nations represented. The priests sang Christian songs in Basque, blessed everyone and wished all of us a safe journey. I am sure that everyone felt a sense of belonging and brotherhood in that loving atmosphere.

On 31 May 2010 I was in Spain for the first time in my life. What a way to see it! My pilgrimage would be different from now on, as the rules for pilgrims' lodgings were 'first in, best dressed' and everyone had to be out by 8.00am. Fair rules, but it would put pressure on me as I would have to walk faster or start earlier to ensure I got a place at a shelter.

The next morning at 6.00am, I was woken by a Gregorian song and as I looked around, I noticed that some pilgrims had already gone. I was surprised to have slept so well through the night and not heard the snoring. After a quick coffee from a vending machine, I left for Zubiri in the semi-darkness, as the sun had not yet completely come out. I could see that the weather was going to be perfect, even with some clouds meandering across the sky. I was well aware of the difficulty of the day ahead with the path going through so many different altitudes: beginning at 900 metres, going up to 950 metres, down to 770 metres and back up to 850 metres, small ups and downs in between over 19 kilometres, before the last three kilometres of rapid descent going down to 500 metres.

After a few kilometres, I turned into a road leading to a forest and was amazed by the number of pilgrims; yes, it certainly was going to be a different pilgrimage! I entered the Sorginaritzapa's Forest, which translates as 'the witches' oak wood', for during the 16th century, witches used to gather in this area. These meetings sparked angry feelings and nine women from that region were burnt at the stake. The white cross was placed as a symbol of divine protection on this road. I was not feeling entirely at ease on this path, I can assure you. Not only would I have to look out for wolves and bears, be careful not to fall or twist my ankles, or watch that I did not get lost and follow the wrong path, but now I would have to add witches to the list of things to beware of! I was glad to have seen the white cross, which would protect me, and, as well as that, the crowd of pilgrims would hopefully act as a shield! At first, it was pleasant to meet pilgrims of all nationalities, but after a while the novelty wore off and strangely enough I began to miss the quietness of the French path.

I arrived safely at the very clean village of Burguete and saw its grand coat of arms on the front of private houses and a scallop shell on the wall of a house. I was passing through some beautiful green scenery and picturesque Basque villages such as Haizea and Espinal. From the summit of Mezkiritz, I could admire more panoramic landscapes and could see from afar the village of Viscarret. The track sloped down to Viscarret through a splendid oak forest before climbing up again and following the edge of the woods. After Viscarret, there was a steep, paved path for about one kilometre and although it was agreeable to march on the pavers for a bit, it was hard on my legs and feet. I tried to walk the way Amar had taught me, to protect my knees. That is to say, I had to shuffle my feet on the road and keep my upper body very straight. This helped a bit, but it was tricky, as after a few steps I kept going straight back to my normal walking rhythm. Surprisingly, I was missing the contact of my feet with the dirt track.

Before the sharp climb up to Lintzoain, I bumped into Gilbert from Alsace in France, who had a heart problem and was doing his pilgrimage accompanied by a friend, Michel, as his wife did not want him to do it alone. We sang some Savoyard and Alsatian folk songs which lifted our hearts. Then I met Monique from Auvergne, France, who happened to be the same age as me. She started her pilgrimage from Le Puy-en-Velay and was thrilled at what she had achieved up until now. A few years earlier, she had started and had to stop due to injury, but she never gave up the idea. She went back home and trained to start again from Le Puy-en-Velay in 2010. I wondered if all the babies born in 1946 were as wilful as we were!

After Alto de Erro, in the middle of a forest, I could not miss a little monument to the memory of a 64-year-old Japanese man who had died on that spot doing his pilgrimage in August 2002. It was another reminder of the difficulty of the path.

Before Zubiri, I met two French women and a French man. Suddenly, I asked him if his name was Claude. The question surprised him and I surprised myself as well. It was the oddest thing. When he replied 'yes', I could not believe it, and then I said to him, 'You must be stubborn'. He became very quiet and gave me a stern look while his wife, who could not believe the coincidence, shouted back, 'Yes, he is!' I told them, 'You have to know one Claude to know another'. We all laughed.

The difficult tracks were full of gravel and small stones

and I was worried about my knees, but surprisingly, I could not feel any pain at all, even on the sharp descent heading to Zubiri. I entered the little village by crossing over the renowned 14th century bridge called 'Puente de la Rabia' ('Bridge of the Rabies'). Up until the 20th century, there was a tradition that the farmers would take their domestic animals to the bridge and make them walk around its main pillars three times to immunise them against rabies. It was said that the pillars' properties emanated energy from the remains of Santa Quiteria, the virgin martyr and saint. She was the daughter of a Galician man who wanted her to marry and to renounce her Christianity. Because she refused, she was killed, and her remains were buried under the bridge. I thought about all the murders that have been committed over the centuries in the name of Christianity and other religions. Since an early age, I could not believe that God, who was so pure and loving, would have wanted us to kill our fellow human beings over different views about religion. I believed it was only a misinterpretation of the message of God, used by those in power to control people over the centuries. Are we, as a human race, playing God? Life could be so easy if we could respect one another and love others as we want to be loved. Is it because we do not love ourselves that we have to impose our will by suppressing others, to allow our ego to become so powerful that we lose the sense of respect for the views of others? Maybe it is time to change, but is it possible to stop this powerful wheel, which is crushing souls?

It took me eleven hours to reach Zubiri, which included the two small breaks I took. The refuge was full and I had to find a private lodging. I shared a small dormitory with a

298

group of visitors from France who were travelling by bus, accompanied by one of their local priests. Somehow, I felt I had to stay put instead of visiting Zubiri. Later, when Josiane came in, I understood why. After a few minutes, Josiane started to open her heart to me. Her pain was so great that it was palpable. I hugged her and when her travelling companions came back, I left the dormitory.

The next morning, I waved goodbye to the French visitors before starting a new day. I was joined by Monique, my fellow pilgrim of the same age, and we had lovely exchanges about life and spirituality. I was surprised when she told me she had noticed how pilgrims seemed to connect with me so naturally and so simply, as if I was attracting them. She had not seen this since she had started her pilgrimage. Monique was a very reserved woman with a seemingly cold approach, though she was very caring. Because of her cold appearance, people could misinterpret her attitude. Very few people approached her, though she was greeted by the usual sign of acknowledgement between pilgrims.

The path in Spain was well-marked with yellow arrows similar to the one I had seen before entering Pellegrue in France. The track was difficult at times. I crossed urban areas and passed an important magnesium factory. The dust from the factory was everywhere and covering the concrete paths. I walked along streams and on the edges of forests, and in the meadows I noticed the famous Basque Pottok horses resting. They are small, short and sturdy horses.

I crossed charming villages like Aquerreta, Zurian and Iroz with its ancient bridge on the Rio ('river') Arga, and later I found another cross where a pilgrim had died in

299

2005. I kept on going through charming forests and steep descents and ascents. Everywhere I looked there were gorgeous panoramas and pilgrims galore. Everything was perfect, yet I was struggling to adjust to the noise around me, as some were speaking so very loudly with no respect for others. Every so often, my throat would tighten, as I was really missing the quietness and solitude of the French paths. It seemed that I had lost my equilibrium; I could not bond with these paths. I felt adrift, disorientated and I was bemused by my transformation after weeks of being in contact with nature. I was able to relate to the recluse or missionary abroad who could never re-adapt to a normal life after returning to their home, and who just wished to be back at the place they had left behind.

I arrived at a very green resting area close to Zabaldika when someone called out my name. It was Josiane, who I had spoken with in Zubiri, and who had prayed and prayed with all her might that our paths would cross again. Her group was on the verge of leaving after a rest when she saw me coming down the path and she asked the bus driver to wait a few minutes. Her wish had been granted and she was so happy. It was nice to see her again. She was feeling better and it lifted my spirits too. I put my hand into my backpack, pulled out a little heart-shaped stone and gave it to her. I had collected it along the way. She was so moved that she could not stop crying. We heard a beep, as her bus was leaving. It had been a matter of a few seconds for us to meet again. As I was climbing up the hill, I looked back and saw her still waving to me, holding on to the side door of the mini-bus which was still open even as the bus was moving. I thanked God for this treasured moment.

At Villava, Monique and I met again over the medieval bridge on the Rio Ulzama with its five arches, and went through an area of chestnut trees. A fierce wind carried the white fluff of the chestnut flowers, and in no time an incredible transformation happened, as it seemed that centimetres of snow had instantly coated the landscape. It was unbelievable. I felt sorry for people with allergies, but to my eyes it was magical. The locals believe that if anyone carries a chestnut, it will protect that person from aches and pains in their bones. Unfortunately for me, it was the beginning of summer and so no chestnuts were available to ease my pain!

I crossed the 12th century medieval Magdalena Bridge with its large, pointed arches over the Rio Arga. At one end of the bridge, there is a stone cross and a carved statue of Saint James, which indicates the main entry to Pamplona for the pilgrims. We passed through what is called 'the Gateway of France', which leads to the historical centre. As we arrived at our shelter in Pamplona, I was in real turmoil, as I realised that I had left the battery charger for my camera behind in Zubiri. I was envisaging walking back the 23 kilometres the next day, as I could not bear the thought of not being able to take photographs. It was my pilgrimage and I wished so much to show my children and my friends where I had been and, for my own personal needs, I wanted to be able to revisit my pilgrimage at leisure. The 'hospitaliers' advised me to keep on going forward, as I would most likely find a camera shop in Pamplona and I could buy a universal charger. Honestly, I could not see myself walking back to Zubiri and adding 46 kilometres and two extra days to my journey. I decided to take their advice, but fear and frustration took hold of me.

Once in Pamplona, I did not find a charger for my camera and my heart sank. Monique and I visited this ancient city, which had been named after a Roman General called Pompey, who had built it with ramparts, baths, temples and houses in 75 BC. Pamplona remains the capital of the Kingdom of Navarre, and since the 11th century it has been on the pilgrimage route. In front of the Plaza de Toros stadium, I spotted the statue of Ernest Hemingway who had made Pamplona world-renowned thanks to his novel 'The Sun Also Rises'. This city is also known for its running of the bulls. Through the Calle Carmen, Monique and I reached the old city with its paved streets and its ancient squares, and after losing ourselves in this part of Pamplona, we came face to face with the beautiful 14th century Gothic cathedral, with its French influence and a neo-classical facade. It has the most outstanding 16th century cloister, certainly one of the most beautiful in Europe that I have ever seen. We could have spent hours in this gorgeous place. We went strolling in the different sections of the city with its splendid squares of houses no higher than five or six floors and magnificent parks. I was told that twenty per cent of the area of Pamplona is reserved for green spaces. The city has a lot of pedestrian malls, squares and streets which give a sense that the pedestrians own the place and I understood why Ernest Hemingway loved it so much. After enjoying a meal in the main street, we went back to our shelter, but I was still worried about my camera. It was obvious that I was still part of the real world. My memories were not enough: I wanted photographic souvenirs.

Very early the next morning, Monique and I left Pamplona, passing through its ancient gates. The day was already hot and I was feeling tired and chesty and had a lot of difficulty breathing. Perhaps it was a result of the cold shower at Saint-Jean-Pied-de-Port or the camping experience at Orisson or the hard climbing over the Pyrenees in the rain and the icy wind. Perhaps it was a combination of the three. I was not at all well, and I knew that there was a straight, but steep 8.5 kilometres climb to access the mountain pass of Alto de Pedron. With the heat, it was going to be quite a testing day.

We stopped at the University of Navarra to have our pilgrims' credentials signed. The Spanish man at reception had a brother living in Adelaide and his dream was to visit Australia. I hope that one day he will be able to realise his dream and I told him that if he got the chance to visit Australia, he should grasp it with both hands. While climbing at Cizur Menor, I saw a tower which belonged to the restored Archangel Michael Church, an ancient monastery and the 13th century hospital of the Order of Malta in Navarre, but sadly the doors to all of these buildings were closed. On both sides of the stony trail there was no shade and the never-ending path opened up to cultivated wheat fields which were in stark contrast to the dry, barren hills above.

Before reaching the village of Zariquiegui with its little San Andres Church, I noticed another cross, this time in memory of a Belgian man who had died there. I was stunned by the number of people who had lost their lives during this part of the pilgrimage. I had not come across a single memorial from Vezelay until I had passed the Pyrenees. At Zariquiegui, I walked close to the walls of the houses, hoping to get some shade, but to no avail.

Gradually, as I climbed, the scenery changed as the mountains became part of the backdrop. Down below, small villages appeared in the valley that I had not noticed when I had passed by further back along the path, as they were hidden behind thickets. The heat got worse as the rays of the sun began to reflect on the gravel track. I was tired, my backpack felt heavier, and I was really suffering when I reached a flat area called the Fountain of Reniega. Legend says that, at this site, a half-dead pilgrim had fallen in front of the dry spring and the Devil appeared and took this opportunity to ask the very thirsty pilgrim to deny God. If he did so, the Devil would show him a fountain. But the brave pilgrim refused. Saint James then appeared and showed him where he could find the fountain. The pilgrim drank the pure water with the help of his scallop shell and was saved. In those days, pilgrims used the handy scallop shell for eating and drinking. I drank from this fountain, happy that the water was still running in this arid mountain. This was a real life saver, even though my bottle of water still had something in it. Water was like gold to me in this area, and I took this opportunity to re-fill my bottle. At the crest of the mountains, I saw many fields of wind turbine power farms and learnt how proud the Spanish are of their environment, and how conscientious they are in looking after it. It was so nice to see and would be a good lesson for all.

It took me nearly three hours to climb these 8.5 kilometres and to reach the pass of Sierra del Pedron at an altitude of 790 metres. At the top was the famous wrought-iron statue of pilgrims bending under the force of the wind and being guided by the Milky Way to get to Santiago de Compostela. As I arrived at the top, I screamed with all my strength, without shame or fear, 'I did it! I did it!' The other pilgrims who were resting after the climb were very surprised. Once their initial surprise had passed, however, they all laughed and clapped and even offered me a glass of red wine, which I politely declined. I knew that I still had to go down a very steep descent, which I had been told was so sharp that I should take the bitumen road. After a short rest, I admired the Pyrenees for the last time as well as the green valley below with its fields of wheat and its small groves of oak and pine trees. There were magnificent views as far as the eye could see. I was going to enter the dry heart of Spain with its almond trees and its olive groves, and I saw from afar what my journey would be from now on: more mountains, more valleys and this for nearly 800 kilometres. But I was not scared by the distance. I was eager to go forward and challenge myself.

I went to explore the downhill track which was made of sharp, stony gravel and it looked quite unstable. The warning from Alain in Benevent l'Abbaye came back to me. He had advised that I should take the road at this point. I pondered for a while before making a decision. I was still concerned about my knee and the number of kilometres ahead of me, but I decided that if I was to descend the steep hill backwards, as I had in France, logically it should work in Spain too. Also, at times, I could use the way Amar had showed me to walk. If I could do it, it would be another challenge achieved. Lately, my body and mind had been looking for a constant dare, like a drug I suppose, and I said to myself,

'Come on, Claude. Be brave. Take the track'. Monique, who had arrived, went ahead and I finished the climb down without any problems and in quite good time. I was proud of myself and also happy to have conquered a little bit more of my fear. My strength of will was growing every day.

I arrived at Uterga where there was a refuge with only 18 beds. Already, some young pilgrims in their 20s had decided to stop their pilgrimage there, as they could not physically continue any further. I went to the lounge room to change the strips of Elastoplast around my knee. I had not had the courage to discard them as Amar had suggested, though I could see that my knee was becoming close to its normal size again. Fear was still my companion, however. A man of European appearance was seated in an armchair opposite me and he was observing, very intently, what I was doing and how I was placing the strips of Elastoplast. I could sense that he wanted to say something and after some hesitation and gestures, I heard him say, 'No'. Bemused, and without thinking too much about what went through my head, I asked him if he was a doctor, as doctor is a universal word. To my surprise, he confirmed it. So, putting my hands to my head, I asked him if he was a brain surgeon. He smiled and pointed to his heart, and I worked out that he was a cardiologist. After many gestures between us, he showed me that the way I was placing the strips meant that I was blocking the flow of fluid along my leg and I should not use them. I thanked him for his advice and reflected for a while on the prospect of pulling off the strips for good. They had helped me so much up until now. It was a difficult decision: a matter of trust. After a lot of soul searching, I came to the conclusion that I should get rid of them and I pulled them off very slowly, one by one, as if I was saying goodbye to some dear friends. I felt I had betrayed them, but I had to be wise and listen to advice. I still had the small, wrapped present that Bruno had stuck on my leg before I had left his home in Casseneuil. I remembered his words to leave it until I was sure I was healed, and not to look inside before that moment. I could not remove it, too fearful that the next day my leg would be swollen again.

That night I did not sleep well, as I woke up at around 2.00am from the sound of eight locomotives around me. Every one of the male pilgrims was snoring and I could not get back to sleep. At one stage, I thought I was going to kill them all. Have you ever slept with eight locomotives beside you? If not, I could give you the following advice: do not do it unless you want to become mad. Monique and I left just after 5.30am, tired and bothered.

On 4 June 2010, I had been walking for two months. It was hard for me to believe, but I still had to cover about 750 kilometres on the map before reaching Santiago de Compostela. It was pleasant to walk in the cool, fresh morning. Monique and I decided to extend our walk that day to visit the Chapel of Santa Maria de Eunate, adding four extra kilometres to the journey, but we could not see inside the chapel as it was closed. We were surprised by its octagonal shape, which gave us the impression that it could have been a Templar church. The chapel was surrounded by partially reconstructed arches, however the cloister had completely disappeared.

The town of Obanos is well known for its legend about Santa Felicia, Princess of Aquitaine. On her return from her pilgrimage to Santiago de Compostela, she had decided to go and live in a cloister. Her brother, San Guillien, tried to talk her out of it, but she refused. He was so angry that, in a moment of rage, he killed her. Later on, he regretted his act so much that he decided to walk the pilgrimage himself to ask for forgiveness. Afterwards, he became a saint. I am sure that, as with this legend, there is hope for all of us sinners!

We arrived at Puente La Reina, which is a very important town, as the path from Arles in France, through the difficult Somport Pass, and the path from Roncesvalles converge there. From now on the pilgrimage would be called the 'Camino Frances' ('the French Route'). I crossed the medieval part of the town, along the Calle Mayor, and there were beautiful residential houses and palaces with balconies adorned with colourful geraniums on both sides of this street. We noticed the Church of the Crucifijo ('crucifix'), which had been built by the Templars. I tried to find a camera shop, but with no luck. It was Saturday and the shop opening hours in Spain were quite different from the French ones and it was hard for me, as a pilgrim, to adjust. They opened around 10.00am or 11.00am, were closed by 2.00pm and re-opened at 6.00pm. I questioned whether my decision not to return to Zubiri to collect my charger had been the right one.

It was very hot. My chest was becoming worse and my breathing heavier. I had to make a mighty effort during the climb as the path was really only a goat track. The lanes were laid with white stones and gravel, and the reflection of the sun's rays on them was affecting my vision. It was hard to concentrate on the trail because of the brightness, even with sun-glasses. There was no shade at all and the heat made it quite a test of endurance and patience.

I had left behind green fields to enter the arid part of Spain. I was burning under the sun. Later on, I passed through the lovely village of Mañeru, with its beautiful houses and coat of arms. Before entering the medieval village of Cirauqui, I saw a line of trees far away in the distance on the top of a mountain, very similar to the ones I had seen in France on my way to Saint-Hilaire-de-la-Noaille. They looked like soldiers. Maybe they were there to provide the pilgrims with a sense of protection as the Knights Templar had done in the Middle Ages. I had asked Monique if we could stop at Cirauqui for the night, as I was too tired and too hot. In the Basque language, Cirauqui means 'vipers' nest'. This village was at an altitude of about 500 metres and since the 11th century, it had grown thanks to the pilgrims going to Santiago de Compostela. We went under a fortified doorway with a disc-shaped stele in front of it. Then we climbed up through a typical steep, narrow and cobbled street with its medieval houses and coat of arms. In the higher part of the village, we passed in front of the 11th century Roman Church of San Roman, which was closed, but we could admire its impressive oriental portal before reaching our lodging.

By 5.30am the next day, Monique and I were already on the road again enjoying the cool air of the morning, as by 8.00am in this part of Spain, the sun was scorching. We left the village of Cirauqui, perched at the top of a hill with vineyards climbing up its side, and we followed the ancient Roman road called 'Calzada', crossing the Rio Salado over an old Roman bridge. My chest was getting worse, but nothing could have stopped me. I had acquired an incredible will. I appreciated having a walking companion and I believed that my meeting with Monique was not a coincidence. I felt she had appeared for a reason at that time of my pilgrimage. She was going to help me go forward. We kept on delving into spiritual conversations and sometimes she would go forward by herself, as I was walking with difficulty, and she would wait for me further down the track. The goat tracks were still the same: stony along quite steep mountains with their ups and downs, and we continued to walk in the Spanish heat.

We crossed an area with a lot of paving stones and in the middle of the footpath, a row of oblong stones were placed in a way to mark a centre line which divided the lane in two. I did not know if the purpose of this was to protect the pilgrims from the cyclists, who did not seem to have much respect for us pedestrians. I imagined that, high up on their bicycles, they felt a sense of power and speed that we walkers could not compete with.

We arrived at Lorca and the name of this little village appeared in the book 'Codex Calixtinus', written by a 12th century French scholar, a monk from the Poitou region named Aymeric Picaud. His book is considered as the first guide for pilgrims travelling the Saint James' Way and, as one person said, perhaps the first travel guide-book in history. In his book, Aymeric Picaud did not have a fond memory of his visit to Lorca. It has been recorded that when he arrived close to the river with his horses, he met two locals who were seated on the bank of the river and he asked them if the water was safe for his horses to drink. They answered with a 'Yes', but in reality the water was salty, and as soon as his horses drank from the river, they fell to the ground, dead. In a flash, the two locals with their sharp knives cut them into pieces. I wondered if it was for this reason that the people of Lorca had built the lovely Church of San Salvador to ask forgiveness for their wicked sins! I was crossing over the bridge and it was getting so hot that I decided to hold on tightly to my bottle of water. Who knows? I did not want to end up like Aymeric Picaud's poor horses. I bent over and looked under the bridge to see if there were any locals waiting. Luckily for me, no one was there. I was safe!

The green colour of wheat and barley fields was disappearing and the heat was becoming harsher, not only for my body, but for my mind too. I carried on along the road to Villatuerta with its Church of the Assumption and its tower which was a real fortress. I went over the Rio Uranzu via the Roman Bridge. As I was going along the path, I noticed a mountain in the distance, which looked very much like the one near my birthplace called Mont Revard. My deeper thoughts went to my Maman, Papa and family. I have heard many times that we have a double somewhere in the world. I had met my godmother's double; maybe it was the same for the mountains!

We were still a fair way from Estella, an important Roman city which had been under the authority of the Muslims until King Sancho Ramirez took it over in the 11th century. He saw the potential prosperity the town could have by attending to the pilgrims, and a thriving economy was created, with six hospitals being built to welcome the pilgrims. Since that time, the town's original layout has barely changed. As I was walking alone at this

311

stage, for Monique had gone on ahead, I kept on the ancient pilgrims' road and passed in front of the spectacular 11th century Church of San Sepulchre, with its 12 statues of saints, six on each side of its main portal. It is the first church the pilgrims would have been able to see before their arrival in the city of Estella.

At the entrance to Estella, pilgrims were coming from everywhere and, for the first time, I saw first-aid nurses busily attending to them with their different ailments and giving them massages to relieve the soreness of their poor, battered bodies. The modern pilgrims are still the life blood of all the villages and towns along the path and the Spanish have used this economic manna to their great financial advantage. I went all over the city, looking for a charger, but again it was no use.

My cough was wearing me down. I was sad, worn out, and the heat was affecting me. I sat down on a bench and began to pray when a man sat down beside me and started talking to me. I asked if he knew where I could find a camera shop and he gave me the address of one he knew. I went there and the shopkeeper had only one universal charger left. I grabbed it with both hands, feeling relieved and privileged. Was it another coincidence?

With the pavement reflecting the heat of the sun, I looked for a cool spot and managed to find a bench with a tiny amount of shade and waited for Monique. I was so physically exhausted that I could not visit this beautiful medieval city properly, but used my time to write some cards. After a rest, Monique and I decided to go a few kilometres further to the refuge of San Cipriano de Ayegui, where we received a certificate testifying that we had walked our first hundred kilometres in Spain from a German 'hospitaliero'.

I went to bed early, but did not sleep well as my chest was painful and my breathing shallow. I could hear a noise coming from what I thought was the bed above. It was not like snoring and it took me a while to realise that, in fact, it was my chest which was making such a racket. I was shocked when I realised that I was the culprit and that bronchitis had started setting in.

It was 5 June 2010 and I was finishing my ninth week of the pilgrimage.

WEEK TEN

The parallel roads

It was still dark when Monique and I left the next morning. There was a hard day of climbing ahead and my spirits were already low. Outside, the cold breeze welcomed us with grey clouds hanging in the sky. We thought rain could be on its way.

To reach the small village of Azqueta, we had two possibilities: either we could go through Irache or directly to Azqueta. To the great dismay of the other pilgrims who went in the direction of Irache, with its old Benedictine monastery, Navarre Nuestro Señora la Real de Irache, we walked straight towards Azqueta. The community of Irache has been known since 958, however, nowadays the place is a must-see for a totally different reason. The pilgrims go there, mainly, to enjoy the 'Fuente del Vino', the wine from Rioja, which comes out of a fountain for free. We were the sober ones, the odd ones out, and did not care much about this tradition, which was talked about among all the pilgrims.

At the top of Ayegui we looked behind and saw the medieval town of Estella and the countryside around it waking up. It was quiet and peaceful at this time as the population was still in bed. We could hear the birds giving their morning concert, for during the hottest part of the day they remained silent. I appreciated this moment, as every day I still missed the quietness of the French path and I was aware of how spoilt I had been in France. The sky was black as ink when we got to Azqueta and the

Heavens opened. We were so lucky to reach the village in time as we would not have found a shelter before this. We spotted a woman opening her café and ran inside it for protection from the downpour and waited for the rain to pass. I asked if there was a doctor in the area, as each breath I took was becoming more painful, but regrettably there was none. The rain ceased and we left. Because of my slow pace, Monique and I separated for a while.

The scenery was majestic with endless mountains. I had to go through red soil tracks between olive groves and vineyards and as a consequence, the dirt stuck to my boots like glue, making each step very slippery, and I had to take great care not to fall. I passed the 12th century Romanesque 'Fuente de los Moros' ('fountain of the Moors') and to reach its spring, I had to go down the stairs that had been eroded by time. Sadly, the water was not drinkable, as it was stagnating in an open cistern.

Further ahead, at the top of a hill, I spotted the newly restored Romanesque Castillo de San Esteban de Deyo. This castle overlooks the village of Villamayor de Monjardin, which is at an altitude of 650 metres. From afar, I noticed the tower of its 12th century Romanesque 'Iglesias' ('church') of San Andre, situated in the middle of the village. The track took me through concrete routes and more red dirt mixed with gravel paths, always with a background of the beautiful mountainous scenery. I met Danni, an 18-year-old German girl, who was also doing the Camino Frances by herself. By the end of her Camino, she wanted answers to the questions she had. I was impressed by her desire to search her soul at such a young age. To do so she had decided to walk the Camino Frances, much to her parents' dismay. What a brave

315

young woman she was. I hope she found what she was looking for and kept on walking.

Suddenly, in the distance, I could see something coming towards me. It was big, like a wave. It was coming closer and closer when I finally recognised that it was a huge pack of sheep: hundreds of them with three black cattle dogs and a shepherd in front. I could hear the lovely sound of a bell, as a sheep at the head of the herd had one attached to its collar. In my mind, I was wondering what my reaction would be when the three black dogs passed by me, but there was not even a flicker of fear on my part. It seemed it was gone forever. I was so happy that my phobia of dogs had vanished.

My head and chest felt as though they were in a cast-iron cage. I was feeling so down and thought about taking a day's rest at Los Arcos. Even the green of the wheat and barley fields could not make me forget my suffering. My backpack was feeling heavier and I started to look with envy at the pilgrims who passed me with a small daypack. I was still annoyed and disturbed by their loud chatting or singing. Where was my 'douce' France and her quiet tracks? Had I become so critical? How easy was it to change one's attitude towards others? For hours on end, I had been walking on a very long, flat trail and for the last few days, the sensation of the path under my feet was different. I did not feel uplifted and was curious to know why. Was it me or was it the track? I stopped for a rest on an embankment, thinking about Godina and Uve from Germany. I had met them in the refuge the day before and there was so much more that I would have liked to talk with them about, if only I had not had to leave so early. Suddenly, out of the blue, they appeared in front of me. We had more good exchanges, trekked together for a while, and then each went our own way, not without giving each other a hug. The path, with its simple life, was making us more aware of our afflictions, even the smallest ones. But one day, we would have to deal with them. Maybe that was our lesson in life: to learn to recognise our faults and then to release them into the universe. As I was trekking, I was more and more convinced that we had been taught from an early age to ignore our deepest emotions, so that we could appear strong and be part of this world the way it was perceived we should be. Boys are the ones who have suffered, perhaps the most, with the 'macho' attitude.

I met up with Monique, who was waiting for me on the side of the road and as we entered Los Arcos, we heard beautiful music coming from the streets. There was a procession with some locals carrying the Holy Sepulchre and from the balconies the inhabitants were throwing rose petals in front of some children who were making their first Holy Communion. The young girls were dressed like little brides in their long, lace dresses and the boys were in smart suits with white shirts and ties. They were surrounded by friends, family and parishioners who were rejoicing at the special time in the children's spiritual lives, as religion plays an important part in Spanish culture. I had the privilege of entering the small town via the narrow, cobbled streets which were covered with a carpet of roses: a real lift for a tired pilgrim. The decrepit look of this 11th century township and its old buildings in disrepair surprised me. It was quite a different look from the towns and villages I had just crossed. It was a happy day, however, and the birds sang on a higher note, trying

317

to cover the sound of the music coming from the loudspeakers.

We arrived at the refuge and took possession of our bunk. Later on, an Austrian woman gave me a foot massage with gentle movements and put some life back into my poor, worn-out feet and body. It was just divine and the lady left me to rest on a table. One hour later, she came back and said that my chest would be better from now on and she asked me to pray for her when I arrived safely in Santiago de Compostela. Feeling revitalised, I went to visit the Romanesque Church of Santa Maria de Los Arcos with its black Virgin. The inside walls were all painted with different Spanish Baroque designs, with no free space between the drawings and frescoes.

After a good night's sleep, Monique and I decided to each go our separate ways, but still stay in touch, as we would meet again at the end of the day. It was nice to walk with someone, but after a while it was restricting, as I was always worried, knowing that I would keep Monique waiting for me. It was crucial for me to be free, in my mind and in my inner self. I needed to know what this part of the pilgrimage was going to bring and walking alone was the only way. Being with someone most of the time meant that I was not free for someone else, and it seemed that I could not capture the feeling or the energy of the trail, as I was worried about the other person. At our first meeting, I had told Monique that whenever she wanted to walk the track totally alone, I would understand. I had waited for her to make a decision without pressure and she came to that conclusion the same morning. She told me that my mannerisms were very much like a member of her family. She liked my

318

presence, but at the same time it was too confronting. We hugged and went our separate ways, knowing we would meet at the end of the day and keep track of each other.

I was feeling better after the foot massage and I did not stop for an extra day's rest at Los Arcos, although I was still coughing and my cough sounded as though it was coming from a cavern. The weather was overcast and I hoped that it would be easier to walk. I was ready to do what I had to do. I could sense something was changing on the path and I was sure it was not because I was alone. There was a different energy. Somehow, I felt as if I was being pushed to go on by an invisible hand. I had a feeling that there were deeper things coming my way, and to discover them, I needed to be alone and available for anyone, or maybe, available for myself.

I passed over the Rio Odron and the Chapel of San Blas. The first section of the route to Sansol was easy; it gave me the chance to free my mind. At one point I prayed and asked God from the bottom of my heart to bring me someone in need every day if I was meant to help, or someone who could help me, and in total humility, I would accept what He sent to me. I kept on walking in the quietness of the morning on this long stretch of gravel road between yellow wheat fields, olive groves and vineyards. I noticed that there were fewer pilgrims, not like the previous days, when the Camino Frances was invaded by Spanish people speaking loudly. I had been told it was Monday and wondered if on Sundays, all the Spanish people living in this area walk a bit of the Camino Frances. Maybe it was their way of doing it, so that after many years of walking a bit every time, they would eventually finish. If that were the case, it would explain why the path was so quiet today.

I reached the village of Torres Del Rio and stopped at a café where I had a sudden coughing fit. I could not control it and I ran outside as I was making such a noise. Two French pilgrims, Catherine and Bernadette, followed me. They had overtaken me along the way and had already heard my cough and noticed that my breathing was quite shallow and heavy. They gave me some homeopathic tablets and sachets of Ayurveda herbal tea from their backpacks. I did not want to take them as they might have need of them at some stage on the way. It was the last of their tablets and tea, but they did not want to hear about it. I had just met two more angels and thanked God for placing them on my path.

Back on the road, there were a number of hills to traverse. The road was covered with small, dry gravel and had a sharp 10 per cent gradient. I was happy not to have to descend in the rain. I was about three kilometres from Viana when I was stopped by two women waiting for a car. They were interested in the pieces of sheep skin attached under the straps of my backpack. These bands had helped to absorb shock and sweat from my shoulders, protecting them from the rubbing of the straps. I was explaining this to them when a young man passed. Our eyes met and I was surprised by the rhythm of his walking. It was a very slow pace for a young person, as they usually run and end up stopping halfway, exhausted. I caught up with Ricardo, as he was still walking at his gentle pace. A force was pushing me to talk to him and after a bit of small talk, I shared some of my experiences, when suddenly, he burst into tears. He was shaking like a leaf in the wind. I felt his pain and put my arm around him and he cried. He could not stop for a while. He was wailing and I let him release his sorrows. He apologised and I dismissed it right away. I was there for him so he could let go of some of his pain. He had lost one of his parents who had the same Christian name as me, and he was still very affected by the loss and his emotions were raw. We strolled as far as Viana, stopping at times when he was overwhelmed by grief and sorrow and he wept on my shoulder and in my arms in the middle of the quiet streets. Some locals glanced at us out of curiosity, but we did not care. I shared with him that I was a firm believer that there was life after death, and that his deceased parent was walking with him. I had a feeling that there was more to his grief, but I respected his silence as anyone should do. The lesson I had learnt in my volunteering in palliative care and in oncology was to live without any regret and without hurting others and to say, with a gentle heart, what we need to say while there is still time. Otherwise the guilt can consume us. I knew from personal experience that it was not easy, but in order to be free after someone's passing, it had to be done, not only for the dying, but for the living.

As we reached the centre of Viana, we ate a 'bocadillo' ('sandwich') in the square in front of the Church of Santa Maria where we met a French pilgrim who had built a hand-cart to carry his belongings. In a way, he had substituted himself for the famous donkey that pilgrims used to take with them to carry their effects along the path. He believed that it was the way to go so as not to hurt his back, and proudly he showed us how he 'harnessed' himself. I was wondering, with the bulkiness of his apparatus, what he did when he had to go up and down steep climbs and descents. He probably needed to walk on bitumen roads instead of the track. This was not for me, but to each their own pilgrimage.

I pulled out my credential to get a stamp at Viana, and Ricardo was amazed to see the number of stamps on it. We hugged, as he was going on to the next town, and my eyes followed him down the narrow lane until he disappeared, still going at a gentle pace. I wished I could carry some of his pain. I had a heavy backpack, but felt that the weight of his misery was heavier than what I had on my back. I could not take his pain away, as each person has to deal with their own hurts before being able to release them into the universe. This does not mean that the suffering will be forgotten, but it would not be as tender. I sent him my motherly love, still wishing I could do more. Shortly after, I put my hand in my pocket and felt the little heart-shaped stone, which I had meant for him, but had forgotten to give to him. I was saddened, but hoped that we would meet again.

I found the shelter where I would be staying that night. Each dormitory had three rows of bunk beds, one on top of the other, but thanks to the kindness of the 'hospitalieros', the lowest bunk was given to the seniors. Before catching up with Monique, I wrote an e-mail to my children. As I was so engrossed in my writing, I did not see the flashing light telling me that I only had 30 seconds left and my e-mail went to cyberspace. I had only one coin left and, annoyed, I wrote another short e-mail, as there were others waiting for the chance to use the internet and write to their loved ones.

Viana, a fortified city and capital of the Rioja region, is at the top of a hill and towers above the Rio Ebro Valley.

There was a pleasant atmosphere in this town and I wandered among its medieval cobblestone streets and sat on a terrace behind the refuge, enjoying the view of the city while reflecting on the day. With humility, I thanked God for putting the grieving young man in front of me and I prayed for him to find peace in his heart.

The next morning before day-break, I left Viana, the last city of the Navarre region, alone. I was headed towards the small province of La Rioja, which is universally renowned for its wine. The Camino Frances crosses it from east to west. I was happy to walk in the dark, knowing that I would see the sun rising above the mountains one more time and I would benefit from the cool air of the morning and be able to hear the first songs of the birds announcing a new day. I had heard a cuckoo over the last few days when my breathing was at its heaviest. My chest was still very painful and each step so hard. I mused that maybe birds have a 'pilgrims' radio' as well and that my French cuckoo had sent a message to his Spanish counterpart, saying, 'If you see Claude struggling on the Camino Frances, sing for her to give her courage!'

I left Viana behind with minimum difficulty and after passing the Santa Maria de las Cuevas Chapel, I went through vineyards and more vineyards. It was still dark when I arrived at La Lagunas de Las Canas, a bird observatory, where I could only distinguish some reeds and heard the concert given by the frogs and the birds. The tracks took me through concrete, bitumen and white gravel tracks with not much difficulty and in the background there was more mountainous scenery. Going downhill on my way to Logroño, I met Feliza's daughter, Maria, who had been following her mother's tradition since her death. Feliza was renowned on the Camino Frances, as for many years she had opened her house to all pilgrims on their way to Santiago de Compostela. She offered them refreshments, cakes, coffee and a well-deserved rest on the wooden benches in her kitchen, or outside, depending on the season. I was welcomed in with much genuine warmth, but when Maria heard my cough, concern appeared in her eyes and with the beautiful language of the hands, she advised me to stop and rest. I could feel her kind heart and her real concern. I picked up from her a similar sort of warmth as my Savoyard family and my heart swelled. I signed her 'Livre d'Or', which she said was a must, and I dropped some coins in a clean cup. I left with her blessing and prayers, asking God to protect me, and then I went down the steep hill. Many Spanish have followed Feliza's example to help others along the path and have placed food and drink near their houses for hungry pilgrims.

From afar, I could distinguish the two towers of the 15th century Baroque Cathedral of Santa Maria La Redonda and crossed the Rio Arga to reach the ancient city of Logroño, with all its historical buildings. It reflected various cultures and its settlement dated from the Romans under the name of Vareia. During the Spanish Inquisition, Logroño saw the witch trials in the Basque country. The narrow, paved Rua Vieja, with its characteristic old houses and stalls on one side, led me to the Church of Santiago del Real. There was an enormous recess on its facade, which represented Santiago Matamoros (Saint James) from the 16th century. He was on a horse, dressed in a pilgrim's cloak and waving a curved sword. I was quite shocked by this carving, which depicted the violent side of religion. Fortunately, inside the church there was a more peaceful Saint James on the altar. The legend of Santiago Matamoros ('the Moor slayer') says that before a battle, King Ramirez of Castile who had a small army, had a dream in which Saint James showed him victory against the Muslims. On the day of the battle, Saint James appeared on the battle field on a white horse with a sword in his right hand and a banner in his left. I was told that Saint James had appeared at least forty times during this period of wars and consequently became the patron saint of Spain.

Logroño is a very pretty city with lots of green parks, and I stopped to rest on a bench along the track for a little breather, as my chest was hurting so much. I met Anna-Maria from Switzerland, who was tired, as she had spent the night in an old bull-fighting arena and could not sleep. I told her it could have been because of the energy of the area, which would have seen quite horrible killings, and she agreed. Anna-Maria left and a few minutes later I followed. I noticed the lace of my right boot was undone and I decided to attend to it once I reached the next bench, as this would save me from having to pick my backpack up off the ground. I could put my foot on a bench and it would be high enough for me to lace my shoe without stretching too much. After a while, I saw the next bench with a woman sitting on it, and to my surprise, it was Anna-Maria. I showed her my boot with the undone lace and as I was doing it up, Anna-Maria said, 'Claude, your chest is so bad. I do Reiki. Would you like me to do it on you?' I had heard about Reiki, as it works with energy, but I did not know much about it. I thought to myself, 'Why not?' Maybe she was meant to help me. It could have been one of the reasons why my laces were undone. I really did need help and for the sake of my chest, I agreed. Anna-Maria did it on the spot and afterwards we separated, not knowing if we would meet again.

I went through the Pantano de la Grajera Park, with its dam and small bridges, and where lovely wild birds and ducks benefited from the cool water. As it was so hot, I enjoyed the shade of the trees, but soon I had to leave this paradise behind and walk through industrial and modern housing areas. The track was next to a main road for kilometres and I had to walk on bitumen and close to fumes. I missed nature more than ever. I came to a hill where there was a giant bull sculpture made out of enormous pieces of metal. It was the symbol of a major winery that overlooks Navarrete. A fence was placed between the road and the track, and pilgrims had picked up small pieces of wood that had been scattered on the ground from the pulp factory and put them on the wire in the shape of a cross. There were hundreds of them. I thought about my Maman and Papa and gathered four pieces of wood to make two crosses, which I placed in the shade of a tree. Somehow, it did not feel right, but I left them there all the same. I did not think they would have wanted me to place them there, so close to such a busy highway and dusty pulp factory, as they were born in the country. I sensed that, deep down in my soul, I felt I had to do something for my parents along the path, but I did not know what and where. I was questioning myself, as we all do. In our lives we often wonder if we are doing the right thing at the right time, creating such a dilemma in ourselves instead of accepting the flow of life as it comes.

I crossed a bridge over a highway to reach the entrance to Navarrete, not before passing beside the ruins of the old pilgrims' hospital of San Juan de Acre. I found the refuge, did my daily chores and for the first time since the beginning of my journey, I lay on the bunk before it was time for bed. It was about 3.00pm and to my surprise I went straight to sleep, exhausted. I woke up at 6.30pm, just in time to buy some food and prepare a meal in the kitchen. I slept the night through. I thanked Anna-Maria for her Reiki and God for having put her on my path, as I assumed it was due to this.

I was feeling a bit better after this restful night and I learnt that the next day was the feast of La Rioja. On the balconies of private houses and on public buildings, the elaborate Rioja flags were flapping. It was a public holiday and I was not sure if the shops would be open. I patiently waited until 10.30am in the hope that I would find one open. This was a risk for every pilgrim, as we are not aware of the traditions in the areas we pass through. Eventually, the baker opened and I bought some bread: I would not die of hunger, after all! In any case, I doubted I would have died of hunger along the path, but if I did not have any water, that would have been quite different.

Since Los Arcos, I had begun to meditate before leaving for the day. I went into the deepest part of my being to ask God to bring me someone in need or someone who would help me on my spiritual path. I was allowing God to take my life into His hands for His bigger plan. This had been a daily ritual and I kept it up until the end of my journey on the Saint James' Way. As I was leaving Navarrete, the skies opened. I scrutinised them in the hope it would be just a shower. God had to be kind: it was a special day for

327

La Rioja! I left in the rain, but it did not last and I walked on a bitumen path along a highway, then a stony track took me through vineyards, and on their edges I saw flower beds with the most beautiful poppies and cornflowers among high grass. Nature was showing me its beauty and then, shock horror, I was back on the bitumen. This happened a few times going from track to bitumen along the highway. Was the highway playing hide and seek with me or did it want to trigger something in me?

Before the little Alto de San Anton Pass, I met a very concerned man at an intersection. Emile from Belgium was travelling with a Korean girl, Inch, who had disappeared. He had walked back to the previous village and could not find her. He had taken care of her when she had a problem with her blisters and he had left some personal belongings in her backpack. I saw fear in his eyes and told him to trust that, sometimes, things are not what they appear. I looked behind me and saw Inch coming out of a bush. I looked at Emile and saw relief on his face. I hugged him and left without a word. Later, they overtook me, and then I overtook them as they were having lunch on the side of the path and I commented on the kindness of pilgrims on the path. Emile got up, emptied out his backpack and handed me some tablets, saying, 'Claude, God has blessed you. You are doing good things on this path. I will ask God to protect you always'. I hugged him and left with tears in my eyes, humbled by his words. The purpose of my pilgrimage was back.

As I was walking along the gravel path I thought how privileged and loved I had been on this pilgrimage, when my eyes spotted a little heart-shaped stone and I picked it up with the plan to give it to Emile as a gesture of friendship and trust. A while later, I noticed that Emile was walking very slowly behind me. I did not turn my head or stop; I waited for him to overtake me, which took a while. When he did, I showed him the stone and asked what he could see in it. He turned it over and over between his fingers describing it, its colour, what kind of stone it was and so on, never recognising its shape. I took it from his hands, placed it at an angle so he could recognise the outlines of the heart in the stone, and gave it to him. He was surprised. I informed him that if our paths crossed again and he needed to talk to a friend, I would be there for him. He did not say anything and he walked forwards with tears in his eyes. Our paths never did cross again.

Further along the track I ran into Rouky from California. As he overtook me, he asked if I was the spiritual one. I was perplexed and replied that he could call me what he wanted, as I did not mind. I was part of this universe and I believed in God. Rouky was a typical intellectual: doing what he was supposed to do for his family, going to church sometimes, staying on the safe side. He was working for NASA and to him, he had done his job concerning his family and work, and that was enough. He did not feel the need to look outside the square. Later on, I met his wife, who worked with horses and was very in tune with energy and with things in different dimensions. What an odd couple, but each respected the belief of the other: a lesson for all couples, I would say. As they were American, I asked them how they had heard about the pilgrimage. One day, Rouky and his wife were cycling from Geneva in Switzerland to Saint

Nazaire in Brittany, France when they came across a symbol of the Saint James' Way. They asked about it and decided to do it at a later date and started from Saint-Jean-Pied-de-Port. As they were used to cycling, walking was a real challenge, especially for his wife, as all the weight of the body is placed on the feet, not to mention the weight of the backpack. She could not carry it anymore and had it transferred from lodging to lodging by private companies. I wished her well and told her to have courage, knowing that her pain would eventually subside, since the first weeks are the hardest.

As I trod along, I pondered why, in general, men are less ready to admit that they are spiritual than women are. Are they worried that it will show a sign of weakness? I was sure that, deep down in their inner selves, a little voice would say that there was something much deeper than just living, creating and dying, and I hoped that, one day, Rouky would find that out. I knew it was his choice and that I should not interfere because everyone has free will.

I passed by a spot of little stone monuments made by pilgrims. They were similar to Japanese garden features and I wondered if they had been built by Asian pilgrims in memory of their passage in this part of the world. I took the little heart-shaped stone out of my pocket that I had collected for Ricardo and left it there, as I felt our paths would never cross again.

In passing through vineyards and almond groves, I went over a hillock, on which there were some ugly radio antennae, to a point called Pyo de Roldan. One person said that, from this point, Roland, Charlemagne's nephew, saw the giant 'Ferragut', descendant of the Syrian Goliath, seated on a bench in front of his castle.

Roland threw a large stone at the giant which landed on the giant's forehead, killing him. As a result of the giant's death, Roland was able to free the Christian knights who were imprisoned.

Soon, I was confronted again by semi-industrial areas with all their pollution. Leaving behind the modern area of Najera, I crossed a bridge over the Rio Najerilla. On one bank there were beautiful green parks and on the other side was the old town with its small, mostly pedestrian streets and its pink-coloured cliffs with caves rising behind it. I also saw storks, which had built enormous nests on top of the chimneys of the old houses. This little town had been under Muslim rule too and was a centre of culture. In 1142, its reputation grew after many visits by Peter the Vulnerable who was a French abbot. He had asked for the translations of important Islamic writings, which involved the first translation of the Quran.

Once I arrived at my lodging, I went for a shower and for the first time since I had the little wrapped package placed on my leg by Bruno, I decided to look at what was inside it. The day was 9 June 2010 and I was strong enough to take it off. Gently, I pulled the plastic covering, wondering what I was going to discover. I was speechless when I discovered it was the Miraculous Medal, the same medal my mother had sent me nearly 30 years ago and that I put with my treasures which I carried with me on the walk. Bruno had no knowledge of how precious this medal was for me. I was so moved by this gesture of kindness and overwhelmed by the coincidence.

At the base of the cliffs in this little town is the monastery of Santa Maria la Real. On a pamphlet it was written that King Garcia Sanchez III had been hunting partridge on the banks of the Rio Najerilla when a strange event occurred. His hawk went into a cave and the King decided to follow it. As he entered the cave, he was astounded to see the Virgin Mary and, close by, the hawk and the partridge sitting peacefully, side by side. Later on, the King and his wife, Queen Estefania de Foix, built the monastery to honour the Virgin Mary and it became an important burial place for Spanish kings.

Inexplicably, I felt I had to go and see this place. As I arrived, I noticed that there were a lot of visitors in the grounds outside, and I decided to visit the church first. To my surprise there was no one inside. I looked around it quickly and felt attracted towards the crypt and the cave. Something very strange happened: it was as if I had been pushed towards the female tombs, of which one was Queen Estefania's, and I felt the need to stroke her hands. I could not control this impulse and tears rolled down my cheeks. I did not understand what was overpowering me. I stayed there quite a while, still stroking the hands on two of the female tombs and scrutinising their faces, as if I wanted to imprint them on my memory. I was trying to understand all these emotions, which were quite out of the ordinary. I felt almost as though I was going mad, then I went inside the cave where I found the 13th century carved statue of the Virgin Mary with Jesus on her lap, and prayed intensely. There was so much energy in this cave: it was incredible. After a while, I left, and to do so, I had to pass in front of the tombs again. The same thing happened: I was pushed towards them. I left, more confused than ever. I wished I could have met up with Anna-Maria again, who had performed Reiki on me in

Logroño. Perhaps she could have given me an explanation, as she worked with energy. I had visited a lot of tombs and churches since I had started my walk, but until now, this had never happened. It felt so eerie. I did not want to leave. It was as though I was saying goodbye to something very important. I had no idea where this had come from.

As I left the crypt, people started to come inside. I was still bewildered when, close to the exit, I ran into Anna-Maria's friend, Margarita, and I told her what had just happened. To my astonishment, Margarita said that this was a message for me. Puzzled, I asked her what she meant and Margarita told me that I would 'find out' in time. Dubious and shaken, I went back to the refuge, hoping to find Anna-Maria. Maybe she could give me a better explanation regarding this weird episode. I started to question myself. Had I dreamt this? No, it had really happened.

I was still hoping to meet Anna-Maria, when suddenly I saw her going up along the same street in the direction of the monastery. I approached her and related to her the events in the crypt. She asked me if I believed in reincarnation, to which I replied that I was open to most things, but one thing I was sure of was that there is life after death. Anna-Maria added that I might have had a connection with the place, that I was blessed, and that I was so lucky. I would therefore have to stay open and listen to all the messages that I was going to receive along the way. She continued that there would be something very important for me to know. The fact that I was alone when this happened was very significant. There was no mistake that the message was meant only for me. She emphasised again that I should stay very aware, and we hugged and separated. I did not know what to think. I had heard that sometimes strange things happen along this pilgrimage, but I did not imagine anything would happen to me. It was so odd.

While walking like a zombie back to my lodging, I met up with Monique. As it was the feast of Rioja, everyone was meeting in the square to dance and have a drink. The music was blaring out of the loudspeaker and I wondered if we would be able to sleep, as I knew the Spanish people did not go to bed early. At least with all the food stalls we would not starve! As it happened, all the music was turned off at 11.00pm in consideration of everyone.

We were sharing our refuge with pilgrims of different nations and I loved the fact that, even if we could not speak each other's language, we could understand and respect one another. There was a rule in all refuges, which had been respected until that day. The rule states that everyone has to be back at the refuge by 10.00pm. As two French men had not made it back by curfew, we all decided to be considerate and leave the light on so they would not get hurt or bump into anyone's bunk. Late in the evening they returned, drunk, obviously having enjoyed La Rioja's wines too much. They made a racket, waking everyone and they were even insulting towards two Brazilian men. We have to love everyone, but sometimes, it can be hard. My experience of the day had left me worn out, but I could not fall back to sleep, as I was revisiting the day's events.

Before starting our day on 10 June 2010, Monique and I went to a post office on the other side of the bridge to send some items back home to lighten our backpacks. We hiked mostly on dirt roads through beautiful fields of cereals as far as the eye could see, and Monique went on ahead of me. It was overcast. There were many tones of green and sometimes yellow due to the ripening of the cereals. I loved the soft track and my feet did too. I was taken by the beauty of the area; it was a perfect place to reflect on the events of the last few days.

Before Azofra, there was a fountain with a bench beside it on the top of a hill with a 360-degree view of mountains, valleys and green fields.

It was in this spot that I met Bernard from Germany. We sat silently in front of this gorgeous landscape, absorbing its beauty, each of us in our thoughts, until one of us broke the silence. Bernard was a very spiritual man. He talked about Saint Francis of Assisi's words: 'Soul and body are two different things', and how the soul has to listen and be open to new things, even if they are uncomfortable or challenging. I always knew from a very early age that body and soul were two different things, therefore, it was not a revelation, but I did not know that Saint Francis of Assisi had said these words. Like me, Bernard worked in palliative care, and this is probably why we connected so easily. One day, we will all die and no matter how many people will be around us, the hard work of leaving our body will be done by us only, as no one can help. This journey of death or birth can be done only by the individual. We are born alone and we will die alone, but not without revisiting our entire life. Both of us understood that at the end of our lives we would ask ourselves what we had achieved. Could we reverse our decisions, our mistakes? How many times has God given us the chance to reverse our bad decisions, but we do not want to listen? How many of us have not dealt with our mistakes out of shame or fear of being judged? Have we helped our neighbours? All the battles, the struggles, the nice houses, the bank account, all of these will become so insignificant and then the real meaning of life becomes defined. At the end, what really counts is how we have directed and lived our lives on this earth. In the last few hours before our passing, we will revisit our time here: the good or bad we have done, and our most intimate thoughts will be revealed to us. There will be no more pretence. Sometimes we meet an individual who is too confronting. I wondered if in that being we see our real selves and are challenged by this realisation. Maybe it is an opportunity to analyse honestly the innermost part of who we really are. On the path, I took the person I was talking to at face value. I did not care if they were a Lord or a pauper: they were just another human being with a burden. Everyone has something to deal with in their personal life on earth, and those on the path were looking for answers. At times along the pilgrimage, I had been the witness of the unravelling of the human soul.

Bernard and I talked for a long time in this ideal environment and hoped that we would meet again. He was quite surprised by the number of kilometres I was covering on a daily basis. He had started from Puente La Reina with a group of friends, but they were going too fast for him. Bernard's backpack was too heavy and he had made the decision to go his own way. I thanked God, as we would not have met otherwise, and I would have missed these wonderful spiritual exchanges. I knew there was a purpose in this meeting, as it would allow me to grow more spiritually. Before we separated, I gave him a little heart-shaped stone in memory of our exchanges on the Camino Frances and we hugged.

The rain had stopped by the time I reached the village of Azofra. At the end of the village there was a fountain known as 'Fuente de los Romeros' in celebration of the pilgrims coming from Rome. I was crossing a valley far from any habitation and I noticed a highway parallel to the path. I could not hear the noise of the trucks and cars. It felt as though they were two different worlds. There was mine and there was the other, with its vehicles and their occupants representing the outside world continuing on with day-to-day life. Two parallel worlds which would never re-join, never know each other's existence and aspirations. This imagery was very powerful, as we all have parallel roads in our lives. I kept on looking at the trucks and cars going back and forth, when suddenly I became aware of a deeper realisation: I was living something wonderful and there beside me was a life I did not want to be part of anymore. On the path, everything was simple. In the past, not long ago, I had a connection with this other existence, but no more. All of a sudden, I became scared of returning to that world, as I had lost the link with it gradually, unknowingly, step by step. An imperceptible change had crept into me. I wanted my children and their love. I wanted them to keep on loving me as much I loved them, but I did not want to be part of that world.

At the entrance to the village of Cirueña, there was a feeling of abandonment and death and I shivered when I crossed it. It was a ghost town, with lots of cold, empty, modern houses with courtyards and an empty golf course. There was no life and the village was dying. A lot of modern houses had been built in this area perhaps to make a 'quick buck', or perhaps someone had had the idea of bringing life to this village and it had not worked. Maybe the global financial crisis was the culprit. All the houses were now empty-looking, like modern, sad concrete blocks.

At the refuge, I was welcomed by a big man. Perhaps he was a twin of 'Ferragut', the Syrian giant, I thought, and so I named him 'Ferragut'. He showed me to a bunk. There was a sense of heaviness in this refuge. Monique was already there and later on Bernard arrived. The refuge was filling up quickly as more rain was on its way and the next village was about six kilometres further along the path. I was checking my backpack when from down below I heard loud voices: 'Ferragut' was screaming at whoever it was, sending away some Spanish pilgrims quite abruptly. I felt ill at ease. I did not like the way he was talking to these people and I saw on Bernard's face that he was feeling the same way.

My sister rang and while speaking to her on my mobile, I could hear 'Ferragut' shouting again. I learnt that he had sent away a father and his 10-year-old son, Roan, because the lodging was full. When I learnt that, I wanted to give my bunk to the little one, but it was too late: they had left. Bernard and I were feeling quite uncomfortable about the way 'Ferragut' was treating the pilgrims and Bernard went to see if there was another place in the village where we could stay. He came back later after having no success: Ferragut's lodging was the only one. I was so sad and could not stop thinking about this little boy who would have to walk six kilometres more to find a place to sleep. My heart was heavy. This was not the way to act on the path.

Bernard and I talked again for a long time in the kitchen where 'Ferragut' was preparing our evening meal of pasta and lentils in a huge pan. We sat around the kitchen table and each ate out of a wooden bowl with a wooden spoon, like real monks, and shared a traditional pilgrim's meal, accompanied by some bread and an apple. To our surprise, 'Ferragut' became quite amicable and the heavy feeling disappeared. After the meal we all went to the Church of San Andres for a blessing. 'Ferragut' was doing the blessing. I could not believe it and I saw his other, gentle side. A group of five Estonian pilgrims who were members of a choir started to sing in their native tongue and a miracle happened, as we were all carried away by these captivating voices.

During the night, I kept waking up as I could not sleep properly. Rain was pouring down and I was worried about the little boy who had been sent away. As I was on the top bunk, I decided to climb down and leave early. I found a note in my shoes from Bernard with the lovely words: 'Keep on opening your heart and arms to people close to you and others. It has been a gift meeting you'. It had been a gift for me too, I thought. On 11 June 2010, I started alone, in the rain. The day would be tough and I got lost. I met Bernard in front of Santo Domingo de la Calzada. It was nice to see each other again so soon, and we hugged, hoping that we would meet again. We never did.

In this lovely medieval town, many shops displayed pictures, carvings and pottery of a rooster, which is the symbol of the most well-known legend on the Camino Frances: the miracle of the hanged man. In 1130, Hagonel, a young German pilgrim, was on his way to

339

Santiago with his parents when they stopped for the night at a refuge in Santo Domingo de la Calzada. A young maid wanted to flirt with Hagonel, but he refused her advances. Angry, she hid some silver in his bag and when he was leaving, she reported the theft. Consequently, Hagonel was hanged. His grieving parents took the road to Santiago de Compostela with heavy hearts and fervently prayed upon their arrival in the cathedral. On their return, they stopped at the tree where their son had been hanged and found him still alive. Hagonel informed his parents that he had been under the protection of Saint James while they went to Santiago de Compostela. His parents decided to go and talk to the judge who was at his table eating roasted rooster and hen. Hearing their story, the judge started to laugh and shouted, 'Your son is as alive as these roasted hen and rooster! Can you bet that they will start singing on my plate?' As soon as he finished speaking, the hen cackled and the rooster sang. The judge was bowled over and asked to have Hagonel taken down, and instead, he hanged the young maid. To commemorate this miracle, one white hen and five white roosters are kept in a splendid hen-house in the centre of the cathedral. I went for a coffee and enjoyed a delicious pastry in the shape of a rooster in commemoration of this event, but I did not give it a chance to sing!

Santo Domingo de la Calzada was named after Santo Domingo who was a builder. He erected a bridge over the Rio Oja to help the pilgrims cross the swamp. Along the Calle Mayor, there were beautiful 16th and 17th century manors with their coat of arms on their facades. The Santo Domingo hostel still welcomes pilgrims and this has never stopped since the 12th century. Soon, I was out of the town and found my way through majestic green fields. It was cold, raining on and off, and the sky was looking more threatening with its heavy grey, black and white clouds. I was concerned that this was not good for my chest, but I had to keep on going. I arrived in the village of Grañon, which had been built on the top of a hill. Close to its church, I met a group of French pilgrims who had been walking for one week. They had covered 100 kilometres over the space of a few days and they were on their way back to France. They invited me for a coffee, but I declined their invitation. Something or someone was stopping me and I listened to my intuition. On the side of the church, there was a tower. As curiosity overpowered me, I walked up the steps and noticed the sign: 'Take your shoes off before entering'. I did so and kept on going up, and to my surprise, it led to a refuge run by Franciscan monks. I was welcomed by a warm atmosphere: peace was coming from everywhere. I was offered a lovely hot chamomile tea and rested for a little while. I spotted a piano and a guitar, presumably left there for the pilgrims. Shortly after I arrived, the little boy, Roan, appeared with his father and grandfather. I approached them, wondering how they had managed the night before. Roan's father had a sharp manner and I was told in a few words that all went well. They had stayed an hour in the village waiting for the rain to clear, had a meal, and walked the last six kilometres to Santo Domingo de la Calzalda. They had covered 36 kilometres and would be doing a small walk today. My heart went out to Roan and I gave him a big hug and he went with his father to play some music on the piano. I knew that under the father's cold appearance there was a warm heart beating. I was amazed at Roan's endurance: he was such a brave little boy. He was looking after his backpack and all his belongings like us grown-ups. What a lesson of courage he was giving to us all. As I left, I told him how proud I was of him. Two young Australian men from Mackay came in and we had a quick chat, but I had to leave so that I could reach my next destination of Viloria de Rioja. I had been very worried about Roan, and God had directed me to this refuge so I could find peace within me to continue my journey.

I left the main road for the countryside. I got so used to climbing up and down that I did not seem to take notice of the hills anymore. I was just enjoying the moment when the skies opened up close to Redecilla del Camino, the first village of Castile. It was bitterly cold. In no time, the track became barely passable. The mud was thick and deep, it was slippery and I was scared that I would develop another cold, but I had no choice: I had to be strong. I was halfway up the climb when a car passed me, and without any consideration for the pilgrims, the driver splashed mud all over us. I got frustrated and I wondered how anyone could be so stupid to drive a car on such a road. The car then skidded, but without damage, and the driver made the wise decision to drive back.

It was still very cold when I arrived at the little village of Viloria de Rioja, in the province of Burgos where Santo Domingo de la Cazalda was presumably born. The refuge was a little bit out of the way, but it was worth it as Orietta's whole-hearted welcome made me forget all the challenges of the day. Some wood was burning in the stove in the dormitory to warm my heart and body and dry my clothes and boots. Orietta and Acacio were friends of the world-famous writer, Paulo Coelho, who had helped them to create this simple little Heaven for pilgrims. They greeted us in the spirit of the Camino. They informed me that they had done the pilgrimage many times from Saint-Jean-Pied-de-Port and had measured the distance between the two cities with a metric wheel and had come to the conclusion that one would have to add another 60 kilometres to the official calculation of the distance to Santiago de Compostela. Monique had already arrived and informed me that she had learnt about a geographer, Madeleine Griselin, who had studied the gradients of Saint James' Way, starting from Le Puy-en-Velay. The geographer discovered that the total of the gradients over the 1,500 kilometres was 21,040 metres, which is two and a half times that of Mount Everest. The total gradients from Saint-Jean-Pied-de-Port to Santiago de Compostela are 8,300 metres, that is to say, one Mount Everest. This information was good for my ego, but I will always wonder how many Mount Everests I climbed, as no study has been done from Vezelay!

Refreshed by a good night's sleep in this lovely lodging, Monique and I left Orietta and Acacio's refuge the next morning. It was still raining and a penetrating cold wind was getting through to my bones. We were high in the mountains. I would not have been surprised if it had snowed. It was a day of mud, wind and rain, and I needed to focus all my concentration on the slippery track. There were very few pilgrims and from time to time, the Spanish police in their police car would come along, checking that no one had injured themselves. This kind of consideration generated a sense of safety.

I passed Villamayor del Rio in the province of Burgos,

and at Belorado I rested for a little while at a coffee-bar, which was very inviting with its display of international flags on each side of the driveway. Not far from the castle there were the San Caprasio grottos used as dwellings by some hermits. The rain had stopped, but the muddy paths were still requiring all my attention. I did not mind: I was becoming stronger as the days passed.

I stopped in Tosantos at a café for a light lunch and some warmth, as the wind had not eased. At a table, I talked with Joseph from Serbia. He had a big burden to carry and as he was leaving the café, I took a little heart-shaped stone that I had carried from the Massif Central out of my pocket. I did not know why I had to give it to him, as it had been in my pocket for so long. I guessed he needed it more than I did and it would be a reminder of our meeting. I also met Arlette and Pierre from Clermont-Ferrand in France. They were leaving the dangerous, muddy track for the main road, and I decided to do the same. As soon as I was on the main road I realised that the danger was worse here, as the trucks did not reduce their speed and they even drove over the embankment. At the first opportunity, I went back to the slippery track; I preferred the danger on the trail. I did not want to be crushed or end up under the wheels of a monstruous truck. The state of the track was difficult, but the task did me good. I was accepting the track the same way that I accept what comes my way in life, as nothing happens without a reason. With the difficulty of the track, I was getting stronger. I had to learn to have God more in my life and to trust that, at the end, all would be well.

At San Felices, in the middle of the fields of wheat, I passed beside the ninth century ruins of Santo Felices de

Oca's old monastery, which only had one arch left. Eventually, I made it to Villafranca Montes de Oca, where I would be staying for the night. I found the refuge and Monique was already there. I had finished the 10th week of my pilgrimage on 12 June 2010.

WEEK ELEVEN

'The madness of the Meseta and two little crosses'

I was ready to go by 5.00am on 13 June 2010. It was pitch black and with the rain, the state of the track would be precarious with a climb from 900 metres to 1,163 metres in the space of three kilometres. I had not slept at all, as in this 38-bed dormitory, half of the pilgrims had 'rocked' me with their snoring lullaby! By 4.00am, I could not stand it anymore, earplugs or not, and I had to go to the kitchen where I lay down on a wooden bench. I could not sleep there either. I thought I would have to complain to God about this human attribute and ask him to modify it! For safety reasons, I had to wait patiently until 6.00am before I could head out on the path again. A pilgrim from Mongolia joined me in the kitchen and went directly to the fridge to look for something to eat and I realised that he was probably expecting a breakfast to be provided or he had nothing to eat in his small backpack. I had a cake left in mine and I handed over half to him. He hesitated, and there seemed to be a sense of embarrassment on his part. I insisted and wondered whether it was my white hair and the fact that I was a mature-aged woman that made him feel ill at ease in accepting this little bit of cake. I did not know the traditions of Mongolia. I boiled some water and offered him a cup of tea and we shared our frugal breakfast of half a piece of dry cake and tea in silence. Then, hurriedly, he left without saying anything.

At day-break I was ready for the challenge of the day ahead. At first the steep track was very muddy and slippery, and I was quite proud of myself when I got out of a difficult section with my two legs not broken and no twisted ankles. Some pilgrims had slept in the dense oak forest under a protected area, probably caught by the rain in this dangerous stretch. They would not have been able to go forward. Lucky for them it was 2010, for in the Middle Ages, this range was teeming with brigands and wolves. The wolves are still in these forests, but they are scared of the humans and that was lucky for me too, considering my fear of dogs. Besides, it was not advisable to trek this area alone. I had heard this before. At a look-out I could see the mountains I had crossed and further on there was a cross marking the death of a pilgrim. This did not dampen my will and I accomplished the climb in the wilderness alone, enjoying the challenges with my whole being. My exhilaration changed when I reached a tableland with forest and conifer overgrowth on both sides. Thanks to the rain, the wide track of red soil had become a hideous, impassable path of slippery mud. After a while, the slippery mud ahead of me was transformed into a stony track. I thought it could have been a mirage.

I walked among a plantation of pines for kilometres and I saw another cross which marked a pilgrim's death. I had been well protected and I was safe. At times, annoyance would flare within me because of the state of the track, but my faith that I would make it never failed. The more I walked, the more certain I became.

In this area, a miracle happened in 1108. A sinful Frenchman had decided to marry and have a family. But he could not have a child and thought it was because of

347

the life he had led and so he decided to walk the Saint James' Way and implored the saint to help him. Eventually, his wife gave birth to a son named James. When James reached the age of 15, the family left France for Santiago de Compostela. As they arrived at the Montes de Oca, James became unwell and died. The mother begged Saint James to return her son to her. At the burial, the young man got up and they kept on walking to Santiago de Compostela, just as the saint had asked them. Maybe this legend shows us to have faith.

I was walking day in and day out in this area and loving it. I crossed over the ravine of the Cerrada de la Pedraja, over the Puerto de la Pedraja Pass and into the Montes de Oca. I passed in front of the hermitage that San Juan de Ortega built for the pilgrims after his return from Jerusalem. At the Alto de la Pedraja, suddenly the forest ended and far away, I could see the village and monastery of San Juan de Ortega. The monastery is still used by pilgrims as a refuge. The church there was constructed in 1147. San Juan of Ortega's remains are in a very simple, unadorned sarcophagus in this church. In 1960, the sarcophagus was opened and inside some Roman cloths were found, along with San Juan's paten and chalice. There is a statue of Saint Domingo de la Calzada represented as an elderly man with a long, grey beard like a hermit. He is covered in a black monk's cloth, holding a staff and he is bare-foot. At his feet are the legendary hen and rooster. Both San Juan of Ortega and Saint Domingo de la Calzada were great builders of bridges and routes to make life easier for the pilgrims.

As I was leaving San Juan de Ortega, I took a very rough, stony path, which led me through an oak forest. I looked back at San Juan de Ortega's village. Soon I was in Atapuerca where, at the entrance to the village, I saw a big sign on which the face of an ancient western European was drawn. I was mesmerised, as some of its facial features were similar to the first inhabitants of Australia: the Aborigines. As always, Australia was never far from me. The findings at Atapuerca were discovered when the mountains were cut to make way for a railway line. Tools from more than one million years ago were found in the area. The site is now UNESCO World Heritage listed. While I was looking at the poster at the entrance to Atapuerca, I met a French couple, Michelle and Robert from Limousin in France. I exchanged just a few words with Michelle, as I noticed that Robert was in a hurry to take to the track: he was walking as fast as a hare. Seeing this little scene, I was thankful not to have a constant companion and to be able to walk Saint James' Way alone at my own pace.

At this altitude, it was windy and the wind was going through to my bones. As I reached our destination first, I waited patiently on a bench until Monique arrived and later on we were joined by Arlette and Pierre, who I had met the previous day. I had a good night's sleep that night, having been spared the snoring lullaby, and the four of us left late at around 8.00am, each going our own separate ways. The next stage was Burgos. It was still bitterly cold - minus four degrees - and very windy. The uphill, rocky trail took me along the edge of an oak-tree forest before I reached the Termino de Atapuerca Pass at 1,060 metres, where a tall cross and a cairn (a pile of stones) stand. My path crossed with that of a young man, Jonathan from Austria. We connected right away and we talked about spirituality and direction in one's life. As we were exchanging our views, I was bowled over at the similarities between this young man and my son, David. Both young men had the same visions for life, such as honesty, integrity and doing good in the world. They were even physically similar. It was Jonathan's 29th birthday and bit by bit I understood why it was that I had to meet him. He was born the same year I had lost my unborn child and, strangely enough, it felt as though my child was talking to me through him, but I kept that special moment in a little corner of my heart. I asked him what he would like to have for his birthday and, to my surprise, he said, 'A can of coke and a big Mac!' As we were trekking we shared more about our experiences on the path, then Jonathan said the most beautiful words to me. 'Claude, I knew I would meet an angel along the Saint James' Way and today I met her'. Tears came to my eyes. I was touched and humbled by his words. My thoughts went to my children, grandchild and their partners who I was missing so much. I also thought about my unborn child, who always had a special place in my heart.

Along a long, flat stretch with cereal fields on each side, we saw a drink machine and I offered Jonathan his birthday present: a can of coke. At the entrance to Burgos, we separated and I gave him a little heart-shaped stone. To get to the centre of Burgos, the pilgrim has to go through eight kilometres of an industrial zone. After being in the full wilderness, I could not face it and joined Monique who was waiting for me at a bus stop at Villafria. I did not enjoy the bus ride, and my conscience was killing me. It felt as though I was betraying everything I had stood for during so many weeks. However, my scruples eased a little bit at the number of young and old pilgrims who were doing the same. But I promised myself that one day I would walk these eight kilometres.

In Burgos, it was raining and cold. Monique and I looked for a refuge and found one with only bunks and showers, which was close to the cathedral in the centre of Burgos. I dropped my backpack to visit this wonderful Gothic cathedral, dedicated to the Virgin Mary. It is one of the biggest cathedrals in Europe. Its construction began in 1221 and its works went on and off for another two hundred years. Its main facade was inspired by the French Gothic cathedrals, like at Reims. Inside there were some Renaissance and Baroque decorations. From the outside of the cathedral you can see the 15th century steep spires of German influence. The cathedral is so big that I needed more than a few hours to visit this magnificent work of art and as I came out I ran into Jonathan, who had not yet found a McDonald's, but was sure to find one!

At the refuge, the 'hospitaliera', Udi from Hungary, gave me a foot massage and to my surprise, she said, 'Claude, you have to let go of all the sorrow and pain you are carrying in your heart. Now is the time for you to do it'. Startled, I smiled and without a word I went back to my bunk. There were a lot of pilgrims going back and forth, but I did not hear them, as I was so deep in thought, trying to analyse what had happened since my meeting with Amar at Orisson and the intriguing events in the monastery of Santa Maria la Real at Najera. Had other pilgrims had similar experiences? Could it be that there was more than meeting pilgrims? Was this another explanation for why I wanted to do this pilgrimage: to have these experiences? I knew I had been pushed to do it,

351

but why? Do we leave our burdens behind along this magical path? I was engrossed in my thoughts until my eyes caught a little man coming into the dormitory: it was Roan. He smiled at me and took possession of a top bunk just in front of me. He unrolled his sleeping bag, took out some exercise books and did his homework.

It was late and night was falling as Monique, Arlette, Pierre and I went out for dinner. As we were walking along the narrow streets, we met Udi, the 'hospitaliera'. We ate together and for the first time I had some tapas and the best thick hot chocolate ever. Udi said that she could tell me a lot of things that I needed to hear, but her English was not good enough and restrained her from doing so. The rules in all of the refuges in France or in Spain state that you are allowed to stay only one night unless you are sick. As I was still chesty, I was allowed to stay another night. Monique could not see herself starting out alone again, after so many days of starting our daily trip and meeting up again at night, so we stayed at a hotel where I enjoyed a long, hot bath. I visited the monastery of Santa Maria la Real de Huelgas, which was founded in 1187 and still used by the nuns, but was open for one and a half hours every day. After this visit, I spent time in the streets of Burgos looking for fruit, as it was fruit I missed the most on the path. Eating sandwiches every day after a while was kind of boring. I could not find any fruit shop in the centre of Burgos and I asked a Spanish woman where I could find one. She told me I would find them only in supermarkets. With my limited Spanish I asked her the way and she gave a detailed reply: left, right, across, left, first, second, third street and so on. I would get lost for sure, as her explanation was like a maze. My confusion would have shown on my face as I was distracted by her hand gestures and also, she spoke Spanish so quickly. Then she decided to walk with me and left me at the entrance of a supermarket. Both of us had a lovely time, even though neither of us could speak the other's language. She explained, still in the language of the hands and in Spanish, how to find my way back to the cathedral via a short-cut.

On my way back, I crossed over a bridge and somehow I turned right instead of left and took a small alley on my left and was drawn towards a shop window with different Christian items, books and paintings. I went in and asked the sales person, who could not speak either English or French, if she had two crosses made of wood. I used my new-found knowledge of the language of the hands, plus a few words in Spanish. I chose the crosses of Jerusalem, which were made from an olive tree. In one corner of the shop there was an easel, some paint and a paint brush, and I asked if she could write with her paintbrush a name on each cross, but I got a negative answer. Then I asked for a pen and on the back of each cross I wrote my parents' names and showing each cross to the shop-assistant, I said, 'Para mi madre y mi padre'. The shop-assistant provided a tin of varnish and put some on each name to seal them. At the thought of my parents, tears rolled down my cheeks and I left with the knowledge that I would have to leave the crosses somewhere. Why in Spain? Where? These were the questions, but I did not have the answers. I just knew that I had to carry them and leave them somewhere on the path, and that I would have to trust and listen to my heart. I was certain, however, that I would find a place much nicer than the one close to the pulp mill before Navarrete.

The next day would be a difficult day, as I was embarking on the high plateau of the Meseta. Since the beginning of my pilgrimage, my sister and I had daily contact by phone and text message. I had made a decision to reduce the amount of contact we were having, but I was concerned to tell her. As I was starting the dreadful climb of the Meseta, I needed to have no contact with anyone, including her, as I wanted to go more deeply into my soul without any distraction from the external world. I knew it would be hard for her to comprehend and I was fearful that she would not understand, but she complied with my wish and I loved her more, as I knew how scared she and my children would be until we spoke again. I told her that I would meet Monique at the end of every day. For everyone's peace of mind, I promised that I would stay in touch by sending her a text message on a daily basis, but that would be all. I did not share what the Meseta was about. It is a long stretch of vast, flat plains in central-northern Spain between Burgos and Astorga, that is to say a distance of 250 kilometres, without much shade or water. Furthermore, it could be terribly hot or bitterly cold. The villages are far apart from each other, but that did not worry me as I had known this experience in France. I had read quite a lot of negative things about the Meseta, such as the loneliness and the monotony of the landscape that can prove quite challenging to the extent that some pilgrims had lost their minds along that track. To escape it, a lot of pilgrims take a bus or a train from Burgos to Leon where they re-start their pilgrimage.

On 16 June 2010, Monique and I left Burgos in the cold rain and blustering wind. The Meseta was showing us what to expect. The rain became icy and on the track I felt I was walking on a lake of mud. My boots were full of rain and I could hear 'clog, clog' at every step. I wished for a bush to protect me even a little bit from the icy wind, but there was nothing for many kilometres. We came to a village and stopped for a coffee and I took off my water-proof jacket. I was wet through. Water had gotten everywhere, even into the inside pockets, and I could see water behind the camera screen and my Dictaphone was wet too. These had been my companions and witnesses to my pilgrimage and my thoughts since the beginning. To finish it off, all the clothes in my backpack were wet. I felt like screaming and suddenly I sensed the Meseta's madness, erupting like a volcano. I was so mad and worried that my camera and Dictaphone would never work again. I did not care so much about myself and my chest, my clothes and my body - all of which could dry out - but I was worried for my camera and Dictaphone.

We left the warmth and comforting atmosphere of the café for the icy wind and rain and the muddy track, which was not flat either. Perhaps the scenery was nice, but I could not appreciate it, as I had to concentrate on the task and not slip. Suddenly, my anger somehow turned into rage. It was so hard to walk in these conditions. It was very treacherous, both on the flat surface and over the hills. I was boiling inside. The reality of the Meseta was taking hold of me. I had been told that if anything like this happened, I should just let the anger come with open arms, as it would be good for me and enable me to let go of all my life's frustrations and sadness. That was easier said than done! This quick anger brought me back to some periods in my life when, at my lowest, I did not want to have God with me.

I had been so furious with Him for bringing so much pain into my being. He had always been part of my life. Over the years, He has been my best mate, my confidant, and He has helped me survive in times of crisis. He was always there for me. He was my trusted companion, helping me to overcome the hurdles of life. I knew that with patience and love, there would be better times around the corner and I knew that after all the sacrifices, all would be worth it, as I had Him by my side. I had built a huge fortress around myself away from the outside world, just keeping God in my heart and soul. He was my saviour at the end of the day. Then one day, my controlled anger and pain had surfaced like the eruption of a volcano. All the softness and love was gone in a second and I left God, not wanting to connect with Him ever again or have anything to do with Him. I felt I was better off without Him and pulled Him out of my heart, thinking it would be forever, as I felt He had abandoned me. But God had other plans. He did not want to lose His child, so He brought me back into His life by sending me people who would open my heart to Him again. It was a slow, very slow process, like taking baby steps. I had to learn to trust Him again and to do this I had to be honest with myself, others and God, as all are inter-connected. I realised that God had put sign-posts throughout my life, but I had not wanted to read them. Too afraid, I had learnt to pretend. It was a kind of security and it all blew up in my face. It had been the loneliest time of my life, as I had lost trust and love in all humanity and God. It took time before I came to accept that God was not responsible, but that it was our environment, our society, our programming and especially myself that was to blame. God had given me tools to be in charge of my own destiny and I just had to take them and follow what I was supposed to do. Events in my life had happened. I had opportunities to change its course, but I did not take them, too scared of the unknown. In time, I started to open my heart and my eyes to messages. I understood why certain events had happened. I had received messages just as everyone receives them if they are prepared to look and listen to their souls and the little voice within. I realised that God would give me the opportunity to see what my life purpose was. He knew that I had to make changes. He had been patient and had waited for me to see and learn. His love had never stopped, even though I had stopped loving Him. With time, the anger left me and as we say, 'After the storm, there is the calm'.

At Rabe de las Calzadas, the real beginning of the Meseta, I could see the start of the desert, which is characteristic of this region, from the top of the plateau I was standing on. I had seen it in the rain, which was strange, as it did not seem to look like a desert. At an altitude of about 850 metres, the plateau was clayish and stony. It did not stop raining all day. I was tired and my rage had quietened down by the time I arrived at Hornillos del Camino. The main refuge was full, but luckily Monique and I found another one, although with very few amenities: one toilet and one wash basin to share with about 20 pilgrims, but we could use the bathrooms of the other refuge. We did not care much, as we had a roof above our heads. In the refuge there were no more newspapers to put in my drenched boots, so I approached the only shopkeeper in the town. She must have felt so sorry for me because she gave me all her daily newspapers free of charge, plus some cheese. I was warmed by her gentle kindness. Blessings can come in little parcels and from anywhere.

On my way back, close to the refuge, I noticed a monument with a rooster on it in the main street. I had heard that during the Napoleonic times, the soldiers had come to this village and had taken all the chickens and hidden them under their coats. The villagers asked for their chickens back, but the soldiers denied taking them until a clever little chicken slipped out from under a coat. Proof in hand, the soldiers had to give back some of the chickens and the rooster became the symbol of Hornillos del Camino.

Back at the refuge, I was informed that the pilgrim in the next bunk, Claude from France, was a terrible snorer and that we would all suffer, again! After writing in my diary, I suddenly got up and asked Monique to hurry up as we had to go to the only café in the street right away. I did not know what the rush was, but it had to be now. We arrived at the little café. I had my hands on the handle when the door opened and I was taken aback. Ulf from Sweden, who I had met in Saint-Jean-Pied-de-Port, was standing just in front of me on his way out of the café, and we fell into each other's arms, so surprised to see one another again. Seeing this, all the patrons laughed and clapped. To be able to stay in the café, Ulf had to order another meal and poor Monique had to endure another English-speaking dinner. She did not mind, but told me that she regretted not having been a good student of English during high school. Later, I left with Ulf and we talked outside for a little while, then we said our goodbyes and each went back to our own refuge. This was no coincidence: I was supposed to meet Ulf one more time and if I had not listened to my intuition and gone to the café, our paths would not have crossed again.

I left alone very early the next morning and it was still incredibly cold, windy, and very muddy. However, there was some blue in the sky and I hoped the sun would come out. I had been told that I should walk the last two kilometres before San Bol alone, slowly and quietly, yet while I was making my solitary way there, I heard some footsteps behind me. It was Ulf who had changed his mind and had decided to start earlier too. We walked hand in hand as far as Hontanas. Ulf said how privileged he felt to have met me at Saint-Jean-Pied-de-Port, as our conversations had opened his heart and he had been able to help himself and others along the path. This time it was me who shared my hurts, my pain, my sorrow, my weakness. I had started to open up a little with Bernard a few days ago, and Ulf was my next listener. Through the sharing, my healing process was slowly taking place. Close to a memorial, I saw Ulf bend down to pick up a small stone and put it in his jacket. Shortly afterwards, we saw the small village of Hontanas down in the valley where Ulf would stop. Before saying goodbye, Ulf asked me to do a little ritual that he had done with other pilgrims. With eyes closed, we faced each other, our fingers touching to allow our healing energy to pass through one another, as two caring friends.

We had our breakfast on the terrace of a small café. Our journey together was to finish shortly afterwards. Ulf put his hands in his jacket and took out the little stone, saying that, once I had finished dealing with my fears and pain, I should let go of the pain to find peace again. I was to throw away this stone, which would symbolise the letting go of all my sorrows. Deep, almost sisterly love empowered me. I was so touched by his words. A young man and a mature-aged woman had met along this path. They had shared precious exchanges and they knew that they would never meet again. I had given support to Ulf in his time of need and it was now his turn. I found this perfect and we hugged and said our goodbyes as two wonderful and caring friends. Two friends had met at this part of the Camino Frances, never to forget each other. Each had been a listening ear and had helped the other to release their pain. From now on they would meander on a new path, released from some of their burdens. For a long time after we walked away from each other, we waved goodbye until I disappeared along the Meseta.

I wanted to walk alone to reflect on what had happened, but another pilgrim crossed my path: Nicole from Marseille. We arrived at San Anton's Monastery where, in 1146, a hospital was founded by the Order of Saint Anthony, but nowadays only ruins remain with the exception of one section. As a tradition, the monks would give the pilgrims a small cross in the shape of a 'T' as a symbol of protection for crossing this arid part of the Castile. This cross is called a 'Tau' and is still carried today by the Franciscan brothers. There was a small gift shop at the monastery, so for good measure I bought a Tau, as one can never be too sure!

On my way to Castrojeriz, I passed under the arch of its ruined church, which went from one side of the road to the other. As the weather had lifted, I could enjoy the countryside with its carpets of green wheat and barley fields: true enchantment to the eye. Then I walked under a row of large trees with green leaves for about two kilometres. This part of the Meseta did not resemble a desert to me!

On a mountain above the small medieval village of Castrojeriz, the ruins of a castle built by the Templars dominated the large plain of the Rio Odrilla. Castrojeriz was built along the Camino Frances, and the path crosses it in its entirety. There is much history from the Middle Ages, as nine churches and seven hospitals were built there. On one of the walls of the Castrojeriz Church, two skulls were carved with two crossed bones under them. It felt gruesome. Nicole and I wandered the streets, blending in with the senior citizens who were happy to live and finish their lives in this lovely village There was a kind of peace and contentment on their rugged faces, as if they had learnt the wisdom of letting the flow of life pass by, and that in the end, all would be well.

The next morning I was ready to attack another day on the Meseta, hoping to leave behind me all the bitumen roads. I took the old Roman road leading to the foot of Mostelares and caught up with Nicole who was at the beginning of her Camino and therefore feeling the difficulty of the physical pain of back and leg aches that all new pilgrims experience. The steep, stony hill directed me to the Alto de Mostelares, a plateau at an altitude of 900 metres, and from the top I could see the yellow Meseta spreading in front of me without any end, looking like an arid plain. I crossed the medieval bridge over the Rio Odrilla before climbing down a steep hill to La Fuente del Piojo. A little bit later, we arrived at what looked like a church. The doors were open and I climbed down a few stairs. I was surprised by its small size: it would not take much time to visit it.

Nicole came in behind me. As I entered the church, I was approached by a 'hospitaliero', Christian from Germany, who asked if I was 'Claude from Australia'. Surprised, I replied that I was. Oh dear, would this be a repeat of what had happened along the way in France, at La Chatre and other places? Then Christian asked me if I was planning to stay overnight in this chapel. I had not planned to at all, but I looked around the building and felt a surge of energy coming through my body. I replied in the affirmative and he told me to wait where I was, as in fifteen minutes, someone would bring some messages to me. While waiting, I looked around this little church called Ermita de San Nicolas, which had no electricity or water. It had been founded in 1171 and had been used as a hospital. The nave had been divided into different sections. At the far end, there was the chapel with its altar with some chairs placed in a half circle. In one corner, some capes were hanging on a coat hanger, and in the centre of the nave was a long, wooden table and benches. At the other end of the chapel there were eight bunks and four mattresses to put on the ground for pilgrims and a spiral staircase leading to the sleeping area for the 'hospitalieros'. It was run by the Confraternita di San Jacopo di Compostella of Perugia in Italy. This place felt mystical. I was waiting patiently for my messages, when I saw Udi, the 'hospitaliera' from Burgos, arriving. Udi hugged me and gave me caring words and messages of love and friendship. A few minutes later the doors of the Ermita closed: I had been fortunate and blessed to have arrived just before the place closed, as it would not re-open until mid-afternoon. I could have missed this magical event and the lovely messages that Udi passed on to me. I thought that when things are meant to be they will happen no matter what. At the back of the Ermita, I found a building with showers and a kitchen and I took this opportunity to do my chores. After that, I sat outside listening to the lovely concert given by the birds and I felt blessed to be in this environment. I did not care that the cold wind was neither good for my bones nor my chest.

I saw pilgrims passing by who I had already come across and asked them to inform Monique of my decision to stay at the Ermita if they met her. I had sent her text messages, but not having heard back from her, I was not sure whether she had received them.

By mid-afternoon, the doors of the Ermita opened again. Nicole and I met some young pilgrims from Ireland who were accompanied by a young Spanish priest, Juan. They played some hymns on their guitar; it was just simple and divine. At dusk, the doors closed again, the candles were lit and the magic and mysticism of the place surrounded us all. We went up to the chapel area, sat on the chairs, and soon Udi came carrying a jug of water and Christian a water-basin. Both had their shoulders covered by a cape with the emblem of Perugia on it. We were asked to remove our boots and socks. Udi poured some water on our left feet and collected the excess water in a basin, while Christian, his eyes fixed on our eyes, washed and dried our feet with gentleness and love in his movements, while saying a prayer. The energy of love for all humanity was caught in that moment. I was humbled by this rite and wondered if Christ had felt this humbleness when Mary Magdalene did this for him.

After the ceremony, we all ate around the long, wooden table. I was still overcome by these enchanted moments and how blessed I had been to stop there. At the end of the meal we washed the plates and all participated in a mass said by Juan. Each pilgrim added a few words in their specific language about their day and what had affected them the most. After a reflective time of meditation and personal prayers, I put my hand up and shared with everyone the story of the two crosses I had bought in Burgos for my parents. I asked if it would be possible to leave them in this special place, as I felt deep in my heart that it was where they belonged. I did not know the rules of the Ermita and told them if this was not possible, I would accept their answer with humility. After a little deliberation, Udi and Christian agreed. I went to fetch the crosses at the bottom of my backpack and asked Juan to bless them. He replied, 'Everyone will participate in their blessing'. At the end of the benediction, Juan delicately deposited the two crosses on the altar. The spirit of love was tangible in this chapel and my heart swelled at so much affection. In 2010 and 2011, some French and Australian pilgrims who are friends of mine visited the little chapel and saw the two crosses left for my parents. They were still there on the altar.

The next morning we all ate our breakfast together. I said a few words of thanks to all and hugged everyone, wishing them a good Camino. When I passed under the arch of the doorway, Udi started to sing a Hungarian folk song in my honour. I was overwhelmed. So much love was filling up my soul. Christian came towards me, gave me a hug and thanked me, as my request had touched his heart because he too had lost his parents. I took the road with Nicole, leaving behind the Ermita de San Nicolas, which would always have a special place in my heart and which I will never forget until the day I die, and even afterwards. We went over the Roman bridge of the Rio Pisuerga, known as Filtero, built during the 12th century. I looked back at the Ermita with some nostalgia as I was leaving my Maman and Papa there, but I knew they would be happy in that mystical place full of love. At the end of the bridge, a sign-post indicated we were entering the region of Palencia. The gravel track took me under some poplars, which ran parallel to the river, and we passed in front of the Ermita de la Virgen de la Piedad. It was going to be a hot day and we had been informed to make sure we were carrying enough water.

At the entrance to Boadilla del Camino, I saw a crumbling, rectangular building on a hill, and I wanted to go and investigate it. I asked Nicole whether she wanted to either wait or come with me. She decided to wait and I went on my own to see this strange building. The roof had fallen in and inside there were two circular buildings with a courtyard in the centre. I had to access it through a small opening. I walked around it a few times, still questioning the use of such a building, wishing I knew what it was, when suddenly I was overcome with sobbing. I did not know how long I stayed in this dilapidated, crumbling place, crying my heart out. I saw myself again going through the different stages of my life with its pain and sorrows. It felt like a small load had been taken off my shoulders, as if a small part of my past had left me. Like the transformation of a caterpillar, a new Claude was emerging. I stayed a bit longer, shaken, but I did not question why all these things were happening. Later, I

365

learnt that the building was used to keep doves and then I understood. A dove is a symbol of love and peace and represents the renewal of life. In the Bible, a dove symbolises deliverance and God's forgiveness.

Back at the village, I could not find Nicole. Worried, I went everywhere and asked everyone, but still I could not find her. I decided to walk forwards in the hope that I would catch up to her. I passed in front of the Santa Maria Church, which is impressive compared to the little village where many of the mud houses were crumbling down.

These last few days had been so important for me. I was happy to walk leisurely in nature all along the canal of the Castile with no one; it was like a breath of fresh air. This quietness was sent by God so that I could regenerate and listen to my heart and soul without interruption.

Slowly, I reached Fromista and ran into Juan and his group who informed me that they had passed Nicole at Boadilla del Camino and that she was waiting for me back there. I felt guilty, as I should have been more scrupulous in my checking, and I waited in the main square of Fromista, hoping Nicole would catch up to me. An hour and a half later, I again saw Juan, who was quite surprised to see me still waiting. He suggested that I keep on going to my next stage and he would contact me if he saw Nicole. Before leaving Fromista, I visited one of the jewels of Spanish architecture: the 11th century Church of San Martin of Tours.

I arrived in the village of Poblacion de Campos, which originated from the ninth century. By the middle of the 12th century, it was under the Order of Saint John of Jerusalem. At that time, this town had two hospitals and the beautiful Church of Santa Magdalena.

I was finishing the 11th week of my pilgrimage and I did not know which day it was or how many kilometres I had covered. Nothing mattered anymore except the path at my feet.

WEEK TWELVE

'Why are you leaving me?'

The 20 June 2010 was a sunny, but cold day. After a good night's sleep in a quiet refuge, I picked up my backpack once more, not knowing what the day ahead would bring. As I took to the road I was horror-stricken, for the path went along a main road for kilometres and kilometres. I found a symbol indicating a variant which would extend my journey. I did not care about the extra kilometres in this case and I went in the direction it suggested. On the way, I met Juan the priest walking over a bridge. He too had wanted to take the variant away from the busy road and, once more, I was protected, as the track was badly sign-posted and Juan pointed me in the right direction.

The trail followed the Rio Ucieza in the direction of Villovieco. The grass and the flowers were knee-high. With the recent rain, the ground was so wet that my boots and socks became drenched in no time, though I was not bothered by this. How strange! We strolled together, but after a short time I went my own way, as I needed to be alone. I had felt that a special hand was taking me and that Juan also wanted space. I covered a bit more ground and then sat on a fallen tree. Slowly, I started contemplating things very deeply and without any distraction in this quiet and peaceful area.

At the sight of the red poppies along the embankments, my thoughts went to Ulf who loved them so much and in this enchanting spot, I recalled his words about the 'little Claude' who would have to release her pain at the right moment. Was today going to be the day? Slowly, I focussed my total attention on the red poppies, blue cornflowers, yellow buttercups, daisy flowers and thistles that had grown among the high grass. The gorgeous array of colours was similar to a rainbow. It was as if God wanted to give me a message of peace and hope. Gradually, the vision of the 'little Claude' came to me and I had a compulsion to nurse her and hug her so tightly, then she transformed into a teenager and then a woman, going through all the different stages of her life. I stayed in that position for a while, when a young female pilgrim passed by and I asked her to take Ulf's stone from the outside pocket of my backpack. I sensed how important the next moments were going to be. I looked at the little stone, weighing it up in my hands. I had the desire to keep it. I would have loved to have held on to it, but I had made a promise to Ulf and meditated a bit longer. I was growing more and more peaceful, smiling, sending 'goodbye' kisses, steadily leaving behind sorrows and pain and, little by little, my heart felt at peace. It was such a very emotional moment. In this little part of Spain, I was leaving a part of my past behind. There was to be less guilt, pain and sorrow from now on. Slowly, very slowly, that part of the past was leaving me. I would never forget it, but it would never hurt so much if I had to revisit it. Among the flowers, the birds' songs, the croaking of the frogs and the tranquil water, I threw the little stone into the river, which caused just a small ripple when it touched the water. I had turned a page. I would be walking more freely from that day onward. I was taking the new me with both hands and aspiring to my new life. I stayed a bit longer in this idyllic environment to pray, when an angel with her wings spread suddenly appeared. She had a lovely smile and flew away, waving goodbye and sending kisses. With tears in my eyes, I walked out of this beautiful paradise, lighter and full of new dreams and ready for what was ahead of me. I promised myself that from now on my life would be joy and happiness and if unhappiness was to come my way, I would accept it with a peaceful heart. In doing so, I would become a stronger person, ready to help others with their progress through their lives.

I got to the chapel called Ermita de la Virgen del Rio, but it was closed for refurbishment. I could hear the workers inside, yet there was no chance to have a peek and I kept on going towards Villalcazar de Sirga where I visited the impressive Templar Church of Nuestra Señora de la Virgen Blanca. Inside the church, the display of sounds and lights overwhelmed me, erasing the sensation of austerity, which some churches have. It was built by the Cistercians under the supervision of the Knights Templar, to whom King Alfonso X, the Wise Templar, belonged. Near the doorway of the church there was a poster and I read: 'Santiago 418 kilometres'. I was getting closer.

At Carrion de los Condes, I stayed at the 13th century monastery of Santa Clara near the entrance of the town, and I met up again with Juan who informed me he was finishing his Camino there due to clerical commitments.

I was on my way to visit the 12th century Santa Maria del Camino Church, which is known for the story of the rescue of 100 virgins. The story goes, that, following an agreement between the Moors and the Spanish, every year, the Moors would come and collect some virgins from Carrion de los Condes. In 826, there was a young girl called Maria among the virgins who was very scared and decided to pray fervently for help from the Virgin Mary, who intervened by sending a herd of bulls towards the Moors, driving them away. This young girl became a saint under the name of Santa Maria del Camino.

A local woman in Hornillos del Camino had told me to use the electric hand dryer placed in the toilet of a restaurant and very gently dry my wet camera. I was scared of doing further damage to it, but it did the trick, though one small drop of water was still showing behind the screen. From then on, I was able to use it again and I was photographing the Romanesque portal of the church when I ran into Monique. We were happy to see each other, as we had not been in contact since Castrojeriz. Monique had hoped to meet me again and was so surprised by the coincidence. During our conversations, I had told her that if we were meant to meet someone and if she wished it earnestly, it would happen. It was an eye opener for her.

In the monastery I gave my cough medication to a sick South-African woman, hoping that she would be better soon, and I went into the kitchen to prepare my backpack for the next morning. Upon my entrance, I found three young Spanish cyclists who were having a drink. We started a conversation using the language of the hands, as well as some Italian and Spanish words: a real mixture! We talked about walking versus cycling and the pros and cons of both. For them, cycling was the harder of the two, as they had to cover more kilometres per day. I argued for walking, 'Fortunately for you, wheels travel faster than feet. Walking is harder, as we always go through very difficult stony paths and the weight of our backpacks and our body puts pressure on our feet. The cyclist takes the road and down a slope it is free sailing, almost like a bird flying'. Our conversation was leading nowhere and I reiterated the weight of a backpack, when I heard one of them say, 'Piece of cake'. Not to be put off, I asked the 'clever one' to come and pick up my backpack. As he lifted it, I thought he was going to fall to the floor, for his arm was pulled down so fast. With a stunned expression on his face, he said, 'I can't believe it. Congratulations to you on the number of kilometres you have covered with this weight on your back. You win'. Everyone laughed and he gave me a high five. I was accepted into their clan, which felt good, and my ego did not mind it either!

I had a terrible night, as the other pilgrims in the dormitory were very noisy and the night was extremely cold. I became frustrated and would have left at 3.00am if I could. On 21 June 2010, the first day of summer, I was on my way at day-break. It was three degrees: cold and windy. Each year, the Meseta has nine months of winter and three months of hellish heat. Because of this potential quick change of temperature, I had to carry more water just in case. I was prepared for the heat and made sure I had food with me, such as some packets of delicious Spanish almonds. I would have to walk 17 kilometres of flat, straight road without any shade or villages or fountains: nothing.

At first, it was a pleasant change to walk on such a flat, gravel road, but soon the monotony overpowered me. I became bored. I missed the mountains with their diverse contours. With the mountains around me, my eyes and my mind had never gotten tired of looking for some new shapes or trees. Here there was nothing, only endless fields on both sides. It was so tedious. After a while I could not bear it. In front of me there was just an immensity of yellow fields like a desert. Boredom was my challenge, when suddenly a group of cyclists overtook me, calling my name loudly and clapping. My new Spanish friends from Carrion de los Condes rode past me and their cheers gave me courage.

Little by little, the temperature increased, the hot wind got worse and I dreaded finding out the actual temperature. I was missing the path after Villovieco, with its wildflowers, the calm river and the songs of the birds. I visualised myself back in this delightful place, but the Meseta with its heat overpowered me and swept my thoughts away. As a Queenslander and Savoyard, however, I was not going to be defeated. Far away in the distance, I saw a church tower on my left and thought I was close to it, but I never seemed to reach it. It was always further and further away, as if the heat was playing tricks on my mind. Was it a mirage? Many kilometres later, at last I saw the tower of a church on my right. I was not dreaming and below, in a hollow, there was a village with old buildings and houses, a few in a very poor state. Some voices came from the terrace of a café-hotel where a few pilgrims were having food and refreshments. To my delight I saw Monique. Some of the pilgrims - young and old - were questioning whether they should continue on the Meseta, or whether they should take a bus or taxi to Leon because the challenge was too hard.

Monique and I walked to the village of Ledigos. She stayed and I went ahead: I did not like the energy of the place. On my way out, a man was sitting on the front stairs of the café-hotel and said, 'I have been watching you

373

walking. I really admire you. I am dead, my body is collapsing and you, on the contrary, you are still walking and with such a big backpack. You are unbelievable'. He told me he had started from Belgium. 'No wonder you are tired', I said. 'I just started from Vezelay in France'. Then he let me know that he had crossed France on a bicycle and had only just started to walk. 'Walking is so much harder than cycling', he said. He asked me how many kilometres I had covered. I informed him that I was not sure as I had stopped counting. After a while, the number of kilometres does not matter anymore. How my thoughts had changed since the early days in France!

I was leaving the last section of the path in the Palencia region before the Leon province. I reached the refuge of Terradillos de los Templarios in no time. There was a washing machine and I gave all my clothes a good wash. The wind dried them quickly, and when I went to gather them in again, I found that my two pairs of trousers had disappeared. I could not believe it and I looked everywhere without any success. I had my pyjamas on and I could not imagine myself walking the track in them. There were no shops for kilometres. I was perplexed and tried to explain my dilemma to two Spanish women who were sipping some fruit juice close by. They described to me a man who had been near the clothes line just a few minutes earlier. I had noticed him. He was American with a small moustache: very neat and proper-looking. I explained my plight to the attendant and with discretion we went and knocked at the door of the well-dressed American. There on his bed were my two pairs of trousers. He apologised and gave me my trousers back, saying, 'I have no use for women's trousers, you know'. As pilgrims, we do not carry too many clothes and I wondered how my trousers could have ended up with his. I felt uneasiness at his reply. I had been travelling for quite a while and I had met a lot of different pilgrims along the way - some with tattoos, funny hair-dos or torn clothes - yet I had felt quite at ease with them as if they were my brothers and sisters. I had seen inside them how they were scarred, yet loving and gentle, and how some of them had been bruised during the course of their lives. Judgment would have come their way on a daily basis due to their appearance. This man, however, was all proper, clean-shaven and people would have easily trusted him. I thought it could have been a genuine mistake too, but I was still feeling uneasy towards him.

The refuge was divided into small bedrooms of four or six bunks and that night I slept alone: I would not hear any snoring. In Burgos, I had had the 'clever' idea to cut all my dead toenails. My boots were always drenched with the rain so the constant rubbing had torn the tender skin where I had cut my toenails, and each step was so painful. I promised myself never to do such a silly thing again. I had managed to cover nearly 30 kilometres during the day, and when I looked at my toes that night, I found them all red raw and bleeding.

The next morning, I left refreshed on my way to the Valdeginate Valley, and just a few kilometres into the walk I knew what to expect: heat, dry wind, no shade and kilometres of wheat fields getting more and more yellow. The Meseta was going to be a hard teacher. The track followed the toll road. It was flat and I tried to see its beauty, but I did not find much to admire. As the day was advancing, the heat was battering me. Staying positive was a real test and on the side of the track lay some crosses as mementos for pilgrims who had died doing what they had wanted to do: walk the Saint James' Way. The path was covered with small, white gravel stones which caused havoc for my feet, as the soles of my boots had become thinner. I could have bought another pair, but the fear of blisters had stopped me. I had bought some innersoles just to have a bit of cushioning and protection. Once the sweat set in, the padding did not protect my feet and I could feel all the pebbles under them.

Walking along the toll road was a real nightmare with the sound of cars and lorries in the background. I went through the villages of Moratinos then San Nicolas del Real Camino, where I crossed the Rio Sequillo over a concrete bridge, and at a high point I could distinguish the town of Sahagun in the distance. I walked among a sea of wheat fields for kilometres to Sahagun, which is renowned for its red brick buildings. Since the 11th century, Sahagun has been one of the most important towns on the Camino Frances and the first big town you arrive at in the Leon province. It was named after San Facundo and San Primitivo, the martyrs. I stopped at the municipal shelter 'La Trinidad', and in no time it was invaded by buses full of noisy Spanish tourists. After my credential was stamped, I left. Their chatter was too much for me. 'La Trinidad' was connected to the Benedictine Order of Cluny in France, which followed the strict Order of Saint Benedict, and it was called the Spanish Cluny. I sensed that I should not stop in this town. I did not know where I was going to stop; I just knew that I had to keep walking.

While passing through the San Martin's quarter square,

I ran into Nicole. We were quite surprised to bump into each other again. I had been wondering about her. Nicole had previously waited at Boadilla del Camino for me, but thought that I needed some space and we had not run into each other since then. Through the pilgrims' radio, she had heard that I had been worried about her, but she had had no way of contacting me. I had prayed to God that I would meet her again and say goodbye. My wish came true and all was now well. It had been meant to be, as she was returning to Marseille that same day. Nicole told me that some shelters had been infested with fleas and one of the pilgrims who had been accompanying her had been covered in bites. I had a bottle of anti-flea liquid in my backpack, but its contents had leaked out. Bed-fleas are one of the hazards of the path and feared by all. I had never been affected by them, thankfully.

After leaving Nicole, I passed along the streets of this brick city, visiting some churches and I made sure not to leave without going under the 17th century Arch of Saint Benedict, known for its coat of arms and sculptures.

After Sahagun, the landscape was very dry, like a desolate land. My left knee was starting to give me trouble and I wished I could meet Amar so that he could attend to it and give me some healing. While passing through Calzada del Coto I met Ralph, a young German man who was sitting on a wooden bench, boiling some water to make a cup of coffee. He was carrying 30 kilograms in his backpack to be totally self-sufficient and he had walked from Germany. I could not stop to join him for a coffee because I felt I had to keep on going. I did not like the heavy energy coming out of Calzada del Coto.

In Spain, the path was well-marked. I just had to follow

the yellow arrows: no need to carry a book. I am not sure whether it was the heat, my tiredness or if I misread the direction of the arrow, but I ended up in complete wilderness. I rested under a tree, hoping for a pilgrim to come by, but no one did, and the sun was going down. It was time to go back and retrace my steps. I noticed a barn and as I could hear a lot of barking, my heart was beating fast. Luckily for me, someone was there and put me back on the right track. It was so very hot, but I had to keep on going no matter what. These last few kilometres were extremely challenging. Eventually, I arrived at Bercianos del Real Camino where, at the entrance of the village, I was confronted by another cross in memory of a pilgrim. This time I was not surprised: that day had been difficult and the heat had been excessive.

Close to the refuge, I spotted some familiar faces, and one of the pilgrims came running towards me. It was Jose, a Spanish pilgrim whom I had met in Castrojeriz, and he screamed, 'Claude, you are mad! In Spain, you should not walk anymore after 2.00pm. You are going to kill yourself. Give me your bag and promise me you will never do it again!' I laughed, very touched by his concern. It was probably 6.00pm and I had walked 12 hours without much rest, but I had arrived safely. I was welcomed by Alea in this old refuge. I embraced the coolness of the shelter, which helped me to re-charge my batteries. Alea brought some water and lollies for a pick-me-up. The tiredness had left me.

Alea and I connected right away and had some profound exchanges. Afterwards, she came and handed me an Irish prayer and said, 'This prayer must have been written for you. Keep it'. I read the words on the sheet of paper she had given me:

> *May the blessing of light be on you, light without and light within.*
> *May the blessed sunlight shine on you like a great peat of fire,*
> *so that stranger and friend may come and warm himself at it.*
> *And may light shine out of the two eyes of you,*
> *like a candle set in the window of a house,*
> *bidding the wanderer come in out of the storm.*
> *And may the blessing of the rain be upon you,*
> *may it beat upon your Spirit and wash it fair and clean,*
> *and leave there a shining pool where the blue of Heaven shines,*
> *and sometimes a star.*
> *And may the blessing of the earth be on you,*
> *soft under your feet as you pass along the roads,*
> *soft under you as you lie out on it, tired at the end of day,*
> *and may it rest easy over you when, at last, you lie out under it.*
> *May it rest so lightly over you that your soul may be out from*
> *under it quickly, up and off and on its way to God.*
> *And now may the Lord bless you, and bless you kindly.*
> *Amen.*

My heart swelled with the love I had received all along the path and I knew why it was I had to stop at this little village.

We all shared the same meal in the dining room which had been cooked by the 'hospitalieras'. We all washed the plates and went to the chapel for the benediction. In the small chapel, everyone talked about their personal journey in their mother-tongue and what the pilgrimage had brought to them. This exercise allowed me to see the softness of the men's hearts as they were talking. Over the years, they had created a wall around their real selves and it was just starting to crumble, thanks to the Camino. This exercise was very touching. No one was judging; we were all in harmony and I was feeling the pain of each person, even though I did not comprehend what they were saying. They were speaking in their native-tongues, but their facial expressions, their tears, the sudden leap in their chests gave it all away. That night they could not hide it anymore and in the presence of other gentle souls, they let go of whatever was inside and started their healing process. The macho man was crumbling and he showed, without shame, his soft and gentle heart as each pilgrim related to his personal pain. It was a privilege to witness the renewal of a whole or part of a new person. After the benediction, we watched the sunset and I hugged some of the men who cried in my arms. Tomorrow would bring a re-birth for them as well as another day. As the sun gradually disappeared, so did the past of many pilgrims. It was 22 June 2010.

As I was leaving in the morning, Alea said to me, 'Claude, keep on giving joy like you have done along this path, and God bless you'. With these words in my heart, I left Bercianos del Real Camino in the freshness of the morning. However, in no time, the temperature reached 37 degrees, with my hat the only shade. The markings were non-existent and there was no pilgrim in sight. They had all disappeared as if by magic and there were only pilgrims' crosses: a reminder of the perils of the path. At one stage I went through 12 kilometres of flat, straight paths, with only my shadow, the ochre colour of the dirt and the yellow fields as companions. My watch had stopped working. I felt I was the only thing moving in this part of the world with my house and all my possessions on my back. I had to trust my intuition and God. A few cyclists passed and waved at me.

As I kept walking, I recalled my meeting with Edith whose eyes were without light in the street of Benevent l'Abbaye and suddenly I heard my mother's voice saying again, 'Why are you leaving me?' I was taken aback. Those were my Maman's words when my son and I had informed her of our return to Australia all those years ago. I slumped down onto the hot embankment as though I had been shot by an arrow, and I revisited the moment after my Maman had said these words and become silent. I had witnessed the light in her eyes disappearing like a flash, leaving a dead look in its place. The light was gone. At the memory of this event, I felt a sudden jolt of pain and lost track of time until I felt the arms of my mother and father around me, nursing me. I cried in their arms. They had forgiven me for having left them to start a new life in Australia.

I started walking again under the torrid sun, but my mother's words hung in the air. There was another message, I was sure. I was scared to return to the normal life in the world I had known before my pilgrimage. I did not want to be part of it anymore and I felt I would no longer belong there. Along the way, I had grown and after my experiences on the Camino, I now wanted more from life, more meaningful experiences. This did not mean that I wanted to forget about my family, but I wanted to be able to give myself more to others. I was terrified, as each step was bringing me closer to the end of this beautiful experience and towards the reality of the old world, where everything seemed so futile and foreign now. However, I could feel that my Maman and Papa were sending me their love, so that my heart would be full forever.

I arrived at Reliegos, where I had heard that many

Roman routes cross, one of which is the road joining Bordeaux to Astorga. I was worn out and my feet were killing me, as I had hiked all day on gravel. This stage of the path had been hard emotionally and physically, and I was feeling the strain of it all. I looked for the refuge where I met yet another Claude from France. We were enjoying a well-deserved cold drink out the front of a café, the facade of which was painted like a face, when we saw Ralph, who I had passed briefly at Calzada del Coto as he was boiling water for a cup of coffee. He joined us. Later, Ralph and I talked. His burdens were heavier than the 30 kilograms he was carrying. I gave him my advice and love, but to no avail: his demons were with him, sucking out his life. I felt so sorry that I could not help him. As I was leaving, a group of young American teenagers arrived. They were doing part of the Camino and their bubbling youth was a nice distraction, as my heart was so heavy because of the powerlessness I felt in not being able to help one of my fellow human beings.

The next morning, I left early and I stopped at Mansilla de las Mulas. In the village square there was a big cross with the sculpture of two exhausted-looking pilgrims sitting under its protection. I could really relate to them. Mansilla de las Mulas was a very nice, clean town, which had been fortified during the Middles Ages. It used to have seven churches and four hospitals. I went through it so early that everything was closed except for a café. The owners asked me to write some words in their 'Livre d'Or' when they learnt where I had started my pilgrimage. They were so surprised and I was offered a lovely strong coffee. I went over a medieval bridge on the Rio Esla and kept on going along the track not far from the noisy highway 120, which seemed never-ending.

At Villamoros there was a large stream, its embankments covered with green grass and trees. It felt like I had reached a magic oasis compared to the dry, arid parts I had crossed the previous days. My joy was short-lived, however, for once outside the village, I found myself among the ochre colours of the dirt with the sun giving me a hiding. It was going to be 38 degrees and still there was no shade. My body had not recuperated from the effort of the last three days and my pace was somewhat slow, but I did not have to cover 30 kilometres that day, only 25. The dust of the track, the gravel and the very noisy highway 120 caused horrendous mayhem for pilgrims. As I was walking, I saw some pilgrims taking buses or flagging down cars. They had given up because of the difficulty and the heat. I passed a few pilgrims who were resting under a shelter while waiting for their saviour - the bus or taxi - which would take them to Leon. I was exhausted, but I did not give up and kept on the dusty track under the Spanish sun.

At the end of the bridge in Villarente on the Rio Porma, I found a 16th century hospital for pilgrims. After a long, dusty road, I went through Arcahueja, where I stopped at a fountain to fill up my bottles of water. On the top of the fountain the following words were engraved: 'Santiago 307 kilometres'. The end was close and my heart sank at the thought. I crossed Valdelafuente and again I walked back along the highway to the Alto del Portillo, where far, far away I could distinguish Leon in the haze. It was getting hotter and hotter. The sun was not a friend: it was burning everything that moved, including me. I was thankful to have trained at times in the heat of the day during the summer in Brisbane. I was very tired, as at this stage, the kilometres I had walked were really weighing on my body. It was only sheer determination and will that kept me going. At the end of a slope, I increased my pace to reach what I thought was Leon, but to my annoyance it was not the city itself, only the outer suburbs, and I gasped when I realised that the centre of Leon was still six kilometres away. How I had misjudged the distance! As I was getting closer to the centre, I was surprised to see deserted streets with only very few inhabitants going by. I thought the heat must have been keeping everyone inside, but it was San Juan's feast day, a public holiday, and everyone had gone away. All the shops were closed too.

I did not have a map and I felt like an insect caught in a spider's web in the maze of Leon's streets and I wandered along the empty streets hoping to run into someone. I needed a bit of extra help from 'above', and as I was asking Him not to forget me, an elderly Spanish couple came up the street. Believe it or not, they spoke French after having worked in France. They pointed me in the right direction, kissed me goodbye and wished me good luck. Once more I had been helped. Thanks to their clear explanations, I reached the convent of Benedictine nuns where, to my amazement, I met a tired Monique. The heat had given her a beating, but she said she had enjoyed walking the Meseta!

After my chores, I visited Leon, the capital of the province of the same name. It is built along the banks of the Rio Bernesgar and is a major city along the Camino Frances before the mountains that separate the province of Leon from Galicia. Leon is a beautiful city which was founded during the first century BC. In 1188, the city hosted the first Parliament in Europe's history under the reign of Alfonso IX. A large part of the medieval walls still remain in the old quarters and there are some remains of the original Roman streets. Scaffolding was going up everywhere for the San Juan feast festivities. At night there would be concerts, fireworks and bonfires, and knowing that the Spanish people come alive at night time, I was sure I would not get much sleep. Our two parallel worlds were so different: the pilgrims go to bed early to rest their poor bodies so as to be ready at dawn to start again, and the outside world first comes alive at night, only going to bed as the pilgrims are waking up.

I visited the Gothic Santa Maria de Leon Church, also called the 'House of Light' in reference to the 1,800 square metres of stained-glass windows dating from the 13th and 15th centuries. They are among the world's finest examples of stained glass. The church was built on the site of previous Roman baths. Everywhere I visited, I wanted to stay longer to enjoy the beauty of the place, but I did not have time and I was also very tired. I had covered nearly 100 kilometres in three days, under very difficult weather conditions.

As I was hungry and every shop was closed, I bought an ice-cream at a stand in a square against my better judgment. A little while later I had cramps, but then I remembered Claude's advice to drink a Coca-Cola for any tummy upsets. I had to drink that 'medicine' and magically it worked: the pain vanished. As usual I did not listen to my body, which was craving a rest, and I decided to keep on visiting this beautiful city. I passed the Casa de los Bottines by the Spanish sculptor, Gaudi, a renowned contemporary artist from Castile. His real masterpiece is the basilica called the Sagrada Familia in Barcelona. Gaudi was called 'God's architect', and seven of his works are declared World Heritage listed by UNESCO.

After a collective meal at the convent, most of the pilgrims attended the daily benediction and the voices of the Benedictine nuns transformed the chapel. I burnt a candle for Ralph, who had been the one I was unable to help and I could not stop feeling guilty about this. I asked God to protect him, as God loves all his children, and I asked for His forgiveness, as this time I felt I had not helped my 'neighbour'. Ralph wanted to meet me again in Santiago de Compostela and I had agreed on one condition: that he leaves his demons on the path. However, I had seen him out of the corner of my eye, carrying his huge backpack with his mates that afternoon in Leon, and I knew he was not ready yet and my heart cried. I hoped that, for the sake of his family and especially for himself, he would find the strength to do what was needed, as there were only 350 kilometres left before Santiago de Compostela. I really hoped he could fight his demons. I went up to him and told him to be kind to himself. We hugged and I left. How many times, out of fear, have I not had the courage to tell the truth to someone for fear of hurting that person? How many times as a child had I been punished for something I did not do, accepting the blame for someone else? This time I told Ralph what I really thought, hoping to shock his psyche, but later on I regretted my harshness. Had I been loving or had I let down someone in need? After the benediction, an elderly American priest celebrated a mass in English in a private chapel. Among the pilgrims were two young

American nuns who were walking in their habits, which were ankle-length, cotton dresses. I was amazed that they could walk and climb mountains in their outfits.

My dormitory for that night was comprised of women only and I rejoiced at this news, thinking there would be no snoring. How wrong I was, as one woman was louder than the men I had shared accommodation with along the path.

The next morning, council workers were busy washing the streets after the celebrations, which had lasted all night long. Between the snoring and the festivities, I had had very little sleep. As Monique and I were leaving Leon, we could already feel the heat; it was going to be a very hot day ahead. We passed in front of the San Marcos Monastery, which had been refurbished into a luxurious hotel. The monastery was a most important monument of the Renaissance, a real jewel of Spain, with its carved facade of Saint James Matamoros on his horse and with a sword in his hands. My heart flinched at seeing Saint James portrayed as a warrior, for it was still impossible for me to picture him this way. Now that the monastery had been transformed into a hotel, I wondered what the monks would think! When I had arrived in Leon the previous afternoon the city had been empty, and as I left, it was empty still: no noise or movement.

On the way out of Leon we traversed the same desolate area of any big city, with its big stores and storage places. I was happy to leave it behind me. At Trobajo del Camino I found the endless highway 120 again, with its noise, pollution and cars going at 120 kilometres per hour instead of 60 without any respect for the pilgrim or pedestrian crossing the road. One car almost cut the

387

remaining years off my life. We reached the village of Virgen del Camino where, in 1505, the Virgin Mary appeared to a shepherd and asked him to throw a stone and erect a sanctuary where it fell. A contemporary church now stands there and on its facade are thirteen statues sculpted in metal. At this point, Monique and I parted. I wanted to follow 'La Calzada de los Peregrinos' away from the highway 120. The dirt track would hopefully give my poor sore feet and numb toes a breather.

I passed under a modern bridge and somehow I got lost. I stopped at a bar and asked for assistance, but I was informed that I was on the right track. I was going along the original path, which was good news, but I remained wary, for in Spain, all villagers want to be part of the pilgrimage and all say that they were part of the original ancient track. Soon, I was in the wilderness again and my heart was singing. I was alone for a very long time, it was so hot and there was still no shade. Over the centuries, all the countryside had lost its trees. Deforestation had been the key to feeding its inhabitants and to producing extra food for sale abroad, but no one had thought about reforesting. Very quickly I became a 'cooked pilgrim' once again! At Oncina de la Valdoncina there was a fountain. I put my head under the cool water for a while and then wet my hat to keep my head and body cool for a little longer before starting again under the torrid Spanish sun. It was early, but the temperature was already 37 degrees. At another fountain, I met Marcus from Germany. Our footsteps joined the millions of others: a thought that always made me feel humble. Marcus was doing the Camino as he was frustrated by the direction that the world was going in where there is little place for ethics. We talked like two old friends. He told me I reminded him of his wife who had the same way of seeing the world and life. My views were a challenge to him and the fact that his wife's name was Claudia gave him the impression that he was listening to her and not me. I told him to be very aware and open to the messages he was receiving, as there was no coincidence in our meeting.

We entered the village of Villar de Mazarife and the storks welcomed us from where they stood at the top of the church. At the refuge I met June and Mick from Woodford in Australia, which is a little village just outside Brisbane. They could not walk all of the Camino Frances as they had to be back by 11 July 2010 due to commitments, but it was nice to see two Australians. In my dormitory there was an elderly woman who was surprised by how the pilgrims seemed attracted to me and wanted to know why and how I could have this effect on people so easily. I told her that every day I put my trust in God and thanked Him for whatever he was bringing me. I sensed that she was a very intellectual person, with a lot of anger and sadness in her heart. Maybe she had to try to let go of her analytic mind, her judgment of herself and others, and let the acceptance and love of God into her soul, for we all have this ability. She started crying and told me how right I was and wondered how I knew. I said that I did not know, I just sensed things in people and I wished her well.

Once again, I left at dawn the next day, tired, yet happy to take to the road again. It was as though walking had become such a powerful drug and I could not imagine myself not being able to walk every day. I was always in awe of what the day would bring. Once more, I was alone with my shadow as my only companion. At first, the straight path was all bitumen with wheat fields on each side as far as the eye could see. Then there were stony trails and I re-joined the highway 120. It had been a solo hike until I came across Tony and Cathy from Majorca on a bridge over an irrigation canal before the village of Puente de Orbigo. It was their second pilgrimage and they had started their Camino as a family with their young son, but two of their bicycles had been stolen, along with most of their clothes. Bravely, they had decided to walk the Camino, leaving their young son to do the pilgrimage with the only bicycle left. They kept in touch by mobile phone. As Tony and Cathy had lost nearly everything, they were walking with the only shoes they had: crocodile sport shoes for Cathy and sandals for Tony. They were heartbroken when they had to leave their young son, but they accepted the challenge given to them. Cathy was a social worker who rehabilitated addicts and Tony was giving his time, on a volunteering basis, to the same cause. God had sent them to me. My heart was still hurting because I was not sure that I had said the right thing to Ralph. They brushed aside my worries, but somehow I was still feeling guilty, thinking I could have done more.

We arrived at the town of Hospital de Orbigo and crossed the famous Roman bridge, Paso Honroso, with its 19 arches over the Rio Orbigo. We stopped at a 12th century refuge that was organised by the Order of Saint John of Jerusalem, where Cathy and Tony had stayed years earlier. Coincidentally, after they arrived, they met the priest who had welcomed them 12 years ago. I went into the garden to enjoy the coolness of a shady area where a young man, Jokubas from Lithuania, was resting. This young man had encountered lots of challenges in his short life. He had survived brain cancer and a heart attack. Fearlessly, he had left his home town, leaving behind his wife and baby girl, to walk the Camino. He had started it on 5 January 2010, crossing Europe in winter and having covered about 4,000 kilometres by the time of our meeting. He had been able to cover this distance thanks to the generosity of people he had met along the way who had given him shelter and food. This terrific deed had been done only once previously in Lithuania by a priest during the 16th century. What a courageous young man! He was surprised by my achievement, but I thought it was nothing compared to his. I left him, hoping we would meet again.

I survived another very hot day. My body, though fit and strong, started to play up a bit more and I made a point of not covering the 33 kilometres I had planned to. I had been in Santibañez de Valdeiglesias for a little while when the Spanish skies opened. Within a few minutes, a deluge fell onto the village and I was thankful for my decision to stop. A collective meal was provided and we enjoyed each other's company. That night, America was playing in the soccer World Cup. The two young American nuns who had arrived after me stayed up to watch the match. Unfortunately, America was defeated, to their great disappointment.

There was another reason for me to stop at this village, as I met two more American women who were travelling part of the Camino Frances together. I was happy to provide a bit of solace for one of them and I thanked God with humility for this opportunity to be able to help one of my fellow human beings.

I finished week 12 of my pilgrimage on 26 June 2010 at Santibañez de Valdeiglesias.

WEEK THIRTEEN

'I place some heart-shaped stones at Cruz de Ferro'

The next morning I was feeling refreshed and I left with Tony and Cathy. No shop or café was open and I wondered how I would survive without any coffee or food, as the next stop was at Astorga, 12 kilometres ahead. In front of a farm, I had to pass two huge dogs that were sleeping in the middle of the muddy track. I was challenged again. I had to step over them, nearly touching their heads, however, the animals did not even open their eyes and I did not feel fear. I had definitely overcome my terror. In various ways since I started this pilgrimage, I had grown so much. I was getting stronger and stronger in my determination and will, fighting each test with love and trust in God.

All along the Meseta plateau I had hiked at high altitudes, which had represented for me the harsh reality of life with its ups and downs and illusions. Now the ground, the climate and the scenery were different. I was back in the higher mountains and my heart was singing again and I took a different route to lengthen my journey. Along the Meseta, my leg muscles had had some rest, as it was mostly flat ground, but now there were more up and down climbs, and my muscles were reminding me with a vengeance that they had not been used in a while and did not like what I was putting them through. I was in the beauty of nature with the fragrance of wild lavender and oak trees. My cuckoo was back too; it was nice to hear him again. I had not heard him since I had started the Meseta. I was leaving the somewhat arid part of the Castile and my next challenge, Galicia, was not far ahead. I walked for two hours in an idyllic environment and reached a plateau. In the middle of nowhere, among the high grass, I noticed a concrete tank with a red heart painted on it. I questioned its significance, as for me this pilgrimage had been a pilgrimage of the heart. A few steps further in front of a derelict barn, like a mirage on the side of the track, was a stand with organic foods, drinks, cereals, nuts, fruit, as well as hot water for coffee and tea: a real feast, but no one was around. It was as if an angel had placed the stall in this area to sustain weary pilgrims passing by so that they could have a rest and restore themselves before starting again. Around the symbol of the heart was written 'La Casa de los Dioses' ('house of the Gods') and I also saw a little toy koala had been attached to one side of the stall. An Australian would have passed by and stopped there previously, leaving behind this little souvenir. I wrote a note of thanks in the 'Livre d'Or' and as I was putting some money in the 'donativo box', an old car appeared driven by a young man, David. He was living by himself like a hermit in the derelict barn where part of the walls had fallen down. He felt he did not fit into the outside world anymore and he was the one who had left all the food on the stall for the pilgrims passing by. He showed me his lodging: one very neat, simply furnished room with a bed, an old settee and a tiny wardrobe. There was no electricity or toilet. There was an old sofa in one section of the barn for any weary pilgrim who was caught by the rain or the dark. David collected water from the roof for his personal use and every two days he went back to the city for a bath and to wash his clothes. He stayed in his little castle all year round, devoting himself to the pilgrims. At such high altitude, the winter would be very harsh, but he seemed to have adapted to it. His deepest desire was to be able to find enough people who could donate money to build a refuge for street kids. I wished him well. With the money left by pilgrims in the 'donativo box', he would buy food for the next lot of pilgrims passing through. If no one left any money, he would always make sure the pilgrims had coffee or tea. It was his way of giving back what the Camino had taught him. As he was talking, my heart sank. He was verbalising my thoughts and fears about the end of my magical journey. It was just around the corner and coming too fast. I was not yet ready for my return to the world; I was so unprepared.

At the Cross of Santo Toribio, I could see the city of Astorga in the distance, as well as the Mountains of Leon as its back drop. Along the Meseta, they had looked so far away and now they were so close that I could see some of their peaks covered in snow. It was very hot when I arrived in Astorga, which was formerly a Roman stronghold and the cross-roads for the Camino of the Via de la Plata from Seville in Andalusia and the Camino Frances. I re-joined Cathy and Tony on the terrace of a charming plaza when sounds of church bells filled the square. The facade of the town hall with its three towers had an animated clock with a man and a woman moving backwards and forwards and striking a piece of metal with a hammer, telling the inhabitants and the tourists the time of day. As I was resting, I saw Monique crossing the plaza.

I called out to her and we enjoyed a coffee and some delicacies of Astorga: exquisite puff pastries called 'mantecadas', which are made with lard and loaded with sugar and chocolate. I found they were similar to the cakes and biscuits baked by my Maman and the ones we found in the patisseries in Savoy.

The Romanesque Cathedral of Santa Maria was worth a visit. It is considered a masterpiece of Spanish Renaissance sculpture. Next to it stands the neo-medieval Episcopal Palace, designed by Gaudi and built with grey granite from El Bierzo. It was the second work of his that I had seen along the Camino: the first was in Leon. I went through the city and passed the village of Valdeviejas, stopping at the lovely 15th century Ermita del Ecce Homo Chapel where I put some water on my head and hat, as the sun was scorching. At Murias de Rechivaldo, the houses were made of large stones. I left the road in the direction of the village of Santa-Catalina-de-Somoza. Tony and I talked together along the dirt track. We both agreed on how hard it is for anyone to let go of the pain accumulated in one lifetime. I told him I hoped that by the end of their Camino, most people would be able to do it.

I went to have my credential signed in the little church of the village dedicated to the Virgin Mary where the relics of San Blaise, patron saint of the village, are kept. Inside the church, a 10-year-old Italian boy was having his credential signed, as he was doing part of the Camino on a bicycle with his mum and dad. His father had his son's bicycle cleverly hooked onto his own bicycle in such a way that if his son was tired, he could pull him forward. It would certainly be quite a learning curve for this young boy.

Santa-Catalina-de-Somoza saw the end of the Meseta after I had been walking it over 12 days. I rang my sister who was relieved to hear my voice and have some fresh news. The monotony of the Meseta was finished; I had survived it and I was so happy. After a coffee at dawn the next day, I left the village of Santa-Catalina-de-Somoza, but by 8.00am it was sweltering. After the evening rain, the dirt track was muddy and the air was humid. As I was going higher in altitude, the flora was parading its colours of blue and yellow, the grass was high and the chains of the Mountains of Leon were getting closer and closer.

The village of El Ganso was somewhat strange with its derelict houses. I saw one part of a house standing, refurbished, while the other part was falling down. I thought it would not be long before the second part ended up in a pile of dirt and stones.

I could not face the road and so I went through the forest with its narrow track covered with tree roots, which made the hike quite tricky. A man was coming around the bend in the opposite direction, and while he was still a few metres ahead of me, he nearly lost his balance after tripping on a root. I asked him if he was alright. He was and he smiled. As we passed each other, it was my turn to trip on a tree root and lose my balance. I laughed and turned to him, noticing a French flag on the top of his hat. This was how I met Marcel from France who was returning to his home town in Alsace from Fatima via Santiago de Compostela, Saint-Jean-Pied-de-Port and Vezelay. Not too many pilgrims do the return journey on foot, so it was a privilege to meet him. He asked me if I could read French. As I confirmed it, he invited me to read a prayer which was hanging at the back of his backpack. As I read it, I noticed his signature at the bottom of the page. When I lifted my eyes I saw he was crying. He told me that he had been moved by my soft voice and the way I read it and that I had touched something very deep within him. Then he asked me to turn the page and read the other prayer, which would be for me. I turned the page and by then my throat was so tight that tears rolled down my face and not a sound could come out. It took sheer effort on my part to regain control and through the tears I read it. At the end I could not remember one word of the prayers. We hugged and said our goodbyes. He told me that he would always remember me as I have the same hat as his when he did his first Camino. I smiled and waved at him as I walked away, certain that our brief meeting would remain with both of us, always.

At the entrance to the little village of Rabanal del Camino was the Ermita de Bendito Cristo de la Vera Cruz from the 18th century. Also there was Saint Gregory's ancient hospital and the Casa de Las Cuatro Esquinas where Philip II, the King of Spain who had married Mary I of England, had stayed. Under his reign, Spain reached the height of its influence and power, directing explorations and colonising territories all over the world. It was hard to believe that such an important person had been involved in this small village. After a break and some food at one of the cafés along the Calle Real, I met Rita from France. She and her husband had started from Le Puy-en-Velay. Her husband was walking the Camino alone, as she had broken her foot and had to discontinue her pilgrimage, but lovingly, she waited for him at different places and organised their accommodation. Rita was devastated and each day was difficult, as her heart wanted so much to walk, but like the difficulties we encounter in life, she had accepted her predicament.

It had been a nice and gentle climb up until now, but things were about to change drastically, as I had to pass through Rabanal del Camino at an altitude of 1,156 metres and within seven kilometres, I would reach the famous pass of Cruz de Ferro. The path took me along the main street of Foncebadon where a strange sensation overcame me. It was as if the village was abandoned or a bomb had been dropped on it. I felt a sense of devastation and shuddered. During the 10th century, a hermit, Gaucelmo, had welcomed and looked after pilgrims in the hospital and refuge of Foncebadon. It was sad to see the death of this village where, so many centuries ago, so much love for others had filled it. Pilgrims were still staying at the half-crumbled church, as I noticed towels floating in the wind and backpacks in front of the entrance. Some music came from a refuge where pilgrims were enjoying refreshments, giving a sense of normality to this village, but for some reason I had to get out of the place. Outside Foncebadon, the ruins of some farms looked like burial grounds where nature had taken over with weeds and wild flowers.

At the end of the dirt track outside the village, I was suddenly surrounded by an invasion of young and old people. I had not noticed them before and wondered if they had followed the road. The young ones were noisy and shouting and some of them were running as if they were in a competition. The narrow dirt trail was above the road and to overtake me, the young ones were pushing me out of the way, without any respect. I reached Cruz de Ferro at 1,504 metres - the highest peak of the Camino Frances - where I saw a bus waiting for them. No wonder they were fresh: they had walked a total of two kilometres at most and without any backpacks.

The Cruz de Ferro is a very symbolic part of the Camino. At the top of the mountain there is an enormous cairn, maybe 10 metres high, with millions of stones in all different sizes and shapes, and in the middle of it, there is a metal cross on top of a high, wooden post. The tradition is that each pilgrim leaves a stone brought from their country at the foot of the Cruz de Ferro. Before I left Australia I did not know about this tradition, but I had heard about it along the path in France. I had collected lots of little heart-shaped stones along the way for my children, my immediate family, my French and Australian friends, those who had left my life through various personal circumstances and those who had left this world. I had placed them where I felt my heart was telling me to leave them. I had collected a heart-shaped stone for all the special people who had crossed my path since my birth. I had kept one last heart-shaped stone, which I had collected in the Massif Central, for Christopher, with whom I had spent many Thursdays in Brisbane. Christopher was a special young man who had difficulty dealing with and accepting his sickness. He used to ask me to read him The Little Prince by Antoine de Saint Exupery. I had shared my 'secret' plan of the pilgrimage with him before his death. He must have known about this tradition because he made me promise to leave a stone in his memory at the base of Cruz de Ferro. After a few

400

minutes of meditation, I delicately deposited the stones and I climbed down slowly with everyone in my heart, bidding them goodbye. At this time I was missing my children even more than usual.

At the entrance to the refuge at Manjarin there were sign-posts indicating: 'Jerusalem 5,000 kilometres', 'Mexico 9,376 kilometres', 'Rome 2,475 kilometres' and so on, but none for Sydney, Melbourne or Brisbane! The person in charge, Thomas, was meditating and while I was waiting in the shade, an uneasy feeling overtook me, similar to the one I had had in Foncebadon. I had planned to stop in Manjarin, but I decided to walk to the next village of El Acebo, which was eight kilometres away through mountains. I would have to hurry. At last, Thomas returned from his meditation and I passed on a message to him that I had been given from Amar. Later, I learnt that this refuge was very welcoming, however, I felt that there was a reason for me not to stay. Maybe I had to meet some pilgrims in need and I took the road to El Acebo.

The panorama was majestic. In the distance, my eyes could see mountain after mountain - similar to Savoy, the Auvergne region and the Pyrenees - as well as green grass, trees on the hills and villages. I was looking ahead as I walked along the path, seeing the bitumen road below, when I suddenly became very happy. With a light heart, I was singing with the freedom of a child, until I reached a very steep slope on a track covered with unstable stones. I could not look at the scenery anymore; I had to concentrate on where to put my feet. I was so close to my main objective of reaching Santiago de Compostela, so this was no time to get hurt. I had heard some pilgrims had injured themselves just before entering Santiago, and even though they had walked hundreds of kilometres, maybe thousands, they were not able to receive their Compostela (the certificate awarded at the end of the pilgrimage). After all I had been through, I did not want to be in the same predicament. The climb down was hard and risky. I thought about Cathy with her crocodile shoes and wondered how she would make it. Slowly, but surely, I found my way down and at last I saw the small village of El Acebo at the bottom of the steep hill. It is a typical mountain village where the walls of the houses are made from large stones and their roofs covered in slate. I found lodging in a private refuge.

During the night at around 4.00am, we were all woken up by very loud music coming from outside the refuge. A pilgrim went out and found the culprit. The music was coming from a locked car. We could not do anything about it and so we all decided to get up and start the day's walk. It was pitch black and I walked down along the road for a while when I realised that there was no one behind or in front of me. It was so dark that the yellow arrows were not visible anywhere and I decided to climb back up the mountain to see which way the other pilgrims had gone. I was halfway up when I met three Spanish men. They told me that there was no problem, as I was following the original track. Relieved, I climbed back down again and far, far away in the valley I could see the lights of the city of Ponferrada.

I reached Riego de Ambros at dawn. There was no noise in the village as all its inhabitants were asleep. I passed in front of the Church of Saint Mary Magdalene and found the track. It was a peaceful and charming village. As I was climbing down I saw some very big trees, which were quite unusual. Their twisted trunks reminded me of long, wavy, cooked spaghetti. Two people were sleeping under the branches of this tree.

The climb went through magnificent areas, but the trail was only made of rocks with sharp points and I understood why I had not met any other pilgrims. The track was steep and dangerous, as it was cut into the rocks with very little room for mistakes. At one stage I had to put my backpack to the side and scramble down on my bottom, dragging my backpack alongside me, hoping that the two of us would not end up at the bottom of the hill. It was not a long section, but it was enough to scare me. I was overtaken by a lovely couple who walked this section of the path in no time and without any difficulties. Talk about young ones! When they reached the bottom of the cliff, they waved at me with two big smiles. I smiled back, hoping to reach the bottom safe and sound, a bit envious of their youth and agility. However, each challenge was making me stronger mentally and physically, and carefully I kept going on down the hill at the speed of a snail. At the end of the climb down, I had breakfast at 'Mahou', a lovely place full of a wonderful energy of peace and calm. I was alone and took pleasure in the simple food, music and landscape in front of me. Soon it was time to start again and I found it was hard to go and get back on the trail, as my mind and body had been relishing the break in this peaceful environment.

The difference from the top of El Acebo to the bottom of the hill was 1,000 metres, and my knees and feet received a pounding, but I was proud of my achievement. At one point from the top of the hill, the view had been stunning with the little village of Molinaseca below. I was entering this fortified town over the Rio Meruelo through a Roman bridge when I spotted a young man waving and running towards me. He and his girlfriend were the ones who had overtaken me when I was climbing down the steep slope. Gently, he took my backpack and carried it to where his girlfriend was having lunch. Hendricks from Denmark and Claudia from Romania offered me a coffee. We had a lovely time with a meaningful and profound conversation about their views on life. The two of them touched my heart. As I left their company, Hendricks informed me that Claudia had sensed that there was something special about me and he felt she was right. We hugged goodbye.

I was in the plains of the Bierzo Valley. It was quite flat and pleasant after the ascending and descending of the previous mountains. Along the road around Campo there were cherry trees loaded with delicious, red fruit ready to eat: manna for the thirsty and starving pilgrims and quite a temptation. I did not take any, but a pilgrim offered me a handful. At first, I refused, but he insisted and I accepted. They were juicy and flavoursome and I forgot my guilt for a while, but afterwards, I have to admit, I carried the guilt for some time. I would have to pay later on for my sin! Hopefully, Saint Peter, the young atheist from Yorkshire who I had met in Crozant in France, would remember me when I knocked at the Heavenly Gates and I would be forgiven!

I was walking along a stretch of road when I heard a shout. I turned my head and saw a young girl waving at me with something in her hand. I stopped and as she came closer to me, I realised that she was holding my credential with all the stamps I had collected along the path. This document had so much sentimental value; it was the proof of the places I had been through and it also had some kind words written by the people I had stayed with overnight, as well as their addresses. The bottom of my plastic front pocket had torn and all its contents had fallen on the embankments. Meredith from America had found my credential and she showed it to people she came across, as it had my photo on it, and luckily someone remembered seeing me passing through. She had been running and had been trying to catch me for a while. The chance of her finding me must have been one in a million, and as such, I felt so protected. I walked with Meredith until we came to an intersection where we each went our own way. I was following my intuition. This was going to be a fateful decision with dire consequences.

Hendricks and Claudia's paths crossed mine another two times before Ponferrada, capital of the El Bierzo, and I offered to meet them at a café for a cold drink or an ice-cream. I arrived first at the Castillo de los Templarios ('the Templars' Castle'). I was surprised by the sense of power that was emanating from this 16,000 square metre fortress with its fortified doors, high walls and tower. Claudia, Hendricks and I sat at an ice-cream parlour and they confided in me about their personal situation and I shared with them some moments in my life. As I was talking, I noticed that I had triggered something in Hendricks and he got up and left. On his return, he informed me that he did not like me anymore. At these words, it felt like an arrow had gone through my heart, and still in shock, I told him that I could not see what I had said that could have upset him so much. I had merely been sharing with them my personal emotions at a certain time in my life. We said

405

our goodbyes. Claudia hugged me, but Hendricks did not. We left and I went to visit the Saint Francisco Church founded in 1285. The coolness of the church was welcoming and I tried to put my thoughts in order.

I was so sad. I had lost two friends and my heart was heavy. Later on, as I was crossing a square, I saw them seated under a tree, talking to each other. I kept going in spite of the heat; I had to process the aches in my heart. Alone, I talked to God. I had shared honestly and without judgment. Why, then, this outcome? I could not comprehend it. What message was God trying to give me? It was so hot and walking on the bitumen road felt similar to being in a sauna. My feet were burning and swelling. I was wet with sweat, and with the moisture my feet became more and more tender at each step. I was still thinking over Hendricks' words when I saw the doors of the little Columbian Church open and I entered to have a bit of a rest. The coolness of this building was soothing to my poor body. There, I met a lovely young couple from Rome, Nicoletta and Carlo, who were doing the Camino by bicycle. It turned out that they had relatives living in Brisbane. Coincidence! After cooling down and resting, I went to the little fountain in front of the church and poured water over my clothes and left the water running on my head for a while, drenching my hat. My heart was still feeling miserable about what had happened with Hendricks.

I did not remember how I reached Fuentes Nuevas, where there was no refuge, and it was nearly dark when at last I found a lodging on the far side of the village. Thankful that the shops were open late in Spain, I bought some food for my evening meal and for my breakfast the next day. It was 29 June 2010. Spain was playing in the soccer World Cup and during the middle of the night I heard the honks of the cars parading in the streets and the sound of firecrackers. The Spanish were exultant, thrilled at their victory, and the festivities lasted most of the night. I was happy for their win, but I could not participate in their joy, as my heart was sad and still questioning. Had I used the wrong words? I had talked honestly as I had done before. What had been different this time to cause such a reaction? Should I stop being so honest and upfront? What had Hendricks heard through my words? If expressing my personal feelings was going to hurt people, I did not want to do it anymore. I promised myself that from now on, I would finish my pilgrimage alone. I would close the gates of my heart to all pilgrims I came across. My Camino would be different, but I was ready to accept it.

At dawn, I was on the road to exit the town. Leaving was a challenge in itself, as there were no markings. I eventually found my way through farm tracks, passing by Camponaraya and trekking across vineyards and gardens. Then at Cacabelos, I ran into Michel from Belgium, who was running 6,500 kilometres across eight different countries in Europe to collect money for a Belgian organisation involved in organ donations. He was trying to raise people's awareness and encourage more people to become organ donors. After Pieros, I took a different track, always preferring to add a few kilometres to my pilgrimage. This variant would also take me closer to nature, where I was happiest. I crossed hill after hill covered in vineyards, which reminded me of the Bergerac and Bordeaux regions in France. There was no shade at all, as the trees had been pulled out to make way for the

407

vineyards. The Romans were the first ones to bring grapevines to the El Bierzo region. On one poster I read that a French pilgrim had planted some Cabernet grapes in this area, as he had found that the soil of El Bierzo region was suited to it. Consequently, this district had become the second wine region of Spain after La Rioja.

I arrived at Villafranca del Bierzo, capital of the El Bierzo region, in the provinces of Castile and Leon. I made sure that I went under the famous 'Puerta del Perdon' ('Door of Forgiveness') at the 12th and 13th century Romanesque Chapel of Santiago of the Apostles. Just in case I could not make it to Santiago de Compostela, at least all my sins would be forgiven as I went under the Door of Forgiveness! I crossed a lovely town called Little Santiago de Compostela, which is so named because of its numerous medieval buildings, such as the 13th century Saint Francisco Church, the Santa Maria de Cluniaco with its medieval tower, and many more, which are similar to those in Santiago de Compostela. Some of its streets are cobbled, however, the cars are allowed to drive on them, which makes a terrible and deafening noise in the narrow streets.

After the bridge on the Rio Burbia, I decided to take a variant up to the mountain top. I was stopped by an elderly Spaniard who grabbed my hand. He did not want me to go up the mountain as it was too dangerous and people had been killed going down the slope. Of course, I did not want to listen to his warning; I was not going to give up a challenge! There was honest concern in his eyes and he did not let go of my hand until I gave in and agreed to take the pedestrian track along the national road, which was protected by concrete blocks. It was hot and I did not like the track at all, except for the section that ran along a river sheltered by trees. I could visualise and feel cool river water running over my feet, imagining how delightful it would be, but there was a little slope and fear took hold of me. I did not try putting my feet in the water and so I did not get to experience the sensation of coolness on my burning feet.

I arrived at the village of Pereje and called into the lovely little Santa Maria Magdalene Chapel where the pilgrims who had come from Vezelay used to make special devotion to the Saint. I saw Claudia and Hendricks coming out of the little church through another door. I wanted to call out to them, but a strange force stopped me. As they had not seen me, I restrained myself.

At the entrance to Trabadelo there was a nice refuge, but somehow I did not want to stay there and stuck to my intuition and walked further on. On a terrace of a small café, Michaela and Tony, an Italian couple with whom I had dinner at Santa-Catalina-de-Somoza a few days ago, were enjoying a cool drink. Our paths had crossed three times that day and each time Michaela would take my hands and kiss them, saying nothing more. We were meeting again, but this would be the last time and we had to say our goodbyes, as I thought we would never see each other again. My hands were in Michaela's hands when she told me that she and Tony had so much to reveal to me about myself, but they could not say much because of the language barrier and what they had to say was too important to be misinterpreted. However, they divulged a bit and with the little Italian I knew, I found out that they could see I was a sensitive being and I did not have the harsh and coarse ways of viewing the world as others do. But they told me to learn to trust myself in what I was doing and to keep my heart open to others. Before Tony and Michaela left, Michaela kissed my hands for the last time. I thanked them with tears in my eyes. So much was left unsaid. We hugged and departed. I watched them disappearing along the road and let the tears roll freely down my face. Her words released my sadness and I kept them close to my heart. Maybe they were God's messengers. Our paths never crossed again.

I did not sleep well that night as I was thinking about the events of the past few days and reliving my meetings since the beginning of the pilgrimage with all the people who had touched me and those who had needed me. I remembered the woman from Vezelay who had pulled out her heart from her chest and placed it over mine and was recalling Michaela's words. I came to the decision that, no matter what, I would have to keep my heart open to all pilgrims who were sent to me and I should not stop under any circumstance.

Early in the morning on 1 July 2010, I took to the road with conviction. To my despair, the track was parallel to the highway. I crossed Portela, with its houses similar to those of Trabadelo. Under a sculpture of a pilgrim in a small square, there was a plaque informing all pilgrims: 'Santiago 190 km. Roncesvalles 559 km'. I was not too sure whether these were the correct distances, as they varied from book to book or map to map. Fear gripped me again. It would all be over in a week's time. I had been on the track for a total of 84 days. It was overwhelming and I made the firm decision not to end my pilgrimage in Santiago de Compostela, but to keep going further. I was adamant that I would not finish up in Santiago de Compostela.

As I was going through Ambasmestas, I was hailed by a group of French pilgrims who were having their breakfast on the terrace of a café and they invited me to join them. As I was leaving their company after the breakfast, Hendricks and Claudia passed in front of the café. Claudia spotted me and she ran over and hugged me tightly. Hendricks, after a second's hesitation, did the same and squeezed me so hard that I could not breathe. He was holding on to me as though he did not want to let me go. He thanked me for my words of wisdom and honesty and he asked me to forgive him. I hugged Hendricks back and told him that there was nothing to forgive. I told them how I had feared I had lost their friendship, but now all was well. The three of us walked together, hand in hand. Claudia was on my left and Hendricks on my right and we lived this special moment in silence and communion. After a while, Hendricks left us to walk ahead. I stayed alone with Claudia, continuing to hold her hand. She thanked me for the words I had said to her a few days before. She felt I had been a channel from God and that He had put me in their path. I hugged her and, still holding hands, we walked and talked. After a while, Hendricks came back and Claudia left to go forward. It was my private time with Hendricks. I learnt more about him and his life. I discovered his gentle and tender heart and his delicate soul. We covered some more kilometres - still holding hands - while being completely open with one another, then Claudia came back. It felt as if the two of them were respecting each other's wish to spend some private time with me and I felt God's love all around us.

We passed through Vega de Valcarce, embedded in a valley, as well as Riutelan with its very old houses on one side and its fields on the other. We walked at times alone, at times together. It was special. After Las Herrerias, the climb was harder. It was hot and I appreciated the shade of the trees along the stony trails on the hillside of the mountains. It was rocky, stony and steep, but beautiful. Over a distance of eight kilometres, I passed from 675 metres of elevation to an altitude of 1,330 metres.

I arrived first at Laguna de Castilla and waited under the shade of a tree for Claudia and Hendricks to appear. Claudia turned up first and told me how surprised she was at the way I was climbing this slope, and how strong and powerful my stride was. As I did not know this, it was nice to hear. Hendricks arrived later and when the three of us were together, I told my two friends that it was here at Laguna de Castilla that our paths would separate. We held each other tightly, shoulder to shoulder, the three of us creating a circle. We stayed like this for some time and Hendricks sang a love song as a goodbye, as well as the pilgrims' song, with his gorgeous voice. All the other pilgrims passing by stopped talking and respected this mystical moment, as if they had sensed they were witnessing something very special. For the last time, we hugged each other very firmly. We understood that our paths would never cross again, but we would remain in each other's hearts forever.

It was so hot that, before I took to the track again for the last climb, I put my head under the cold water in the fountain. Hendricks thought this was really 'cool'. He had never seen a woman doing that as they all seemed to care so much about their hair! The pilgrims who had witnessed our special moment and heard Hendricks' words clapped, and I started the climb again towards O'Cebreiro. Claudia and Hendricks, with tears in their eyes, waved goodbye and I thanked God for this gift. No more words were necessary.

On the side of the hill, there was a café and on the terrace, three young Spanish cyclists were drinking a soft drink. As they saw me coming from the track, they started cheering and clapping. They had done the climb and they knew what I had gone through and were amazed that I had been able to do it with such a big backpack. My heart and my ego swelled. After a 10-minute break on the hillside, I started off again in the direction of O'Cebreiro, which was one kilometre away with a gradient of 150 metres. I could have done it in no time, but I missed the track and extended my walk. I had to hike on the bitumen road all the way up to O'Cebreiro in a temperature of more than 30 degrees. Magical scenery spread as far as my eyes could see, reminding me of the Pyrenees with its similar flora, but this time it was in the Galician heat and humidity.

In front of this stunning panorama, I thanked God for the lesson He had sent me. It was a lesson about trust. I knew that I would always have to speak my mind. Yes, I might lose friends and yes, my heart might be heavy at the loss of their friendship, but it would be just for a while, as, in time, once they understood that my message came only from my heart, they would come back into my life. It might take days, weeks, months or years, but I would have to put my trust in God and be courageous. I also realised that when I stopped complaining and let go of fear, and when I put my heart in God's hands, events turned out right if they were meant to be. During the course of our lives, we all have lost our trust in ourselves or in others at

413

times, and every day I was learning more and more to trust God to the fullest of my being. I had to accept what was sent to me, for with this learning, I was growing and I was becoming wiser and closer to Him. Through our mistakes and different experiences in life we all learn and grow, and through the suffering we learn to connect with others on a different level.

I reached O'Cebreiro. The village was like a beehive with lots of pilgrims and tourists buzzing about the place. Some pilgrims start their Camino from here. I crossed its paved streets with boutiques, restaurants and lodgings on each side of the main street and went directly to the refuge, unsure whether I would find a bunk for the night, as it was still 'first in, best dressed'. To my surprise, I was among the first pilgrims and waited very patiently until the doors of the lodging opened.

O'Cebreiro is a beautiful village with its traditional, prehistoric 'pallozas' ('houses') with walls made of flat granite, one metre thick. Their oblong or round shapes are contained by a sturdy wooden frame which holds a thatched roof strong enough to support the heavy weight of snow in winter. On a pamphlet, I found out that the ancient 'pallozas' were divided into two areas: 'L'Astrago' for the humans and the 'estravariza' for the cattle. Humans were living with the animals, as they provided warmth during the harsh winter months. The 'lareira' was the family area, which had a fireplace without a chimney where the women would attend to the cooking and spinning while the men would repair clogs and tools. Food was kept in a 'canizo', a small, suspended, open cupboard above the hearth. This way, the food would be smoked and preserved. In 'L'Astrago' there were two bedrooms:

one for the whole family and the other one for the oldest couple. Amazingly, I felt as if my roots were in this little village. High in the mountains, the villagers had taken to the tourists and pilgrims who had helped them to survive in their birthplace. Everything was done to please the visitors. There was a wonderful energy in this village, but I could imagine how very fierce the winter would be here.

Before starting my chores, I went to have a shower. Even though this bathroom was for women only, my modesty was challenged, as there were only small partitions to separate the cubicles. No doors! It was going to be quite a challenge. I placed my towel as a door, yet even so, I do not think I have ever had a shower so fast.

The kitchen was bright and new, as if no one had used it before. I learnt that it was for display only, as there were no pans or cooking utensils. I was told the reason for this was that some pilgrims had taken them. I was dubious about this explanation, for who would want to add more weight to their backpack? I visited the Santa Maria la Real Church where the pilgrims had stopped and prayed since the ninth century. This 11th century pre-Romanesque church is the only one remaining fully intact on the Camino Frances and it was said that the Holy Grail had once been hidden in this church. I heard that a miracle had occurred in 1300 in the Chapel of Santo Melago: wine had been turned into blood, and bread into flesh. At the end of the ninth century, a hospital was built to welcome the pilgrims. Later on it became a monastery for Benedictines, but was abandoned during the 19th century. Nowadays, the monastery is the refuge. Outside the church was the bust of Don Elias Valina Sampedo who did so much to restore and revive the Camino. He had the brilliant idea of marking the Camino Frances with a yellow arrow for all pilgrims to follow. I would not be able to express my gratitude to him enough, as he had made my journey in Spain so much easier.

Outside, I ventured into the village's paved streets and saw a huge cross at the top of a peak that I had already noticed during the climb, and I made the decision to go up and visit it. From the top I could see 360 degrees worth of magnificent mountains. To my right, the Castile province stretched out, to my left, the Galicia, and below, the charming village of O'Cebreiro, which was the first village I came to in Galicia. The cross was made of two round, wooden posts. On the vertical post people had inserted coins in the grooves of the wood. Even though I did not know the meaning of this tradition, I too placed some coins into the wood. From up there everything looked so beautiful and I enjoyed the peacefulness of nature, the birds, the view and in the stillness with no one around me, I reflected on my walk, wishing that my children and their families could be with me to enjoy this magnificent beauty. It was dusk when I climbed down, sorry to have to leave this charming place and hoping that one day I would return.

From now on, I would have to wake up earlier and earlier until I reached Santiago de Compostela, for it was the beginning of the 'bunk hunt'. There were more pilgrims on the path now and on 2 July 2010, before dawn, I was already on my way. The first 10 kilometres were like a handsaw with up and down climbs at an elevation of 1,200 metres nearly all the way. The symbol of the typical Xunta de Galicia marked the track. The beautiful scenery was the type that one can only dream of. It was a bit like a mix of the Savoy and Auvergne landscapes, with mountain after mountain, valleys, and small cultivated pockets of fields, forests, streams and green everywhere. After the somewhat dry and arid Castile, this was a delightful pleasure to the eye. The beginning of the track was stony, difficult and quite diverse with its vegetation, as well as its stone houses and Celtic villages that were similar to the ones in Brittany in France. I walked more slowly just to absorb its beauty and possibly also in the hope that I could delay the end of my journey, which I was dreading.

I reached the famous metal statue of a pilgrim fending off the winds at the top of the Alto de San Roque at an elevation of 1,270 metres, and then I made the steep climb to Alto do Poio at an elevation of 1,337 metres. I had been walking alone up until this point. As I was crossing the little village of Fonfria, an elderly Spanish woman offered me some pancakes. How sweet and generous, I thought, until I realised that once you had the pancakes in your hands, she would ask for some money. The reality of the world was back. Along the pilgrimage, the pilgrims give and share and are happy to do so, even if they have very little to offer. It was a reminder that in the real world, nothing is free.

Later, I got lost and had no idea how I would manage to find my way again. I crossed a little village with a paved and cobbled track going through it. It was covered in soft cow manure, indicating a herd of cattle had passed through not long ago. There was not one clean spot to put my feet and I had to walk in the manure, careful not to slip. In France it is said that if you walked in manure, it would bring luck and so I was very happy to do so. There was so much of it, but instead of feeling frustrated, I felt happy: I would have plenty of luck! As I trod through it, the smell brought back memories of my early childhood. Out of the blue, the angel who had appeared before me in Villoveico reappeared. I was astonished. This time she did not have any wings, but she was still smiling and jumping and singing happily. I stopped, rubbed my eyes and turned my head to see if I was dreaming. No, she was still there. She walked beside me for a while on the edge of a stone wall, still jumping and singing, then at the end of the stone wall, she stopped, waved goodbye and blew me a kiss. She disappeared as quickly as she had come. I was shaken, not understanding why she had reappeared in this little village. The track was still full of surprises. I was in a Celtic country full of mysticism, and therefore, all conclusions were permitted.

The villagers were poor in Galicia and the farmers put stands in front of their farm houses with fruit for pilgrims to buy. There were punnets of raspberries and an honesty box for the purchase and I had the pleasure of spoiling myself with the local berries which are grown in high altitudes away from fumes and pesticides. Their flavours were divine, taking me back to a moment in my youth when I was picking raspberries in my parents' garden and making a little piggy of myself!

From an elevation of 1,337 metres, the slope fell away rapidly to 660 metres and I crossed more and more villages such as Biduelo and Filloval, where a landmark indicated that Santiago de Compostela was 133.5 kilometres away, in case I had forgotten. It was prompting my mind about the end of my journey. I was annoyed to be reminded constantly of that fact. I arrived in Triacastela where it was difficult to find a bed for the night, but, as always, providence was protecting me and I found a lovely 'albergue'. I was sharing a dormitory with two French and two Spanish women. The Spanish women asked us if we did not mind being woken at 4.00am, as they wanted an early start, and we graciously agreed. At 4.00am we heard their alarm going off at full blast. That part was ok, until they started putting the light on, talking very loudly, banging doors and making such a racket with no respect for others. They went into the kitchen area and made more noise. I was quite put out by their attitude as, until now, if pilgrims were leaving early they would make sure not to wake anyone and quietly move out of the dormitory so as not to disturb the others. I did not know how I could make them understand that they were disrespectful without being too abrupt, when I remembered that the doors of the other dormitories were wide open as well. I got up and quietly went to close the dormitory doors. The penny dropped and the Spanish women smiled, but without an apology. I smiled back and returned to my sleeping bag.

On 3 July 2010, I left late at 6.30am. There were two ways to reach Sarria and I decided on the longer one, which would take me mostly through forests. This would satisfy my need for peace and solitude. I went through very typical Galician villages with their 'horreos' ('silos') made of stones with stone legs high above the ground to store cereals away from rodents and the humidity. The path took me up hills, down hills, through turns and bends, all the time accompanied by amazing scenery. I had to go across streams, some of which had paved, stone paths to cross them. The Galicia was so beautiful and had such a variety of scenery that the time passed very quickly, not like in the Meseta, where boredom had overpowered me.

I was climbing down a very dangerous and slippery section when a little angel came to my rescue. It was Christian from Germany who saw that I was tense and gave me his hand to walk this difficult part. Later on I met his wife. They were doing the Camino before returning to Canada where they had chosen to dedicate their lives to others, for they told me they could not fit into this world that was based on money and selfishness. They regretted that most of the young people these days had lost their sense of self-worth and respect, only thinking about themselves and drinking and using drugs. They had visited Australia and stayed in Brisbane where they had spent their honeymoon. It had been a joy to meet them, as it was so refreshing to see that some young people have the courage to reject this society of consumerism and are prepared to question where the leaders of this world are taking us. Further on, a young Spanish man helped me too. God, again, had sent me a hand in time of difficulty and I thanked Him. In France, I had gone through difficult tracks, but I had had to deal with the trickiness myself without help. Here in Spain, the pilgrims were numerous and it was so nice to be taken care of for a little while.

I passed San Xil with its magic landscapes and its tracks alongside rows of chestnut trees. Then I went through Montan, Furela, Pintin, Calvor and Aguiada where I met Rita again. Our paths had last crossed at Rabanal del Camino and we stopped for a chat. She was happy to see me again and marvelled at my courage. She called me 'Ma Petite Claude'. Hearing these words, my heart jolted, as they were the words my Maman had used when she was talking to me. Maman was never far away. I carried these blessings to San Mamed do Camino, through San Pedro do Camino and through Vigo.

At the entrance to Sarria I was taken aback by the honks, noise and bustle of the town. I could not stand it: it was as though I had a huge headache which would never cease. I walked further along the path, but not before visiting Sarria quickly. All the medieval churches were closed, as well as the Convent of Mary Magdalene with its exquisite mosaic yard. I could not bear the noise anymore and I ran out of the town like a thief in the direction of Barbadelo, but not before having a last glimpse of Sarria at the top of a hill. I went over the medieval bridge of Aspera and from there the walk was a delight as it went between more stony, shady tracks, the green of the trees and small hamlets, reminding me of my dear France.

I reached Barbadelo where the wind was quite strong in the high mountains. I was visiting the 12th century Romanesque church, with its portal of fairy-like animals on the tympanum, the last remains of the only monastery of this village founded around 1009, when I received a phone call from my school friend, Suzanne. Roger, her husband, was in hospital and wanted to talk to me, but caught by emotion, he could not verbalise one word and cried instead. I was never going to see him again, as he passed away a while later. I remembered the events of 26 April 2010 before my entrance to Limoges. Roger had made a phone call, dialling my number by mistake. It was the last time I ever heard his voice and to me this had not been a coincidence.

The 3 July 2010 saw the end of week 13 on the track.

WEEK FOURTEEN

'I arrive in Santiago de Compostela'

From now on, as I got closer and closer to Santiago de Compostela, it would be a new pilgrimage and I needed to get used to it quickly! The dormitories would be packed full of noisy Spaniards. Spanish people are vibrant and loud; that is how they live their lives. It is their country and everyone had to adapt to their way of living to the disbelief of the seasoned foreign pilgrims.

I left very early and saw the fog covering the valley below, a sign that it would be a hot day ahead. At every intersection the flow of pilgrims was growing; some came by cars and would walk a few kilometres, then a car would wait for them at the next village to take them on further. It was their way of doing their pilgrimage and though I may not have agreed with it, I respected it. To each their own journey.

I was crossing a lot of small hamlets and typical Celtic villages full of characteristic little farms with sturdy houses and fences made of stones. The sound of the streams was music to my ears. Water was plentiful in this region and it was like going back to my early childhood. Nothing could dampen my fondness for this area, not even the cow manure which covered the entire path. I was charmed by Galicia. I had been told that Galicia was humid, and coming from Queensland where humidity is part of our summer, I did not think it would play on my body. But it did. I was getting quite tired at the end of each day, my feet had taken a battering with the ups and downs and I was sweating considerably. However, by the morning I was always eager to start again. It seemed as if the track was carrying me with the energy that had been left by the pilgrims' feet over the centuries. The tracks were covered in large - and medium-sized stones and gravel, which was making my journey difficult. If there was a bit of grass, I would walk on it to give my feet a bit of a respite so they thought they were walking on wool or were in Heaven. I always imagined that my feet were appreciative of this and, as their way of thanking me, they would take me a bit further.

At Vilacha in front of 'Casa Banderas' there was a stall with some fruit, an honesty box and a lot of flags with one from New Zealand. I had planned to enter Santiago de Compostela with the French and Australian flags on each side of my backpack, but I did not know where to buy them. Curiosity overtook me and I entered the property. The owners were from New Zealand and South Africa and they did not think I would find any flags in Santiago de Compostela. That was the end of my idea. They advised me to stay in Portomarin overnight, as there was a festival there for the feast day of Santa Isabella. As I climbed down the hill before seeing the famous bridge of Portomarin over the Rio Miño, I saw the San Nicolas Church with its big rose window, high above the city in the distance. At the end of the bridge I had to climb quite a few stairs, which would take me up to the new town. At the top of these stairs I was welcomed by some young people in their local costumes.

In 1962, a dam was built and the ancient medieval town of Portomarin was submerged. However, each stone was removed and later on the old city with its church was completely rebuilt on higher ground. It would have been a mammoth task, but perfect for the pleasure and enjoyment of pilgrims and tourists alike. There was such a long queue in front of the refuge that I thought I would have no hope of finding a bunk and so I left. I knocked at all the places marked 'Private Albergue' and got the same answer. 'Full'. I was starting to feel disheartened when I came across two Dutch women in the same predicament and I went into a bar full of very noisy patrons, mostly men, to ask if anyone knew where we could find any accommodation, while the two ladies waited outside. I was amazed that the waitress understood my request, considering the noise and my broken Spanish. I was more inclined to think that she simply saw my desperation and gave me an address where the three of us were welcomed. The entire town was geared up for the festivities.

The morning before the procession, some corn leaves and stalks had been scattered onto the paved streets where the virgin would be carried by locals on a stretcher, with the inhabitants of the town behind in procession. Before the virgin was brought back to San Nicolas' Church, which was built by the Templars during the 12th century, there would be a blessing of the parishioners and tourists, and then the festivities would start. I witnessed a beautiful local Galician spectacle with their traditional music and dances. Their music had strong Celtic connections. Musicians played their colourful bagpipes called 'Gaita Galega' and there were drums and tambourines and costumes. An orchestra was playing in full swing and the locals, tourists and pilgrims alike started to dance in the square. Very late in the night, the fireworks went off, and then the festivities were over.

The following day I left at 5.00am and already many pilgrims were on the move. Most pilgrims wanted to sleep in a refuge and the number of pilgrims was getting bigger and bigger. Finding a bunk became a constant preoccupation and it was always at the back of one's mind. The 'bunk hunt' was going to continue all the way to Santiago de Compostela. I crossed the Rio Miño over a long, metal foot bridge in complete darkness and followed a path through a forest of conifers. I climbed hills all day long and my poor feet became so painful that each step was real torture.

As the year of 2010 was a Holy Year, some colleges and schools throughout Spain had sent their students to walk the last 100 kilometres along the Camino Frances to Santiago de Compostela. The students who finished would receive their Compostela certificate. It would count as a reference for any future employer, as this accomplishment would show determination and the personal qualities of the future employee. As a consequence, it was time to say goodbye to peace, as from now on it was noise, loud voices and music, with some students carrying their radios, as they could not leave their modern lives behind them even for a week. For them, it was like a holiday camp and being of such a young age, I could well understand, but still part of me was annoyed.

The pilgrims would acknowledge each other with a wave and it was a nice feeling of belonging, but it was difficult to be alone. I tried to walk in solitude even for five minutes at a time by reducing or accelerating my pace. I ran into Alexander from America who was doing the Camino Frances for the purpose of finding out who he was, the meaning of his life and the part he should play in the world. He was 18 years old and was a very sensitive teenager; he could not fit into this modern life and was suffering deep in the core of his heart. He was a deep thinker and had difficulty adjusting to the modern world, where he felt he was considered as a weak and insignificant human being by his peers. He was hoping to find answers along the path. His family did not understand his views about life and his wishes: they thought he was wasting his time and that he should accept and adapt to the modern world. I felt how hard his road would be and how much he was hurting and I knew that the hurt would last until he became stronger and accepted himself as a lovely human being. I tried to explain why his parents would be scared of his rejection of this world where competitiveness, money and financial achievements were key and spirituality was at the lower end of the scale. I told him that, maybe, his family who had migrated to America had had a hard life in their country of birth and they did not want him to live and work as hard, or suffer as they had. He had been brought up in a country of plenty, yet his family were, I assume, fearful for his future. I told him his family would eventually come to terms with his desires and that he should give them time. With determination and patience, they would eventually open up and understand him, accepting who he was and the gentle being within him. Alexander was very in-tune with himself and when he talked about his desires, he had stars in his eyes. He was a youth full of simple hopes and aspirations; it was so beautiful to see. I told him that if he followed his heart, stayed strong during difficult times and kept trust in God always, happiness would come, even if his path was hard, and he would be able to achieve what his heart desired. One of his wishes was to walk all round the world. I wished him well and I hoped that everyone on his path would see what a beautiful soul he was and learn from him. He was afraid of the world he was living in and I was worried about returning to that same world after what I had discovered during my pilgrimage. There was not much difference between us. Alexander had come with some friends, but as the kilometres were swallowed up, the gap between them had widened. His friends were walking the Saint James' Way just for fun. It was hard for him to walk with them and he had felt isolated.

Alexander made me think about the extent to which we are programmed by society and the environment we are living in. If someone does not fit within the criteria, that person will be put aside, rejected and teased. To resist the strong current of society, one has to be very strong mentally. How many times have the tides swept away the outsiders of our society, destroying their spirits in the process? Free spirits have been squashed in this globally competitive world where judgment is all around us every second of the day. There is no avoiding it. I was hoping for a change of attitude, for more compassion, more empathy towards one another in our society, and I prayed for this to happen, as I could not see our world going on the way it was for too much longer. I thanked God for putting Alexander on my path so that I could discuss these things that had been on my mind.

As I continued, I saw numerous youngsters stopping, checking their feet on the side of the road or having difficulty advancing. The ups and downs of the track were playing on their young bodies. The loud voices had become more subdued. The girls helped those in difficulty, but the boys looked on with a smirk at the ones in trouble. Only the strongest would win! It seemed they felt no pity, even on the Saint James' Way. Hopefully the stronger ones would learn something before the end of the 100 kilometres.

The stony tracks were close to the main road, but the scenery was beautiful. I saw the branches of the trees tangled together from both sides of the track creating a shady tunnel. As I walked under them I appreciated the cool. Even nature was full of kindness towards the weary pilgrims. I crossed many small hamlets without local sign-posts and I had to rely on my intuition to find the way.

After Gonzar, I passed through Hospital de la Cruz and Ventas de Naron with their 13th century hospitals, built by the Knights Templar. The track passed under enormous chestnut trees giving shade and pleasure to the eyes and bodies of the pilgrims. From Sierra de Ligonde at 756 metres - the highest point of this section - there were majestic views of the valleys below and before Ligonde village. I saw a cross from the 17th century with the theme of the death and Passion of Christ at its base. It is supposedly the most famous cross on the Camino Frances.

I passed in front of more churches, crossed more hills and I reached Alto de Rosario and from there I saw the Pico Sacro ('sacred peak') mountain, which is involved in the famous legend about Saint James' sepulchre. The disciples had brought Saint James's body back from the Holy Land to be buried in Spain and after disembarking in Padron, they approached the cruel Queen Lupa ('she-wolf') to ask if they could travel through her kingdom. Before agreeing to this, she sent them up to Pico Sacro Mountain to look for two bulls to yoke together. If they could manage this task, they would be able to go wherever they wished in full freedom. Queen Lupa knew that they would only find wild bulls, but a miracle took place and to Her Majesty's dismay, the wild bulls let themselves be yoked. Angry, Queen Lupa sent her soldiers to pursue Saint James' disciples. Once again they were protected, as suddenly a huge amount of water came across and separated the soldiers from the disciples. After these events, the cruel Queen Lupa converted to Christianity and offered her tomb, which was under construction in Santiago de Compostela, to the disciples so they could bury Saint James.

I arrived at the town of Palas del Rei or Pallatium Regis, where the last king of the Visigoths, King Witiza, had his residence during the eighth century. I passed in front of the refuge where there was a very long queue; it had been the same at the previous village of Eirexe. I continued on, knowing there would be no hope in finding a bunk. Though tired and bothered, I had to go further. I was descending a very steep, paved street when, in a small square, I saw a statue of two pilgrims dancing. Dubiously, I looked at it. For me, it was hard enough to walk and I wondered where they would have found the strength to dance. I thought to myself that the artist could not have walked the pilgrimage! After Caballal, I climbed up again to access San Xulian with its numerous 'horreos' for storing grains.

The sun was going down and I was starting to get worried. I crossed the bridge over the Rio Pambre and as I had not been able to find any lodging I asked God to come to my rescue. Night would fall soon and I had nowhere to sleep. I arrived at the next refuge which was also full. I glanced at the terrace where I saw a young Spanish couple sipping soft drinks. We had been waving, smiling and passing each other a few times and I asked them if they knew of any lodgings in this area. Immediately, they took their mobiles out and rang around. At last they found a place in the next village for me to sleep, just a few kilometres further on. I was tired and I had to walk more, but I did not care as I would have a bunk for the night. As I got to the lodging, I gave my name to the manager who informed me how lucky I was, as a woman had just cancelled her booking when my new friends rang. He himself found it hard to believe how lucky I was, as all refuges and 'albergues' were fully booked in this area. He was surprised, although I was not. It had happened to me before in France and God had come to my help then as well. God really was taking good care of me and I thanked Him. I met three German pilgrims at the lodging: two young ones and an older one. Our paths had crossed a few times in the past few days. I had met the youngest at Villoveico many weeks before. They informed me how tired and exhausted they were, as they had walked 30 kilometres that day, about the same as me. I felt compassion towards them and while having our dinner, one of them - who probably forgot what they had already told me - said that they had covered half of the walk in a taxi. I did not comment. On the path, I had not met lies up until now. Anyone could open up easily to other pilgrims without fear or judgment, but sadly the world with its deception was not too far away on that day.

At dawn I was up early, ready for a long and hot day's walk as the temperature would reach 38 to 40 degrees. I was covering close to 30 kilometres on a daily basis. It was

6 July and as a mother, my heart flew to Australia even more than usual, as it was my son's birthday. I had hoped to reach Santiago on his birthday as a present to him and my family in Australia, but it was not meant to be.

From now on, at every 500 metres there were landmarks that reminded the pilgrims of the number of kilometres left to reach Santiago. Perhaps it was a way to verbalise, 'Have courage. The end is near', but to me, each sign-post was saying, 'The end of your dream is around the corner'. As I passed each post, it felt like a dagger was piercing my heart and I was very annoyed by their presence. It was such a horrible reminder about the end of my wonderful journey.

On the way to Casanova it was like the previous days: more climbs up and down, dirt, paved and bitumen tracks, streams, and shady tunnels of trees that protected me from the heat. Just before Leboreiro, a sign-post informed me that I was leaving the region of Lugo and entering the province of A Coruna. At a cross-road, I saw the small medieval Church of Santa Maria with a statue of the Virgin and the Child on its portal. Next to the church I saw the strangest 'horreo', which was shaped like a wicker-basket with a thatched cover. It was a replica of one of the first 'horreos' used many thousands of years ago.

Not far from here, I crossed the medieval bridge, Ponte Velha, which has four arches and leads to the medieval village of Furelos and its Church of San Juan. I had been told by Francoise and Jean-Paul from my birthplace, who had started their pilgrimage from their home, to look out for a certain cross in this church. I found it to the right of the main entrance. It was a very unusual crucifix with

431

Christ's right hand not nailed to the cross, but reaching towards the earth, as if to invite people to take his hand. I was so taken by the way the artist had transmitted so much emotion through his personal interpretation of Christ on the cross that I forgot to take a photograph and had to return to Furelos after reaching Santiago de Compostela.

After the paved track there was a dirt track, which made my feet happy as the ground was softer, and I climbed up to Melide where a recent fire had burnt sections of the forest. I had never thought of this prospect previously and realised how fortunate I had been all along the pilgrimage to not have encountered such a drama. Melide was built during the 13th century by King Alfonso IX. Nowadays, the path proceeds through its modern suburbia, which I dreaded, as the roads led to the main road. I passed the Romanesque Church of Saint Pedro and Saint Roque with its famous 14th century stone cross, which was the oldest in Galicia. Another church of interest was the 14th century Sancti Spiritus Church, built with the stones from an old castle. It had once been a Franciscan monastery. I crossed over the medieval town, which is in the lower area, with its narrow and meandering streets, and went through the back streets down to the 12th century Santa Maria de Melide Church. Melide is at the junction of two Caminos: the Camino Primitivo and the Camino Frances. The Camino Primitivo is an inside route, which starts and finishes in Spain, and is the shortest of all the routes to Santiago de Compostela.

Back on the track, the path was winding its way up and down with oak and pine trees on each side. As I was walking through the forest I smelt a familiar fragrance. I looked around and to my surprise I was in the middle of a eucalyptus forest. I could not believe it. I felt as though I was back home in my adoptive country, Australia. What a present from nature for my son's birthday!

I kept on going along this path - intoxicated by the smell of the eucalyptus trees - to Raido, A Peroxa then to Boente. Suddenly, I was overwhelmed by tiredness. My feet seemed to weigh hundreds of kilograms. It was overpowering and I implored, 'Please God, no more hills, no more up and down, please! No more!' It was the first time I felt that my body was really letting me down and I was so close to my objective. Would I fail like so many had done before me? I had heard that some had broken down so close to Santiago de Compostela and I was so close and yet so far at the same time. I had just seen the sign: '45 kilometres to Santiago'. Was it the heat, the tiredness, the number of kilometres travelled since the beginning of my adventure, or was my body just too exhausted? Had I asked too much of it? Was my will, my obstinacy leaving me? I was feeling so down when my thoughts travelled back to my workmates. In a split second, I saw their teasing grins and it was as if an electric shock went through my whole body. No, I was not going to be defeated. I would not let them win. With new determination and a sturdy pace, I started again. I ignored the exhaustion that had overcome me and kept on going towards Castaneda.

At Ribadiso, I crossed a medieval bridge over the Rio Iso and discovered an idyllic spot near the 15th century hospital San Anton de Ponte de Ribadiso, which is still welcoming pilgrims today. I was informed that it is probably the oldest refuge still in existence on the Camino Frances. A lot of pilgrims, young and old, were sitting under the shade of trees and putting their tired feet into the river to cool them down. No way would I find a bunk in this lovely place: same problem as the day before. Oh dear! I kept walking and I went through a tunnel under a national road when I was hailed by a pilgrim, who asked, 'Are you Claude the Australian? Do you know that you are like a shining star on the Camino Frances? You are like a light at the end of a tunnel. A lot of pilgrims are talking about you. Thank you for what you are doing. I am happy that my path has crossed yours. Ultreia!' I smiled and thanked him, but did not enter into a conversation, as I was too exhausted. I had more hills to climb up and down before arriving in Arzua where I rang my son for his birthday.

The next morning I left around 4.30am. It was dark, but I had been informed that the temperature would reach 40 degrees and with the humidity, I had to have an early start even if I had decided to walk only 20 kilometres. I crossed Arzua along its streets made of large, paved stones. My trekking poles made the only noise in this sleepy town with its traditional Galician houses on each side. With a heavy heart, I tried to reduce my pace to delay the inevitable - the end of my journey - but my legs refused as they had learnt a certain rhythm over the months and did not seem to want to adjust to a new one. They were probably very stubborn just like their owner! More pilgrims were coming from everywhere and it was harder to find a quiet place. I decided to go with the flow and went through fields, countryside and eucalypt forests and I made the best of it all. On the top of a landmark at the 30 kilometres mark, an old pair of shoes was left. The owner probably could not finish their pilgrimage with them as the shoes were in such a pitiful state. As I was crossing a dirt track covered with cow manure, I saw that someone had left a sandal at the top of a pile of manure. Humour was everywhere as the end drew near.

I met two young men - Roger from Holland and Cyrus from America - who at first were reserved and quiet, but bit by bit they thawed and warmed to me. Both were very spiritual. They had met on the Camino Frances and they were looking for some new meaning in their lives. Roger's challenge was how to apply what he had learnt during his pilgrimage to his day job where being 'macho' was important. For him it was a dilemma, as he had to live in pretence and not show the real person within. Cyrus, who was a creative man, would be able to apply his learning more easily. Both of them had found what they were looking for and they were amazed at the number of kilometres I had covered at my age and with my heavy backpack.

It was very hot and walking in the eucalyptus forest was a respite and a blessing. The mounted police were on the move looking after the pilgrims to make sure that nothing nasty happened to anyone before their arrival in Santiago de Compostela. I did not feel more secure in their presence, as I already knew I was safe. I arrived at O Pedrouzo where a few pilgrims were waiting for the doors of the refuge to open. As 'first in, best dressed' was the motto, I joined the queue with them. As the doors opened and we went in, the heat coming from inside the refuge nearly suffocated everyone and we had the horrible feeling that there would be an uncomfortable night ahead.

I was more and more convinced and certain that I could not stop at Santiago de Compostela. My mind was made up: I would keep on going further and keep my dream alive a bit longer. I asked about refuges past Santiago at Fisterra and Muxia. The word spread like wildfire among the community of pilgrims. The Spanish pilgrims gave me names and addresses of people they knew as well as advice for that part of my journey. I was very touched by such kindness.

I had noticed a young Filipino man on the track as I had walked. He was smoking like a trooper and he approached me while I was sitting and writing in my diary in the refuge. He was living in Germany and started to talk about religion and how he disagreed with non-Catholics walking the Saint James' Way and he kept talking about it for quite a while. I was surprised to see such a young person so intolerant of different faiths and others. It was the first time I had met a young man like him on the path and I felt a sense of frustration. I talked to him about compassion, about the fact that we are all one in the eyes of God. He was really annoying me with his analysis, so therefore, to put the 'ball' in his court, I informed him that when he was born, God had given him a pure body and he did not come into the world with a cigarette in his mouth! I asked him what he was going to say to God when He would ask him how he took care of the pristine body he received at birth. I said to the young man that God always loves His children and that He would show His love to him, even though he had abused the body he had been given. I told him that if he was expecting God's compassion, then he too should be kind towards others, including those of different creeds.

436

Narrowness is not what Catholicism is based on; it is more about understanding, empathy and love for others and not judgment. I went on to say that God does not like to put people in little boxes, and I am the same. Once our skin is pulled back, all human beings are the same with the same wants, desires, weaknesses and with a body that functions the same way. I told him that I had met atheists, agnostics and Buddhists on this path and I had been privileged to have run into them and my exchanges with them had been uplifting. So I told him to be kind and loving towards others. As I finished my tirade, he jumped out of his seat and left, as if he had been bitten by a bee. Two days later, I met him in Santiago de Compostela and he approached me and thanked me, for he had needed to hear those truths. He told me that he had walked the end of his pilgrimage with different eyes and a different attitude.

After having dinner together with Celia and Ruth from Ireland who were also staying in O Pedrouzo, we went back to the refuge. We did not have a good night's sleep due to the humidity, heat and snoring, yet we got up early as we had decided to walk together in the early morning to catch the cool air after the previous dreadful days. Some pilgrims had already left by 4.00am.

It was pleasant to walk in the cool of the early morning, but the humidity was still in the air. We went through more hamlets, more eucalypt forests, more climbs, more stony and gravel tracks and more bitumen roads. I was looking everywhere with intensity. I wanted to remember every bend, every landscape, the fauna and flora that I found on my way. I wanted to leave an eternal imprint on my brain of these last parts of my journey. Sadness overtook me. My heart was getting heavier and I cried. I told my young Irish friends that I would leave them at Monte do Gozo. As I could not bear to see the end of my dream quite yet, I wanted to lengthen my journey on the Camino Frances. I was thankful to my new young friends, as their youth and bubbling spirits were a nice distraction. We got caught by the rain and stopped for a snack at one of the small cafés along the path, then the rain slowly stopped and we went back on the track. It was very nice to walk in the cooler air after the rain. The path ran along the airport of Santiago and the planes flew over us constantly. The reality of life was so close: it was like torture.

At Lavacolla village, there is a stream with the same name as the village and the tradition in the Middle Ages was that pilgrims would wash themselves in it before entering Santiago. Perhaps it was why this village was named Lavacolla, which means 'washing one's loins'. Nowadays, no one does it, as we have the privilege of always having showers at our disposal. While I was alone, I collected two little heart-shaped stones for Ruth and Celia. These were the last stones I would give on the path.

Soon, we arrived at Monte do Gozo ('hill of joy'), which was full of activity. We had passed the local TV station of Santiago de Compostela and now cameras were in full swing. Journalists were interviewing the Spanish people who were on their way to finishing their Camino Frances and asking them about their reasons and motives for doing this pilgrimage.

At the top of Monte do Gozo, there is an enormous black aluminium sculpture, with an incomplete circle represented. I thought it looked like two arms joined together in the joy of arriving at Santiago de Compostela and on the top of a platform there were two pilgrims protected by a cross. I had no idea really when it came to the interpretation of the sculpture. On one section of the base, there was a drawing of Saint Francis of Assisi who had also walked the pilgrimage and built monasteries along the path.

In 1989, Pope John Paul II had united 500,000 young people for World Youth Day here and this commemoration was engraved on the pedestal of the monument. During the Middle Ages, pilgrims arriving in Monte do Gozo would have been able to see the Cathedral of Santiago and shout 'Ultreia', but nowadays with the haze and the numerous modern buildings, I could not distinguish the famous cathedral. I would have to wait until I arrived in the city to see it, but I was happy to wait and I went into the medieval Chapel of Santo Marcos to collect my thoughts. As I came out, the idea of stopping to sleep at Monte do Gozo became ludicrous and I informed Ruth and Celia that I would walk with them into Santiago de Compostela. Celia and Ruth gave me a souvenir. It was a little pilgrim made out of wire and he was carrying a heart, which had been the symbol of my journey. I was so touched by this delicate thought.

I crossed over the bridge of the A9 highway at the entrance to Santiago de Compostela at 10.31am on 8 July 2010, after three months of walking through France and Spain. The distance between the bridge and the cathedral was a few kilometres, but to be honest, I do not remember much of it except the cross of Saint Peter and my stride through the 'Puerta del Camino' ('Door of the Camino'). The activity and buzz of the city was disturbing me more than ever and tears started to roll down my cheeks. It was the end of my dream, of my journey. It had been three months of challenges, pain, insecurity, questioning, determination, and every day asking a bit more of my body than I had ever asked of it before. My pilgrimage had been made up of beautiful, unforgettable meetings with people who had helped me and people I had helped. All the special moments and events came flooding back to me. It was too powerful. It felt as if my heart was coming out of my chest. I managed to control my erratic breathing, but not my tears or my shaking.

On the bridge at the entrance to Santiago I had phoned my daughter to tell her I was arriving in Santiago de Compostela, and I was on the phone to my son to tell him the same news when I heard someone shouting my name. As I turned around, I saw Michelle from Limousin, who had crossed my path in Atapuerca, more than 550 kilometres away from Santiago de Compostela, and who had recognised me. I could not believe it. The emotion was too much. I fell apart and the feelings from the journey 'exploded' in me. As I was entering this big city that was unknown to me, someone had called out my name, someone had recognised me. I could not breathe and my legs could barely carry me. I was overtaken by emotion as she came close to me and we fell into each other's arms. It was an unbelievably magical moment. We had spoken for only a few minutes in Atapuerca and she had remembered me. This had happened before, but somehow, it felt different now. After a little while I left her, as she was with her cousin. I continued towards the Cathedral of Santiago, still trembling from what had just taken place. It would be an inexplicable moment in my journey, which would stay in my heart forever. As I was coming into the square, the bells of the cathedral started to ring out in joy. It seemed that they too were welcoming me to Santiago, acknowledging my achievement.

My heart was beating like mad when I heard 'Claude, Claude!' coming from all four corners of the square. Many pilgrims were calling out my name. They too had recognised me when I had entered the square. I could not believe that so many had remembered me and were present at my arrival. Claude, the insignificant one, was welcomed by people from all over the world in a strange city away from her birth and adoptive countries. The pilgrims told me what an impact I had had on their journeys and that they would remember me always. I was fortunate that God had given me a strong heart, for, with the shock of it all, I could have had a heart attack. I thanked Him from the deepest part of my heart for all the blessings I had received since Vezelay. What an arrival in Santiago! Ruth and Celia had witnessed the end of my journey and my arrival in front of the Cathedral of Santiago and they were astonished that so many pilgrims had remembered me. They said, 'Claude, you are special. Look at all these pilgrims who remembered you. It is incredible'. I lifted my eyes to the sky and thanked my family, Saint James and God who had protected me all along my pilgrimage. I was certain that without their help in difficult times I would not have achieved what I did. I felt so blessed.

It was no coincidence what happened that day. I had changed my plan in Monte do Gozo because I had been meant to meet some of the pilgrims again for whatever reason. I ran into the two beautiful angels who had helped me find a lodging a few days ago, for without their help I would have slept outside. I had arrived in front of the cathedral at Praza da Inmaculada, where I could see its northern facade. During the Middle Ages, this entrance was used by pilgrims who were coming from France. At the top of the facade there is an 18th century statue of Saint James with the two kings: Alfonso III of Asturias and Ordoño II of Leon at his feet in praying position. In the plaza there were musicians. I listened to them and their music slowly brought peace and calmness to me.

Apparently, it was during the Napoleonic wars that Santiago was captured and raided by the French and, as a result, Saint James' remains were lost for nearly a century. They had been secretly placed inside a cist and hidden in the basement of the cathedral. I passed in front of the cathedral, which is a wonderful piece of architecture that has been darkened by the years. Some pilgrims were disappointed by the fact that she looked so dirty from the passing of time, but for me I was happy to see the cathedral that way. She had lived a long time. She was proud and, like a lot of us, she was not frightened to show her age. In fact, it was only a matter of perception. The cathedral did not need a facelift, like many of the monuments I had seen on my journey, and I liked that. She was a natural - a bit like me with my white hair!

After finding our lodging, we went to collect our Compostela. The receptionist could not believe that I had covered so many kilometres in one go, alone, at my age, and she told me how proud she was to present me with my Compostela. That day I became 'Claudiam', as the certificate is written in Latin. It is given to anyone who has walked, for spiritual or religious purposes, a minimum of 100 kilometres to reach Santiago de Compostela. Those who had not walked for spiritual or religious reasons received a different Compostela. If a pilgrim walked only 100 kilometres, they had to have two stamps per day to prove where they had passed through. If even one stamp was missing, they would not get their Compostela. If the pilgrim had walked from afar and for whatever reasons - health or otherwise - could not walk the last kilometres or metres even, they would not get the Compostela. I found this second rule a bit harsh, as a pilgrim could have covered thousands of kilometres and become very sick at the last moment, or broken a leg, had a heart attack, or something like that.

Later, Celia, Ruth and I went to join a long queue under the torrid sun in front of the eastern facade of the cathedral. Following a tradition dating from the 12th century, we wanted to go from the Praza da Quintana through the 'Puerta del Padron' ('Door of Forgiveness'). The door is opened only during a Holy Year. At other times it is walled up. We had been waiting for nearly an hour and a half in the sun when we realised we were standing in the wrong queue! We went through a side door to enter the magnificent cathedral of 23,000 square metres of pure Romanesque style. The inside is in the shape of a cross with two side aisles along the nave, as well as numerous chapels. The construction of the cathedral began in the middle of the 11th century and it has been modified through the centuries with additional towers, cloisters and facades. It was an overwhelming experience to be there and to feel so insignificant in such a magnificent place where so many pilgrims had put their feet since the Middle Ages. I was humbled.

Over the centuries, pilgrims have entered through the western Baroque facade of the cathedral, the Praza do

Obradoiro. Immediately inside there is the 'Portico da Gloria'. The central tympanum shows Christ's image as Judge and Redeemer with the wounds in his hands and feet. He is surrounded by angels carrying the instruments of the Passion. In the middle pillar, Saint James is sculpted, his face is peaceful and he has a scroll in his hands showing the words 'Misit me Dominus' ('the Lord sent me'). Below him is what is called the 'Tree of Jesse', which is very important for pilgrims, as it is customary for them to touch the left foot of those statues, signifying that they had reached their destination. Over time, so many pilgrims have laid their hands on the pillar that a groove has been worn into the stone. I was not able to put my hands in the groove due to scaffolding and I wondered if all the pilgrims who had passed before me would consider my pilgrimage officially finished, as I had not done this customary gesture! I had reached Santiago de Compostela and I decided not to trouble myself with this detail.

The most captivating element of the cathedral's interior is undoubtedly the tremendously beautiful altar in the main chapel with its glistening 13th century gold- and silver-plated statue of Saint James dressed as a pilgrim. Above him and beside him are angels, apostles and kings.

I completed my visit to the cathedral, knowing that I would return. I went to explore the town. Santiago de Compostela was rebuilt in the 11th century around the cathedral and embellished with Romanesque, Gothic, Renaissance and Baroque buildings. Through its winding, narrow and cobbled streets, pedestrian quarters and archways, there were pilgrims everywhere and many were familiar faces. I had met such a number along the track. It was lovely to see them again and have one last hug. I belonged to the family of pilgrims forever, and no words were necessary between us, as we all understood each other. I saw Tony and Cathy. I had been worried about them, wondering how Cathy had managed with her crocodile shoes along some of the inhospitable tracks. With courage, they had finished their Camino and were eager to see their son after so long, as he too had finished his pilgrimage, but by bicycle. This lovely family would be one again, each enriched by their private experiences.

Early the next morning, I was back at the Praza da Quintana, which was once divided into two parts: one was called 'Quintana de Mortos' (for the dead), for there had been a cemetery in that section in the past, and the other section was called 'Quintana de Vivos' (for the living), formerly used as a market on the upper-side. I was waiting patiently outside, hoping to be able to go into the cathedral through the 'Royal Door', as I wanted to take part in the famous 'Pilgrims' Mass', but already there was such a long queue. My chances of getting in seemed impossible. Somehow, I got in and I was standing against a huge pillar when a lovely Galician woman asked me if I was a pilgrim and where I had started my journey from. As no one would know where Vezelay was, I said, 'Below Paris'. As soon as I told her this, she asked one of her grandchildren to give up their seat for me. I ended up in the central nave with a full view of the ceremony. At one stage, the archbishop read aloud all the names of the different countries where the pilgrims who had arrived the day before had come from. It was quite emotional, especially when I heard 'Australia' and 'France'.

The hymns were beautiful and created tangible warmth among the congregation. Emotions crept into my soul and

I remembered all the members of my family, the people I had met during my lifetime who had passed and the ones still on this earth, as well as the ones I had met along my pilgrimage. All of these people joined as one in my heart in this beautiful cathedral, which was a witness to the end of my endeavour.

The unique moment of the 'botafumeiro' ceremony, which was anticipated by all the worshippers, arrived. It was a ritual dating from the 14th century, originally thought to cover the body odours of the pilgrims. The 'botafumeirio' is an incense chalice that is 1.6 metres in height and weighs 80 kilograms. It swings on a long rope through the central nave and is pulled by eight men for at least three minutes. The incense flew everywhere, the organs filled up the cathedral with their music and a nun with the voice of an angel sang in Galician. It was like listening to a mass in Latin and I recalled the masses of my youth.

As 2010 was a Holy Year, the 'botafumeiro' was used at every Pilgrims' Mass. It was an impressive ceremony that lifted the hearts of all the pilgrims. We all felt the love of Saint James enveloping us: it was just magical. In a wonderful finale, there was a crescendo of sounds from the organs with hymns sung by the nuns in their angelic voices. The ambiance was such that it felt as though Heaven had opened its doors. After the mass, I went to a side chapel where there is a sculpture of Saint James and had a photo taken of me holding my credential and my Compostela. My credential was more than two metres long with 176 stamps in it - much to the amazement of those assembled - and flashes came from all directions.

I had sent a text message to Monique from France,

Jonathan from Austria, and Marie from Belgium to notify them of my arrival in Santiago, and I was on my way to meet Monique. She had just arrived in Santiago de Compostela. As I crossed the Praza do Obradoiro, I saw a man in a T-Shirt with 'Australia' written on it. I could not resist and went to ask if he was Australian. No, was the answer. I was then dragged to the Spanish priest of this group who had been in Adelaide and Melbourne just four months previously. After some exchanges and to my surprise, the priest took my hand and put me in the middle of a circle made by his group and blessed me. This was happening on the most important square of Santiago de Compostela at the entrance to the cathedral where all pilgrims end their journey. It was amazing. Many pilgrims were still arriving from their pilgrimage and they too called out my name. The magic kept on going and this lasted until I left Santiago de Compostela.

I found out that I had walked faster than many of the pilgrims and this surprised me. I told Monique that I would be going on foot to Fisterra and Muxia, but Monique could not. She had had serious health problems along the way and was happy to have made it to Santiago de Compostela. We hugged, as we knew we might not see each other again, but God willing, we could perhaps meet again in 2021 - the next Holy Year - and walk the Saint James' Way again.

As I was on my way to meet Jonathan, I met more pilgrims and the streets of Santiago de Compostela seemed to be resonating with 'Claude! Claude!' Jonathan had come back from Fisterra. We were so happy to see each other. I had presumed that he would have been back in Austria by that stage. We met on the Praza do

Obradoiro and he had in his hands a bottle of red wine, two glasses and a huge cigar. He laughed at seeing my astonishment. Before leaving for his pilgrimage, he had made a promise to himself that if he made it to Fisterra, he would share a bottle of wine and smoke a huge cigar, just to experience it. I was going to be the witness of his extravagances. We walked to the lovely Park Alameda, where we sat down and enjoyed each other's company, sharing the experiences we had had along the path. Jonathan got up to find a match or a lighter to light his precious cigar. He was struggling to get it lit. During that time, I had been left by myself on a bench with a bottle of wine and two glasses beside me. The Galician women walking through the park were giving me strange and judgmental looks. I found this scene hilarious, for I drink very little and I thought of how, just a little while ago, I had been blessed by a Spanish priest in the middle of the most important square of Santiago de Compostela. Jonathan did not finish smoking his cigar. I had a small sip of wine and thought how my children would not have recognised their mother. We talked more and then we each went our own way. Tomorrow, Jonathan would return to Austria with his mind full of dreams for his future. The pilgrimage had made him a stronger person and given him the certainty to attempt every endeavour to realise his plans for the future. I had had the pleasure of meeting this young man on his birthday before Burgos, some 330 kilometres ago. He had helped me heal one part of my heart and I hoped that, through our exchanges, I might have helped him too. I wished him well and prayed that his dreams would be realised and that life would be kind to him.

I have always been a people person and the path had shown me where my next steps might take me. My heart had been filled up, but first I would have to leave the path and let myself be led into my future. Would I be strong enough to do it? On that day, I did not know where and what my future was going to be, and the sadness of the moment overtook me. Yes, I had achieved it: I had arrived in Santiago de Compostela in front of the cathedral. It had been my dream, my desire, my wish from the start, but so what? It was all over now. Had I done something special by covering so many kilometres day after day over all types of terrain and in all conditions and weather? I did not think so. I had just walked each day and added the number of kilometres to those of the previous days until, eventually, it became a bigger number. At the end, the kilometres had no significance. I was empty, as it was over. Would I survive in the world after what I had known? I was not sure.

What had been most important for me was not the number of kilometres I covered, but the meetings, the sharing and the honesty. People along the path were not master of this or that anymore or just a junkie down the alley. They all had a name, a face and a heart, which beat just like any other human being's with their joys and pains. Young and old carried their own personal burdens and walked their pilgrimage for different purposes, all looking for something that had disappeared in this modern world. Our 'baggage' differed, but they were burdens, just the same, and each one of us was looking for an answer to our dilemma or for a real purpose in life. Some started their journey of the Saint James' Way as a personal physical challenge, however, bit by bit, their perception changed and, with time, new individuals appeared within themselves and they were changed forever. Each one of us had a special pilgrimage. A pilgrimage of a lifetime and a pilgrimage of renewal, which meant a new beginning. Different energies come out of the path. It was said that, in earlier days, the dust coming off the track was from the steps of the walking pilgrims, which created a cloud as they were following the Milky Way. This pilgrimage still lives on in 2010 and the magic of this path will keep on going forever over the centuries.

Did I find myself along the path? Did I find what I had been looking for before I started my journey? I did, yet there was something else to do, but at that time my heart was still in too much turmoil to think about it.

'My last burden left behind'

It was time for me to leave Santiago to go towards Fisterra and Muxia. I sat on the edge of the bed and remembered all the pain, the fears and the insecurities I had experienced along the way. Surprised by these feelings, I questioned myself. Why was I hesitating? Then, in front of my eyes, as though I was watching a film, I saw the people and the meetings that had filled up my soul. Something triggered in my inner self and there was a desire to go forwards. My pilgrimage was not finished: there was something else that I had to discover. Just like the beginning of my pilgrimage, something or someone had been pushing me and all doubts left me. With a sturdy hand, I put my backpack on and as I felt its weight, a strong feeling of determination came over me. I opened the door and ventured into the deserted streets of Santiago de Compostela in search of the track, happy to be back on the path. I could only hear the noise of my trekking poles on the pavement.

Before the hamlet of Sarela de Abaixo I could see the towers of the Cathedral of Santiago on the horizon behind me. The sun was just rising and its rays emitted an aura behind the towers, making the cathedral look even more magical and mystical. My heart was beating powerfully as the realisation that I was leaving Santiago hit.

I crossed eucalyptus forests, the familiar smell of which was intoxicating. Soon, I would go back to Australia where they are so plentiful. The track was full of stones and gravel and with the soles of my shoes so thin, I could feel every single pebble and stone. The extra innersoles did not seem to have made any difference. Each step caused me excruciating pain, but courageously and full of faith I kept going forward. Why was I going to Fisterra and Muxia, apart from the fact that I had agreed to it when I first enrolled for my pilgrimage in Vezelay? Was it because of my desire not to stop?

After the discovery of the tomb of Saint James during the ninth century, pilgrims would go on to Fisterra and Muxia, located in the western-most part of the Galicia region on the edge of the Atlantic Coast. Its coast is very atmospheric with turbulent and rough waves. Many shipwrecks occurred in this dangerous coastal part and it was called Costa da Morte ('Coast of Death'). Until the Middle Ages, the Costa da Morte was the last explored land of the most western part of Europe. The Latin name for Fisterra means 'the end of the world' and at its most westerly point, there is a piece of rocky land called Cabo Fisterra, meaning 'Cape Finisterre'. To find their way, the Romans used to follow the stars. It was the stars of the Milky Way which brought them to Cabo Fisterra where they saw the sun disappearing into the sea for the first time. At the time, they thought the world was flat and Cabo Fisterra became known as the end of the world. Then, this place grew into a mystical site and a lot of pagan rites and rituals were practised in the area. In the middle of the first millennium when the disciples of Saint James brought back the saint's body, the region of Fisterra began to develop an interest in Christianity and Cabo Fisterra became known as the place where most pilgrims would finish their pilgrimage at the landmark 0 kilometres.

Muxia is a small, coastal town north of Fisterra that relies mostly on tourism and the pilgrims to survive. In front of the Church of Nosa Señora da Barca, there are strangely shaped stones that, for Christians, were understood to be the wreck of the Virgin boat and its sails that had been transformed into stones. It was said that the Virgin Mary appeared on a boat to Saint James at Muxia when he was discouraged about the few conversions he had accomplished, and she ordered him to go back to pursue the evangelisation of Spain. Maybe this legend was a message of bravery for all of us not to despair and to keep on trying when challenges arise in our lives.

I crossed more eucalyptus forests with small, stony tracks, more climbs and descents and more streams. The birds were singing. I was back in the quietness of nature after the noise and cacophony of the last sections of the track before Santiago de Compostela. I passed through a lot of hamlets and at the top of one landmark there was a bag which had been abandoned, possibly by a pilgrim who was too sick or too tired to carry it any further. Or was it a symbol of someone who had left their burden on the path and who was now walking freely for the rest of the journey, relieved of their load? I would never know.

On the outskirts of Puente Maceira, I was approached by Maria and her partner, Philip, from Sydney. Maria was quite taken by my desire to walk the Saint James' Way and she was wondering if the pilgrims pay for their lodging in the shelters. I told her that a fee of five to six euro a night, or sometimes even less, was asked. I also told her that, in France on the other hand, you give whatever you can afford. In the past, the Spanish shelters also operated on a donation basis, however, some people had abused the kindness of the municipal associations, and gradually a small fee was charged to cover the expenses for electricity and water. A lot of private refuges had popped up along the way, and the fees for a night could reach up to 10 euro.

As in the Meseta, the weather in Galicia changes very quickly from cold to very hot in no time. At that moment, it was very hot - maybe 40 degrees. I went across the 14th century Roman bridge over the fast waters of the Rio Tambre. Its tempestuous waters were a deep azure colour and the white foam looked like cream on top of a cake: the perfect contrast to the grey stones of the bridge.

From now on, I would follow either the yellow arrows or the symbol of the blue and yellow stylised, ceramic shells with the sun's rays pointing in the direction I had to take. I arrived at Negreira, a small medieval town snuggled in a valley with hills and mountains on either side. Negreira was in full excitement, for Spain was in the final for the soccer World Cup and people were heading towards the park where a huge screen had been erected for everyone to enjoy the game. In the middle of the night, I was awoken by fire crackers and cheers: Spain had won. I was happy for them.

Galicia is beautiful, with its forests, mountains and old villages, although some villages were almost abandoned. The few faithful farmers who stayed in their villages were planting cereals in the fields. At the top of each mountain and hill, there were wind farms generating electricity for all the surrounding villages and hamlets. The Spanish people are so conscientious when it comes to saving the environment.

Maurice from France arrived at the San Marina

lodging at the same time as me. He had lost his wife to cancer and he had decided to start his pilgrimage from Saint-Jean-Pied-de-Port. His health was precarious and walking was very difficult for him. He had to stop to catch his breath every 50 metres. We had something in common, however, and that was our determination and strength of character. It was the magical power of the walk: nothing would have stopped him, just as nothing would have stopped me.

It was raining and cold. For a long time I had to walk along a road, when at the top of the mountain, I got a magnificent view of an artificial lake. Since I had crossed paths with Maurice, I had met no one. It was just like the beginning of my pilgrimage in France. I was returning to the source. In this peaceful environment, I was receiving God's message. I had the power within me and I had to find the strength and courage to let go of all the scars that had been my companions for so long. In this serene environment where the birds sang their melody in a high pitch, their lovely notes resounding like the voices of angels, I would have to be strong. The wounds would have to be closed so that no more pain could enter my heart. I sat on the trunk of a tree and, once more, I held myself tightly, but I was not quite ready to let go.

As I walked, everything around me was fresh and green after the rain. There was gentleness and a soothing harmony in the countryside. In Santiago de Compostela, I had lost myself among the cheerful crowd of pilgrims. My ego had been boosted since I had led the simple life of the path in which my only worry was to find a bunk or a mattress for the night. I had worked hard and had a simple life, yet the new me was craving an even simpler one, and I was no longer the person who had started the pilgrimage three months ago in Vezelay. When one walks in solitude for a long time, there is no escape from oneself. Self-discovery is inevitable. I had to accept myself with both my faults and my good qualities. I also had to learn to forgive others and forgive all the emotional pain that had been imposed on me during my life, which had been so hard to carry. Most importantly, I had to forgive myself, as sometimes, unintentionally, one can hurt another human being with a word or a look, neither knowing, nor grasping the consequences of one's actions.

At Olveiroa, I was having a hot chocolate in a café with other pilgrims when I noticed Paula from Argentina looking at me with intensity. She asked me if we could speak in private. In the freezing cold, we went outside and sat on one of the stone benches in the park. Paula, an athlete, had been covering a minimum of 36 to 40 kilometres on a daily basis, but had not managed to let go of her sorrows. She was desperate and saddened to return home without achieving what she had hoped to gain. As her remaining time in Spain would allow it, I advised her to finish at Fisterra, then walk another route and walk it in a different frame of mind. She could start in Arles and stop at Puente La Reina, where the Camino Frances and the Camino Aragones join. This track, which starts at Arles and stretches across a large section of France before passing through the Col du Somport, is called the Camino Aragones. This path is more arduous and is the wildest of all the routes of the pilgrimage. Not many pilgrims use it because of its difficulty. I advised her also to go at a slower pace and to switch off her competitive, sporty brain. To cover 36 or 40 kilometres a day, she had to run part of the day, but the pilgrimage is not a competition. By going slower, I told her she would have to go quietly into her inner self and, if she wanted, she could cry or scream and let go of her sorrows, bit by bit. It is very important for peace to be able to enter our hearts so that we can move forward in our private lives.

Due to the isolation of this path, I had to be aware and to listen to what was brought to me. Paula was a messenger with the following advice: do not run away from yourself and your future. God had a plan for me, as He does for every one of us. I was in His hands: He just had to direct me. He knew my future, my new path, and I would have to be a willing participant in this last part of my life, though I still had to do one more thing. It was 14 July 2010. My children contacted me for Bastille Day and my heart was filled with their love.

The next day, I was following a very wet footpath along a bubbling stream. While climbing a hill, I passed under many powered wind turbines and I was amazed, as I could hear very little noise from their huge blades. Again, I climbed up and down in divine scenery. As I was passing through a forest, I noticed some wild horses. This part of Galicia is more rugged, its streams are very plentiful, and as I walked I could hear the lovely sound of rushing water. I got lost again, but somehow I found my way to the village of Hospital. I had been told by pilgrims who I had met at Olveiroa that there was a very steep descent in this area and that I should be extremely careful, as one could easily lose one's footing. At every bend I was expecting this difficult slope, which never seemed to arrive, and I thought to myself, 'They have had me on'. I was in the province of Dumbria, heading in the direction of Fisterra, and I was still waiting for this terrible slope. I arrived at the 18th century shrine of Da Nosa Señora das Neves, with its miraculous water. There was a 'Livre d'Or' left in a little niche and I added my message to those written by other pilgrims from around the world. A Japanese pilgrim had scribbled words on a piece of paper and left his boots behind. There were pictures of young children who had maybe been taken away from their parents at an early age or had perhaps been healed by the miraculous water. I would never know.

Later on, I went to the shrine of Saint Peter the Martyr, with its miraculous water for rheumatism and other ailments. I drank a large amount of this water, as I was thirsty, and I filled up my container with this precious liquid, sure that I would be well protected from these ailments for the rest of my life. After all, it is better to be safe than sorry! As I was leaving this shrine, my footsteps cut across those of Roberto, a Galician who was living in England and who was walking with his best mate, a Labrador. They had started from Saint-Jean-Pied-de-Port. I was amazed by the courage and endurance of his dog and I noticed that his feet were in much better condition than mine!

At the top of a plateau, I saw the Atlantic Ocean for the first time - the famous Costa da Morte. I related to the feeling of awe that the Romans and the pilgrims from the Middle Ages would have felt after walking for so many months across mountains, and then seeing the ocean for the very first time. I descended the Caminos Chans - the name given to the walk from Olveiroa to Fisterra - where I found the famous slope that I had been warned about. It was not so much difficult, but somewhat unpredictable.

At the entrance of Cee I saw Monique waiting for me. She had decided to walk with me once again, after all, but this time would be the last. On 15 July 2010, we left for Fisterra in the morning. Straight away, I became aware of Monique's struggles; her pace was very slow and I witnessed the pain she was putting her body through. I became worried. At the Arch of San Roque, we got our first glimpse of Cape Fisterra on the horizon. Seeing it, Monique broke down. Her emotions were too great and she had to sit down to get her breath back. It had taken a lot of will and determination to complete her pilgrimage and she was so close to having achieved what she had hoped for. After her first failed attempt, she had started all over again in early 2010 from Le Puy-en-Velay. She was 64 years old when she set out on her second attempt, and this time she knew she would make it. Respectfully, I waited beside her as she regained her composure. I knew what she was going through and I had been the witness of a very special moment in the life of an individual. In silence, we slowly walked along the beautiful scenic roads, dunes, spectacular beaches and steep cliffs. We were in communion with our surroundings. There were gorgeous views of small bays with turquoise water and beaches of white sand to enjoy along the way before we reached the long Praia de Langosteira. Then we headed towards Fisterra, which is a famous fishing village in north-west Galicia. We fetched our 'Fisterrana' certificate at the municipal refuge, which stated that we had arrived at the end of the earth on foot. On our way to the lighthouse and to the mystical Cape Fisterra, which is the final destination for many pilgrims, we waved at a pilgrim who passed us. She was an Australian from Melbourne.

459

At Cape Fisterra, there is a ritual that dates back to pre-Christian times. The pilgrims would burn their shoes as well as some of the clothes they had worn along their pilgrimage, signifying that they had reached the end of their journey. The burning of the clothes was symbolic for the pilgrim, as after the burning, a new person could emerge the next day. We did not see the magnificent sunset, which had created such fear in the Romans when they saw it for the first time, as it started raining. When I set foot on the rock near the lighthouse, I was affected by strong emotions, but nothing like the ones I had experienced in Santiago de Compostela. I caught sight of the landmark which reads: '0 kilometres. THE END'. As it was not quite the end for me, I did not burn my boots or my clothes because I needed them to finish my journey to Muxia. Tourists and pilgrims alike stopped us and were amazed at our achievements. They took our photographs, and those who were not able to finish the walk, due to pain or injury, were in awe of the two 64-year-old women who had done it. Obviously, we enjoyed the popularity.

As we were leaving, we stopped at the medieval Church of Santa Maria das Areas with the impressive sculpture of the Santo Christo. The legend said that the statue had appeared on the beach after being thrown from a boat during a storm. The next day, Monique decided to join me yet again. She could not stop and so we started our walk, which would take us to Lires. The fauna and flora were stupendous and the scenery was out of this world with the Costa da Morte nearly always in view. My feet were still hurting, but nothing would have stopped me. I was still pushed by the energy of the track. Monique was exhausted and I was praying that she would be able to reach Muxia without too many problems. Bravely, she kept on going. At Lires, I climbed up the Monte Veladoiro and was engulfed by the beauty of the place. I went to the beach to dip my feet in the water when something black and sticky landed on my toes. To my horror, it was some oil residue that I could not get rid of, as it went into the grooves of my skin. In 2002, an oil tanker sank in this area, which created an oil spill off the coast and polluted thousands of kilometres along the coastlines of Spain, Galicia, France and Portugal. This spill had been the largest environmental disaster for Spain and Portugal, and here I was in Lires, eight years later, with remnants of the oil on my feet. I was flabbergasted. What are we doing to our planet to satisfy our worldly needs? I compared this residue to what was left for me to get rid of in my personal life before I finished my pilgrimage.

The next day we would reach Muxia. Would I stop there, or go back to Santiago de Compostela on foot? I still did not know. To cross the Rio Castro we would have had to go over very slippery, slimy stepping stones. Because of the recent rain, the current in the river was too strong. I went to check it and realised it was too dangerous to cross. On my way back I met a young jogger, Noemie, from Adelaide, who was teaching English in Spain.

Monique was waiting for me and I informed her that we should take another route. We crossed through Frixe. In Orzon, we saw the largest 'horreos' of Galicia. Mount Aferroas was the last ascent before Muxia. We kept on walking along the roads, the dunes, the forests of pines, of eucalyptus and heath moulds. I could hear the waves crashing on the coast. Soon, it would all be over. The emotions of Santiago flashed back and I started to walk alone. I did not want to have anyone witnessing my distress, but most of all, I felt lost with my conflicting feelings. Would I be strong enough to go back into the world, away from what had been my life for the last three months? Would I be a lost soul among the crowd, drifting like a boat taken by the treacherous current, with the waves smashing it against the cliffs? How could anyone understand what I was feeling? I was in turmoil. I would have to re-adapt to what made no sense to me anymore and what I did not want to be part of. Just like a snake, I had shed my skin, replacing it with a new one.

Along the dramatic coast line, someone had left their boots on a dune. They looked like lost souls that had been left, waiting to be gradually covered by the sand. They were of no use to anyone anymore. I saw the sign for Muxia, and waited for Monique. Once she arrived, the two of us entered the little town, our footsteps in unison and our voices silent. No words were needed.

We saw Galician women doing lace-making under the porches of a cultural centre as we entered the town. Later on, we walked along the coastal route of Camino da Pel ('way of the skin') to the Church of Nosa Señora da Barca, which was built on the Cape of Muxia. Outside the little church stand the famous 'Piedras Santas' ('Holy stones') and the 'A Pedra dos Cadris' stone. The latter is in the shape of a kidney. It was alleged that if one passed under these enormous stones nine times, one would be healed of kidney and rheumatic ailments.

On 18 July 2010, Monique took the bus back to Santiago, whereas I stayed behind an extra day. I still had to make one last decision. Would I return to Santiago on foot? I had not slept well, as every part of my body was aching. In fact, I was in agony and through the pain, a message was sent to me. It was freezing, as it was only 10 degrees and windy. I walked back to the sanctuary and sat on a rock, close to the coastline. The waves were beating fiercely against the rocks of the shore. I was admiring the beauty of the place with its wind-power farms on the hills and its lighthouse. I went more deeply into my soul and gradually, against my will, I capitulated, surrendered and bowed down like a solider in front of the enemy. I would have to stop at Muxia: I would walk no more. With this decision, heaviness engulfed me and coldness enveloped my heart. Just like this frosty morning, I was cold inside and outside at the thought that everything would soon be over. Slowly, I got up and, like a very old woman, I walked towards Mount Corpiño. It would be my last climb, my very last mountain. I was in turmoil. I had to bring peace into my soul and I prayed with all my might.

The meetings I had had along my pilgrimage were not simply coincidences. Albert Einstein once said that: *'coincidences are God's way of remaining anonymous.'* Through them, I had constantly received messages, but at the same time, this did not mean that I wanted to confront all the messages that were given to me. Through my pilgrimage, I had been helped mostly by men: caring, wise men who had been there for me at the appropriate time. I could hear again their words of courage and wisdom and thought to myself that they were possibly not even aware that they had helped me to grow and heal. They had helped me heal my heart, just as I had helped them heal theirs. 'When you give, you receive'.

A little while ago, I had bowed down like a soldier in front of the ocean. Now, at the summit of this mountain, I had to perform one last act. I had to make peace with men, as men had been the ones who had hurt me so much during my lifetime. I had to release the pain and I had to forgive, for without forgiveness, my new route would never open and I would never be able to walk it freely. Suddenly, as if by magic, a gust of wind came and carried away my sorrows and pain into the universe. From now on, I would be able to fly high like a bird that trusts in the power of its wings when it leaves the nest for the first time. On that day, 18 July 2010, I was set free.

After a while, I pulled a little heart-shaped stone out of my pocket. I had gathered it somewhere in France with the intention of laying it down wherever I ended my journey. I held it tight and searched for a place where it would be protected from the wind. In a similar way, I wanted my heart to be protected. Delicately, I placed it beside a small boulder under a wild plant to leave it there forever. As I was doing so, my heart started to beat so hard and so fast, that it seemed as though it wanted to jump out of my chest. This little stone had been the symbol of my journey. I stayed still for a while, just looking at it, and then I called it a day.

A young Spanish couple nearby could see my emotions and they approached me and gave me comfort before I climbed down again. As I was doing so, the full realisation that it was all over hit me harder than ever. From the Church of Nosa Señora da Barca, a Spanish tenor sang powerful Galician songs and his voice stirred me even more.

The 18 July 2010 was the last night of my journey on the Camino and I did not sleep well. My dream had been realised and now it was all behind me. I would have to have the courage and strength to go forwards. The next morning I left for Santiago by bus. Seeing a few pilgrims walking was hard for me. I recalled Monique's last words before she had gotten on the bus to return to Santiago de Compostela the previous day. 'I thank God for allowing me to meet you, Claude. You have brought a lot to me and, most of all, you have taught me how to interact with people in a simple and easy manner with honesty and love. Thank you, thank you so very much'. I had had to control myself and not explode into tears upon hearing her kind words. We had hugged and promised to keep in touch and yes, God willing, we would meet again and walk the Camino Frances in the next 'Anno Santo'.

As I arrived in Santiago de Compostela, I strolled to the Franciscan's convent that Jonathan from Austria had mentioned to me. On the door there was a piece of paper with the words: 'Open at 4.00pm'. It was 10.30am. I could not wait that long, as I needed to talk. My inner self was in chaos because of the emotions in my soul. I felt completely lost. I prayed and asked God to send me someone who could listen to me while I let go of my emotions. After a few minutes, the doors of the convent were opened by a nun and a Galician woman. I approached them, but no word came out of my mouth. I was sobbing and, upon seeing my distress, they let me in. By chance, two more angels, in the forms of Sister Anna and Marisa the 'hospitaliera', had come across my path. I entered and, patiently, they listened, then they hugged me, spoke peaceful words and gave me advice of faith and courage. They made me aware that I could do the same thing in the real world that I had done during my pilgrimage. I just needed to open my eyes and let my heart go free and this would lead me in the same way it had on the Saint James' Way. The de-briefing with these two beautiful angels and their words of wisdom were God's message so that acceptance and peace could enter me. Afterwards, Marisa took a basin, washed my feet and kissed them. Her gesture made me feel so humble. Tears rolled down my cheeks again, as I had received so much love and so many blessings along this path.

I left and went strolling in the streets. Nearby, there was a little square close to the convent where I saw a young woman, Beatrice from France, with her donkey and Raymond from Switzerland who was holding her hand. Her body language showed that she was in much distress. I asked if I could help and although her answer was negative, her eyes were telling me differently. I sat beside her on the bench and patiently waited until she felt confident enough to open up. She had had a terrible encounter, however, with Raymond's gentle and patient help, she was learning how to trust again. Maybe in that moment I was receiving my new direction from God. Maybe He was leading me on my new road, so hope and deep peace could enter. The words of Amar resonated in me again. Would I be stopped in my endeavour? I did not know, but I doubted it.

On that day, 19 July 2010, I ended my pilgrimage full of hope and eagerness for the future. A few days later, on the eve of Saint James' feast day, I noticed a familiar face sitting on the steps of the cathedral. It was Jokubas from Lithuania and he looked so lonely. Both of us had achieved our dreams. He had finished his pilgrimage after nearly six and a half months on the road and he did not want to face the world again. His wish was to go back home by foot, but it was not possible, as his wife and his little daughter were waiting for his return. On the steps of the cathedral, our two souls cried in unison, as they could understand each other's feelings. We hugged and said goodbye.

I wanted to take part in the festivities in Santiago, and so I arrived at the Praza do Obradoiro at around 5.00pm. The square was already fully packed. It was hot and there was no entertainment at that early hour. This was not a problem, however, as the young and old sang Spanish folk songs and kept the crowd entertained. To the delight of the crowd, at 10.00pm the King of Spain, Juan Carlos I, his wife, Queen Sofia, their family and prominent Spanish notables appeared on the balcony of the Rajoy Palace parliament building. A stupendous display of sound and light started from the facade of the cathedral. When the 'Fuego del Apostol' ('Apostles' fireworks') started, it seemed as though the whole cathedral was on fire.

On Saint James' feast day on 25 July, the plaza was jammed full of pilgrims. I was determined to pass through the cathedral's 'Door of Forgiveness', which is opened only on a Holy Year, and to visit the crypt of Saint James on his feast day. Well, what a queue! I stood under the scorching sun for more than three hours before entering. In the crypt it was an emotional moment for all the pilgrims. We all knew what personal challenges we had been through on our private journeys, but we all felt as one. Peace and love fell on us. It was an amazing and powerful moment.

While wandering the winding streets of Santiago, I felt compelled to go into a church. I was drawn towards the altar, when my eyes caught sight of a little chapel on the left-hand side. To my amazement, it was a chapel dedicated to the Miraculous Medal. I sat on a pew and felt my Maman and Papa putting their arms around me with all their love, saying, 'Bravo, little one'.

EPILOGUE

'The realisation of a dream'

Quite a few years ago, a seed was planted by my friend Anna. On 4 April 2010, I took to the road on foot to bring that seed to fruition. I wanted to walk the Saint James' Way in its entirety and in one go. I was oblivious to what was ahead of me; I just had a desire - a strong desire - to fulfil a dream. Somehow, I knew deep down in my inner self that I would finish the walk. I never doubted it. In all honesty, however, I did not know that I would accomplish all that I did. I walked day after day as though blindfolded - a bit like in our every-day lives - not knowing what was in front of me or what I would have to go through to reach the next shelter. I crossed villages, towns and cities, which were just dots on a map, sleeping in a different bunk every night, walking in the rain, wind, cold and fog, along stony tracks, dirt and muddy paths, as well as through beautiful, untouched scenery. I climbed and descended many mountains across France, over the Pyrenees and across the Castile region, with its dreaded Meseta of terrible heat and cold, and to the north-west of Spain to the 'Coast of Death'. I experienced terrible pain as I pushed my body to undertake more physical challenges and I had to deal with a lot of my own uncertainty and fear. And I grew. I met some pilgrims who did not see any change occurring in themselves and who had by-passed the beautiful discovery of who they were. Perhaps their eyes were closed or maybe they were not ready yet. This would be for another time, if there was

469

to be another time.

For me, my personal journey was different. All along 'The Way', I had beautiful meetings. I opened my heart to pilgrims in need and they opened theirs to me. Most of the pilgrims were searching for something special, perhaps a nirvana or an answer. I met challenges as well as the kindness of the human soul and I had been blessed.

Whether they were religious or not, the walkers, cyclists and pilgrims along the path who had noticed changes in themselves had been stirred forever. They would return home as new people. We all had something in common: we were 'one' in the search for something. We were walking the Saint James' Way, following the stars and the Milky Way. Consequently, all of us had grown on a more personal level and we had allowed ourselves to be more open to the brotherhood of humanity so as to live in this modern world the best way possible. I learnt that we have to create a balance between the human world and nature. This balance is delicate, but we can achieve it.

I was saddened to see the end of my journey, but, at the same time, I had lived an exhilarating experience and I had made it. I had covered more kilometres than I thought possible. My fellow pilgrims said that I had covered 2,500 kilometres. As the days passed, the number of kilometres had very little significance. What counted were the meetings, the discovery of unreal, mystical moments and the realisation of who I really was.

I had put my footsteps on this ancient path along with millions of pilgrims from over the ages. I now look at my boots with tenderness. They were my faithful companions and they carried me to the end of my journey as dutiful, trusting servants and friends. There is a bond between us that will never be broken. I will never have the heart to discard them, as they served me so well.

Through the experience of the Saint James' Way, I have become a stronger person and more assertive and confident in my abilities. I left my burdens behind me and since then I feel lighter, true to myself and happy. In front of the cathedral in Santiago, I was proud as I saw the end of a magic moment and my soul was filled up and full of emotions.

My journey was not finished exactly: it was time for a new beginning, but a different one. I was sure that, just as the doors had opened for this pilgrimage, so they would open and show me the way of my future life. This path with its special energy and strange experiences is for anyone who wants to unlock their heart. The really magical lessons of the path are to unleash our past, be more aware of the present and live in the moment, for then you will flourish.

A lesson I learnt was: 'Do not despair. Have a dream and follow it through'. We can all conquer the world - our little, personal, private world - in different ways. Our dream can be small, but it is our dream. If we want to be a willing participant, we will make it happen and the doors will open in front of us. If we are afraid of tackling it, we will learn courage and strength and, after learning, we will not be afraid. The world will be our oyster. We will triumph over our fears and in doing so we will take control of our lives for bigger and better things.

All of us face challenges through the course of our lives. These challenges are our personal mountains and it is the way we climb them that will make the difference. Age is irrelevant: it is all will and determination.

Learn to trust yourself, God and the universe, or any other power. Have honest and sincere wishes and desires. Know that God will never let you down. If you have the courage to walk the pilgrimage, you will return changed, free or more free from your emotional burdens. Know that there is another way to find your own personal freedom. I had to discover myself right within the deepest part of me. I wish for you all that you accomplish your dreams in your lifetimes, for then the stars will glitter in your eyes and you will reach the top of your own mountains where the beautiful landscape will never end.

Dream big, for your dream will be realised. Take life in both hands and enjoy its discovery. The light will always direct you.

ACKNOWLEDGEMENTS

I would like to thank my children and their partners for their love and faith in me: Sabine, David, Brett and Alexandra; my grandson, Alexander; my sister, Michele; my brother, Philippe and all my friends who had trust in me to achieve the unthinkable. I am grateful to Anna Chambers from Melbourne who inadvertently planted a seed which germinated and helped me become a stronger person and discover a new me: the real me.

My thanks also go to all the people who helped me along 'the way', especially Monique and Claude Fortin from Reims who showed me the ropes at the beginning of my pilgrimage, Cristele and Bruno Guillier from Casseneuil who took me into their home and hearts when I could barely walk and, of course, to Dominique in Australia for placing these wonderful people along my path.

I have to thank my fellow workmates and my sister's partner, Bernard, who had doubted my ability to finish the Saint James' Way. When I felt I could not go on anymore, I remembered them and pushed my body even more.

I want to thank Gerard Benjamin for his advice and William Borbasi for encouraging me to pursue my writing.

Most of all, I thank with all my heart Jeanette McDonald, who put in me the first seeds of faith in my ability to write, as well as Dr Maureen Bella and Dr Kay Fraser, my readers, for their continual advice and trust in me so I was able to conquer my second mountain: the writing of this book. Without their constant love and friendship I would never have had the courage to publish this story.

And finally, I want to thank two beautiful young ladies: my editor, Clare McEniery, and my book designer, Katie Farmer. I hope that my book will open some new doors for their futures and I wish them well in their careers.